The Italian
Political Filmmakers

Other works by John J. Michalczyk:

André Malraux's Film Espoir: *The Propaganda/Art Film and the Spanish Civil War*
    (1977)

Ingmar Bergman: La passion d'être homme aujourd'hui (1977)

The French Literary Filmmakers (1980)

Costa-Gavras: The Political Fiction Film (1984)

The Italian Political Filmmakers

John J. Michalczyk

Rutherford ● Madison ● Teaneck
Fairleigh Dickinson University Press
London and Toronto: Associated University Presses

Associated University Presses
440 Forsgate Drive
Cranbury, NJ 08512

Associated University Presses
25 Sicilian Avenue
London WC1A 2QH, England

Associated University Presses
2133 Royal Windsor Drive
Unit 1
Mississauga, Ontario
Canada L5J 1K5

*The paper used in this publication meets the requirements
of the American National Standard for Permanence
of Paper for Printed Library Materials Z39.48-1984.*

Library of Congress Cataloging-in-Publication Data

Michalczyk, John J., 1941–
     The Italian political filmmakers.

     Bibliography: p.
     Includes index.
     1. Moving-pictures—Italy—History.   2. Moving-
pictures—Political aspects—Italy—History.   I. Title.
PN1993.5.I88M48   1986   791.43′0945   84-48807
ISBN 0-8386-3250-5 (alk. paper)

Printed in the United States of America

To Susan:

"Men che dramma
di sangue m' è rimaso che non tremi:
conosco i segni dell' antica fiamma."

Contents

Acknowledgments

An account of the research for this work is a tale of many cities. In my travels to and research in these various places I was in contact with many individuals and institutions crucial to my academic progress. For this I am most grateful.

In Boston, the base of operations for my scholarly activity, I am most appreciative of Boston College for a grant to complete the manuscript; of my wife Susan Ross Michalczyk for the very practical Index; of Carol Maryanski O'Neill for the distinctive jacket design; of Claire Murray for her patience with the extensive task of typing the manuscript; of the O'Neill Library staff, especially Monique Lowd, for their generous assistance with the documentation; and of Rev. Joseph Gauthier, S.J., for his reading of several sections of the manuscript.

The Museum of Modern Art in New York offered me a wealth of information from its archives in the earlier stages of research.

In Washington, D.C., Patrick Baliani's insights into Italian film, his encouragement, and his scrutiny of the final text have been most helpful. He has also provided invaluable assistance in his translations from Italian. (All translations from French and Spanish, however, are my own.) The Library of Congress was also useful in basic film research.

The archives at the British Film Institute in London were most useful for film criticism of the sixties and seventies.

Three film libraries in Paris provided me with countless articles, references, and important data: Institut des Hautes Etudes Cinématographiques, Fédération des Organismes de la Communication Sociale, and Centre Pompidou. Critic and historian Jean Gili furnished me with many leads to further my research in Rome.

Rome was the center of my major research for more than six months, during which time I had the assistance of the staff from the Cineteca Nazionale, as well as Titanus, Lux, and Clesi Films. The filmmakers Francesco Rosi, Gillo Pontecorvo, Bernardo Bertolucci, Lina Wertmüller, and Marco Bellocchio offered me firsthand data on the films and biographies. The recently deceased screenwriter Franco Solinas assisted me with many profound insights into political film. The film critics Lino Micchichè and Aggeo Savioli, with their vast political experiences and ideologies, furnished me with a wealth of invaluable information. Alberto Moravia, author of *Il Conformista,* offered his personal ideas about Bertolucci and Pasolini.

Lastly, critic Luigi Bini, S.J., of the San Fedele Cultural Center in Milan, read the final manuscript and made several important suggestions.

I am indebted to the above and hope that the final results do not in any way misrepresent their views on political film.

The Italian
Political Filmmakers

Introduction

Neorealism has not ended, I believe. It has evolved. And I think that the French New Wave and the British Free Cinema reflect this evolution, and are a revolutionary continuation of neorealism. In Italy also neorealism has not completely disappeared.

—Pasolini, 1966

For most critics who judge Italian cinema, the post–World War II period of neorealism serves as the common measuring rod. This movement provides a concrete and convenient means of situating a film and a director in Italy's cinema history. To document and analyze the work of seven politically oriented directors—Pier Paolo Pasolini, Francesco Rosi, Marco Bellocchio, Bernardo Bertolucci, Elio Petri, Gillo Pontecorvo, and Lina Wertmüller—we must also return to the neorealist epoch. The roots of these directors who best represent the political cinema are imbedded in this movement. Most of the filmmakers claim Roberto Rossellini, Luchino Visconti or even the early Federico Fellini as their cinematic father(s). Their first works, whether Rosi's *La sfida (The Challenge)*, Bertolucci's *Prima della rivoluzione (Before the Revolution)*, or Wertmüller's *I basilischi (The Lizards)*, were made on small budgets, with nonprofessional actors playing alongside professionals and reflected deeply existential sociopolitical themes. Most of the seven filmmakers were in their impressionable teens or early twenties at the height of neorealism. Some of the senior ones, such as Rosi and Pontecorvo, had also known the fascism that created a "big silence" in the film industry prior to the neorealist explosion.

With a crucial cinematic event of 1946 the seed was planted, and within twenty years it would yield a hundredfold. In September 1946, just a little more than a year after the Liberation, Cannes hosted its first festival. Rossellini's *Roma, città aperta (Open City)* was given international recognition, but it was its Paris screening that made of the film a major success. The film was hailed as a significant breakthrough in cinema, radically different from the Hollywood-like, unrealistic, "white telephone" films of pre–World War II.[1] Rossellini's *Open City*, a tragic account of the heroic collaboration of Communists and Catholics in their struggle against fascism, became the paragon of new cinema for most of our seven filmmakers. Despite its birth out of necessity, the movement represented a fresh technical approach to cinema and a penetration of the complex socio-

13

political problems of the reconstruction period. This cinematic thrust inspired these younger cinéastes to continue the work of the neorealists, but in a modified form.

In the thirties, as Mida and Quaglietti point out, realist tendencies and socio-political themes already existed in the cinema.[2] They only reached maturity, however, in the postwar climate of Italy in the neorealist movement. *Open City* received all the international fanfare, but it was Visconti's *Ossessione (Obsession)* of 1942 that would be labelled in retrospect the first neorealist film. Umberto Barbaro of the Centro Sperimentale published a manifesto in 1943 in *Cinema* setting the tone for the future of the movement.[3] He fostered a rebellion against the "white telephone" mentality of filmmaking, and at the same time urged the directors to be more personal and realistic in their works.

The sources of the neorealist movement could be traced back to the *verismo* or realistic atmosphere especially found in the novels of Giovanni Verga (1840–1922).[4] His was a literary quest for truth. The directors of the neorealist movement such as Rossellini, De Sica, and Visconti, were further impressed by the realism that they had already seen in the French classic filmmakers, Marcel Carné, Jean Renoir, and René Clair. The American social novel of the thirties and forties, in the tradition of John Steinbeck, Frank Norris, and Dashiell Hammett, provided them with further inspiration. Over all, it was this search for truth in the depiction of sociopolitical situations that guided the directors and screenwriters in their first neorealist works. Lino Miccichè, film critic for the Socialist newspaper *Avanti!*, reminisced: "We were hungry for reality in film," and later, "The filmmakers wanted to be in constant contact with reality. Zavattini [screenwriter for De Sica's *Shoeshine* and *Bicycle Thieves*] was always concerned about the people's problems."[5]

The purpose of the neorealists in filmmaking was *to witness* to the ills of society and then *to state* them before the public in order to raise their consciousness. The results would represent a double approach—a naturalist slice of life in such films as *Obsession*,[6] and a sociopolitical perspective in *Open City* and *Bicycle Thieves* in which antifascism and class consciousness emerge as principal themes. A film such as Visconti's *La terra trema (The Earth Trembles)* in Sicilian dialect combined the slice of life in a fishing village with a class-consciousness motif. Ugo Casiraghi in the communist newspaper *L'Unità* for 4 September 1948, called this cinematic masterpiece "the first Italian film that reflected a socialist spirit." It was this very humanistic sociopolitical vein as well as the dual perspective of the neorealist vision that would greatly attract the seven directors at the heart of the present study.

After a decade of international popularity, the neorealist spirit began to evaporate. The cinematic idiom had become banal, a technically prefabricated cliché. Postwar problems for the most part had been resolved. Financial backing was no longer given to films with this style. Legal snares also prevented the neorealist filmmakers from pursuing their original interests. The public itself had had enough of the negative image of Italian society represented in the neorealist films.[7]

While this movement began to wane, another group of filmmakers was in the ascendant, from the young rebel Bellocchio to the older, more experienced Rosi. The up-and-coming cinéastes' steady diet of neorealist films over a decade supplied nourishment beyond belief. These new filmmakers were the direct heirs of this tradition of political commitment and social consciousness. Some worked as assistants to the neorealists directors. Others organized screenings through the cinema clubs to promote these films. The rest absorbed the works of these masters at every opportunity, either at the university or the Paris Latin Quarter or Cinémathèque. They would take up the sociopolitical torch in the Italian cinema world.

Like their neorealist forefathers, Bellocchio, Pasolini, Pontecorvo, Wertmüller, Petri, Rosi, and Bertolucci were, in varying degrees, exposed to the political tenets of Marxism, and the Communist and/or Socialist parties. Besides reading the ideological works of Karl Marx—for the European Communist a household name—they devoured the writings of Antonio Gramsci, one of the founders of the Italian Communist party. Gramsci died in 1937 after ten years in a fascist prison. He left a socialist heritage of 428 letters that influenced several of the new breed of filmmakers in the areas of a national-popular literature, education of the proletariat, cultural revolution, and the southern or Mezzogiorno question, dealing with the need for socioeconomic development.[8] In postwar Italy the Communist party was interested in supplementing the ranks of the old diehard Bolshevists with new blood. It made a deliberate appeal to the youth, especially from 1944 to 1946, just as Mussolini and Hitler had done in the thirties. The Italian Communist party attracted to it many young upper class men and women who had a strong negative reaction to the bourgeois, a reaction perhaps not as drastic as that of the later terrorist sons and daughters of wealthy businessmen.[9] The party promoted a radical cultural philosophy directing the ciné-club or sponsoring Brechtian-style theatre.

The new generation of filmmakers thus built on the old systems of neorealism and Marxism, which had also merged in the works of the preceding generation. The political scene of the sixties and seventies obviously differed from postwar Italy; so these directors were obliged to transform their masters' guiding principles. A criticism of the supposedly superstitious Catholic Church and the ineffective state, already treated by De Sica in *Bicycle Thieves*, attains much more lucid and often bitter proportions in the films of Petri and Bellocchio. The resistance against fascist oppressors in *Open City* becomes applied to all power systems in Italy and the world. The sociopolitical tone of *The Earth Trembles* is made more intense but also given a greater psychological depth in the treatment of the Mezzogiorno question in Rosi's films. Color photography, internationally famous stars, and links with major American productions replace the stark, black-and-white films using many nonprofessional actors paid from a shoestring budget. To the clear-cut and at times melodramatic presentation of issues and confrontations are added satire, surrealism, and sarcasm that make each work more complicated than its predecessor.

Although some of the same themes of neorealism are repeated in the new wave of Italian filmmakers, they have a freshness and vigor that make them equally or more appealing than the themes of their cinematic progenitors. For the most part it is a cinema of denunciation, as Pierre Billard recounts:

> What do Italian filmmakers denounce in their work? Police brutality, and judicial inadequacy, abuses of the wealthy and extortion in public office, the plotting of secret services and racketeering by political parties, moral and religious hypocrisy, social inequality, and the tacit complicity among all levels of authority to maintain power. In varying degrees these ills have weakened the credibility of the Italian state and, as a result, have debilitated the national consensus.[10]

Very concretely, the subject matter of the younger directors becomes the Army and machismo (Bellocchio's treatment of the military in *Victory March*); the Catholic Church and the Christian Democratic party (Petri's *Todo modo*); colonialism and imperialism (Pontecorvo's *Battle of Algiers* and *Burn!*); sexual perversions of representatives of power (Petri's *Investigation of a Citizen above Suspicion*); Mafia and underworld corruption (Rosi's *Lucky Luciano* and Petri's *We Still Kill the Old Way*); and the glories of socialism and communism (Bertolucci's *1900*).

In general, the products of many of these directors are didactic, at times in a positive sense of Rossellini's *"didascile"* (instructive or didactic) film. They teach a necessary truth to the film audience. The seven film directors go beyond the neorealist approach by not only stating the problems, but adding commentary and critique. They are more bitter in their denunciation, usually settling personal accounts with institutions, such as Bellocchio's scathing attack against a religious institution, the Catholic boarding school. They prefer to take on such institutions because of the latter's neofascist or Establishment behavior. The directors in these modern works at times apply a revisionist thinking in their application of contemporary insights into historical situations of twenty or thirty years ago. Since censorship has lessened, without having totally disappeared, there is greater opportunity for these cinéastes to approach their controversial subject matter with a highly critical attitude.

Although the filmmakers profess a leftist creed, their ideologies evolve with the existing political situation. Pasolini will show the "historic compromise" while a Rosi or Petri may show the "strategy of tension" of the Left. Following the strong antifascist political trend in the mid-forties reflected by the neorealists, there emerged widespread sympathy for the Left, especially for the Communist party. During the Cold War many of the Italian intellectuals, both filmmakers and critics, harbored pro-Soviet sentiments. They were, perhaps, not as strong in their leanings as French critic Georges Sadoul, who considered almost every American film a piece of propaganda. Some of the same intellectuals relinquished their membership in the Communist party after the Soviet invasion of Hungary in 1956, as others would do in 1968 with the invasion of Czechoslovakia. The Hungarian crisis above all divided the ranks.[11]

When the first film of this new generation of filmmakers was released, Rosi's *The Challenge* (1958), a new political sentiment was developing.[12] Between 1958 and 1960 the strong centrism was losing its political hold, and for the next few years, 1960 to 1963, there were premonitions of a Center-Left developing. From 1965 to 1967 certain crises emerged from the Center-Left alignment. Then student and union unrest burst upon the national and international scene in 1968, the effects lasting until the early seventies. This caused a counter-push in 1969, "the strategy of tension," the attempt of the government to discredit the Left. Soon afterwards the major coalition took place in the government which brought together the conservative Christian Democrats and the Left of the Communist party, after more than three decades of their being at each other's political throats.[13]

The early leftist and/or antifascist political formation of Petri, Bellocchio, Pontecorvo, Pasolini, Bertolucci, Rosi, and Wertmüller colors their work. Their reaction to their bourgeois upbringing and the historical evolution of the Italian political scene from the Cold War to the present also has had a significant bearing upon their politics and cinema. Their fertile imaginations and technical expertise, however, help them transcend party lines to create a successful national cinema which rivals their neorealist predecessors.

The results of the artistic and critical endeavors of these seven filmmakers emerged in a new Italian political fiction cinema. These works are documented but few are documentaries. On occasion they resort to thrilling entertainment, but their films are primarily meant to be consciousness-raising. In general, they run a gamut of political, ideological, social, and historical perspectives. Many of these directors preceded Costa-Gavras whose celebrated *Z* brought international attention to the political fiction genre from 1969 on.[14] Their films would be instructive and moralistic, in Rossellini's terms, theses through fiction, but based on the sociopolitical reality of the times. On occasion their self-conscious aesthetics or fascinating entertainment have interfered with the message, militating against the political purpose of the filmmaker. Lino Miccichè in this case stresses the responsibility of the director to achieve the fine balance between politics and aesthetics.[15] These directors' films were made, ideally, to persuade the viewer to think and act differently, without being a brainwashing experience. In effect, the cinéastes reduced complex social issues to a two-hour film, most often commercially distributed. The resulting film ordinarily reflects the values of a director in a specific political time frame. In 1972, Joan Mellen considered the genre still in transition, but nonetheless had hope for its continued self-renewal:

As critics have long been aware, film has a particular affinity for recording social life in flux. Those now working in fictional documentary are in the process of rediscovering and revitalizing a mode which may yet generate a new engaged cinema, aesthetically creative, politically daring and capable of direct bearing on our immediate lives.[16]

The political fiction films of our seven filmmakers should be situated in a larger picture of Italian cinema. Although political films comprise only 3 or 4 percent of the 150 works in the annual vintage, they have nonetheless made an impact on the general public, according to Lino Miccichè. The small percentage of films of this genre still represents a greater sociopolitical consciousness than in America or even France. Furthermore, it is inevitable to be political in postwar

Italy, observes novelist and film critic, Alberto Moravia.[17] He explains the phenomenon of a political cinema in light of Italy's large Communist party. The bourgeois class is weaker in Italy, in comparison with Germany. Hence the class struggle is much more intense in Italy. It makes some citizens fight for revolution and others desperately try to avoid it, in Moravia's mind. The arts in general represent this conflict, while the cinema in particular serves as a perfect vehicle to capture this political atmosphere.

The following study of the political fiction film of seven directors has as its purpose the basic neorealist principles of witnessing and stating the truth as far as this is possible. It will *witness* to the political fiction film production in Italy over the past two decades relying upon the critical viewing of films, many of which have never been distributed in the U.S. or France; interviews with the directors, screenwriters, and critics whose work is at the core of this analysis; and research in Paris (I.D.H.E.C.), Rome (Cineteca Nazionale), and New York (Museum of Modern Art) where most materials have been gathered. Then, this work is further designed *to state* results, revealing patterns and examining the political and technical evolution of each director. It is chiefly meant to be historical and critical, but takes on a biographical and political perspective in order to trace various currents in the lives of these directors. The voices of other critics and historians are included in order to furnish a dialectic. Given this approach, it becomes the task of the reader to continue the process of reflection and healthy dialogue, thus fulfilling the intentions of the cinéastes in the creation of their films.

1
FRANCESCO ROSI:
The Dialectical Cinema

> I feel that a filmmaker more than ever has the obligation to witness to the times. He must also indicate and suggest the limits of a discussion about this period. In this way one can provoke an uninterrupted dialectical rapport between the individual and reality.
>
> —Rosi, Cannes, 1972

The Italian Renaissance man knew war and art, languages as well as courtly music. His talents were many, his education all-encompassing. Above all, he was a humanist. Francesco Rosi, another Renaissance man, exhibits some of the same qualities, talent, and education. He possesses a profound knowledge of the entire film industry, owing to multiple experiences as actor, scriptwriter, editor, assistant director, and eventually filmmaker. The labels of historian, journalist, sociologist, and more recently ethnologist, have also been pinned on him, not without justification. Rosi reflects all of the above, but still manages to escape categorization. His far-reaching, humanist spirit transcends labels and categories.

Rosi has been known as a politically committed filmmaker of the Left. He is foremost an artist. Through his complex works—thirteen to date—he personally reflects that very narrow juncture of aesthetics and ideology idealized by Lino Miccichè. He has produced brilliant, searing exposés of various segments of society: Big Business in oil monopolies (*The Mattei Affair*), real estate speculation (*Hands over the City*), the Mafia (*Salvatore Giuliano, Lucky Luciano*), the military (*Just Another War*), and white collar terrorism (*Illustrious Corpses*). Rosi's lyrical film *Eboli* portrays the Catholic Church and the Italian government as either disinterested in or incapable of improving the tragic lot of the southern Italian farmers. In his most recent work, *Three Brothers* (1981), the director reveals a crosscut of contemporary Italian society and uncovers tension within and among several sectors of society. Rosi believes that even certain respected institutions are not completely free of corruption and hypocrisy. With these insightful cinematic statements,

Rosi provokes, stimulates, educates, and elevates his audience. He never allows them to be passive.

With other political artists—André Malraux, Bertolt Brecht, or Pablo Picasso—aesthetics and politics cannot always be separated. Not totally distinct entities, they must at times overlap, nourishing each other in the process. At different moments, nonetheless, one is in high relief while the other fades into the background. With an evolutionary and quasi-developmental approach, we will select elements from Rosi's biography to show the genesis of his political vision, and then its reaching fruition in the political fiction film. Some of his personal life, like that of the protagonists in his films, will become secondary to this vision.[1]

Political-Cultural Biography

Naples has left its indelible mark on the filmmaker's repertoire. Throughout his works, Rosi shows concern, nostalgia, and sympathy for this southern city and its colorful residents. Full of life, rich with culture, Naples, nonetheless, has been relegated to a position of inferiority when compared to the capital Rome or other northern industrial cities such as Milan or Turin. It was in Naples that Francesco Rosi was born in 1922 at the dawn of Italian fascism. His family was certainly not actively antifascist, but had its share of socialists and masons. It would nonetheless be difficult for any individual to be aloof from fascism as it began to spread. Politics filled the air, punctuated sidewalk conversations, and covered the front pages of newspapers. As Rosi grew up, the daily news would deal with the power of the Third Reich and the glories of Il Duce, as well as the Abyssinian crisis and the Spanish Civil War. Nationalization reached the most obscure corners of society. The film industry did not escape its tentacles. This could not help but mark Rosi's generation of filmmakers, as we will later observe. In recounting the political atmosphere of the time, he recalls how he returned home one day after hearing a typical discourse by Mussolini, not unlike the one at the conclusion of *Eboli*. The fourteen-year-old lad began to repeat some of Il Duce's slogans on the grandeur of the Empire. The father immediately gave the boy a sound thrashing and then explained the political reasons behind the chastisement. Gradually the young Francesco began to understand the gravity of the situation.

Rosi and his comrades at the *liceo* and then at the university (Raffaele La Capria, Giuseppe Patroni Griffi, and Antonio Ghirelli) lived more under the influence of Benedetto Croce's idealism and Antonio Gramsci's historical materialism than Mussolini's fascism. Ettore Giannini was their *maestro*. At the university, these comrades ironically belonged to the GUF (Gruppi Universitari Fascisti), the only culturally advanced organization in Naples. The fascist organism bred its own brand of antifascists. Rosi jokingly observed in our 11 May 1981 interview in Rome, "I was formed in my antifascist spirit in the heart of fascism." In the GUF Rosi had the opportunity to read the Soviet classics, French and American novels, and Neapolitan literature. He was involved with experimental theatre, staging plays of Eugene O'Neill, Ivan Turgenev, and the Neapolitan journalist and playwright Roberto Bracco. The group of young intellectuals with new cultural horizons published a journal called *Sud* with Pasquale Prunas as editor. Rosi was responsible for the film articles, for example, on Rossellini. Rosi initially studied law, but his heart was primarily in the arts. Since the completion of his secondary school education, he longed to enter the Centro Sperimentale di Cinematografia, the prestigious film school in Rome. Instead, he was obliged to live vicariously in the cinema world through his reading of *Illustrazione* and *Bianco e nero* and writing of film critiques.

The war altered any plans Rosi had for either legal or cinematic training. In 1942, at the age of twenty, he began his military service. The following year marked the end of fascism in Italy, but created for the country a moment of political and military chaos. Separated from his military unit in northern Italy, Rosi and his four comrades hid for six months. In the evenings, the art historian Carlo Ludovico Ragghianti, head of the resistance in Florence, spent hours with the group, giving them a course on the history of art. It was a curious blend of politics and aesthetics. Rosi was also exposed to the antifascist sentiments of his relatives like Ernesto Rosi. Arrested several times by the Americans who had landed in Sicily and were already moving northwards at a rapid clip, Rosi finally arrived in Naples in September 1944. The war had brought with it to Naples diverse problems which awakened Rosi—the black market, prostitution, and another occupation, this time by Americans. All of this activity provided Rosi with a new perspective on life, especially Neapolitan life. It would eventually come to the surface in his films such as *The Challenge* on the illegal profiteering of the *camorra* and *Hands over the City* on speculation scandals.

Following the war Rosi became more and more interested in history and Marxism, in particular the writings of Antonio Gramsci. He had first been exposed to Gramsci's ideology in Florence. From his work he gleaned a methodology of a dialectic, obvious in the form of the director's works, as well as an interest in propagating a popular culture for the masses, evident in his selection of subjects. Both Gramsci and Rosi, for example, sought to delve into the conscience of the masses, explaining the crucial sociopolitical problems of the south. At this time Rosi came into greater contact with both Communists and Socialists; he felt closer to the Socialists, but preferred to remain independent of political responsibility and duty.

Through a friend he was able to begin work with the Americans on radio broadcasts for the Psychological Warfare Branch, assuming the functions of actor, writer, and assistant director. Pursuing theatre in Rome and on tour, journalism and graphic design, but still undecided about a future, Rosi had a stroke of luck that finally brought him into the cinema world.

Rosi had been seeing the classics of American film noir, gangster films, and films of John Huston, Elia Kazan, and Jules Dassin. These were interspersed with neorealist films on which he wrote critiques for *Sud*. He was also reading the social novels of American writers. He absorbed all he could from the film journals *Cinema* and *Bianco e nero,* as well as from the writings of Pudovkin, Eisenstein, Umberto Barbaro, Luigi Chiarini, and the French critics Georges Sadoul and Georges Charensol. He was still eager to enter the Centro Sperimentale in Rome. He prepared a study of *I Malavoglia* (1881) by the verist novelist Giovanni

Verga. By a fortunate coincidence, an actor working with Visconti, Achille Millo, was asked to be Visconti's assistant for the screen version of Verga's novel. Rosi, in light of his own work on *I Malavoglia*, was very much interested in this venture described by Millo. He was accepted by the Marxist filmmaker for the filming of the adaptation entitled *La terra trema (The Earth Trembles)*, to be sponsored in part by the Communist party.[2] This is the turning point in Rosi's life, as cinema and ideology first become for him compatible bedfellows.

On location at the Sicilian port of Aci Trezza along with Visconti's other assistant Franco Zeffirelli, later director of *Romeo and Juliet* and *Brother Sun, Sister Moon,* Rosi had several functions. He assumed the usual extensive tasks of an assistant director, but was also responsible for the script, technical precision of the filming, and sketching of the peasants for continuity. Later he would take charge of the dubbing of the film from Sicilian into standard Italian. Only three years after Rossellini unveiled to the world the hidden power of the neorealist cinema with *Open City,* Visconti did the same with *The Earth Trembles* in 1948.[3] Rosi was an integral part of this creation. Here he learned a precise method of working and acquired an intense desire to create his own dynamic style in filming. At Visconti's side Rosi further learned to capture struggling humanity in a slice-of-life fashion but with technical precision. While politics merged with art, art flowed into the living experiences of the fishermen and film crew. Visconti, Rosi, Zeffirelli, and the others on location were able to abide by the tenets of the newly established neorealists' code, witnessing and stating what they personally experienced. Looking back on this period from a 1964 vantage point, Rosi remarked that this experience was absolutely fundamental to him, for it gave him an opportunity to know the richness of the professional yet human character of Visconti. It also provided him with the chance to be present in the creative process of a film which stands as a landmark in Italian cinema. Lastly, he felt that this serious and intense work had contributed most significantly to his cinematic formation.[4]

The collaboration with Visconti would be Rosi's first step toward forming a political consciousness in cinema. The style that he would gradually develop would reflect constant flux as he came into contact with several filmmakers for whom he worked as assistant over almost a decade. His apprenticeship to them was impressive: Luciano Emmer *(Una domenica d'agosto; Parigi è sempre Parigi; Il bigamo);* Raffaello Maltarazzo *(Tormento; I figli di nessuno);* Luchino Visconti once again *(Bellissima; Senso);* an early Michelangelo Antonioni *(I vinti);* Ettore Giannini *(Carosello napoletano);* Mario Monicelli *(Proibito);* and Gianni Franciolini *(Racconti romani).* A script which he had written in 1946–47 about a trial against the *camorra, Processo Cuocolo,* later became Luigi Zampa's *Processo alla città* (1951). This experience with screenwriting already underlined his interest in the relationship of the Mafia, politics, and hidden truth.

In two cases Rosi's duties took him further into the film industry. When Goffredo Alessandrini had difficulties with the producers over the filming of *Camicie rosse,* Rosi undertook the completion of the production. When the actor Vittorio Gassman decided to film *Kean, genio e sregolatezza,* he entrusted Rosi with the technical aspect of the production. This extensive experience was never underestimated by Rosi, for he felt that in the process of working on this production, he had an excellent departure point. We must see *only* that, however, for soon his first few films—far from being imitations of his masters—would manifest an individualism, though tinged with a neorealist aura.

Constants

Rosi deeply appreciates and often praises the collaboration he had with the Italian directors one generation before him—Ettore Giannini and Luchino Visconti close up, and Rossellini from afar. Throughout his interviews, especially with Jean Gili and Michel Ciment, he has underscored the importance of artistic cooperation in his own work over more than two decades. He has realized that a film production is not a one-man show, although as the director—the person ultimately responsible for the film—he supervises the work from the first comma of the script to the final cemented image on the editing table. Around him, producer, scriptwriter, photographer, actor—all form concentric circles, at times their functions overlapping. He insists on working with professionals he knows and trusts, and from them he obtains their confidence, expertise, and constructive criticism.

Producer Franco Cristaldi, always eager to accept a challenge, has often fought alongside Rosi for a more sophisticated style of film that could still be directed toward a commercial audience. With an occasional exception, he helped finance Rosi's films from *The Challenge* (1958) to *Eboli* (1979). For screenwriters, the director has often turned to the literary trinity of Enzo Provenzale, Raffaele La Capria, and Tonino Guerra, with others assisting as the occasion warrants it. Forming a veritable "think tank," these three writers cross-pollinate their ideas with Rosi's. When Gianni Di Venanzo, the director of photography, died after working with Rosi on his first four films, the cameraman Pasqualino De Santis graduated to the position. For each film, beginning with *Moment of Truth*, Rosi describes to De Santis in precise terms exactly his expectations of visual effects. He takes the photographer to the location several times. They discuss possibilities. Rosi allows some experimentation in order to discover the correct lighting and composition, and then they come to an agreement. De Santis's success with "de-coloring" the image in Ettore Scola's *A Special Day* to produce a convincing Rome of 1938, his vibrant colors for Zeffirelli's *Romeo and Juliet*, and the haunting compositions in Visconti's *Death in Venice* only partially reflect the range of his talents. Throughout Rosi's entire repertoire are carefully woven the musical compositions of Piero Piccioni, evoking a full gamut of psychological moods. Rosi says music accompanies him on every set. It generally serves as a type of inspirational background. When he was shooting *Giuliano* he used to listen to Stravinski's *Le Sacre du Printemps*. The symphonic jazz of Stan Kenton, Count Basie, and Duke Ellington followed him around the set of *Hands over the City*. During the shooting of *Three Brothers* his constant companion was Bach variations played on a guitar. Later on during the filming Rosi would talk with Piccioni, and they would analyze the possibilities and then exchange ideas for the sound track. Each film would have its own need.

Perhaps the most visible part of the collaborative process can be witnessed in the choice of Gian Maria Volonté as protagonist from *Just Another War* to *Eboli*. Although Volonté resists the label of "political actor," which he believes is rather simplistic on the part of the critics, he is nonetheless an actor who has a strong leftist ideology. He is a militant member of the Communist party and has played the lead role in leftist-oriented productions of Rosi, Petri, Bellocchio, Pontecorvo and Montaldo. Known in Italy as a gifted stage, screen, and television actor, he is primarily appreciated in the United States for his role in Montaldo's *Sacco and Vanzetti* and more recently Rosi's *Eboli*. What is significant in the Rosi-Volonté rapport is their sharing of a revolutionary vision of their work. They comprehend and live out the intertwining relationships of art, politics, and daily life. Volonté often becomes a spokesman for Rosi. In order to achieve the maximum quality of acting, they collaborate for a long time before the production begins. Volonté testifies that for Rosi the actor is not the object in the production, but a subject involved in the creation.

Besides these personal forms of potential energy that burst into life under Rosi's directorship as with assembled musicians at the first sweep of a conductor's baton, there are other constants in his work. These are leitmotifs that punctuate most, if not all, of his films.

William Faulkner, James Baldwin, and Flannery O'Connor have given a unique, provincial image of the American Deep South to the rest of the country. Rosi on his native soil has accepted the same mission. This cinematic and cultural son of Naples has decided to take his slice of life from the landscape of southern Italy, as opposed to his predecessors of the neorealist persuasion who used primarily Rome for their backdrop. A few exceptions would be those directors who sensitively treated the south such as Visconti *(The Leopard)*, Rossellini *(Paisan)*, and De Sica *(Gold of Naples)*. Images of Naples and the south of Italy—considered symbolically by some as part of the Third World—haunt the majority of Rosi's films, as *The Challenge* and *Hands over the City*. Sicily, home of the novelist Leonardo Sciascia, playwright Luigi Pirandello, and political thinker Antonio Gramsci,[5] makes its way into *Lucky Luciano*. The primitive region of Lucania appears in *Eboli* and Apulia in *Three Brothers*. Even when the action does not take place in the south of Italy, Rosi's work resounds with Neapolitan images or Southern themes. In *The Weavers*, a sly Neapolitan travelling salesman sets up shop in Germany; the bullfighter Miguel in *Moment of Truth* begins his austere life under the southern sun of Andalusia. In his regionalism, not unlike that of Marcel Pagnol's view of southern French life, a universal spirit emerges from the provincial.

In these southern locations Rosi sets out to reveal the inner workings of institutions. With an acerbic camera he denounces all power systems, especially as they pass from beneficial and utilitarian to established and corrupt. When asked in our interview about the origins of his political interests, especially in power, he replied, "Naples." This city, he explained, just a few hours south of Rome, is in itself a most complex society in which the reality is dialectic. This, he felt, was most important for his political formation.

Italians need a "Big Mamma" to survive, Rosi is wont to remark. This maternal figure can take the shape of the Catholic Church, the Virgin, or the state. Rosi's films often show the collusion of the Catholic Church and the state. He does not attack religion as such, for he feels the necessity of freedom of expression in this regard. When the faith assumes a physical, corrupt form, however, it becomes his target. He calls this institution a type of cancer that has plagued Italy for centuries, inhibiting its growth. He further criticizes any institution which claims to have full possession of *the* truth, be it cultural, religious, or political:

> It is necessary to flee those institutions which claim they have *the* truth. I have no certainties; I have doubts. I don't trust those men who claim to have absolute certainty. I think all power must submit itself to and regulate itself with culture, that is, with truth and, therefore, with liberty.[6]

The Italian state fares no better than the Catholic Church, especially as it is represented by the Christian Democratic party in office since 1948. The director does not shy away from confrontation with the government. He often presents it as a powerful oppressive and corrupt force, as in *Hands over the City* and *Illustrious Corpses*.

Rosi's films highlight class tensions, whether it is in the forgotten countryside of *Eboli* or on a bloody battlefield of *Just Another War*. Although he admits that his education was completely bourgeois, Rosi feels that his contacts with the lower classes throughout his life made him aware of the destiny of the poor. Every shot in *Eboli* reveals this sensitivity. Some of his more negative critics may refer to this sympathy for the lower classes as a type of compensatory reaction of a bad bourgeois conscience.

Rosi is none too gentle with the Mafia. In *Salvatore Giuliano* the Sicilian underworld enigmatically appears on the scene. A Mafioso Judas is responsible for the betrayal and death of the guerrilla. With the cryptic death of Enrico Mattei, oil industrialist, the name of the Mafia is also linked. The director is less subtle with the subject in *Lucky Luciano* where he depicts the radicalization of the Mafia through the efforts of the Sicilian-born gangland leader. The myth of Cosa Nostra thus haunts the various productions of Rosi.

When once asked if he would like to make a film on fascism, Rosi said he was not interested. Historical fascism was too far in the past, and he grew up under it, although not very consciously, he admits. What he is more interested in, however, is the present-day fascism exhibited in various institutions. Whenever a free-thinking, nonconforming individual, be he guerrilla or socialist, challenges society, he is automatically eliminated by some fascist power. This oppressive phenomenon is thus a many-headed Hydra that roams about today and did not die with Mussolini or Hitler.

Throughout all of these themes there runs one that is inescapable: death. Ordinarily it does not come naturally for Rosi's protagtonists, except in the case of Lucky Luciano's heart attack or the mother in *Three Brothers* who passes away peacefully at an advanced age. Firing squads, vendettas, professional risks, as-

sassinations, and "accidents" untimely rip them from life. Death becomes the
spontaneous reaction of participants in an repressive labyrinthine system that is
threatened by their presence.

Style and Methodology

In the history of film, European as well as American, the fiction film has been
generally considered a means of entertainment, and the documentary a medium
of enlightenment. The fiction film most often appeals to the emotion, and the
documentary to the intellect. Rosi's films, however, testify to a wide range of
nuances between these two categories of cinema. The line between fiction and
documentary fades in each film, as can be seen in his biographical sketches of
Lucky Luciano, Enrico Mattei, and Salvatore Giuliano.

Rosi laments the fact that the production personnel of the film industry have
often caricatured the spectator as a passive individual who only seeks amusement
in a film. Box office receipts prove this, producers repeatedly protest to political
filmmakers seeking financing. Rosi has personally rebelled against this attitude
and has combatted it directly in his films. If one had to schematize on a line the
film style of a director's work from emotional entertainment to provocative realism, or from fiction to documentary, Rosi's films would consistently be situated
closer to the latter. He would be displeased to have his work called documentary,
suggesting, nonetheless, that they are "documented" but not documentaries,
more precisely sociopolitically oriented, but not militant.

Rosi's cinematic style derives almost directly from his political ideology. This in
turn is dependent upon his vision of cinema and his perception of his role as a
filmmaker. He comprehends the immense power of the cinema to modify people's perceptions of reality, although not the reality itself. The cinema, he stated
at the release of *Just Another War,* has become one of the most important means of
provoking a profound intellectual awakening.[7] Rosi feels that the individual is
eager to know and to understand what is happening in the world today. During
the 1972 Cannes Festival he discussed the role and responsibility of the director:

> I feel that a filmmaker more than ever has the obligation to witness to the
> times. He must also indicate and suggest the limits of a discussion about this
> period. In this way one can provoke an uninterrupted dialectical rapport be-
> tween the individual and reality.[8]

Rosi goes further than the neorealists who also witnessed their epoch; he wants
to *interpret* reality, not reproduce it or invent it. He advocates an aggressive role
for the filmmaker: "But I am convinced that a film should be made to touch the
conscience and the intelligence of the spectator, to assault him if necessary."[9]

Rosi's own conscience is not left untouched in the process. From script to edited product, he engages in a profound self-questioning. Before the audience
experiences its own awakening which he provokes, he undergoes it first in confrontation with the sociopolitical situation and the data at hand. His guiding light
in the personal reflection and data-gathering process is truth, truth through doc-

umentation. Rosi is quick to point out that what he presents is *"one* truth," one vision of the specific material, and not an *absolute* one.

At the heart of Rosi's methodology is the dialectic in the historical and current realms, as well as on the interior and exterior levels. This is a process that pushes him to the limits of art, politics, and psychology. The same principle dominated Eisenstein's theory of montage. For both filmmakers the thesis-antithesis-synthesis model is utilized to raise the consciousness of the viewer. In each sociopolitical circumstance, Rosi juxtaposes the obvious visible forces with the more subtle invisible ones, at each turn challenging the commonly accepted perspective. This procedure ordinarily results in an enlightening and credible exposé which challenges the viewer to reflect and to take a position. It is not far removed from Brecht's approach to theatre, although Rosi came to an appreciation of Brecht late in his cinematic development.

Film critics and historians such as Freddy Buache of the Swiss Cinémathèque have on occasion referred to Rosi's films as epic theatre. For certain films such as *Mattei* they hit the mark. As in the Brechtian theatre, Rosi offers a detached, almost clinical approach to the characterization. He does not attempt to force identification of the spectator with the character, but instead objectively tries to oblige the viewer to reflect on the situation in greater depth. In a sense this does have a moralizing or didactic aura about it, given Rosi's philosophy of the cinema of enlightenment. In a dialectic frame of reference, Rosi does not anesthetize the critical faculties of the viewer but sharpens them. Going one step further, he resembles Brecht in his antifascist play *Rise and Fall of Arturo Ui*, intent on modifying, although slightly, the current social, economic, or political situation. Rosi understands nonetheless the incredible forces of inertia that control society.

A direct correlation exists between Rosi's ideology and cinematic technique, between the dialectical process and the means of achieving enlightenment. To show the constant dialogue between reality and himself, he uses the medium of the documented reconstruction of a precise controversial event or character's biography. He speaks in the historical present, and the result is a narrative with the tone of a reportage. It is deliberately fragmented, set out in a nonlinear, nonchronological order. Flashbacks punctuate most of his works. They are, however, not used with the traditional intent of creating *temporal* relationships, but are destined to be *psychological* and *judgmental* means of assisting the viewer to come to some decision about the material presented. The public, for exammple, is invited to arrive at a conclusion or judgment concerning the possible "assassins" of Mattei—Sicilian Mafia, Big Business, American CIA or French OAS. Via these intricate flashbacks one has the grounds for judgment. The works of Rosi are structured dialectically and therefore are open-ended but not transparent. The visual dynamism of De Santis's and Rosi's compositions and orchestration of light and color are essential components in the process. They carry the heavy burden of the complex content to the audience so that they can reach their personal decisions.

The dialectic development goes on over a period of almost two years before a film such as *Hands over the City* or *Illustrious Corpses* reaches the theatre. It usually begins in Rosi's mind with an insight, an uncomfortable feeling about some element of society, or on occasion a literary work such as *Christ Stopped at Eboli* or *The Third Son*. From a succinct sketch the idea finds its way to a written subject. A type of dossier is established. Researched and verified, through news reports, books, and television footage, the subject is enlarged in collaboration with one or two scriptwriters. Slowly flesh is added to the skeletal concept. For authenticity Rosi and De Santis usually search out the actual locations. In filming *Eboli* it meant going to Lucania to investigate and then to film. With *Salvatore Giuliano* the challenge came from filming on location in Sicily under the watchful—sometimes hostile—eye of those who had lived through the experiences.

To incarnate the various ideologies at hand and to convey realistically the dilemma of a sociopolitical circumstance, Rosi blends the professional with the nonprofessional actor. Gian Maria Volonté played Carlo Levi in *Eboli* alongside villagers from the region of Lucania, and Rod Steiger the enterprising Nottola in *Hands over the City* with active members of the current municipal government. Since Visconti's *The Earth Trembles*, Rosi sensed the power of the nonprofessional to offer an authentic glimpse of a harsh reality.

While filming the actors on location, Rosi has a clear idea of what he would like to create. He has a tightly written script, but views it as a departure point. He allows his actors the opportunity to get into the skin of the characters, on occasion to improvise their roles. In doing so, Rosi follows a symbolic principle of Jean Renoir: "Always leave a door open on the set!" After several weeks of filming he carefully supervises the editing, going over every frame with a movieola. It is here that Rosi feels the final dialectical process reaches its epitome. With the movieola he creates the lasting image for the spectator. To sign his works personally, he further participates with his own voice, narrating, commenting, or interviewing, as he did in *Mattei, Eboli,* or *Luciano*. With each film his presence is felt in every aspect of the evolution of the work, testify his actors, director of photography, and screenwriters. The audience can detect this hidden presence throughout his sociopolitical repertoire, as an analysis of each film demonstrates.

Cinematic Repertoire

Ten years of apprenticeship had passed since Rosi went to Aci Trezza to film the Sicilian fishermen with Visconti. In 1958 the time had come to launch out into the deep on his own. One film would soon lead to another, one contact to a second, one reflection to a further one. Over a period of twenty years, with a film almost every two years, he has accumulated thirteen films in his cinematic repertoire.

The Challenge and *The Weavers:* The Twilight of Neorealism

Rosi pinpoints the origins of his evolution to the political cinema in this way: "In *The Challenge* and *The Weavers* I was solely interested in the social aspect of reality. It was only with *Salvatore Giuliano* that I truly discovered the political and ideological aspects."[10] From an actual historical fact the narrative of *The Challenge (La sfida,* 1958) takes shape. In July 1955, Pupetta, the wife of a Neapolitan fruit dealer, killed the murderer of her husband, who was eliminated because of a conflict of interest.

The southern city of Naples under the camera of Rosi becomes an asphalt jungle, harboring gangsters, profiteers, and black marketers, each instinctively guided by a personal territorial imperative. Beneath the intrigue and corruption there is still a law that reigns supreme. Not too subtly it states, "Macht macht recht" (Might makes right). Violate this unwritten code and you risk liquidation. The ambitious, brazen Vito Polara (José Suarez) chooses to take the risk. From a small contraband cigarette dealer he rises to a position of importance with his own terrain to guard. The camorra, *the local profiteering combine, in an attempt to get maximum prices for its vegetables, requires that all dealers hold back their products. Vito, newly married to Assunta (Rosanna Schiaffino), fails to heed this edict in his attempt to amass more wealth and power. He does not live long to profit from the experience. He is gunned down by the powerful boss Salvatore Ajello (Decimo Cristiani) before the very eyes of his bride.*

Twenty years of living in Naples before his war experiences gave Rosi the background for this social study, but his awareness of the corrupt system after the war was more significant. Superficially, the network of crime and monopolies was hardly perceptible. Rosi's purpose, therefore, was to reveal the Neapolitan world, to describe the component elements of a cultural tragedy. More particularly, Rosi wished to understand and present the inner workings, the intricate mechanism, of the system.

In Naples, the power is in the hands of the legal and illegal authorities. Helpless with respect to criminal law, the former allows the underworld corruption and injustices to continue. The latter, in the form of the *camorra,* aggressive and enterprising, but without an ethical sense, monopolizes and bullies its way to the core of power. The victims are legion. The vegetable and fruit growers must abide by the law and sell at the low prices of the *camorra.* The subproletariat must serve as the gears in the well-oiled machine. They are trapped in their slavery. The focus in *The Challenge* is a third category, the individual who is part of the operation but who no longer wishes to be a pawn. Vito becomes the catalyst in the system. He challenges the power elite by choosing to deal on his own terms and at his own discretion (or indiscretion). His ambition intefers with the machine, and he is disposed of immediately.

Overseeing the "business" sector of society is the Catholic Church which attempts to impose its own power, a moral order, on the injustices. Rosi depicts it as a traditional, ritualistic church trapped in its heritage on one hand, and a mercantile institution on the other. Vito's significant contribution during the procession of the statue underlines both his own hypocrisy and the business side of a religious system. This will be the beginning of Rosi's attempts to elucidate what he sees as the ambiguous status of the Catholic Church.

In this first cinematic venture of Rosi, highly praised at the 1958 Venice Film Festival, we can already see the germinal sociopolitical concerns of the director.

Although his individualism will gradually become apparent, two areas of influence can be readily detected in his film. Rosi still lives under the sign of the neorealists. Alberto Moravia, the critical pen of the neorealist movement, considers the film an almost documentary glimpse at reality, in *L'Espresso* of 21 September 1958. The director can hardly be absolutely free of the power of the movement, given his exposure to the manifestos and screenings, as well as his encounters with the pioneering filmmakers. The sordid side of reality is certainly observed and then accentuated in *The Challenge*. Vito, like De Sica's bicycle thief Ricci, falls victim to a system that suffocates, breaks, or destroys.

The social realism of the American cinema also filters through the various sequences of *The Challenge*. As noted earlier, the gangster and the film noir classics greatly delighted Rosi and his companions. Continued, tense excitement, ambiguous morality, along with a tightly knit plot and natural low-keyed acting (Robinson, Cagney, Lorre, Bogart) were responsible for the popularity of both genres. The European political filmmakers of the fifties and sixties claim to be highly influenced by these works. Rosi especially appreciated such films as Howard Hawks's *Scarface* and Elia Kazan's *On the Waterfront*, both not too far removed from the Neapolitan *camorra*.

I magliari (1959), translated literally as *The Weavers*, or more figuratively as *The Con-Men* or *The Swindlers*, followed quickly in the footsteps of *The Challenge*. Where Franco Brusati's tragicomic *Bread and Chocolate* (1973) graphically and surrealistically presents the picaresque adventures of the Italian worker in self-imposed exile in Switzerland, Rosi concentrates on the more somber side of Italian carpetbaggers. These crafty migrants sell their supposedly luxurious wares to unsuspecting German clients.[11]

In *I magliari*, eerie and dreary Hamburg and Hanover serve as a contrast to the colorful southern climate to which the Italian travelling salesman was accustomed. The subject of the itinerant vendor has as its source the Italian traffickers in goods, both contraband and legitimate, who reigned over their private kingdoms in Cologne, Frankfurt, and Hamburg after the war. The little migrant salesman was soon initiated into a larger system that provided products and protection, but not without its own demands.

The unemployed Mario (Renato Salvatori), discouraged, abandons hope of finding work in Germany and wants to return to his native Grosetto, north of Rome. In a chance meeting with Totonno (Alberto Sordi), he is encouraged to stay. Mario is then introduced into the system of i magliari, *a highly developed organization of salesmen under the thumb of Don Raffaele (Carmine Ippolito). When Mario, like Vito of* The Challenge, *attempts to exhibit some independence from the system by allying himself with a German merchant, he is excluded from the clan. Pressured to move off, Mario embarks for England where he hopes to capitalize on his newly discovered charlatan skills.*

Once again Rosi submerges the spectator into the grimy sea of contraband and illegal operations. He structures the character Mario as a type of foil for the organization. Mario's presence among the *magliari* reveals this small caste system as part of an already existing system wherein Germans and migrant workers are pitted against each other in the market place. The hierarchy in the Italian order becomes more and more perceptible in the course of the film. The age-old maxim of the rich getting richer and the poor poorer is most applicable here. The enterprising, unethical salesmen live with few pains, despite their exile in a northern climate. It is a tight circle; only a few are entitled to penetrate it. The honest, hardworking immigrants on the other hand, do not fare well, as Mario observes when he visits a disadvantaged family. The destitute hang onto life by a flimsy thread. These are the individuals who deeply sense their alienation. Uprooted, they nostalgically long for Italy. Like countless others before them over the past few years, they left behind Italy for an economically progressive Germany. Their pockets were empty, their heads filled with pipe dreams.

The social and psychological portrait that Rosi paints of the human components of this multileveled world is bleak. The antihero Mario is nonetheless a survivor. Unlike Vito, he does not allow the system to break or eradicate him, but relies on his own inner powers to start anew.

Rosi is operating here with the same Gestalt as in his first feature. The sordid, corrupt world of Naples is transposed to the industrial cities of Germany. Human nature, still suffering, still triumphing, remains the same. Traces of the illegal rackets in the American gangster films of Dassin and Benedek which marked Rosi can be found in *The Weavers*. Some of the romanticized elements of both directors are further evident. This influence carried over into the first two films of the director, but with his next work he will break the cinematic umbilical cord.

Salvatore Giuliano, The Mattei Affair and *Lucky Luciano:* Polemicized Biographies

In speaking of this biographical triptych, Rosi remarked, "Giuliano, Mattei, Luciano serve as a pretext for a global analysis of the world. They are like litmus paper."[12] He further delineates these films by putting them into the context of Italian history: "These are three contemporary narratives which deal with the total postwar reconstruction period in Italy. They depict this reconstruction in light of the confrontation of the two world blocs, East and West."[13]

For the first of these nontraditional political portraits, Rosi chose the Sicilian Robin Hood, Salvatore Giuliano (1922–50), a ruthless outlaw and colorful defender of justice for the little people. In his earlier films Rosi took a social approach to his material. With *Salvatore Giuliano* (1961) his perspective would be political and ideological. "Here I explored the dichotomy between the actual truth and what one pretends to be the truth. The latter is a mask fabricated by institutions, by power structures, in order to manipulate the uninformed public."[14] Once again, following a dialectical process, Rosi elucidates the inner workings of various sectors of society which control the strings of power and claim unquestionable truth. In doing so, Rosi proposes a profound examination of society's collective conscience with the trial of a bandit as a departure point.

The subject of banditry lends itself well to the film medium, with the elements of myth, legend, adventure, and excitement carefully orchestrated by a director. Vergano's *I fuorilegge* (*The Outlaws*, 1950) and Amato's *Morte di un bandito* (*Death of a Bandit*, 1961) more than Rosi's film, leaned toward perpetuating the glorified image of the guerrilla. With his radical technique, Rosi analyzes but does not romanticize the character of Giuliano. Pierre Leprohon gives a succinct glimpse into the director's purpose and technique in the film:

> Rosi's aim is not to explain, to defend or to accuse: he gives evidence, merely in a dynamic and effective style which is all of a piece. It has been asserted that his account of this complex affair only goes half way, in that it is based on a rigged trial which shielded those really responsible, the Sicilian barons. But a film director is neither a judge nor a lawyer. The indecisive way in which Rosi leaves the drama is the very stuff of reality.[15]

The facts of Giuliano's life can be readily documented. In 1943, Giuliano was involved with the black market and killed two *carabinieri*. He escaped into the hills. At the end of the war, following his many adventurous exploits, he met with separatist leaders from the Esercito Volontario Indipendenza Siciliana who promised him a position in the new government as chief of police or minister of justice in the event of Sicily's independence. At this point he primarily saw himself as a patriot.

By spring 1946, Giuliano had earned a reputation for being the defender of the poor. He then met with Mafia leaders who wished to support his adventures, promising their backing, their "law" in exchange for the fruits of his labor.

In the wake of World War II communism began to spread throughout Europe. Promising to wipe out communism, Salvatore Giuliano wrote to President Truman in 1947 requesting arms. He also asked that Sicily be annexed to the U.S. and made "the 49th American star." No deal was transacted. An inexplicable massacre of the people gathered at a Communist rally on 1 May 1947 at Portella della Ginestra resulted in eleven dead and fifty-six wounded. This gave Giuliano's gang a bad reputation, even among the poor. In 1948 and 1949, he challenged two power structures: he killed key Mafia leaders and published a taunt of the government in the newspapers. The government reacted and set up an antiterrorist corps headed by Colonel Ugo Luca to eliminate the bandits. On 5 July 1950 the bullet-riddled body of Giuliano was found at Castelvetrano, forty miles from his native Montelepre.

Time magazine of 17 July 1950 referred to Giuliano's Robin Hood status among peasants and his "Public Enemy No. 1" role among police. The published photo of the dead body of the bandit was reproduced exactly by Rosi in the film. The project of making a film on bandits was the lure used to ambush Giuliano, according to the *Time* news report. The editorial in the *New York Times* of 6 July 1950 is much harsher. "Giuliano, in short, was typical of the unbalanced, amoral, vicious killer that we knew to our cost during the Prohibition era."[16] The articles published at the time of his death revealed the controversial and ambiguous nature of Giuliano that Rosi wished to clarify in his film.

Rosi's film was entitled *Sicilia 1943–1960* during the production itself to avoid needless problems. It was to provide a historical sketch of Sicily during that time frame, as well as a graphic sense of the collective tragedy of the Sicilian people. Giuliano became the focal point of this tragedy, for he was a major political catalyst in this history. His biography cut through various periods and levels of Sicilian society, so it was only fitting that he be the center of this cinematic project. In *Les lettres françaises* Rosi specified that his real subject was an unfortunate oppressed country, and that Giuliano was "the fruit of his own native land, and the social and political conditions of the forties." In this way the director makes the inevitable link of the guerrilla to the history of Sicily. He unravels the story of the bandit as if it were a lengthy discourse over the cadaver of Julius Caesar.

The film begins: "This film was shot in Sicily, at Montelepre, where Salvatore Giuliano was born. In the homes, streets, and mountains where the bandit reigned for seven years. At Castelvetrano, in the house where he spent his last months. In the courtyard where, one morning, his corpse was found." The police examine the body of Giuliano (Pietro Cammarata), stretched face down in the dusty courtyard. A series of flashbacks fills in the biography of the bandit as it intersects with historical events in Sicily from 1945 to 1960. Kidnappings, confrontations of Giuliano with the carabinieri *and Mafia, shoot-outs, all reflect the everyday life of Giuliano, until that fateful day when he is lured into an ambush at Castelvetrano, betrayed by a Mafia traitor. Following the trial at Viterbo of the men purported to have massacred a group of peasants at the May Day activities of Portella della Ginestra, Gaspara Pisciotta (Frank Wolff), Giuliano's lieutenant, is found poisoned in his prison cell. A Mafia Judas is eliminated in 1960.*

The manner in which Rosi established this plot is referred to as *dialectical* by the director, and as *inductive* by his screenwriter Raffaele La Capria. These views are perhaps two sides of the same coin. At each step of the process Rosi challenged the data and confronted the reality.[17] It was already more than a decade after the actual events and the collective memory of the people was encrusted with the legend. Other documentation derived from literary sources. Rosi consulted books published by Carlo Levi *(Le parole sono pietre)*, Danilo Dolci *(Banditi a Partinico)*, and Gavin Maxwell *(Dagli amici mi guardi Iddio)*. Then there were reports published in *Oggi, Crimen,* and *L'Europeo.* He had read an article from *L'Europeo* by Tommaso Besozzi, who, following his own investigation, challenged the authorities' version of the details in Giuliano's life and death.[18] Daily Sicilian chronicles from 1943 on gave a blow-by-blow account of Giuliano's adventures. The parliamentary discussions of 22 June 1949 on the bandit problem in Sicily were equally revealing. Newspaper photos were invaluable to Rosi in reconstructing the period. During the trial at Viterbo initiated to assess the guilt of the *picciotti* who supposedly fired on the crowd at Portella della Ginestra, testimony was offered on motives and little known actions of Giuliano's men. Court material was clandestinely procured by a bailiff. Further firsthand information on the separatists and bandits came from persons on the scene during the difficulties. The Portella della Ginestra scene, for instance, was shot with some farmers who participated in the May Day rally.[19] The women rushing the *carabinieri* in the streets in the film did it with the same hostile attitude as the original Furies. This research on location proved important, for it offered an on-going dialogue with reality, an integral part of Rosi's dialectical process. Alternating a week in Rome writing with a week in Sicily documenting, Rosi developed the creative tension necessary to construct an authentic dossier of the piecemeal material.

Salvatore Giuliano was a breakthrough in the area of technique, flowing once again from his methodology of historical materialism. Dialectical in principle, the director's technique challenges the viewer to come to personal conclusions about the death of the guerrilla. Rosi declines any use of "invention" in the content. Everything that is seen in the film had to be verified, sometimes from multiple sources. The dialogues emerged from the reality of the experience. The discussions during the trial in the film were drawn from the *Corriere della Sera*'s transcriptions of the actual trial, published 15–19 May 1951. The conversations of the villagers come right out of the *picciotti*'s mouths, set into a functional dialogue form, and rehearsed with the villagers, a technique used by Visconti with the fishermen in *The Earth Trembles*. Originally Rosi was going to intersperse newsreels into the fiction film. Instead he reconstructed the actual scenes from documents and testimony.

Flashbacks are creatively used here, not merely in the temporal sense as a return to the scene of the crime, so to speak. On the one hand they proposed material for the viewers' value judgments on the responsibility of Giuliano's death. On the other, they established cause-and-effect relationships necessary to understand the ambiguity about the bandit in July 1950 as well as at the time of the production.

Building on the social perspective of his two earlier films, Rosi took a more political approach to his materials in *Salvatore Giuliano*. First of all he chose Sicily for the setting, a Sicily quite distinct from the mainland of Italy. Using the controversial character of the guerrilla, Rosi lays bare two decades of conflict. In one interview with Michel Ciment, Rosi stated that his primary interest was Sicily itself, human values, the human tragedy born of relationships between Giuliano and the other Sicilians, Giuliano and the *carabinieri*, and Giuliano and the other political figures of the time.[20]

Rosi portrays Sicily as a conglomerate of powers, effective, lethal, and omnipresent. He analyzes them as socioeconomic principles and subtle legal forces. The director tries to understand their functioning, often hidden from society's eyes. On location in Sicily he found that the *omertà*, or self-imposed silence of the local people, created great difficulties in obtaining the precious truth. One of the first targets Rosi chooses is the Mafia. Maria-Teresa Savage in her article on the Mafia in *Salvatore Giuliano* writes:

> If bandits are always romantic subjects for legends and if these legends were fertilized by the actions of an insensitive and incompetent government which provided the humus where social inequity could flourish, no matter. The Mafia above all always was, and still is, reactionary: one of the most savage, lasting, well-organized reactionary forces ever devised.[21]

This solidly entrenched force views Giuliano as a threat, just as the *camorra* considered Vito in *The Challenge*. The bandit's personal independence is frowned upon, discouraged at all cost. Showing the eternal tension of such power systems,

Maria-Teresa Savage points out at the end of her article on the Mafia that the Giulianos always die, while the Mafia always survives.

Quebec, Brittany, Corsica, Ireland, and the Spanish Basque region have all witnessed waves of separatist activity. In *Giuliano,* Rosi illustrates the struggles of their comrades in arms in Sicily, the members of the EVIS, militant arm of the MIS. Discovering their own power, their alienation from the activity of the mainland, their distinctiveness in language, culture, and history, the Sicilians of the postwar period felt compelled to wage war for their physical independence. In 1945, the separatist leaders who had roots in the Resistance movement against the Nazis saw the advantages of a revolutionary leader like Giuliano. His highly organized group of bandits could be useful in the struggle. The leaders met with the guerrilla, offering him the rank of colonel and a position in their government if they were victorious. Their quest for independence turned out to be "la grande illusione." In presenting this encounter Rosi was able to focus on two forms of power, neither free of opportunism or manipulation.

In general, Rosi believes that Giuliano became "too big for his own boots." He threatened a certain balance of power—government, Mafia, police, and perhaps even the American OSS (in the pre–CIA days).[22] At all costs this individualist was to be prevented from developing his own kingdom. He could not be taken alive, obviously, lest he expose all the clandestine links he had with the legal and illegal power structures. It was expedient, therefore, that one man die for his country.

The neorealist, gangster, and film noir elements of Rosi's earlier works tend to disappear in *Giuliano,* although the subject matter could lend itself to any of these cinematic styles. In this reconstructed and dramatized document, Rosi makes no concessions. He purifies the narrative of the escapism, adventure, personalism, or romanticism which characterized the American films of the thirties and forties and the Italian films of the forties and fifties, despite the neorealist philosophy of certain directors. The story of Giuliano in conflict with the societal forces of separatists, government, Mafia, and police is stripped to its essence. The result is a study of a particular yet universal confrontation of forces, not unlike those seen in the Soviet classics of Eisenstein, Dovzhenko, and Pudovkin. The viewer experiences here the cult of the heroic dead in all of its poignancy. Rosi recreates a type of *Pietà* of a mother weeping over her dead son, as Geoffrey Nowell-Smith also points out.[23] During the actual shooting of the Portella della Ginestra scene, Rosi mentioned in our interview, a woman screamed bitterly, "My two sons were killed that day! Where are my sons?" Although Rosi wanted to dispel the myth of the bandit, his enigmatic portrayal of him—seen from a distance in a white raincoat—only heightens the mythical aura surrounding the bandit. Not filming those who fire on the crowd during the massacre further preserves the myth. The Sicilian novelist Leonardo Sciascia suggested to Rosi that there were some mythical aspects in the treatment of Giuliano, and the director was in agreement.[24]

The sharp, political rhetoric of his characters like Pisciotta during the trial, the flood of flashbacks, the deliberate open-ended narrative and technique, and the clinical approach to characterization, made *Giuliano* a unique contribution to the

Italian cinema of 1960–61. A brave new example of cinema of the Left, *Salvatore Giuliano* could certainly hold its own among the other Italian contributions of the period by Pontecorvo *(Kapò)*, Antonioni *(La notte)*, Petri *(L'assassino)*, and Pasolini *(Accattone)*.

The second film of the biographical trilogy, *The Mattei Affair* (*Il caso Mattei*, 1972), was made more than a decade later with the experience of several other diverse films in the interim. Rosi links Mattei with *Giuliano*, for both give a crosscut of Italian history through an individual agent who is a menace to the existent power centers. Like the bandit of the Sicilian hills, Enrico Mattei was already a romantic legend and rapidly becoming an all-encompassing myth in his own lifetime. Called the Czar of Petrol, compared to Caesar Augustus or Marco Polo, Enrico Mattei (1906–62) was for some the real Emperor of the Republic of Italy, and for others a White Communist. Mattei, a self-made man from a poor background, rose quickly in industry from laborer to director and finally principal employer. Near the end of the war he became a leader in the Resistance and accepted a Bronze Star from the U.S. for his work as a partisan. At the close of the war Mattei aided in the economic rebirth of Italy, maintaining a very strong nationalist perspective. His obituary in *Time* of 2 November 1962 read, "More than any other man, elusive Enrico Mattei, 56, influenced the sustaining postwar boom known as the 'Italian miracle.'" P. H. Frankel captures the psychological and political essence of Mattei four years after his death:

> Mattei's mainspring, his driving force, must have been a sense of deprivation; an Italian, born at the outset of this century, he objected to a state of affairs in which his country failed to join the ranks of the real political and economic powers. This general attitude of protest was for him superimposed upon the perennial antagonism of the "little man" against the Establishment, against the *Grandi Maestri* whom Savonarola singled out as his targets. Mattei, thus an underdog twice over, knew how to seek out and make use of the *ressentiments* of others, not only in his own country, but eventually anywhere in the world; this explains much of his success and most of his failures, resentment being an effective spur but a deceptive guide.[25]

The film covers the postwar phase of the life of Enrico Mattei (Gian Maria Volonté) up to the fateful airplane crash of 27 October 1962 that killed him along with Time-Life *journalist, William McHale (Peter Baldwin), and the pilot Irnerio Bertuzzi (Luciano Colitti). Mattei was about to sign an oil agreement with Ben Bella in Algeria. A string of flashbacks from the plane crash near Milan offers the pieces to a grandiose, colorful, and intriguing puzzle. In 1949, Mattei chanced upon methane and attempted to use the discovery to make the country independent in the area of petroleum. Soon Mattei, an ambitious agent provocateur, witnessed the demise of the petroleum enterprise A.G.I.P. and assumed the responsibility of the National Hydrocarbon Authority (E.N.I.).*

Mattei challenged and provoked a number of institutions such as the "Seven Sisters" of petroleum (creating an imbalance in the oil production world); the Mafia (threatening their power); the CIA (dealing with the Soviet Union); the multinationals (attracting Big Business on his terms); and the French OAS of the extreme right (selling arms to Algeria in the war of independence). He continued to grow in power, establishing his own newspaper Il giorno, *not too different from the Orson Welles of* Citizen Kane. *The industrial tycoon reasoned and battled in hopes of creating an economic renaissance in postwar Italy. His ultimate aim was to destroy poverty, break foreign hegemony in Italy, and restore human dignity to the people. He was essentially idealistic, a crusading Don Quixote on one hand, but also an ambitious, rationalizing Machiavelli on the other.*

The film is cyclical, opening and closing on Mattei's "accident," over Bascape in October 1962, a minute before his private plane was to land in Milan following a business trip to Sicily. Apparently during the heavy storm the plane blew up in the air. Accident or sabotage? Rosi, through interwoven flashbacks, suggests the possible reasons that could justify Mattei's elimination. At the close of the film, the spectator is still left in the dark about the case, but has ample information to come to some personal conclusions based on Rosi's verified facts.

What is most striking about this film is its prophetic air. The film concludes with the voice-off of Mattei: "If I don't succeed, the people with oil under their feet will." A year after the film's release, the economic power shifted from the capitalist and communist blocs to the Third World and Arab nations which had oil to wield as a political weapon. This anti-American little Caesar who broke the monopolies had already wooed Russia. He had also visited China, Algeria, Iran, Tunisia, Libya, and Saudi Arabia, in a significant way, laying the groundwork for the OPEC politicization of world economy.

This testimony to a man and a prophecy was long in the preparation. Approximately two years after the death of the industrialist, Rosi was first interested in making the film. One film project after another, one production problem after another, prevented him from undertaking the film. Several years after Mattei's death, there was a new impetus to make the film. The brother of Mattei said the crash was the work of the CIA, the police suggested the Mafia, and the USSR undertook its own inquiry. During the filming of *Just Another War* in 1970, Rosi had a greater urge than ever to reopen the Mattei case. He discussed the plan with Gian Maria Volonté who agreed to play the complex role of Mattei. Franco Cristaldi found the means to produce it. The machinery was in operation.

Rosi's basic underlying principle was not to present Mattei's life story in a traditional fashion—birth, education, family, profession. In telling of his death and the enigma hovering over it, Rosi instead wished to get at the power structures at play in postwar Italy, but also in the world today. In *The Guardian* of 17 June 1975, the London journalist Derek Malcolm quotes Rosi about his purpose in making *The Mattei Affair:*

> Some people thought that I was so fascinated by the man that I ceased to be objective about him. But I don't believe that is true. He was certainly a complicated and unusual man, with a negative as well as a positive side. But the film is really a pretext for telling 20 years of Italian history.

With his usual dialectical intention and persistent desire for collective truth, Rosi and his screenwriter Tonino Guerra began to accumulate material for the Mattei dossier. The many books, articles, political debates, and conferences dealing with Mattei's business practices all served as a departure point for director and screenwriter. Rosi also went one step further than he did with earlier films, using the media (television and journalists) to help in the investigative process. He viewed foot after foot of television clips and inserted them in his work. Rosi also sought the help of the journalist Mauro de Mauro from the leftist journal *L'Ora* (Palermo) in order to establish Mattei's activities in Sicily shortly before the oil magnate's return to Milan on 27 October 1962. The director was in touch with de Mauro in Sicily by phone during the course of the data gathering. Then suddenly on 16 September 1970 three men confronted de Mauro as he got out of his car. He was never heard from again. The hypothesis was that de Mauro touched a sensitive nerve in the body politic of the Mafia and was necessarily eliminated.[26] Other speculation ran from ideology to drugs; de Mauro may have uncovered a link in drug traffic from Sicily to America. Rosi himself appears in the film to testify to the work of the journalist in the investigation of Mattei's business connections. Nerio Minuzzo and Tito De Stefano, both journalists, also offered their services in the gathering of information for the screenplay.

Pushing the structure and general style of the film to their absolute limits in fiction film, Rosi approaches the documentary or semidocumentary. Several factors account for the heightened realism of his film. Choosing to have authentic locations, Rosi gathered permissions from all corners of the world and was able to film in Saudi Arabia, Iran, New York, Libya, and Sicily. The red tape in the USSR prevented him from filming in Moscow. The actual offices of the E.N.I. reveal the original sites of the radical business transactions. Interviews in the film with Senator Ferruccio Parri and Honorable Michele Pantaleone, government officials, offer further documentary traces and blur the area between fiction and reality. Arrigo Benedetti, the director of *L'Europeo* at the time of Mattei's work, appears in order to reiterate what he wrote in his journal. Finally, to incarnate the character of Mattei engulfed by both enigma and truth, Gian Maria Volonté studied with Rosi the tapes for voice tones, television footage, and then read and studied the person from the inside out.

It is precisely this many-sided, almost cubistic portrayal of the oil king that is at the heart of the criticism of the film and its director. Rosi primarily develops the character of Mattei in a favorable light through Volonté. Mattei, at the pinnacle of his fame, is characterized on one hand as a charismatic individual with a Nietzschean "superman" power. He comes across on the other hand as the little spoiler, a crafty David pitted against the Goliath of the oil monopolies, the Seven Sisters. He helps give the Third World an identity, but it is not at all clear whether he operates under the principle of enlightened self-interest or of farseeing opportunism. He appears to fight for justice on behalf of the poor and the underdog. Apart from his modest salary for his Rome apartment and daily expenses, his wages went back into the corporation. His life became his work.

The other side of Mattei is glossed over. To many, especially his competitors, he appeared to be an abrasive and ambitious manipulator for whom the end justified the means. He was perceived as a cunning individual who used the system to build his own empire in a quest for personal power. In Africa, for example, he toyed with the politics and economy of certain countries in the hopes of future gains. Politically, he never denied the fact that he was an opportunist who rode the convenient ideological wave until it was time to get off. With some basis in truth, he was considered a ruthless and unethical entrepreneur, a megalomaniac, and a socialist in capitalist clothing. This negative aspect of Mattei, however, is hardly perceptible in the film.

Seen as a model of the political fiction film, *The Mattei Affair* raises the consciousness of the spectator—Rosi's ultimate goal in filmmaking. We watch individual power in conflict with diverse collective blocs of power—Mafia, Big Business, CIA, OAS, and so on. Mattei consciously or unconsciously takes on the role of catalyst, bringing into play all of these forces. The recherché form which closely approximates Jean-Luc Godard's anticommercial style militates against the total comprehension of all the links among these political and economic organisms. As a result, British and American critics referred to the film as an "honorable" one, but not without its faults. It has a frozen and distant air about it. Irony of ironies, notes one critic, although *The Mattei Affair* vehemently attacks the monopolies of the oil companies, Gulf and Western had its Paramount cinema branch distribute the film in the U.S.

The following year, 1973, saw the last installment of the controversial biographies. *Lucky Luciano*, a sociopolitical sketch of the Mafia leader, is not just another cops-and-robbers or "Family" picture. The public had already been deluged with exciting underworld films, starting in the thirties with *Scarface, Public Enemy*, and *Little Caesar. The Untouchables* on American television made the underworld all the more fascinating. Then came *The Valachi Papers*. The popularity of Coppola's *Godfather* gave rise to *Godfather II*. American television merged both films with the ironic disclaimer: "*The Godfather* is a fictional account of the activity of a small group of ruthless criminals. It would be erroneous and unfair to suggest that they are representative of a particular ethnic group." This series of Mafia-oriented films indicates that the organized crime film possesses its own history as well as its own code.[27]

In 1972–73, Rosi deliberately set out to create his own dossier on the Mafia's relationship with society and Charles "Lucky" Luciano (né Salvatore Lucania) is the focal point.[28] Rosi succinctly elucidates his intentions: "I wanted to recount the sunset of a caesar, the inglorious end of a *capo* who knew how to stay in the game till the bitter end, or who perhaps *had* to stay in the game till the end."[29] Rosi's *Salvatore Giuliano* had the Mafia in the wings, with more implications than outright statements. In *Luciano,* he places the clan front and center, in an even less favorable light at times.[30] His attempt in the film is to utilize Luciano as a historical character who cut across several decades of Italian and American sociopolitical life and modified it in doing so. For Rosi, Luciano is a personal microcosm of a larger system that in its totality is almost incomprehensible. In his interview with *Cinéaste,* Rosi reads the definition of the Mafia given by a judge at a Sicilian Mafia trial:

> The Mafia is an association with criminal intentions for the purpose of illicit enrichment of its members and which, by the use of violent means, imposes itself as a practical intermediary between property and labor, between production and consumption, between the citizen and the state.[31]

Tullio Kezich expands upon this notion. He quotes the statement of Nino Sorgi, the attorney on the set of *Salvatore Giuliano,* that the Mafia is "an instrument by which economic structures are maintained in a medieval situation in Sicily or an industrial area as in the U.S."[32]

In 1946, Lucky Luciano (Gian Maria Volonté) is deported from the U.S. to his native Italy. An extensive series of flashbacks covers the periods of 1931 starting with gangland murders and Luciano's rise to power; then they describe the American Army's arrival in Naples in 1944. Further details of the Mafia leader's activities come to light in Joe Valachi's testimony in 1952, the United Nations meeting on drug traffic in the early fifties, and a high-level meeting of the Mafia in Palermo in 1957 with Luciano presiding over the congress. The thread of continuity through most of the film is the U.S. Narcotics Bureau's pursuit of the gangland figure in an attempt to link him with organized crime, especially the drug traffic between Italy and America. The Narcotics Bureau chief, Harry J. Anslinger (Edmund O'Brien) puts Charles Siragusa (played by himself) on the trail of Luciano. Siragusa finds Luciano an ordinary citizen above suspicion. In the course of being questioned at police headquarters, Luciano is found innocent of participating in organized crime but suffers a mild heart attack. Another cardiac arrest at the Naples airport where he is awaiting the arrival of a journalist friend (Martin A. Gosch in reality), terminates the life of this "little caesar." Over a freeze-shot of the dead body of Luciano, the voice-off of Rosi concludes: "We chase Luciano, Dewey chases us, Kefauver chases Dewey, and after all this running around, we all end up right where we started."

The starting point for this technically dense film was Rosi's analysis of a confrontation with power. He elaborates on his conception of the film:

> I do not pretend to offer the filmviewers a lesson on power, but to expose them to this continuous debate . . . between my two selves which every one has, to have them share this research with me and come to understand what I have understood. This is not simply a given, but an exploration.[33]

This inner debate of Rosi and his documentation of the actual reality of the Mafia give rise to the director's desire to explore with the audience the various facets of Lucky Luciano as a microcosm of power. No work of art is absolutely free of subjective interpretation, for if it were it would be a banal imitation of the reality. Yet, in the process of investigation dealing with the personage of Luciano and the preparation of the scenario, Rosi's original conceptions were modified, especially on location in New York. In presenting the Mafia he wanted to break the stereotypes of the organization that the audience might have entertained, and to dispel as much as possible any preconceptions of the underworld film genre.

To begin with, Rosi amassed an extensive body of data to draw from for the script. The life of Luciano touched upon a multitude of historical events on both sides of the Atlantic. Rosi was determined to select material that best showed the leader at the core of legal or illegal power structures, on the national and international levels. At his disposal he had the research of Sid Feder and Joachim Joesten in *The Luciano Story* (1954), the United Nations transcripts on international drug traffic, court records from Mafia trials, but above all the continued collaboration with the investigating agent, Charles Siragusa, who assumes his original role in the film. The latter was able to provide the "inside story" about the trailing of Luciano, especially documenting the New York and Paris scenes. Rosi accentuates the importance of Siragusa in the production:

> He was of some assistance to me in discussing the Luciano case in conversations in which Lino Jannuzzi [journalist from *L'Espresso*] participated in Chicago and New York. Siragusa confirmed for us the exactitude of the facts that we learned from written documents. As technical consultant he offered us invaluable support, for he had lived through the actual events.[34]

Rosi uses Siragusa in the film in a symbolic manner as well. He puts into his mouth certain revelatory dialogue, for example, about Luciano's financing of Dewey's political campaign, that represents a type of American understanding of the existing collusion of organized crime and politics.

Rosi went on location in the United States with Lino Jannuzzi to assure the heightened realism of the general setting and the complex psychology of the character who had lived there almost thirty years. He carefully researched every detail—friends whom Luciano frequented, the books he read, the clothes he wore, and so on.

In the sociopolitical sphere Rosi raises many questions, some of which he prefers not to answer but leave open to the public. Several systems are intimately linked in *Luciano;* some are legal, others are illegal. He shows them at their unethical, hypocritical, and manipulative best. The purity of intention of each organization is thus challenged in the film. At the opening of the film we learn that (on 3 January 1946) Governor Dewey suddenly releases Luciano from prison after only nine years of his thirty- to fifty-year sentence for running a prostitution ring. Only later do we discover the reason: Luciano and his contacts helped to fund Dewey's gubernatorial campaign in New York with a contribution of approximately $90,000 and a promise to get the New York vote. It is said that, although in prison, Luciano helped organize the Sicilian Mafia during World War II to facilitate the American landing.[35] Thus "for services rendered" Luciano is freed and allowed to return to Italy.

The American government and the military do not hesitate to use the Mafia as on later occasions in the struggle against communism. During World War II, the Mafia was already organized and the U.S. made use of the system in operation; the American government only had to provide a target. In reality, the cooperation is concretized at the entry of American troops. The "Family" became legitimized. The American military was greeted in July 1943 by the Mafia chiefs such as Calogero Vizzini and Gienco Russo. The Italian-American Vito Genovese served as guide and translator for such officers as Colonel Charles Poletti, the head of the Allied Forces in Sicily. This period especially interested Rosi, for he always wanted to make a film about the arrival of American troops in Naples. He once had wanted to adapt John Horne Burns's collection of short stories in *The Gallery*.[36] In *Luciano* Siragusa's observation of the American soldiers in Naples asking Luciano for his autograph helps to create some of the ambiguity Rosi intended with his characterization of the Mafia chief.

The Mafia, working hand in hand with the American government in the forties, does not come across sympathetically in the film. The local "petty thugs," observe Rosi and his collaborators in their interviews, left Italy for America, and returned to their homeland with a corporate, multinational image. The Prohibition period provided the opportunity to organize, to make the "Family" dealings a sleek, well-established big business. In the film Rosi attributes the responsibility for the spread of drugs, organized crime, and exploitation of the weak to the Mafia.

With his choice of material from the vast quantity available, Rosi was able to situate Luciano at the crossroads of power where Big Business, the Mafia, the American government and military, and international politics intersect. He places the mob leader in a neutral and at times favorable light. When asked if he became sympathetic with Luciano during the production, Rosi stated that he did not feel *sympathy* for him, just *pity*.[37]

Part of the realistic view of "the man with the sad face" results from Gian Maria Volonté's interpretation. The actor attempted to capture not only the gestures and voice patterns of Luciano, but also the whole subculture of the Mafia. He tried to portray him as an individual who is responsible for the Italian-American power system but is also a product of it, perhaps even a victim of it. Volonté plays him as an antihero. In reality there was a Jekyll-and-Hyde ambiguity in Luciano's life. He walked his dog, was friendly with his barber, frequented young ladies (but discreetly), and even paid his taxes, he boasted. The film shows this side of the Mafioso leader, not lingering on the fact that he was responsible for lethal power plays, the drug traffic between Italy and the U.S., and prostitution rings in the sphere of organized crime.

To offer a foil for Luciano, Rosi developed the character of Siragusa. This was the other side—the legal one—of the same Sicily that engendered Luciano. Rosi cast him as an individual who had the same existential and political choices as Luciano, but followed the straight and narrow instead. For the director, he was an honest man who was a good and faithful servant of the power structure, but yet did not want to get mixed up with the politics of it. He only wanted to do his job as a policeman. This contrast of the two Sicilians highlights the character of Luciano and the sociopolitical nature of the Mafia as well.

The tone of the film is pessimistic, yet the director also considers it most realistic. We live in a world built around violence, he believes. Because of the chronological shifts through the flashbacks, the work is dense but comprehensible. The graphic, visual image carries the necessary ideological and psychological narrative in an enlightening manner. Rosi's treatment of the violent and bloody massacre of the forty or so Mafia leaders in 1931 illustrates the power of the director's images. The executions, for example, are jolting, filmed and edited in a stylized fashion and in slow motion, not unlike the conclusion of *Bonnie and Clyde* or the symbolic massacre of the competition during the ritualistic baptism in *The Godfather*. The death of Gene Giannini (Rod Steiger), a Mafia Judas in Luciano's eyes, among the trash cans of a New York street was less stylized. Here Rosi deliberately borrows from the American gangster film, such as Howard Hawks's *Scarface* (1932), Mervyn LeRoy's *Little Caesar* (1930), or William Wellman's *Public Enemy* (1931). Since Rosi was first nourished on these films he wished to offer a tribute to their creators. Colin McArthur in *Underworld USA* analyzes this conventional type of death:

> That the gangster must ultimately be dead in the street became perhaps the most rigid convention of the genre, repeated through successive phases of its development . . . and extending into European films like *A Bout de Souffle*.[38]

He includes this violent scene with irony and affection. Rosi reflects on his original purpose here:

> My intention with *Lucky Luciano* was not so much to portray the horror of the violence but the horror of living in a world which is built around violence. We know that certain things for which Lucky Luciano was responsible are undeniable, even though no one was able to make him pay for his misdeeds, either because the proof was insufficient or didn't hold up in the government. That accounts for the pessimism which permeates the film. The film's ambiguity is intended to reflect the ambiguities amongst people who actually held state power in their hands.[39]

Luciano has its own real political sequel. In the sequence of the 1957 gathering of the Mafia leaders in Palermo, Rosi had proof that Filippo Joe Imperiale and Francesco Scimone attended the session. In November 1973, both attempted to have the Italian court confiscate the film, but to no avail. The film came too close to the truth, as Norman Mailer wrote in the publicity for the film:

Rosi's **Lucky Luciano.** The classic slaying of the gangster in the refuse-strewn streets. *(Courtesy of Movie Star News.)*

... It is the finest movie yet made about the Mafia, the most careful, the most thoughtful, the truest and most sensitive to the paradoxes of a society of crime. So it is a picture with marvelous episodes, a fine sense of irony and the breath of art in every sordid detail.[40]

Hands over the City, Just Another War, and Illustrious Corpses: A Triple Denunciation

With *Hands over the City* (*Mani sulla città*, 1963), and the three films of the polemicized biographies, Rosi felt he created a type of montage or anthology of the history of Italy since the war. If he were to construct a strict chronological narrative of the material, he would begin with the landing of the Americans in Sicily in *Luciano*, chronicle the awakening of Sicily in its struggle for independence in *Giuliano*, then parallel this with the oil magnate's discovery of methane in *Mattei*. Rosi would note that in the case of Enrico Mattei, the rebirth of Italy came about at the same time as the action of *Hands*. The anthology would conclude, suggests Rosi, with the 1972 investigation into Mattei's death.[41]

French television for 27 February 1981 carried a five-minute news brief on Naples which revealed the actuality of the political-economic situation seen in *Hands*. Shots of Naples with crumbling buildings and others with ugly scaffolding, followed by interviews with the citizens, not unlike those of St. Andrea Street in the film, prove that the building speculators are still at work, and the government inactive. The poor continue to receive eviction notices, as in *Hands*, with nowhere to go because of the predominance of high-income housing. The French newsclip concluded with one of the more powerful trade unions in Naples protesting against this abuse of human rights. Rosi's cinematic protest is far from dated.

Prior to the credits we are thrown right into the middle of the action. The enterprising real estate speculator Edoardo Nottola (Rod Steiger) tells his associates he wants to make 5000 percent profit on this remote area of Naples that must be developed. Another brief scene shows a discussion among city leaders over municipal expansion. As the helicopter glides over the city, the credits begin on the screen. Rosi thus dramatically introduces the theme of the collaboration of business and politics.

A building collapses on St. Andrea Street. Two persons are dead and a child gravely wounded. Nottola's son is construction manager here. The site is also one of the elder Nottola's many investments. In a sense he may share the responsibility for this, the entrepreneur's critics feel. The city officials set up an investigation since elections would be approaching. No blame, however, can be attributed to Nottola.

Nottola wishes to get a position as building commissioner so as to shift funding to the area that he would like developed. Seeing the tension on the Right he shifts to the Center. His party wins the election, much to the chagrin of the outspoken member of the Left, De Vita (Carlo Fermariello). In the final sequence speeches and blessings are given by the local dignitaries at the new site for development. The film concludes: "The characters and events shown here are imaginary. The social reality which produced them is authentic."

Hands over the City touches upon a dangerous current situation. The scandal in Naples prior to the filming was referred to by some as "The Affair of the Magnificent Seven," and by Rosi as that of "The Seven Whores" who shifted their vote from Right to Center. In *Hands* Rosi blended fact and fiction, unlike the other films in his repertoire which demanded authenticity, meticulous documentation, and minimal invention. His screenwriter Raffaele La Capria first had an idea about a building crumbling and killing people. Rosi had for his point of departure a construction manager who wanted to evacuate people for reasons of safety. Newspapers reinforced their original ideas, and Rosi felt that now reality illustrated and reinforced art.

To build on this nucleus with the intention of denouncing the obvious corruption involved, Rosi wandered through the streets of his home town, feeling like a ball of wax ready to be molded, shaped. The shaping came in various ways. He attended Naples council meetings in January and February 1962, some of which were documented by Ciment in the appendix of *Le dossier Rosi*. He thus got an on-the-spot feeling for the political atmosphere—language, ritual, tensions. The engineer Luigi Conzena who inspired the leftist council member De Vita provided him with an insight into the politics of the council as well as the evolution of the city. Rosi interviewed countless workers to get their impressions of politics and business in Naples. For further documentation the director turned to architects, urban developers, and entrepreneurs who seemed to him to play roles in a "commedia dell' arte." Journalists such as Enzo Forcella, ideally more objective by profession, also assisted Rosi in penetrating the complex political and socioeconomic scene. With the further collaboration of La Capria and Enzo Provenzale, Rosi was able to give the material a final taut form.

The narrative develops along the double axis of Big Business and politics. Between the two there exists a rich symbiotic relationship that reinforces the belief that money and power corrupt. Edoardo Nottola represents both interests. His primary concern is to amass a fortune at all costs. In his machinations, like Richard III, he could "set the murderous Machiavel to school." He is the vulture of speculation that preys upon weaker or unsuspecting members of society. These are to be his victims cast from their homes for the sake of progress, urban development, expansion, or security, but more basically for Nottola's profit. The people protest this injustice, and council member De Vita takes up their cause, only to be silenced when the police step in. Nottola's white collar crime of unethical speculation within a legitimate enterprise and the widespread corruption in the business and political sectors of Naples have thus become Rosi's targets. On a more profound level Rosi observed, "If I had to explain my film, I would say that it is a debate of ideas, mentalities, but above all moralities."[42]

Nottola's desire to run for office as building commissioner points to the link of economics and politics. The film sketches three lines of political thought in the characters of De Vita (Left), Balsamo (Center), and Maglione (Right). Nottola abides by the political policies of the Right but, like Enrico Mattei, changes direction when the political winds are not favorable. In a spirit of opportunism he moves to the Center in order to be assured of a position in the new municipal government. On the human level, he even suggests that his son be delivered into the hands of the police for the responsibility of the St. Andrea crisis. In that way Nottola's political record could appear clean. Rosi saw Nottola as a sympathetic figure with boundless energy and progressive ideas. Nottola's ethics, however, are obviously misguided.

To oppose Nottola is De Vita, the leftist council member. Patterned on an actual council member, he is played by Carlo Fermariello, Secretary of the trade union C.G.I.L. in Naples. De Vita, in a sense, becomes the spokesman for Rosi. He is idealistic and courageous in attacking the two-headed monster of corrupt politics and unethical business. This council member brilliantly denounces scandals, warns exploiters, and confronts reactionaries. He thus comes across as the only real hero in *Hands*. One key sequence in the film shows De Vita challenging Nottola at a construction site. Nottola emerges from the confrontation as a realist who earnestly wants Naples to progress and people to have better homes, but not without his share of the booty. De Vita may be an incurable romantic, a Don Quixote figure who fights against the never-ending injustices of society. Perhaps Rosi may imply that the solution to some of the social woes of Naples may be found in a combination of both philosophies.

On the periphery of these two areas of politics and business lies Rosi's perception of the Catholic Church. The Church as an established religion is seen as sanctuary, a refuge for Nottola when he considers which direction he should take with his life. The conclusion of the film, however, shows the Church in a different light. It is simply another institution that is in collusion with business and politics. During the groundbreaking ceremony for the new development, the cardinal blesses the enterprise. His shaking of hands symbolizes his cooperation with the municipal leaders. "Thank you. It is with great pride that I am present at this ceremony. I am most pleased to inaugurate a project undertaken by the city government and warmly supported by us." The cardinal then steps into his Cadillac.

The style of *Hands* is linear, unlike the previously discussed political biographies. It is more message-oriented than the others. The film in some respects is a sermon or thesis put into the mouth of De Vita; other ideologies, however, are not excluded. The audience thus has less of an opportunity to make a decision about the collaboration of the legitimate powers at work here than it had with *Giuliano, Mattei*, and *Luciano*. The tone is pessimistic, for with the evolution of the film we see that the realization of the development plan was inevitable. In a supposedly democratic system, Nottola, the town dignitaries, and the Church align themselves financially and politically. The people of St. Andrea and the embattled Left lose out against such strong opposition.

Although this type of exposé of political corruption had already been popular in the American cinema with Capra's *Mr. Smith Goes to Washington* and Preminger's *Advise and Consent*—but not with such starkness and force—*Hands* has been hailed as an international landmark in the political fiction genre. Lino Miccichè of the Socialist paper *Avanti!* saw it as a film with an ethico-political rigor, without precedent in the Italian cinema. Ugo Casiraghi in the Communist daily *L'Unità* sang its praise and noted that it was on the same track as the neorealist film. More flattering was John Francis Lane who considered Rosi the Neapolitan Eisenstein.

Hands touched a raw nerve at the 1963 Venice Film Festival where it received the Golden Lion prize, despite its being hissed by an upper-class audience in attendance. Rosi also projected the film on location in his native Naples for a debate among several sectors of society. It served as a type of catalyst for a confrontation with city problems. The film raised the consciousness of those who were open to being enlightened but was dismissed by others as being partisan. The film itself further raised the issue of aesthetics versus politics and brought into question artistic freedom in filmmaking. On 21 October 1963, Rosi was taken to court for "contempt for the police force." A film such as *Hands over the City*, concretely revealing the strangle hold of power structures on the city, can hardly remain neutral in the political or public forum.

Although World War II has provided the more popular material for films over the past three decades, World War I has had its classics: *Westfront 1918*, *Farewell to Arms*, *All Quiet on the Western Front*, *Road to Glory*, *King and Country*, and *Paths of Glory*, with Renoir's *La grande illusion* still the chef d'oeuvre on war and peace. In Italy, prior to Rosi's *Just Another War* (*Uomini contro*, 1970), Mario Monicelli's *The Great War* (*La grande guerra*, 1959) had already dealt with the first major conflagration of the century. Given Rosi's sociopolitical perspective, however, it would be difficult to conceive of a work similar in tone and technique, especially in light of the director's sharp denunciation of militarism and class distinctions.

Rosi clearly states his intentions in making *Just Another War:*

> What interested me above all was the need to shed light on the clear separation between the men who had decided to initiate the war and those who had been mobilized to fight it. On one hand you have the power structures, the bourgeois who defend class privileges; on the other hand the masses of peasants who were asked to identify with an abstract ideal. These were poorer class people who submitted to the war with the same resignation that they accepted natural cataclysms.[43]

For the first time in his film career Rosi used a literary work for the basis of his film. For *Just Another War* he adapted the memoirs and testimony of Emilio Lussù in *Un anno sull'Altipiano* (1938) which traces the author's personal evolution. Lussù had felt that the war was not one of liberation and that it only caused more and more injustices in the army and in society. As an antifascist and Socialist, he was imprisoned by Mussolini but escaped to France where he wrote his experiences of World War I. Rosi did not just transpose Lussù's reflections onto film, but interpreted, developed, and politicized them. The director found no major producer willing to touch the subject; so he and Luciano Perugia put their own salaries into the production and received some assistance from Prima Cinematografica (Rome) and Jadran Film (Zagreb).

In 1916, the Italian-Austrian phase of the war continues. A strategic position, Monte Fiore in the Carso Mountains, shifts hands from the Italians to the Austrians, a severe loss

for the Italians. General Leone (Alain Cuny), patriotic and fanatic, feels he must retake the
position at any cost. Thousands of lives are needlessly sacrificed because of the obstinate
general's wishes. Lieutenant Ottolenghi, an anarchist (Gian Maria Volonté), tries to appeal
to the general but is mortally wounded in action. Lieutenant Sassu (Mark Frechette), in
contact with the dying Ottolenghi, experiences a traumatic change of heart. When he is
given an order to command a firing squad to shoot those who have refused to enter into the
fray, he adamantly objects. He is executed by order of Leone, stoically dying for his princi-
ples.

In the adaptation of the book, Raffaele La Capria and Rosi modified Lussù's
vision of the war. They wanted to show the absolute lack of a humane spirit
among the generals as well as the total absurdity and inhumanity of the war. The
scriptwriter and director did so by politicizing the memoirs. They brought the
original ideas in the text into sharper focus and invested them with a post-1968,
anti-war philosophy while the Vietnam War was still blazing. At the same time
Rosi wanted to make a universal statement about all wars.[44]

To obtain convincing realism, Rosi studied World War I photos and documents. His father, an amateur photographer, had taken many shots of the
trenches. In the photos some of the men were strapped to the trees between the
lines. This punishment served as an example of the fate of mutineers and deserters.[45]

Needless to say, war brings out the best and the worst of a society, the heroic
and the cowardly, the idealistic as well as the absurd. It further reveals the inner
tensions, conflicts, and contradictions within the society. In *Just Another War*, Rosi
concentrates on the sociopolitical comportment of the embattled men thrown
into the bloody campaign. As Sassu visits the medical station teeming with
wounded men, an exhortatory message beams over the radio speaking only of
glory and honor.

To show the diverse reactions to the war and in particular to the Italian-Austrian campaign, Rosi allows the three principal characters to support the ideological weight of the film. All three are trapped in a system. General Leone, a
composite of several generals, is both executioner and victim in the system. For
him discipline, honor, and sacrifice are the primary guiding principles, even
when it means sending wave after wave of his soldiers to their death. Although at
times he appears to be outrightly fanatical, he is a man of good faith as long as he
feels he must remain in this setup of war. Leone is part of the bourgeois class
responsible for calling the war and must therefore stand up for the privileges of
the wealthy right to the end.

The Socialist and anarchist Lieutenant Ottolenghi represents the revolutionary force of society. The philosophy of Ottolenghi is closely related to that of
Gramsci. His appeal to Leone is rational, responsible, and humane. He finds
himself torn between the concern for the soldiers and orders from the general.

Sassu is the focal point of the film. His conscience is enlightened when Ottolenghi dies, victim of the bloody absurdity of war. His evolution is highlighted
by Rosi. When Sassu revolts against the system he is removed by the forces then

in power. He becomes a martyr for pacifist or, more specifically, humanitarian ideals.

Sculpting all of these characters, Rosi creates a merciless denunciation of inhuman powers. The real enemy of the troops proves to be not *before* them but *above* them. The troops are only pawns. Rosi here dialectically brings out the class distinctions existing in the army. The poor male of conscription age, sometimes older it appears, and usually from the Mezzogiorno area, is ordinarily the one called up for battle. The rich intellectual generally manages to escape. With absolute blind faith the mobilized soldier is asked to fight for his country to the bitter end. Patriotism must come before human concerns. The officers, normally of upper-class backgrounds, desire to be there and have trained professionally for the occasion. Generals like Leone and his colleagues have a taste for blood, exemplified by the firing squads or decimating attacks.

Besides treating the idiocy of war in light of class problems, Rosi continues aiming at other specific targets that he hopes would be generalized throughout the world by the viewers. The colonialist spirit of Italy vis-à-vis Austria can be witnessed by its display of greed and fanaticism. The Church, as in *Hands,* shows its complicity with the power system: the chaplain blesses the men to be executed by the firing squad without raising a voice of protest. The soldiers are exploited by the government and sent the worst supplies. On a national, political level, Rosi shows that there is a subtle and at times less subtle repression of individuals; on the philosophical level, he uncovers a sense of metaphysical fatalism that cuts through the ranks of the little people.

On a more positive note, the director indicates that World War I is the dawn of another civilization in Europe and across the world. This war marks the birth of a new vision of reality, for better or for worse. Rosi further feels that these trenches were the breeding grounds for the fascism that Europe will experience over the next several decades. His film forces one to look at the phenomena of the world historically and existentially. The viewer now must come to his or her own conclusions.

Less positive factors tarnish the political import of the film, though they do not interfere with the aesthetic beauty of the work, for example, the night battles and winter scenes. Following a principle already established by Brecht in *Mother Courage,* Rosi imposes our current political consciousness upon a historical situation of an earlier period. It may be valid to unravel the complexities of the original situation, but it may be a purely historical misreading of the data, despite the origin of the film in Lassù's personal testimony. With respect to the characterization of the individuals in the film, the ideologies may be somewhat schematized into three clearly defined positions.

The publicity for *Uomini contro* from the Venice Festival in 1970 indicates that the film essentially is only a microcosm:

> Within history, events have a logic of their own. But, by placing himself outside it, Rosi sees the war strictly from the viewpoint of behavior patterns. He describes it almost biologically, to draw attention to the utter horror and utter absurdity of war. War as nonsense. War without meaning.

The wiretapping of *The Conversation*, the political intrigues of *All the President's Men*, the injustice and hypocrisy of *And Justice for All*, as well as the subtle power plays of *Three Days of the Condor* have their Italian parallels at different moments in Rosi's other film of denunciation, *Illustrious Corpses* (*Cadaveri eccellenti*, 1976). Rosi's work goes beyond the American political fiction film, ideologically calling into question contemporary power systems of the government as he did in *Hands over the City*.

Rosi's making of the film goes back to 1971. At that time novelist Leonardo Sciascia published *Il conteso (The Contest)*.[46] The plot of the novel (with its basis in reality) takes place in an undefined country and has an almost metaphysical, kafkaesque absurdity to it. Procurator Scaglione was assassinated in Palermo. The story of the original character known as Procurator Varga in the film had appeared in a literary review, *Questioni di letteratura*, in the beginning of 1971. A few years earlier, Commissioner Tandoï was murdered in Agrigento in Sicily. Another political crisis, the Montesi affair, also caused a major stir in Italy. Violence and intrigue in political life thus provided the raw material for the literary work, according to the author.

Rosi, an admirer of Sciascia, read the text. He was immediately taken by it and saw in the work an apology, an allegory, an intellectual game, a philosophical detective novel, and a pamphlet. He had understood it more specifically as a type of requiem for the revolution, but perhaps also as a cautionary signal and a message of hope. The novel itself nonetheless was written by Sciascia from within the bosom of the Italian Communist party.

Rogas (Lino Ventura), sporting the Latin name meaning "ask," is a police investigator. The case he is presently working on involves the assassination of high-ranking officials, like Procurator Varga (Charles Vanel) and Judge Sanza (Francesco Callari). In his investigation Rogas discovers that the private lives of these men are hardly above suspicion—links with the Mafia, unethical real estate speculation, corruption. The possible suspects are a leftist homosexual, a truck driver, and a pharmacist. When another homicide victim, Judge Rasto (Alain Cuny), is discovered, the case is handed over to the political police. In his own investigation Rogas suddenly becomes aware that these murders are all part of a superplot. He wants the truth made known and asks his Communist friend Cusano, a journalist (Luigi Pistilli), to publish the exposé. During an encounter of Rogas with a leader in the Communist party, Amar (Giorgio Zampa), in an art museum, they are both assassinated. The official report will read that Rogas, fearing a conspiracy, killed the Communist leader and then shot himself. The party accepts the report. The Deputy Party leader (filmmaker Florestano Vancini) explains to Cusano that the reason the party had to accept the official line, even though it was not true, was that they could not yet provoke a revolution.

A comparison with the novelist's original political allegory (of parody as the subtitle reads) would indicate that Rosi has remained faithful to the novel, at least in spirit. The director is quick to assure the public that an adaptation takes on a creative and aesthetic life of its own, separate from that of the original work. Sciascia agreed with this. The novelist was further aware that more and more characteristics of his imaginary country were taken on by modern day Italy, and in particular Sicily. Sciascia's metaphysical atmosphere was changed into an ultra-realist and concrete one, although the situation in the film is universalized, as in Costa-Gavras's *Z*, with reference to "the capital," "the provinces," "the minister of security," the "revolutionary party," and so on. The literary metaphor had to be translated into a graphic image, given the demands of the medium. Essentially both novel and film succeed in sounding a warning to the public about the dangerous future ahead if we are not careful.

Rosi has a double objective in *Illustrious Corpses:* on one hand, to expose the corruption of a moribund society that in its final stages deteriorates, decomposes, and then is mummified; on the other, to describe how power operates in the past, present, and future. In essence the film became a funeral dirge for the bourgeois ruling class. At the conclusion of the film the director indicates that a type of ultrapower still reigns supreme. Jean Gili observes that the Mafia of *Luciano* has turned into a superMafia in *Illustrious Corpses*.[47] Wealth, modern technology, and political contacts are all invaluable tools for keeping the power in the right hands. This has gone on for centuries, as seen in the monologue of the elderly magistrate Vargas among the cadavers in the catacombs. He resembles them more and more each day. The existing government with its "strategy of tension" attempts to discredit or disgrace its leftist opposition. It cooperates with the police in a cover-up of the assassinations of the magistrates. Their deaths were only used as sacrificial distraction, in one way to draw attention from the real plots and corruption on hand, and in another to traumatize the masses. The power structures stop at no extremes of violence to keep the elaborate machine in operation.

Rogas, like the uncorruptable investigating magistrate in *Z* (also from the Establishment), wishes to pursue the truth. He is of the race that asks questions, even when it hurts. In Rogas's confrontation with the sources of power, Rosi, for the first time, casts a policeman in a positive light. This differs from the director's view of the police force in general in the film, an oppressive group of fascists who pry into the private lives of the citizens.

What is Rosi's depiction of the Communist party here? Following his awakening to a disquieting reality, Rogas wants to have the truth published. He trusts his Communist party friend in this delicate matter. Both become victims when it is discovered that they are too close to the truth. The image of the Communist party leadership is hardly favorable. The supposed "party of the proletariat" gathers at a lavish reception. The revolution that is part and parcel of the party's ideology is easily snuffed out by the fascist elements. In this manner Rosi proposes that the Communist party was not ready for revolution and casts his doubt on the possibility of its occurring at the time. The ending of the film implies that the Communist party was in collusion with the current Christian Democratic government on the details—known to be incorrect—of the double assassination. This political relationship, referred to as "the historical compromise," was seen as a possibility in 1975.

Although ambiguous and somewhat open-ended, *Illustrious Corpses* is still pessimistic in its approach to hidden, yet omniscient and omnipresent forces which destroy any element of society, threatening its proper functioning. These established forces of military, law, business, and politics are complexly intertwined. The dynamic principle that guides the film is Rogas's investigation of these forces. He assembles the pieces calmly and meditatively. While watching the news one evening he has his insight into the conspiracy. Rogas's quest for truth is the quest accentuated by Sciascia and Rosi. Each artist offers *one* aspect of the truth, not the whole or *absolute* truth. In this respect, the ending of the film elicited stronger criticism than the conclusion of the book. Following the assassination, the Communist party journalist modifies the oft-quoted Gramsci maxim of the truth always being revolutionary to "the truth is not always revolutionary." Rosi defends his alteration of the principle by saying that ideally the truth should be revolutionary. In reality, however, one has to accept concessions and compromises. The road to revolution today, believes the director, must pass through certain frustrations. This attitude, along with the critical image of the Communist party in the film, provoked a strong reaction from the party. It would be understandable that the party would feel sensitive about this type of compromise depicted in the film.[48] The Right also attacked Rosi. On 27 April 1976 a Roman court denounced *Illustrious Corpses* for its offence to a government institution. For the director the film was a pebble cast into the murky political waters, creating greater and greater waves. Through all the reactions Leonardo Sciascia and Francesco Rosi stood side by side, changing neither a comma nor a frame in their creative works, for these represented their personal quest for truth.

Moment of Truth and *More Than a Miracle:* Marginal or Meritorious?

Il momento della verità (1965) and *C'era una volta* (1967), filmed eight and ten years into a career that already proved Rosi to be a sociopolitically engaged filmmaker, may appear to be on the periphery of this reputation. In his repertoire gradually built up from 1958 to the present, these films are the most commercial and international, an integral part of an industry. At first glance they do not fit into our political fiction film schema. Thematically and technically, however, they have something in common with Rosi's other works.

Ernest Hemingway's *The Sun Also Rises* and *Death in the Afternoon* gave a national Spanish sport an international image. Under his pen the running of the bulls at Pamplona on the feast of St. Firmin and the destiny of bull and matador in confrontation with each other provided alluring, dramatic moments for the reader. A mythology was created, one that Rosi was about to dispel when he undertook *Moment of Truth*.

The film opens with the famous religious procession of Holy Week at Seville. Miguel (Miguel Mateo, called Miguelin), a poor lad from southern farmer stock, witnesses it. He also enjoys the challenge of running the bulls in the streets. Returning home, Miguel only finds misery making further inroads into his life. He is bored with his work and tells his father, "It is better not to live than to live badly." Off he runs to Barcelona to escape the poverty, only to find himself alienated and unemployed. The contrast of a simple rural existence with fast-paced urban life jolts him. Once he lands a job he is manipulated by the "employment agency." At night he learns bullfighting from an old master (Pedro Basauri Pedrucho) who lines him up with an enterpreneur (José Gomez Sevillano). Miguelin penetrates the innermost circles of bullfighting, discovering for the first time in his life money, women, and glory. His agent exploits him. Depressed and exhausted one day in the ring, he discovers his moment of truth, the ultimate one between toro and matador. He has had his time in the sun. Miguel dies in the hospital thinking of his poor mother in Andalusia, while the Holy Week procession weaves its way through the spectators.

Spain always attracted Rosi with its characteristics of grandeur, confusion, generosity, as well as its aura of destiny and death. His mother's side of the family, once wealthy, was of Spanish origin, for the Spanish had occupied Naples for five centuries. Rosi set out for Spain to do a type of travelogue. Once there he was moved by what he saw around him, from the ever-recurring duel of a bullfight to the heartrending poverty of certain areas. Rosi then decided to make a film on the rise and fall of a matador from Andalusia. For his protagonist he chose the actual matador Miguelin. Born in 1939 in Algeciras, Miguelin was the son of a *banderillero*. At the age of seventeen he became a bullfighter, then shot upward until he ranked just behind Cordobes. Miguelin agreed to make the film with Rosi, but on the condition that he retain his bullfighting commitments. Taking the risk of a fatality or an injury to the matador (which did occur on one occasion), Rosi was able to use him as the focal point of his sociological and psychological study. For four months Rosi learned the customs, language, and history of Spain, trailing Miguelin from town to town, filming the actual *corridas* on location. Miguelin shot the nonbullfighting sequences on his free days, following his already exhausting schedule. For the dialogues, Rosi sought the same realism of *Giuliano*, asking the characters (nonprofessional actors) what they would say in certain circumstances.

The results—Rosi's first color film and last collaboration with Gianni Di Venanzo—were far from the romanticized travelogue that would be expected with this subject matter. The film manifested a sociopolitical tone, different from *Giuliano* or *Hands,* but still having a basis in Rosi's personal ideology.

Andalusia is to Spain what Naples is to Italy, believes the director. Rosi wanted to enter into the anguish of Spain. When asked why he was not making a film against Franco, given his own sociopolitical heritage, Rosi replied that he wished to study Spain, a more eternal subject than "El Caudillo." Franco had a beginning and would have an end (he died in 1975). Centuries, however, have marked the present subjects.

Using Miguel as a link, Rosi was able to study the poverty of Andalusia, the life of misery led by Miguel's parents barely above the subsistence level. The director tried to suggest the reasons for the poverty and unemployment which forced the young into the big cities. Once there, as Rosi illustrates, these uprooted individuals experience great frustration, alienation, and unemployment. The harshness of life is obvious in shots of the working class in the factory. The exploitation and oppression of those who migrated to the major cities are worse than their original state of poverty. Contrasted to the poorer conditions in the south is the lavish social life which Miguel falls into once he earns a reputation. This *"dolce vita"*

Rosi's **Moment of Truth.** The young Miguelin (Miguel Mateo) leaves his poverty-stricken Andalusia for Barcelona where he pursues the career of a matador. *(Courtesy of Movie Star News.)*

existence seems vapid and void. It highlights class differences. The wealthy American woman (Linda Christian) represents the nonagrarian, capitalist world, ever exploiting. In such a class-structured society ruthless and complex forces are at play. Miguel, like countless others from his generation and stock, easily falls prey to the social piranhas.

The Catholic Church, as Rosi presents it, is medieval and in collaboration with the ruling class. Jean Gili underlines this collusion:

> In *Moment of Truth,* Spain is living under the domination of the collaborative forces of the Church, the army, and the police. During Holy Week in Seville, members of the Church hierarchy and the military who process side by side recall the classical collusion of those forces that oppress the body and others that oppress the soul. Rosi speaks of the Church as "a cancer which devours Italy," and "a mother who has abandoned her own to ignorance and who despises the true country."[49]

Bullfighting is also the terrain for Rosi's critical camera. He films the actual liturgy of death, a matador and bull violently and yet ritually locked in mortal combat while the spectators call for blood. Both bull and matador become victims and sources of pure entertainment.[50] In this tragic and sacred rite Rosi demythologizes the hero and films his psychological and physical demise.

Although a folkloric tone may exist in *Moment of Truth* which could run the risk of making it a tourist film, on the whole the work is a sound, almost documentary social study. In some respects the film reflects a neorealist approach, a slice of life dealing with an Andalusian youth seduced by visions of grandeur. The squalor, pessimism, violence, and psychological despair witnessed in the film are part of Rosi's neorealist inheritance. The exotic color photography and clever cinematic technique, on the other hand, enhance the aesthetic statement of the issues. It is not without reason, therefore, that the Spanish critic Cesar Santos Fontenla in *Nuestro cine* (1965) praises Rosi and Di Venanzo for their extraordinary filming of the most remarkable shots of the *corrida* ever seen on film.

Of the entire repertoire of the politically oriented Rosi, *More Than a Miracle* is challenged for its complete disregard of social realism as well as for its escapist qualities. La Capria refers to it as a "jungian project." Other critics label it "a fairy tale for adults." *Variety* calls it a "tepid Cinderella story shot down by [a] heavy-handed tract," and the *New York Times*, "a pointless comedy." Rosi himself finds a soft spot in his heart for the film.

In the kingdom of seventeenth century Naples, the young prince Ramon (Omar Sharif) must select a wife from the seven princesses proposed by his domineering mother (Dolores del Rio). His interests lie more in horsemanship than in marriage. He is thrown from his stallion and later comes across the horse in the possession of the ravishing Isabella (Sophia Loren), unfortunately for him a member of the peasant class. After a stormy initial relationship with Isabella, he falls madly in love with her. She competes with several princesses for his hand by entering the dishwashing contest, but loses because of a competitor's cheating. In the end she still wins her handsome prince, and, as expected, they live happily ever after.

The scriptwriter Tonino Guerra first had the idea of the adventures of a woman helped by unbelievable characters. The story had its basis in Italo Calvino's fable "I cinque Scapestrati." Once Rosi and La Capria came on the scene, the trio began to work for producer Carlo Ponti. This altered the original plans. In their script preparation they would have to keep in mind the superstars Sophia Loren and Omar Sharif. A new fable was chosen, from Giambattista Basile's seventeenth-century Neapolitan work *Lo cunto de li cunti overo lo trattenimiento de li peccerille*. It was also known as the *Pentamerone*. Over the course of a year the scenario changed four or five times.

In this hybrid production, can there be found any trace of the ideology of the sociopolitical cinéaste? Alberto Moravia points out that Rosi has blended a "dialectical realism" with a rustic sense of wonderment.[51] Superficially it can be taken as the "fairy tale for adults" with a rags-to-riches theme. Scratch the surface of the romantic fantasy and one can discover another world, where power, poverty, class distinctions, and injustice are as present and evident as they are in the Naples of *Hands*. Amidst the elements of fantasy are interspersed realistic concerns. The peasants fall under the occupation law of the Spaniards. The ruling

Rosi's *More Than a Miracle*. Prince Ramon (Omar Sharif) falls in love with the peasant girl Isabella (Sophia Loren) in this seventeenth-century setting. *(Courtesy of Movie Star News.)*

class has all the privileges; the peasants, none. Hunger marks the lot of the disadvantaged, as seen in the episode of the starving man coming across another eating walnuts. Rosi discussed this realism with John Francis Lane:

> You must remember also that most of our fairy tales come from Southern Italy and so are tied to values which are extremely realistic. That's why I believe that *C'era una volta* was close to my world of expression. I was telling a fairy story as if it were something that really happened, because Neapolitan fairy tales correspond to real life. The dream of a poor person is, at the most, the dream of being able to eat until he bursts. It's not a dream of escape from reality as in your fairy tales. . . . So, I can say that the film, though a quite simple story, belongs to my "realistic" world in so far as it reflected a certain type of Southern Italian reality, not shall we say as "documentary" as in some of my other films but none the less corresponding to a real life situation.[52]

With *Moment of Truth* and *More Than a Miracle*, Rosi demonstrates that there were certain compromises that had to be made as he became part of a larger commercial enterprise. He feels that they were minimal, and that his entire production still retains an integral, sociorealist tone to it, but in varying degrees. Above all, his aesthetics show through these two films colored by Spain and its pageantry and folklore. He is not ashamed of this hiatus in his political fiction film career.

Eboli and *Three Brothers:* Social Lyricism

Rosi's most recent films are not a detour from his political path. They are essentially social and lyrical milestones along the way. In a sense they also reveal a creative director coming to grips with aesthetic and social issues that are both personal and collective.

In the era of fascism in Germany, political dissenters who challenged the Third Reich were sent to labor or extermination camps. In a fascist, but more "humane" Italy, political dissidents like Carlo Levi (1902–75) were sent into exile. Ostracized in a distant region, their political ideology would not contaminate others. Levi, whose personal and political experiences are at the heart of Rosi's film *Cristo si è fermato a Eboli* (*Eboli,* 1978), studied medicine but never practiced it. Art and politics interested him more. In 1929 he belonged to a circle of artists called "The Six Painters of Turin." The following year he founded the Socialist and antifascist movement "Giustizia e Liberta" (Justice and Liberty). In 1935, during the Abyssinian War, he was shuffled off by Mussolini to a deserted area of Lucania. For almost two years he lived in exile before he was offered amnesty. At the close of World War II he wrote and then published his classic work *Cristo si è fermato a Eboli.*[53] Reflecting with almost ten years of hindsight, Levi shows his evolution of consciousness in a closed world, a destitute region that Christ supposedly never reached. He stopped short at the neighboring village of Eboli. This book marked a significant step in Levi's psychological and literary evolution.[54] It has had a longer-lasting effect than his Resistance work in Florence, his direction of a Roman newspaper (the party organ *Action*), and his senatorial work in 1963.

Shortly after its publication, Levi's chronicle was seen as a book full of denunciation, condemnation of a regime, discovery of the south, and a consciousness of serious social problems.[55] It greatly influenced Rosi and his peers who were in their early twenties. In 1960 Carlo Levi visited Rosi in Sicily during the filming of *Salvatore Giuliano.* After carefully observing the director at work, Levi asked him if he would like to adapt the book. Rosi had a keen interest in the adaptation, but for one reason or another was unable to undertake the project. Finally, fifteen years after Levi's request, Rosi fulfilled it with a work that reinforces his earlier sociopolitical perspective, but adds a new dimension of lyricism.

Eboli starts out meditatively with the reflections of an elderly, bearded Levi (Gian Maria Volonté) surrounded by haunting paintings. A flashback reveals that he was sent into exile for his antifascist beliefs during the Abyssinian conflict. Beyond the railway station of Eboli lies another deserted planet, the village of Gagliano in the southern province of Lucania. Once housed among these "damned of the earth," Levi chooses only to observe. His dog Baron is his only companion on the periphery of their poverty. After some hesitation he gradually becomes interested in these people as human beings, abandoned by the state. Most civilly, the fascist mayor (Paolo Bonacelli) discusses with Levi the sociopolitical milieu of these disadvantaged villagers. Levi's sister Luisa (Lea Massari) visits him and offers her very rational view of the situation.

The exiled artist takes up his painting again. His housekeeper Giulia (Irene Papas), bred on supersitition and hard work, shows Levi another side of peasant life. The last stage of his evolution occurs as he involves himself with the villagers as their doctor and spokesman. Levi now totally integrates himself with their lives, but, at the capture of Addis Ababa and the conclusion of the Abyssinian war, he leaves the village a changed man. He realizes that these poor, forgotten people helped him more than he had helped them.

The production of the film differs from Rosi's earlier works. Besides the usual financing by Franco Cristaldi, fifty percent of the production cost was assumed by the Italian television RAI. There would be a double production—a two-and-a-half hour film, and a four-part television program of three-and-a-half hours.

As with his other films, Rosi sought authenticity. For several months he researched sites in Lucania. Ironically, with only small modifications, the director was able to reproduce Levi's original village of exile forty years later. Much of the modern world, like Christ of their legend, had not yet made it this far. With a dialectical sense he was able to confirm Levi's observations that there were indeed two Italys, a split that had existed for centuries. One segment of society—northern, progressive, urban, and technologically developed with the aid of the state—went in one direction and entered into the twentieth century. The other— southern and agrarian—remained static, a *huis clos*, resisting change or being refused change, or worse, being ignored by the government. In an interview with Gian Luigi Rondi in *Il Tempo* of 8 March 1981, Rosi described the dry, unembellished area in the province of Lucania:

> Desert-like, despoiled, stripped. These are areas so poor that not many years ago families still rented their children as shepherds; they called that "the dog sale." Later those poor children would have such a hard life that one day a boy of twelve killed himself in despair with a rifle placed between two rocks with a cord to pull the trigger. The images of the film reproduce that poverty of color as well: the white farm, the whitewashed interiors, the opaque stones, the crumbly rocks, the silver grey of the olive trees, and for the rest little or no vegetation. The life of the fields, in short, seen not as a refuge, an elegy, an escape, but as hard work. That is reflected in the framing, the decors, in the entire representation.[56]

Rosi faithfully follows the tracks of Levi into the burnt-out regions of this inferno. Levi's eyes are opened wider and wider to the abominable realities of life as he encounters the inhabitants of the village. The mayor speaks for the state and on one occasion tries to link Levi with him, saying that they are of the same class: "We are the state, you and I!" In his speech the cultivated fascist condescends when referring to the villagers of the lower class. He and his political affiliates are ignored by the villagers although they force the people to listen to their burlesque speeches. Rosi uses the mayor to represent the state which ignores the lot of the peasants. At the close of the war *Il Duce* announces, "Africa is in Italy!", reflecting a greater interest on the part of the government in war and taxes than in the human condition of the poor. As a result the disadvantaged people barely survive. Their sickness endures without medication or capable physicians. Their strenuous labor on the one hand or unemployment on the other, their ignorance of their sad political lot, and their collective cultural genocide make up their everyday subhuman existence. Yet, as Levi and Rosi observe, fraternity makes the burden of suffering much lighter.

The Catholic Church has made few inroads here. The spiritual shepherd, Don Trajella (François Simon), is as doomed as his flock. Alcoholic, eccentric, and irresponsible, the dissipated clergyman hardly represents the Church's reaching out to the poor. The villagers ridicule him for his comportment. At the Christmas Midnight Mass Don Trajella supposedly is drunk. He turns the sermon, however, into a brilliant display of politics, humanity, and rhetoric in a plea for human rights. The Fascists leave the ceremony in protest. Baron Rot (Alain Cuny) resides in his own feudal world. With his outlandish religious customs and attitude, he reflects an irrelevant, constraining medieval influence and force in the region.

The feminine element comprises one small part of Levi's new world. Giulia, somewhere between a slave and a sorceress, enlightens the artist-doctor to the lot of the peasant women. She is a veritable baby-factory with her seventeen pregnancies. Superstition and hard work dominate her reality.

Finally there are those residents of the forsaken village like the barber and carpenter who had momentarily escaped to a paradise, America, the land flowing with milk and honey. They have since returned to their own sealed-off world armed with photos and nostalgic memories of the New World. The young who

Rosi's *Eboli*. Carlo Levi (Gian Maria Volonté) is exiled in southern Italy for his antifascist sentiments. *(Courtesy of Franklin Media Corp.)*

found no employment in Lucania, and a husband of Giulia, have made a permanent residence in America, far away from the destitution and solitude of southern Italy.

Through Gian Maria Volonté's portrayal of Carlo Levi, Rosi attempted to create reactions of enlightenment and disturbance among the spectators. He remains faithful to the author's personal and literary trajectory. If the director had fulfilled Levi's wishes after the shooting of *Giuliano*, the film would have been cast in a neorealist mold—no doubt in austere black and white—using the same raw material that Rosselini, De Sica, Visconti, and Germi all wished to film. Instead, Rosi's social, critical lyricism rings out clearly in *Eboli*. Rosi reveals this world of destitution for our scrutiny but does it with a poetic vision. The film is slow-paced, meditative, and follows a linear development with only one major flashback. Through it Rosi is able to capture aesthetically the collective conscience of a village, a people, and give them an eternal aura.

In *Eboli* Rosi abandons his early aggressive and denunciatory style and makes his sociopolitical statement much more subtle. When asked if the results consisted of a political thesis, a social fresco, or a personal work, the director replied: all three. Rosi has thus made *Eboli* a work of art that can honestly rank with Bertolucci's *1900*, the Taviani Brothers' *Padre padrone*, and Olmi's *Tree of Wooden Clogs* in their unforgettable depiction of provincial life.

On location in Lucania for *Eboli*, Rosi came upon Andrei Platonov's short story, "The Third Son." He was immediately taken by the work. Discussing the genesis of the film *Three Brothers* (*Tre fratelli*, 1981) which resulted from this discovery, Rosi recounted:

> For a long time I had a desire to make a film about a family . . . and naturally, to talk somewhat about life, death, sentiments, and solitude—but especially through a family whose members had gone to search for work away from their place of birth and were compelled to face destinies in other cities. . . . But it wasn't until Tonino Guerra suggested Plantanov's [*sic*] story that I found the key needed to open the door of the house of the family that I wanted to enter. After that we invented all the rest from our personal experiences.[57]

Rosi was interested in getting at the personal and social elements that normally bind or divide members of a family. He recalls having talked to Tullio Kezich about this subject while filming *Giuliano*. For many years he had kept notes. He personally witnessed a certain continuity with the issues and questions of the past.

> And the facts of Italian life haven't changed: the coexistence of different cultures, the continuing problems of emigration, the quest for work, desertion from the villages, the fate of people from the South cut off from their cultural origins and the traumatic effect this has on the way they think and live. . . . In Italy, moreover, politics are becoming increasingly tangled with private concerns. I felt that to tell the story of a family from the South in Italy today was an opportunity to deal with every aspect of our lives, and that I could symbolise the country's three major problems through the choice of professions for the three brothers.[58]

His observations and insights came to fruition when he interested Gaumont and Giorgio Nocella of Iter Film to produce *Three Brothers*.

The wife (Gina Pontrelli) of the octogenarian Donato Giuranna (Charles Vanel) dies suddenly and the old man sends telegrams to his three sons. "Mother is dead. Your father." The three men return to their family homestead in the southern region of Apulia for the funeral. Their encounters over the next day trigger deep-seated feelings about their lives by way of hopes, fears, and dreams. The older son Judge Raffaele Giuranna (Philippe Noiret) experiences a vivid nightmare about being gunned down by terrorists in Rome as "an enemy of the people." His wife (Andrea Ferreol) is anxious about his court work. The second son, Rocco (Vittorio Mezzogiorno), is unmarried and cares for juvenile delinquents in a correctional institution in Naples. He has a blissful dream of guiding youth to help straighten out society. The third son, Nicola (Michele Placido), is an unsettled, angry young man working in Turin. His wish-filled dream depicts a reconciliation with his estranged wife Giovanna (Maddalena Crippa).

While the brothers converse in the adjacent room, the father develops a tender relationship with Nicola's eight-year-old daughter Marta (Maria Zoffoli). As the three brothers carry off the coffin of their mother in the funeral cortege, Marta and Donato wait back at the house. She finds an egg; he finds his wife's wedding ring. There is hope.

Working with Tonino Guerra, his scriptwriter, Rosi takes Platonov's seven-page tale, "The Third Son" (1936), published in *The Fierce and the Beautiful World,* and vivifies it. The provincial yet universal Russian tale becomes a parable of modern Italy. Rosi and Guerra telescope the four days into a period of twenty-four hours of grief, eliminating three of the six brothers and the requiem service of the timid priest with socialist hopes. They then fill in the narrative with images of Nature in peaceful rhythms, as well as of the personal problems of the three sons. Through it all the narrative speaks profoundly of the death/life juxtaposition in the family members.

With disarming honesty Rosi raises critical questions. He does so on a human and sociopolitical level, witnessing to the issues that stretch the fabric of contemporary Italian society, almost to a breaking point. The director designs a microcosm that could be both a typical southern family and a universal situation. Rosi places the family in a three-dimensional temporal realm. He shows the characters' links with their past, their roots in an agrarian society. These three men are now uprooted and face many challenging, complex issues. They also have illusions and anxieties about the future.

Each character not only has a particular temperament but also reflects a certain sociopolitical problem. They come from three key cities, professions, and ages. Raffaele, in his fifties, is an integral part of the Establishment. As a judge involved with a terrorist case, he fears being assassinated. Rosi's depiction of him was timely. On 12 May 1981, the day prior to the opening of the Cannes Festival with *Three Brothers*, there was an assassination attempt upon the life of the Roman Catholic pontiff John Paul II. Part of the film was shot in Piazza Aldo Moro in the southern village of Cassano delle Murge where the story takes place. Rosi recollects, "It was a strange feeling last summer to shoot a scene in which the dialogue was an exchange of ideas about terrorism in a bar which was located just under the plaque bearing the name of the square."[59]

In his forties, Rocco holds a very humane, idealistic view of society. In our interview of May 1982, Rosi referred to Rocco's dream as "utopian," a synthesis of the eastern and western cultures. In his dream—filled with brilliant live animation—Rocco sees himself a hero. He and his contingent of youth sweep away weapons and syringes. Dollar bills float in the air while a Russian church looms in the background, a juxtaposition of capitalist and socialist elements.

Perhaps the most complex brother is Nicola, a handsome man in his thirties. He still agonizes over his separation from his wife. With his roots in the south and hers in the north, they have strong temperamental and cultural differences to work out. In the past he has run into problems as a militant factory worker in Turin. His solution to the social problems of the blue collar force is hard-line confrontation. He is not alone facing the problems of the Italian working class. The husband of his former girlfriend Rosanna works as a *Gästarbeiter,* a foreign worker, in Germany in order to support his wife and himself.

Carrie Rickey of the *Village Voice* succinctly sums up the sociopolitical perspectives of the three brothers:

> Their interactions are convincingly those of fraternal embattlement. The eldest wants judiciously to maintain the status quo. Middle brother aims to rehabilitate those denied the privileges of the state. The youngest inflammatorily rails against the state's built-in inequalities. The three constitute a trialectic, together they are the eternal triangle, a trinity both holy and unholy.[60]

The elderly and simple father, Donato, poses a vivid contrast to these contemporary problems in society. He is from another time zone, living in an agrarian, nontechnological age. Leading a modest existence on his southern farm, he is immune to the chaos and confusion that fill his sons' lives. Daily and seasonally he follows the rhythms of Nature; stars and roosters serve as his guides. Living close to the earth he is one with Nature, unlike his sons who have become alienated from its rhythms. Rosi himself finds nothing nostalgic about this pastoral existence. He views it in a political light:

> What it stands for is the possibility of rediscovering the tough peasant strain that exists in all of us, the values of an older civilisation. That civilisation is disappearing. The state can profess a clear conscience because it offers aid, but it's also destroying the man of the South by taking away his sense of responsibility. Many young people in the South today seek security in routine clerking jobs, abandoning all desire to work productively.[61]

The characterization and structure of *Three Brothers* may be slightly artificial and schematic, and the dialogue didactic in the mouth of the judge or bluecollar worker. Stanley Kaufmann comments, "It's less a story structure than a recipe."[62] The film, however, succeeds. It is a most convincing testament to Rosi's human sensitivity and abiding concern about society's ever-increasing and complicated problems. Being part of the diaspora from the south, Rosi renews himself psychologically and nostalgically by filming the issues of his native land. David Ansen sums up his view of the film and offers at the same time an insight into the lengthy evolution of a political filmmaker:

> It's hard to convey the luminous quality of this deeply moving film, the modesty of style with which it addresses enormous issues and its seamless flow of moods—sensual, melancholy, terrifying, fantastical. It's the "political" movie of a man who has stepped back from ideology to a place where the topical and the metaphysical meet—a movie of wisdom and experience, the rarest kind.[63]

2
PIER PAOLO PASOLINI:
The Epical-Religious Cinema
of Political Sexuality

> All my works are concerned with human beings in their
> dealings with the sacred, with the presence of the sacred in
> everyday life—which bourgeois capitalist society does its
> best to repress, but which always ends up by breaking out
> anyway.
>
> —Pasolini, 1968

At the age of fifty-three, Pier Paolo Pasolini met an untimely, horrifying, and symbolic death in 1975 on the night between All Saints and All Souls days, 1–2 November. At that time some of his colleagues and admirers canonized him, à la Jean-Paul Sartre, St. Pier Paolo: Homosexual and Martyr. Others were quick to exorcize his spirit, referring to him as diabolical, perverted, and heretical. *The Sun* (England) on 3 November 1975 proclaimed: "X-Film King Murdered." Posters of mourning were distributed by the Communist party and defaced by his enemies, including a priest. The mildest epithet of this group was "pig." The compromise about his worth came from those who blessed his genius but cursed his "immorality."

Pasolini's brutal death on Ostia beach at the hands of a seventeen-year-old *"ragazzo di vita,"* was symbolically seen as emerging from the very fiber of his novels, poetry, and films.[1] "Death imitates Art!," the critics murmured. As with Pasolini's protagonists, Accattone and Ettore, Destiny and uncomprehending society supposedly teamed up against the innocent, nonconforming protagonist and did him in. His early death mythified him. It came to him following a series of interviews in Italy and France wherein he stated his absolute disillusionment with life, violence, and consumerism. His murder evoked a score of allegations— victim of a plot by the CIA or Fascists, or at the hands of several ruffians. Ettore Scola, director of *A Special Day,* referred to the incident as a "political homicide" in the strict sense, for Pasolini had become too dangerous. "He spoke too much. He had to be silenced."[2] The journalist Oriana Fallaci implied the investigation was a cover-up.[3] Bernardo Bertolucci appeared in a short film by Dimitros Mavrikos, *Portrait of P. P. Pasolini* (1975), to bear witness to the passing of a true *fratello*.[4] He accused society of killing the director for it could not accept him. It always prevented him from speaking out. Pasolini's intimate friend, novelist Alberto Moravia, reinforced this in *Paese Sera* of 15 November 1975. He pointed out that our gross society, not only wanting to be masculine but virile (we could say "macho"), treated Pasolini during his life, but also at the moment of his death, with infinite prejudice, hatred, and ignorance.[5]

Michelangelo Antonioni lamented: "In the end, he was a victim of his own characters—a perfect tragedy foreseen in its different aspects—without knowing that one day it would end up overcoming him."[6] In this way Antonioni reiterates what Pasolini's poems already prophetically pointed out in 1963 about his own vision of death:

> —I'm like a cat burned alive
> crushed by a truck's tires,
> hanged by boys to a fig tree,
> but still with at least six
> of its seven lives, like
> a snake reduced to a bloody pulp,
> an eel half-eaten
> —the sunken cheeks under the dejected eyes,
> hair horribly thinned in the skull,
> arms skinny as a child's
> —a cat that doesn't die, Belmondo
> who "at the wheel of his Alfa Romeo"
> in the logic of narcissistic montage
> detaches himself from time, and inserts in it
> Himself,
> in images that have nothing to do with
> the boredom of the hours in a line,
> the slow shining till death of the afternoon . . .
> Death is not
> in not being able to communicate
> but in no longer being able to be understood.[7]

The death of Pasolini, Antonioni further remarks, is "one of the most upsetting events of recent times, partly because it comes in a context which Pasolini—with his numerous works—tried to define: Italy today, youth, the flat contradictions."[8] Pasolini, like modern-day Italy, was full of these "flat contradictions":

—His father was a fascist officer and his mother a sensitive, peasant woman who was anti-Mussolini.
—He was a Marxist, but the Italian Communist Party expelled him in 1949 for reasons of homosexuality.
—A strong believer in the sacred, he gave up the Catholic faith at the age of fourteen and fought against the Vatican institution.
—In the late sixties, during the student revolutions, the leftist-oriented Pasolini sided with the police ("sons of the proletariat") against the student rebels ("daddy's boys").

—He criticized television for initiating an era of hedonism, yet his *Teorema* and *Arabian Nights* are deliberately and overtly sexual.

—His *La ricotta* on the commercial filming of Jesus' Passion earned him a four-month sentence for blasphemy, while his *Gospel According to St. Matthew* merited the international Catholic film prize just two years later.[9]

—This "man of deep goodness, mildness, gentleness" (says Alberto Moravia) and "gentle, thoughtful, unsuspicious soul" (observes Andrew Sarris) who criticized increasing violence in society, filmed *Salò*, using some of the most violent and sexual images seen on screen, derived from the works of the Marquis de Sade.

—Right until the end, on moral issues he fought for the respect of homosexuals but saw the propagation of abortion as fascism.

Well before the death of the director, Marc Gervais in *Sight and Sound* points out the paradoxical side of Pasolini:

> In any case, Pasolini is a very disconcerting figure, both to his friends and to his foes. To many he is a living source of contradiction and confusion. To others (including myself), he is a sort of central reflector of the contemporary maelstrom, a desperately honest and sincere artist-intellectual searching after "reality," influenced by any number of conflicting forces; but pointing the way, too, perhaps, to an over-all conciliation of scientific materialism with the spiritual view of life, of Marxism and Christianity. Paradox again, surely, for a man who, anything but the spirit of conciliation himself, upsets *all* systems by his contestation.[10]

In light of the above, Pasolini could honestly say in his last interview destined for *Tuttolibri:* "There lie within me enormous contradictions, nostalgia but also malaise."

Analyzing a filmmaker who has died (and most violently at an early age) differs greatly from studying one who is still directing, his repertoire still evolving. Pasolini's death in 1975 added a period to his work, which can be readily changed to a question mark or exclamation point. In the last few years of his life and during the past several years since his death, many studies and biographies have been published.[11] For the most part they attempt to come to grips with his gossamer-like genius in poetry, theatre, novel, and film. To date novelist and literary critic Enzo Siciliano's biography of Pasolini furnishes the most comprehensive view of the man. Siciliano is able to show that the spiritual, sexual, psychological, cinematic, and lyric are all intrically intertwined in Pasolini's life and work. His character and his creative production merge—or perhaps collide—providing a unique Rorschach blot for his viewers and readers to interpret.

Pasolini looked back on the origins of his film career in this manner:

> I came to direction when I was forty. I made my first film simply in order to express myself in a different medium—a medium I knew nothing about and whose technique I had to learn with that first film. And for each subsequent

picture, I have had to learn a different technique. . . . I am always trying out new means of expression.[12]

Pasolini's aesthetic training was elaborate by the time he entered the film world. He had already been lauded as poet and novelist. Once a member of the Communist party, he now reflected a Marxist perspective on life and creativity. This triple undercurrent will graphically break through the surface of his film repertoire.

When Jean Cocteau was received into the French Academy in October 1955, he was hailed as a poet, having created artistic, dramatic, graphic, and cinematic poetry. Although Cocteau was well known for his quasi-surrealistic films, *Blood of a Poet* and *Orpheus,* he was first a poet. Luigi Bini points out that this also holds true for Pasolini: "The story of Pasolini's life is identified with the evolution of his poetry. However he expressed himself (through discourse, cinema, theatre, novel, essay), he always felt himself creating and living his poetry."[13] Moravia called him one of the foremost poets that Italy has produced. Pasolini was heavily influenced by the French *poètes maudits.* He was enamoured of the poetry and the character of Arthur Rimbaud, controversial "mate" of Paul Verlaine, encountering the poet-prodigy's work for the first time in 1938–39 at the Liceo Galvani in Bologna. He also appreciated the esoteric poetry of Stéphane Mallarmé and the surrealists.

Pasolini's own active participation in this adventurous world began at the age of seven in the northern village of Sacile when he first wrote verses in response to his mother's very elementary sonnet on her love for him. His first volume of poetry appeared in 1942, at the age of twenty, *Poesie a Casarsa,* dedicated "To my father." In Casarsa, in northern Italy, he lived and breathed the sixteenth-century atmosphere of his mother's native village. He rebelliously wrote his early verses in the local Friulian dialect which Enzo Siciliano calls a "literary koine." This was at a time when major efforts were made nationally to insist upon standard Italian.

> Friulan [*sic*] is my mother's dialect and obviously my father was against it both as an Italian coming from Central Italy, who consequently in a somewhat racist way considered that anything that came from the margins of the country and had to do with dialects was inferior, and also as a fascist (because fascism was hostile to dialects, which were a form of real life it wanted to conceal). So it was quite a bold gesture to dedicate this volume of poetry to him.[14]

By publishing in this dialect he confronted the official Establishment which wished to ignore the peasants, the workers, and their rustic dialects. During the state's quest for uniformity and conformity Pasolini used the dialect as a political weapon to capture the forgotten realism of peasant life. For the poet, as Siciliano writes, "dialect was above all the privileged language of the poor blessed by God."[15]

During the same period he founded the Friulian Language Academy (Academiuta di Lenga Furlana), a literary club that had a unique credo. At the Yale

University symposium on Pasolini in October 1981, Pasolini's painter friend and
militant Communist with him prior to World War II, Giuseppe Zigaina, spoke of
this early poetic activity in dialect. In a type of "manifesto" for the Friulian Language Academy, Pasolini stressed the blend of tradition, linguistics, art, and politics. Political and literary autonomy was to be preserved at all costs.[16]

At the University of Bologna during the war, he aspired to work with the
celebrated art historian Roberto Longhi on a thesis dealing with contemporary
painting.[17] After doing brief chapters on Carra, De Pisis, and Morandi his work
was interrupted by military service in 1943. Following the war he completed his
thesis on the poet Giovanni Pascoli (1855–1912):

> I chose Pascoli because he was a poet who was very close to some of my own
> interests at the time, and very close to the world of Friulan [sic] peasants. Pas-
> coli's characters and his settings, his children, the birds and all that, his magical
> and *highly* artificial world, which is falsely ingenuous—all this was very close to
> my taste.[18]

Literary minded youths of Pasolini's generation were influenced by Benedetto
Croce and by Gabriele D'Annunzio's overwhelming presence in the Italian world
of ideas and letters. Pasolini, however, went beyond their inspiration in his
creativity and travelled in another direction. His revolutionary poetry was vis-
ceral, graphic, and sensitive to the substructures of humanity. By his literary
production and character he would fit well into the controversial literary pantheon of Oscar Wilde, Jean Genet, François Villon, André Gide, Allen Ginsberg,
and Dylan Thomas. His poetry, *The Ashes of Gramsci* (*Le ceneri di Gramsci*, 1957)
and *Poetry in the Form of a Rose* (*Poesia in forma di rosa*, 1964), was published while
he was writing his novels. His controversial *The Ragazzi* (*Ragazzi di vita*, 1955) and
A Violent Life (*Una vita violenta*, 1959) were both heavily marked by a Roman social
realism.[19] In these novels he used the common street language of the subproletariat. Enzo Siciliano appraises Pasolini's literary work in this fashion: "Pasolini was a noted novelist and essayist and radically changed the traditional
image of twentieth century literature."[20] In the mid-fifties he published his short
critical works in *Officina*, a literary and political journal, collaborating with Francesco Leonetti and Roberto Roversi. From these essays he later published *Passione
e ideologia* (1948–58), suggesting that poetry and ideology share a symbiotic relationship. It was with the novelist Alberto Moravia, however, that Pasolini made a
significant leap into politicized literature. Through Moravia's influence Pasolini
was able to publish *The Ashes of Gramsci* in *Nuovi argomenti,* a journal of politics
and culture, in the November 1955–February 1956 issue.

Pasolini's interest in aesthetics carried over into his literature and film. He took
to painting at first, in an impressionistic style. From his studies in art, he was to be
able to compose his shots in filming with an aesthetic vision rooted in classic
painters, primarily Italian masters. In his commentary to *Mamma Roma* he recalled that his cinematic style and taste did not originate in the world of cinema
but painting:

What I have in my head as a vision, as a visual field, are the frescoes of Masaccio, of Giotto—who are the painters I love the most, along with certain Mannerists (for instance, Pontormo). And I'm unable to conceive images, landscapes, compositions of figures outside of this initial fourteenth-century pictorial passion of mine, in which man stands at the center of every perspective. Therefore, when my images are in motion, it is a little as though the lens were moving on them as over a painting; I always conceive the background like the background of a painting, like a stage set, and for this reason I always attack it frontally . . .[21]

Ettore's death in *Mamma Roma,* for example, is a foreshortened study of Mantegna's *Dead Christ,* not too dissimilar from Rosi's composition of the martyred Salvatore Giuliano.

Besides the literary and aesthetic origins and interests of Pasolini there are ideological ones which are complex and controversial. Of all the cinéastes under consideration in our study, he is the most ideological and involved. This militant noncomformist fought in the center of society's ongoing fray. Moravia, showing the link between politics and poetry in the character of Pasolini, provides the germ of his political consciousness:

Pasolini was what can be termed a citizen-poet. He was concerned with his homeland and expressed his feelings in his work. Patriotic poetry usually comes out of a right-wing tradition and is nationalistic, but Pasolini's great originality was to be a citizen-poet of the left.

He wept over the ruins of Rome but without a hint of rhetoric. He was a modern who used the classical tradition. Rimbaud, the poet of the Paris Commune, remained his greatest influence. In the years after the Mussolini dictatorship, he adhered like many of his compatriots, to an unorthodox brand of communism that was both Christian and utopian, and these feelings for the poor and underprivileged motivated his own poetry and films.[22]

Some might say that Pasolini's anti-Establishment aesthetic and political credo emerged as a strong, negative reaction to his father, Carlo Alberto Pasolini. Carlo Alberto was a career army officer, pro-fascist, hypocritical practiser of the Catholic faith, and egotistical. Siciliano analyzes the character of the father:

That such a man could become a fascist is not surprising; it would be surprising if he hadn't. Fascism was biologically part of Carlo Alberto Pasolini: it was part of his vanity, of his obvious vitalism, of the look of suspicion in his eyes, and it was part even more of his ruined social position, of his aristocratic origins reduced to the desolate realms of the petite bourgeoisie. His having become a soldier is an unmistakeable sign, because of the authoritarian, anti-democratic tradition that the Italian army stood for at that time, and because of the way such a career provided an answer to the fate of economic degradation.[23]

This could explain in part the younger Pasolini's evolving leftist ideology and perhaps be the psychological basis for his political thought, writings, and films. Simultaneous to his father's fascist presence was the antifascism of his mother,

Susanna Colussi Pasolini. She was a simple sensitive woman of peasant stock. She was no admirer of Mussolini, under whose star her son Pier Paolo was born on 5 March 1922, and constantly ridiculed *Il Duce*. She referred to him as "the buttocks" *(una culatta)* among other things. There are, however, several stages of Pasolini's political development that must be further accounted for here.

As a youth, he later reminisced, he was politically naive. He was born into a fascist world and did not know it. In his university years, like Rosi, he participated in the Gruppi Universitari Fascisti but reacted against certain fascist attitudes toward literature and culture. In essence he saw himself "a papa's boy," born into the middle class. He came to despise the upper class with a passion. He admitted to a traumatic hatred for this class and saw it in a Manichaean way not only as an evil, but as Evil personified.

At the age of twenty, in the midst of his studies at the University of Bologna, the war disrupted his scholarly life. His military service lasted hardly a week: the Nazis captured his unit on 8 September 1943, the day of Italy's truce with the Allies. He managed to escape and went into hiding; he constantly feared discovery. His brother Guido, three years younger, fought in the Resistance as a Communist and then as a Nationalist. He died in the mountains around 10 February 1945 under mysterious circumstances.[24] This incident engraved an indelible mark on Pasolini's political conscience and emerged in his poetry.

Like Tommaso of *Una vita violenta*, Pasolini believed he could find salvation in the bosom of the Communist party. In Friuli, he once witnessed the peasant struggle against the wealthy landowners. He recounted this experience to critic Oswald Stack:

> As I told you, I discovered the Friulan [*sic*] peasants objectively through the utterly subjective use of their dialect. In the immediate post-war period the *braccianti* (day-labourers) were engaged in a massive struggle against the big landlords in Friuli. For the first time in my life I found myself physically absolutely unprepared because my anti-fascism was purely aesthetic and cultural, it was not political. For the first time I found myself faced with the class struggle, and I had no hesitation: I sided with the *braccianti* at once.[25]

The Communist party in Friuli was a peculiar one. In the party office a portrait of Joseph Stalin would hang side by side with a crucifix. In this atmosphere, on the eve of the Cold War, Pasolini pursued his political studies with the religious spirit of a convert. He devoured the works of Marx and Lenin. His readings in Marx reinforced his interest in class struggle. This helped him open his naive eyes to the political injustices rampant in Italian society. His contact with Gramsci's writings made him more conscious of creating art for the masses—and not the elite. Through Gramsci's national-popular tradition Pasolini aspired to awaken the people to a sense of history. The role of the socialist intellectual, as Pasolini understood it, was to educate the masses culturally in preparation for the revolution. The poet in the late forties and early fifties took this vocation seriously.

Pasolini approached the Communist party as early as 1946, just a year after his brother Guido may have been killed in a Communist-partisan political struggle.

Without bitter feelings and with a populist sentiment, he saw the Communist party as a vehicle to transform society. He joined the Communist cell of San Giovanni di Casarsa, perhaps in the course of 1947. In 1948, he helped found the Communist Provincial Federation of Pordenone. The following year he became secretary of the cell in San Vito al Tagliamento.

Pasolini's relationship with the Communist party was short-lived. In October 1949, the executive committee of the Communist Federation of Pordenone expelled Pasolini from their ranks "for moral and political unworthiness."[26] He had allegedly enticed minors to homosexual activity in the neighboring village of Ramuscello. He responded to the charge that he was acting under the influence of André Gide in a type of literary and sexual experiment.

Aggeo Savioli, film and theatre critic for the Communist daily *L'Unità,* clarified the situation.[27] The decision to expel Pasolini from the party was a local and not a national one. Friuli at the time was a heavy Catholic and anti-Communist region. Three decades ago, Italian society, but more so the Catholic element, could not easily accept homosexuality. Alberto Moravia explained that the people were very provincial-minded and that Pasolini never hid his homosexuality from them. At times, being the complicated person Pasolini was, Moravia went on, he looked for scandal, as a type of revenge against them.[28] As a result of his sexual preference he was thus ostracized by Catholic and Communist alike.

His affiliation with the Communist party did not end in 1949. He insisted, "I am and will remain a Communist." His communism, however, would evolve. Moravia discussed this development: "Pasolini's communism, which originally was most likely Marxist, scientific, orthodox, changed, becoming populist, somewhat Christian—given the Catholic origins of Pasolini—as well as utopian."[29] He continued by stating that Pasolini's Christian communism then swerved toward anthropology with a special interest in the Third World.

Savioli explained that Pasolini's relationship with the party was stormy but healthy, and on occasion even fertile. At one point in the sixties, the party encouraged him to return to the fold, or at least continue the struggle alongside. The poet-director had some difficulties with the current ideology and never rejoined. Although he shared some of their interests, he goaded his comrades to rethink certain ideological and social issues. When he ran into censorship problems, the party often backed him in principle, but not always for his content or tone. At his death, the Communist party organized a party funeral even though he was not a registered member.

In 1949, no longer a member of the party but still abiding by a Marxist diagnostic of life, Pasolini moved to Rome with his mother—a radical change from the northern Friulian countryside. Here in the poorer suburbs of Ponte Mammolo, he encountered other social issues than those of Friuli—prostitution, unemployment, and lack of purpose or drive in life. Soon these factors would be integrated into his literary works and film. He wrote to his friend Tonuto Spagnol on 25 September 1955: "Life is cruel here in Rome, and unless you're tough, stubborn, willing to struggle, you're unable to survive." The lifestyle in the poorer quarters of Rome was in total opposition to his bourgeois education and values. In perceiving these dialectical differences in his exposure to the subproletariat, he was able to penetrate their world physically and intellectually. He became more and more sensitive to their lot.

In the fifties, Pasolini's literary works *The Ragazzi* and *A Violent Life* put the disadvantaged individuals from this milieu into the limelight. Into their mouths he placed the Roman proletariat or subproletariat dialect. In learning this whole subculture, Sergio Citti, later director of such films as *Ostia*, was Pasolini's intermediary, or "my living *argot*," as the poet-novelist expressed it. The atmosphere of these first novels paralleled John Steinbeck's sociopolitical realism in his somber tableau of the lower classes in *The Grapes of Wrath* or *Cannery Row*. With both writers literature and politics merged, but to varying degrees. In 1957, Pasolini wrote *The Ashes of Gramsci* criticizing all ideologies, even Marxism, for failing to understand fully the nature of the subproletariat.

Although identifying with the peasants and the marginal "dregs" of Roman society in a Marxist perspective, Pasolini readily admitted that the legacy of Catholicism also greatly shaped his approach to life, for better or for worse. This became more and more obvious in the sixties, sometimes much to the embarrassment of the Marxists. With the arrival of Pope John XXIII in the papacy, he had a rekindled hope in a smoother relationship between the political and religious worlds. This pontiff was a very human individual of peasant stock, responsible for the ecumenical and open spirit of the Vatican Council in the early sixties. Pasolini accepted Pope John's desire for an overture to a Marxist-Christian dialogue. From this came Pasolini's celebrated *Gospel According to St. Matthew.*

After the successful but controversial distribution of *Gospel*, Pasolini lost his attraction to the Gramscian ideal that motivated his earlier literature and cinema creations:

> Several years ago I aspired to creating what Gramsci called "national-popular works." Years passed. A national-popular film for today has proven impossible. The "masses" have become amorphous and the social classes less distinct, for consumerism makes both nations and classes more uniform. The "vast public" could be seen as a purely numerical term.[30]

With *The Hawks and Sparrows* in 1966, as will be discussed later, the director symbolically revealed his disillusionment with Marxism. The Marxist philosophizing crow is devoured at the end of the film. Over the next few years he criticized Marxism for leaving no room for the irrational and the sacred.

When Europe and America were in political turmoil, spearheaded especially by the student revolutionaries at Columbia, Berkeley, and the Sorbonne, Pasolini published a piece of political poetry in *Nuovi argomenti* in the April–June 1968 issue. "Il P.C.I. ai giovani!!" ("The Italian Communist Party to the Youth") in excerpt form had already caused a controversy in *L'Espresso*. In these polemical verses he attacked the youths for being more spoiled and bourgeois than revolutionary. The police—their enemy—are sons of the proletariat and are better off ideologically. At this time also he refers to the "fascism of the Left", which was in vogue under Stalin and on occasion comes to the surface today.

Although oscillating in a curious love-hate relationship with Marxism, Pasolini felt at the time of *Arabian Nights* (1974) that he was free of its influence. The director spoke with great optimism in his "trilogy of life" films. He emphasized his cult of the past and sense of the sacred, and stressed the goodness of nature. Only one year later Pasolini would be filming what would be his last work. Gideon Bachman recounts a conversation with the director at the time of *Salò:*

> Too many times he has said to me and in print that he is a pessimist who continues to act as if he were an optimist, that he is a disillusioned revolutionary who continues to act as if he believed in revolution.[31]

This last film abounds with pessimism. Shortly before its international distribution and Pasolini's death, the director had prepared a discourse for the Radical Congress which he never had the opportunity to read. He professed his faith in Marxism and urged the young to struggle on.[32]

Especially in those last few years Pasolini showed himself ideologically most provocative. His unsettled spirit of activism motivated him to sign petitions, give lectures, and support certain causes such as homosexual liberation. Throughout his films he shared with Francesco Rosi the central theme of power, as Bachman points out: ". . . he seems obsessed with power and its misuse, power and its various forms of imposition in fascism, consumerism, ecology, human relationships, and modern ways of sociological convention."[33]

Pasolini was also quick to note that the two institutions of Marxism and the Catholic Church are types of power structures which impose an ideology or morality from an *elite,* situated *above* the individual. His ideology, he claimed, was more oriented *toward* the individual. At the heart of his own Marxist ideology is a dialectical process that guided him. In his films it reflected on one hand his vague humanitarian spirit, Marxist in origin; a concern for the lower, disadvantaged classes; and sympathy for Mezzogiorno problems in a "prehistorical" situation. On the other hand, in struggle for an anarchic society which he idealized, at least at the time of *Teorema* (1969), he manifested his hatred for the state, bourgeois domination, puritanical morality, and rampant industrialization. His antagonism and challenges have been met with strong reactions—ink thrown at the screen by Fascists during *Mamma Roma,* protests by extreme rightists against a Communist making a life of Christ, court cases against a film like *La ricotta,* festival scandals for others like *Teorema.* He patiently endured his problems with censors, judges, and critics. The controversy over pornography would even outlive the director of *Salò.*

Pasolini's politics were integrated into his life. From this life of alienation he created his provocative verses and films, illustrating his famous declaration of personal independence: "I decided not to accept, to disobey, to give scandal, to denounce what can happen to a clean man in a horribly dirty country."[34]

While Rosi came to his film direction through a decade of apprenticeship as assistant director, Pasolini arrived there at the age of forty with a more literary, aesthetic, and political background. In his years of Friulian joy and discovery he already entertained an interest in cinema. Living in Sacile, he would attend the local cinema run by the parish priest. He later recalled seeing some of the silent films there as well as watching the transition from the silent to sound film. In

Casarsa he organized a cinema club. Fritz Lang showed his films there. In the late 1940s, with his new faith in a socialist credo, he toyed with making a documentary on the farm workers of San Vito al Tagliamento. He always wanted to study film at the Centro Sperimentale, but the idea came to naught. At the dawn of neorealism he was drawn to the films of these new political masters. He recalled seeing at Udine the films of De Sica *(Bicycle Thieves)* and Rossellini *(Open City)*. The latter for him "was a real trauma that I still remember with emotion."[35] The classics of Jean Renoir, Charlie Chaplin, and René Clair which he had viewed at the University of Bologna during World War II were soon surpassed by these sociopolitical directors. He profited from the Centro Sperimentale film program and was enlightened by what he saw of the neorealist work.

When asked which directors influenced him the most, he replied:

> CHAPLIN (his world of working class poverty; the absoluteness of his images; stylistic blend of comedy and tragedy); DREYER (unorthodox religious inspiration; absoluteness of images); KEATON (perfection of the *General*); RENOIR (nostalgia for the middle class world which I can't learn to love; absoluteness and elegance of images); MIZOGUCHI (epic feeling, absolute and almost obsessive perfection of form); ICHIKAWA (a fluid religious quality, lacking of all limits except the one that Auerbach calls "pity for creation"); BERGMAN; WELLES; GODARD; TATI (the one and only true poet of the petty bourgeoisie)—and probably some others that I don't recall at the moment.[36]

His blessed cinematic trinity, however, that most often appears in his interviews is comprised of Eisenstein, Dreyer, and Mizoguchi.

Pasolini turned to cinema for various reasons. His prior literary works such as *The Ragazzi* he saw as already cinematic. He still had within him, however, a burning desire to express himself in a more direct cinematic way than he did in literature. The crucial link for him was scriptwriting. From 1954 to 1961 he wrote scripts for approximately fifteen films of Mauro Bolognini, Florestano Vancini, Carlo Lizzani, Franco Rossi, Luciano Emmer, Bernardo Bertolucci, and Federico Fellini, among others. He collaborated on his first major script for Mario Soldati's *La donna del fiume* (1954) with Giorgio Bassani and Florestano Vancini. In 1956, Fellini invited him to assist with the script for *Nights of Cabiria*. His responsibility was to capture realistically the dialect of the lower strata of society, especially in the relationship of Cabiria with the prostitutes. With Sergio Citti, Pasolini wrote the dialogue for the homosexuals in the orgy scene of *La dolce vita*. At times Pasolini felt he could do better than these directors with the given material.

When he approached his first film venture his passion for cinema was greater than his experience. He lacked the technical knowledge, not knowing a pan shot from a travelling shot. He compensated for this with his dramatic sense and aesthetic background.

Accattone and *Mamma Roma:* Neorealism and Beyond

In 1960, Pasolini wrote in *The Religion of My Time:*

> . . . Nearing my fortieth year
> I find myself enraged, like a youth
> who knows only of himself that he is young,
> and so rebels against an archaic world.
> And like that youth, without pity
> or shame, I do not hide
> this state of mine: I'll not have peace, ever . . .[37]

With *Accattone* (1961), his first film, he begins his merciless attack on an old, crumbling world. The director prophetically paints a bleak picture of a type of Third-World milieu already grimly depicted in his novels. Moravia documents Pasolini's shift from one medium to another:

> In transferring the world of his novels to the screen, the Friulian writer had necessarily had to drop the ideological catharsis that might have deceived his inspiration and stick to pure representation. Let me say at once that this transfer has succeeded to perfection, so much so as to give rise to the suspicion that Pasolini's novels were an unconscious preparation for the cinema—meaning that his stubborn search for the physical and the authentic by means of dialect had necessarily to lead to relinquishing the ever metaphorical word for the image, which cannot be other than direct and immediate.[38]

The film begins with a quote from Dante's Divine Comedy *("Purgatory," V): "The Angel of God took me and Satan cried out, 'Why do you rob me? You take for yourself the eternal part of him for one little tear which takes him from me . . .'"*
The young Vittorio (Franco Citti), known as "Accattone" (scrounger or beggar) lives in the Pigneto suburb of subproletarian Rome. His wife Ascenza (Paola Guidi) and child have abandoned him to his immoral ways. While his charge Maddalena (Silvana Corsini) remains in police custody on charges of prostitution, Accattone falls in love with the innocent Stella (Franca Pasut). In an effort to reform his life he attempts to work, but finds himself allergic to it. To support Stella he takes to petty stealing. Apprehended by the police who had him under surveillance following Maddalena's denunciation of him, Accattone manages to escape by stealing a motorbike. A fatal accident a few seconds later terminates his tragic life. "Now at last I'll be all right," he whispers as he passes away.

The world to which Pasolini invites the spectator is a Dantesque one where, on the surface, one abandons all hope. The director calls this "a tragedy without hope," a type of *huis clos* in which Accattone and his peers are trapped. Accattone, like the "young bulls" in Fellini's *I vitelloni* or Michel Kovacs in Godard's *Breathless*, is a sympathetic low type, victim of himself as well as of society. To escape his own misery he exploits the misery of others. He lives as a parasite. When he tries to break out of the system, he is isolated, taunted, and scorned by his peers. His momentary hope Stella, literally "the star," fades all too quickly, and he with it. He cannot fit in conventional society.[39]
The subproletariat society that Pasolini knew since 1949 is a Third-World, preindustrial milieu, the director believes, not unlike the poorer areas of Cairo, Algiers, or Bombay. To a certain extent, he feels, they are like the concentration camps under fascism and compares the situation of Accattone to a Black living in

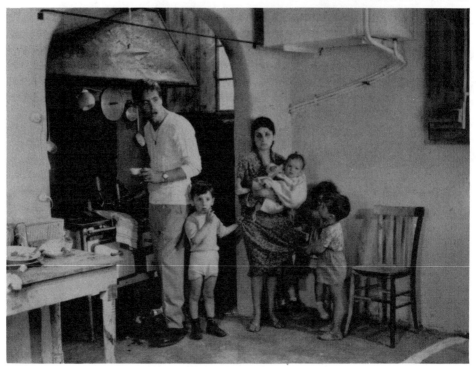

Pasolini's **Accattone**. Vittorio or "Accattone" (Franco Citti) in his milieu of the disadvantaged subproletariat. *(Courtesy of National Film Archive, British Film Institute.)*

Harlem.[40] The author of *Christ Stopped at Eboli,* Carlo Levi, remarked about the bleakness of this sector of society: "It is a world of destitution, of unpredictability, of absolute extreme, where the horizon of the vicissitudes of life is closed, without development or redemption. . . ."[41] In Accattone and his comrades there is no historical sense, no political consciousness. They exist in a pre-Marxist society, which Pasolini simultaneously wishes to document and denounce. He paints these tragic figures without drive—card-playing, taunting each other, lounging about. Those who work or have aspirations are ridiculed. Just a few years after *Accattone,* Pasolini analyzed his reasons for highlighting the subproletariat in his literary and cinematic works. First, he says, psychologically he does not differentiate between one individual or another. Each has the same value. The other reason is more historical and sociological. He sees the tragic division in Italy between the capitalist and preindustrial areas and is concerned about the fate of the poorer classes.[42]

This harsh, pessimistic, almost nihilistic portrayal of Accattone's universe is a powerful sociopolitical study of the same world as Tommaso Puzzielli's in *A Violent Life.* Tommaso passes from fascism to communism via a brief flirtation with the Christian Democratic Party. *Accattone* was filmed at a moment when Pasolini was already politically conscious, a time of discouragement, given his sensitivity to society's pains. For individuals such as Pasolini the government of Tambroni allowed life to remain unimaginative and uniform. At this time Carlo Levi referred to the people, a significant part of the population of twenty million, as belonging to a "grey race" *(razza grigia)*. Pasolini saw the Tambroni government as ending the neorealist phase of Italian life and initiating a reign of officialdom, bourgeois values, and hypocrisy.[43]

Besides this sociopolitical dimension that immediately strikes the eye, the sacral or reverential can be found in *Accattone,* as Pasolini indicates:

> The film, even though it deals with a social theme, even though it is an enigmatic film to me as well, does not only deal with a social problem: it does not only deal with one point of view, but with two, one which is Marxist and one which contradicts and criticizes Marxism. Thus, from the social point of view, it is already complex and ambiguous. But at any rate, both the Marxist and non-Marxist critics are agreed that the film is an outright Catholic one. If not too Catholic, I would say it is a kind of religious film.[44]

There are constant references to the sacred or symbolic, whether it is in name (Maddalena or Stella), graphic image (Accattone's calvary while doing manual labor), dream sequence (Accattone's funeral, not unlike Isaac Borg's experience in Bergman's *Wild Strawberries*), or music (Johann Sebastian Bach). Pasolini is nostalgic for purity, for the primitive sacredness of life, almost totally lost in contemporary society. The initial quote from Dante implies that, beneath the surface, there is a slight hope for salvation for the subproletariat society, more specifically Accattone. (In "Purgatory," Buonconte de Montefeltro was impenitent until the last hour, repented, and was saved.) Pasolini further elucidates his perspective of the sacred in the secular world:

> My view of the world is always, at bottom, of an epical-religious nature: therefore, even in fact above all, in misery-ridden characters, characters who live outside of a historical consciousness and specifically, of a bourgeois consciousness, these epical-religious elements play a very important role. Misery is always epical, and the elements at work in the psychology of a derelict, of a poor man, of a lumpenproletarian, are always rather pure because they are devoid of consciousness, and therefore essential.[45]

He opposed the Communist party on this question of the sacredness of life, saying that Marx wrote in ignorance about religion. At another moment, he stated that Marxism was not necessarily atheistic, much to the dismay of the Marxists.

This sense of the sacred in cinema puts him under the tutelage of Dreyer, even though the neorealists also exert their influence on the raw material of the film. He shared with the neorealists the desire for documentation and the spirit of denunciation. Pasolini, like the early Rossellini and De Sica, filmed an unembellished world most often of subproletarian and bluecollar workers, and not of the bourgeois of the "white telephone" era. The director realized that the misery depicted in *Accattone* would shock the Italian public, and it did. With his camera, however, Pasolini hoped to transcend the neorealists by creating a lyricism that would follow in the footsteps of Dreyer.[46] With this first film he was already on the way to establishing a tradition of "cinema of poetry."[47]

At the Valence (France) Film Festival in April 1981, dedicated to "Cinéma et Histoire," Pasolini's *Mamma Roma* (1962) was one of the forty films screened. The festival was designed to present the various visions of Rome by international directors such as Rossellini *(Open City),* Visconti *(Bellissima),* De Sica *(Bicycle Thieves),* and Fellini *(Roma* and *La dolce vita).* Pasolini's film may be one of the more nihilistic views of Rome, which he calls a *"stupenda e misera città"* in *The Ashes of Gramsci.* Yet for him the capital is still the nurturing yet oppressive mother. *Mamma Roma* provides a matching panel in a realistic diptych with *Accattone,* another world with little hope. It was inspired by the actual death of a young man, Marcello Elisei, in a situation similar to Ettore's in the film.

Mamma Roma (Anna Magnani) views the wedding celebration of her souteneur *Carmine (Franco Citti) as a proclamation of her independence. She henceforth retires from prostitution and recalls her sixteen-year-old son Ettore (Ettore Garofalo) from the country to live with her. She wants to offer him respectability through church attendance, a restaurant job, and better housing. Ettore becomes enamoured of the young virtueless Bruna (Silvana Corsini), a ray of hope, a fleeting moment of blissful love in his aimless life. Like Accattone, however, Ettore cannot adapt to conventional society. He is caught stealing from an invalid in a hospital and sent to prison.*[48] *Feverish, crying out for his mother, he gives up the spirit.*

Once again Pasolini blends the sacred and the social to show the crushing force of society upon the asocial individual. He implicitly asks who is morally responsible for this unhealthy situation, and leaves the reply to the filmviewer. His Catholic background becomes further explicit in his language, for example at the beginning and end of the film. Mamma Roma brings three pigs into the wedding feast and proclaims in biblical style to the gathered assembly, especially directed at Carmine, "Behold your brothers." Ettore calls out for his mother as he lies dying, "Mother, why are they doing this to me?" He questions why she has abandoned him. Aesthetically, he is stretched out in the form of a cross, a shot inspired by Mantegna's *Dead Christ.* In the prison, the men read from Dante's poetic-religious allegory, *The Divine Comedy.* Sacral works of Vivaldi provide the background music for the film. Like *Accattone,* moreover, this film is a tragic story of looking for salvation in a sordid world. Giulio Cesare Castello believes that the sacred, as described above, provides the aesthetic and social tension in conjunction with the subject matter:

> Admittedly here again are Pasolini's familiar contradictions between Marxism and Catholicism, between social awareness and romantic individualism, between realism and allegory—allegory which he carries to the extreme of showing the boy like an adolescent Christ crucified on his prison bed.[49]

No institution comes out well in *Mamma Roma.* The "neocapitalist priest" (in Petraglia's words) to whom Mamma Roma comes for assistance is helpless to find a job for the youth. She and her friends must therefore resort to trickery and blackmail. The victim of the blackmailing plot is a church-going man who cultivates the charms of the local prostitutes. He, like Mamma Roma, attends church services on Sunday more as a matter of social standing than religious belief, just as Pasolini's father had obliged his son to do for the sake of respectability.

The omnipresent police of *Accattone* become ruthless, insensitive, and unjust in *Mamma Roma*. (Accattone once remarked, "There are more cops than people.") The police fail to understand Ettore's offense and his illness, allowing him to die upon their institutional cross.

We have a second glimpse of the underworld of prostitution in Pasolini's repertoire. This world has its own laws, its own code of honor. All the elements of the system have an interdependence. Mamma Roma finds she cannot break out of it when she entertains her bourgeois or idealistic aspirations of education, religion, and employment for her son.[50] Dragging her vegetable cart, Mamma Roma becomes another Mother Courage, trapped in a system, at the end foiled by unrelenting Destiny. Despite Anna Magnani's incredible dramatic acting here, Pasolini felt he miscast her:

> The fact is, if I'd got Anna Magnani to do a *real* petite bourgeoise I would probably have got a good performance out of her; but the trouble is that I didn't get her to do that, I got her to do a woman of the people *(popolana)* with petite bourgeois aspirations, and Anna Magnani just isn't like that.[51]

Claude Trémois is correct in assessing the film as a sad parable which contains in germ the future films of Pasolini, with all the director's questions, anguish, obsessions, revolts, and lost hopes.[52] Like *Accattone*, *Mamma Roma* goes beyond

Pasolini's **Mamma Roma**. The prostitute Mamma Roma (Anna Magnani) creates a stir at the wedding reception of her former "agent" Carmine. *(Courtesy of National Film Archive, British Film Institute.)*

neorealism, becoming a statement of confrontation, calling for a moral awakening of the viewer.

La ricotta, Gospel According to St. Matthew, and Teorema: The Religious versus the Anti-Religious

Although Pasolini always thrived on his love-hate relationship with the institutional Catholic Church, he nevertheless preserved a passion for the sacred and the transcendental.

> My religion is of a fairly atypical kind: it doesn't fit into a pattern. I don't like Catholicism because I don't like any institutions. On the other hand I feel it would be rhetorical to declare myself a Christian—although, as Croce said, no Italian can say he is not a Christian, culturally.[53]

With this next phase of filmmaking, Pasolini moves from the despairing realm of the suburbs to the lofty domain of religion, but in each case his approach radically changes.

In the sixties, the "sketch" film was in vogue in Italy. Many established filmmakers provided personal short films to create a thematic feature. Such was the germinal idea that producer Roberto Amoroso had in mind in 1962, for a film to be entitled *Life Is Beautiful (La vita è bella)*. He was to juxtapose four shorts by Rossellini, Godard, Pasolini, and Gregoretti. Pasolini wrote his script, *La ricotta*, which gravely offended Amoroso's religious sensitivity. Alfredo Bini, the producer of Pasolini's earlier films, took over the production, and retitled it *RoGoPaG*, for the first letters of the directors' surnames.[54] Pasolini's contribution to the feature is a curious piece, a burlesque type of film-within-a-film.

> *The film begins with two scriptural quotes. The first is from Mark 4:22: "For there is nothing hidden but it must be disclosed, nothing kept secret except to be brought to light. If anyone has ears to hear, let him listen to this." The second comes from John 2:15–16: "[Jesus] scattered the money changers' coins, knocked their tables over, and said to the pigeon sellers, 'Take all this out of here and stop turning my Father's house into a market.'" Then follows a third quote form Pasolini about his intentions of filming this "story of the Passion."*
>
> *A film director (Orson Welles) is making a commercial biblical film, "The Chronicle of St. Matthew." The poor, ever-starving Stracci (Mario Cipriani), whose name means "rags," is cast as the Good Thief. His only adequate meal each day comes at the break, during which he gorges himself. When the crew discovers him ravenously devouring his* ricotta *cheese, they heap upon him exotic remnants from their banquet table. Shortly afterwards he ascends the cross for the filming, only to die from having overeaten. The director casually remarks, "Poor Stracci," as the camera ironically comes to rest on the banquet table.*

Pasolini made this short film with a spirit of ingenuity and with tongue in cheek, poking fun at the Cinecittà or Hollywood biblical film. He cleverly uses black and white for the contemporary scenes of the filming and the rich colors of Pontormo and Rosso Fiorentino for the filmed biblical scenes. The funereal "Dies Irae" in Gregorian chant is played by a whimsical accordion. The Mack Sennett gags—homage to the Keystone Kops—are witty. Like Buñuel recomposing the Last Supper scene in *Viridiana*, Pasolini uses the *Crowning with Thorns* and the *Descent from the Cross* of Pontormo (and perhaps Rosso Fiorentino) as a type of pastiche. In the character of the director Pasolini caricatures his own weaknesses. With humor sprinkled with truth, he puts sharp words of criticism in the director's mouth as he is interviewed by Pedocchi of the *Daily Sera*.[55] With this film, the Welles character says, he wishes to express his intimate, profound, archaic Catholicism. He then criticizes Italian society for being the most illiterate, and its bourgeois the most ignorant of all Europe. After a few other banal questions by the reporter, the director reads from Pasolini's earlier poetry, "I am a force from the Past. . . ."

With *La ricotta* Pasolini prolongs his study of the subproletariat. According to the director, Stracci, the Third-World hero, is the saint and martyr of the subproletariat. Alberto Moravia calls the first Christians whom Stracci represents the proletarians of the Roman Empire. Like his starving peers, Stracci makes one attempt after another to survive. He eats like an animal and is mocked by the actors as if he were performing for them in a zoo. This pitiful Keaton-like character cuts a comic-tragic figure, a perfect contrast to the heavyset, bourgeois, decadent director (Welles).

Pasolini touches a sensitive nerve in society when he caricatures religion. He satirizes the commercialization of religion through art/film, showing the bourgeois using religion as a weapon in class warfare. The Church and state did not find this episode of the film very amusing and sentenced Pasolini to four months in prison. He was said to have offended the Roman Catholic Church in twenty-four different ways through his handling of Jesus' passion. The striptease on the set, a high-strung actress (Laura Betti) as the Madonna, and Stracci's blurting out "I'm hungry" to parallel Jesus' "I thirst," were found to be offensive. Pasolini's reaction to the suspended sentence and harassment from the law and press was to say that Italian society was racist and unduly persecuted him.

Two years after *La ricotta* Pasolini made his own film on the Passion of Christ. The regime of authority in the Catholic Church, according to Pasolini (and Bellocchio in *In the Name of the Father*), had come to an end with the death of Pius XII, a statesman and diplomat.[56] The humble John XXIII was to give a different direction to the Catholic Church, a spirit of being open and up-to-date *(aggiornamento)*. A Christian-Marxist dialogue was now more possible with the new peasant-pope. The Center-Left in the government reinforced the possibilities.

In the town of Assisi in October 1962, Pasolini found himself alone in his hotel room. The entire population of the city of St. Francis flooded the streets to welcome Pope John XXIII, the favorite of the poor. The director began to thumb through the Bible and suddenly became fascinated by the image of Christ portrayed by Matthew. Filled with aesthetic emotion, he decided that this would be his next film project. As a souvenir of that day, and as an acknowledgement of this new beginning in the Catholic Church, Pasolini dedicated the film "To the dear, joyful, and loving memory of John XXIII."

Pasolini's *Gospel According to Saint Matthew.* John the Baptist is beheaded by Herod's soldiers. *(Courtesy of Movie Star News.)*

Originally Pasolini intended to film *The Gospel According to St. Matthew (Il Vangelo secondo Matteo,* 1964) in Jerusalem. Once there, having filmed some of the sites, he realized that too much had changed; the setting was far from suitable to a biblical film.[57] Instead he chose southern Italy, which he felt was still in the preindustrial age and reflected a possible biblical milieu. Matera became the old city of Jerusalem, as he began following the principle of *analogy.* A twelfth century castle from the Norman occupation was transformed into Herod's palace. For Christ, using the same norm, he wanted to choose a Polish Jew, an African, or a poet like Yevgeny Evtushenko or Jack Kerouac. Instead he chose Enrique Irazoqui, a young man from Barcelona with an angular, El Greco face. He was an economics student who had phoned Pasolini earlier for an interview relating to culture. Pasolini found him to be a nonbeliever with a strong ideological background. For the apostles he had originally hoped to have bourgeois intellectuals by analogy. He chose Settimo Di Porto, a Jewish subproletarian from Rome, as Peter and the writer Enzo Siciliano for the role of Simon. Eventually he selected a Roman truckdriver (Otello Sestili) for Judas, a poet (Mario Socrate) for John the Baptist, and a lawyer (Marcello Morante) for Joseph. Natalia Ginzburg played Mary of Bethany, and Pasolini's mother Susanna, the elderly Mary, mother of Jesus. For many parts he used other nonprofessionals from Lucania and Calabria who were only briefly rehearsed. These were individuals in whom Pasolini spotted some unique characteristic. He claimed to have an uncanny judgment in sizing up characters for specific roles. This also helped him in the Gramscian principle of reaching out to the masses, even in a commercial production.

Filmed in black and white with relatively modest means, *Gospel* resulted in an almost simple literal translation of Matthew's text. For theological consultants he turned to his friends of Pro Civitate Christiana in Assisi. They helped him to penetrate the very masculine-oriented, Aramaic-Jewish world of Matthew. This evangelist, felt Pasolini, wrote as a proletarian who was very historically conscious. The gospel itself was divided into five parts, alternating speeches with actions. Pasolini's scenario, written with Luigi Scaccianoce, captures the non-Western flavor of the gospel directed toward Jewish converts to Christianity, but without the artificial division of five sections. Instead, Pasolini elliptically proceeds from scene to scene, beginning with a shot of an embarrassed pregnant Mary, through the tragic end of the Crucifixion, finally to Jesus' promise to be present following the Resurrection.

Technically, this third feature demonstrates the mature style of the director. To capture Jesus and the crowds on the move toward Jerusalem, the city of Destiny, Pasolini utilizes two cameras, shooting two or three times as much material as needed. To give an effect of on-the-spot experience, he uses a documentary style of cinéma vérité made fashionable by Godard; at a sermon or the trial of Jesus, the camera-spectator jockeys for position. The compositions form a string of aesthetic references Mantegna, Duccio, Masaccio, and Pollaiuolo. There is a Christ from a Giotto, a madonna from a Raphael or Titian, an angel from a Botticelli, while the costumes come from Piero della Francesca frescoes. The music is a rich aural collage made of the African *Missa Luba,* a Negro spiritual by Odetta, and an excerpt from Prokofiev's *Alexander Nevsky* to accompany the Massacre of the Innocents.

Like *Accattone* and *Mamma Roma,* but without their inherent pessimism, Pasolini starkly presents this biblical world. His is a tender and sensitive view of humanity. The masses are involved with Jesus in a social revolution, but for spiritual ends as well. The mélange of Christian and Marxist principles at work here are obvious. Pasolini's Christ is a realistic one, not the handsome, blond, blue-eyed model used in earlier iconography. Instead he is a dark-featured Mediterranean type, at times brusque, aggressive, and vehement. Yet he laughs, cries, and loves children. A friend of the masses, the poor, the prostitutes, he preaches to them a subversive religion against the will of the Establishment. With them and for them he wishes to create a new order, destroying social injustices, materialism, and hypocrisy. To do this he forcefully attacks two power systems, the synagogue and the pharisees. He overturns the tables of the materialistic vendors at the temple. His enemies are "a brood of vipers," not unlike the pharisaical foe of Jesus in the biblical section of Griffith's *Intolerance.* They look ludicrous in their tall hats as they confront Jesus or conspire with Judas behind his back. The soldiers—save one—are gruff, hostile, and greedy. In essence, like the director himself, the protagonist of *Gospel* is a bearer of contradiction: neither comes to bring peace but the sword.

Pasolini does not separate his form from his content. Through this aesthetic medium with a plethora of cultural references, he manages to allow a message about contemporary society to emerge, a poignant message that he detected in Matthew's gospel. In western civilization of the sixties, he sees the sacred disappearing. He struggles to recapture it, and in doing so challenges Marxist rigidity. "My film is a reaction against the conformity of Marxism. . . . The mystery of life and death and suffering—and particularly of religion—is something which Marxists do not want to consider."[58]

Some who went to see the film expected to catch an Italian version of *King of Kings*. Others, knowing Pasolini's political record, anticipated a Marxist interpretation of the gospel with Jesus a radical leftist, agitating for social revolution. The second group was closer to the truth, but was thrown off by the literal rendering of the miracles, the walking on water, curing of a leper, and multiplication of loaves. What the spectators witnessed was Pasolini's attempt to intertwine the sacredness and the humanness of Jesus and his profound desire to get at the "myth" of this person.[59] Although he had not been a believer for the past thirty years, he was still marked by his early exposure to Catholicism. Like André Malraux or Albert Camus, who claimed to be agnostics, Pasolini may not have believed in God but had a deep-seated respect for the sacred and the mysterious. He called it at times a nostalgia for Catholic belief.

Pasolini's creation also drew strong political reactions and polarized society. The Communists reproached him for not making a demystified Christ. The youth of the Right picketed the film with signs calling it blasphemy to have a Marxist make a religious film. Pardoning Pasolini for *La ricotta,* Catholics lauded him for the straightforward adaptation of Matthew's gospel. René Jordan in *Films in Review* interpreted the work with a different vision:

> Pasolini adopted for *The Gospel According to St. Matthew* the hyperbolic style of Soviet-film hagiography: lingering close-ups, exophthalmic grimaces, 'posy' compositions, declamations à la *Chapayev* and Lenin in *October,* and hairy men in hairier shirts crawling in dungeons to Prokofiev's score for *Nevsky.*[60]

In the end, although Pasolini may not specifically show the divine nature of Christ that Matthew does, except through the miracles, and does not treat of salvation and the supernatural mission of the Messiah, he proves beyond a doubt that he can give a sympathetic view of the sacred. He does this while painting his portrait of Christ as a powerful social figure in a battle against injustice.

When interviewed by the press following the international success of *Gospel According to St. Matthew* in August 1966, Pasolini mentioned a forthcoming project—"The Visit of God." If some spectator had expected a similar but modern sequel to the *Gospel,* he or she may have been gravely disappointed, shocked, or delighted, depending on the religion, politics, age, or aesthetics of the viewer. As it occurred, *Teorema* (1968), a "visitation according to Saint Pier Paolo," primarily sent shock waves through many sectors of society.

Beginning in black and white, Teorema *reveals the messenger Angelino (Ninetto Davoli) delivering a telegram to a wealthy bourgeois Milanese family. It enigmatically announced the arrival of a visitor. With a shift to color, the film then depicts the coming of the young, handsome, but mysterious guest (Terence Stamp). He gradually and instinctively becomes a catalyst for the five members of the household, offering them sex and sympathy. When this dionysian emancipator suddenly leaves, they are radically transformed. The father Paolo (Massimo Girotti), after a quasi-Rimbaud-Verlaine relationship, abandons his factory to the workers and dramatically exits from bourgeois life. Lucia (Silvano Mangano), his nymphomaniac wife, cruises through town trying to pick up young men in order to relive her privileged moments with the guest. Odetta (Anne Wiazemsky), the daughter, falls catatonic, a type of refusal to live in bourgeois society, analogous to that of Elizabeth Volger (Liv Ullman) in Bergman's* Persona. *Previously uninspired, the son Pietro (Andres José Cruz) takes up art once again and urinates on his canvas as an act of artistic self-expression. The family servant Emilia (Laura Betti) returns to her village and becomes a saint, working miracles and levitating. The final scene shows the father in the Milan railway station, stripping himself naked, and scurrying off into the desert, uttering a primal scream.*

Pasolini meant *Teorema* to be a modern-day parable with a type of hypothesis—"supposing that . . ." He sends a triple electrical charge of religion, sex, and politics running through what some critics may call a "neosurrealistic" work. Most critics of the film nonetheless touch upon the possibility or impossibility of secular and spiritual redemption in contemporary society.

With Mozart's *Requiem*, and excerpts from Psalm 58 and Jeremiah 20, all shrouded in mystery, Pasolini leads the spectator on an audio-visual odyssey of religious interpretation. When Leonard Berry of *The Guardian* of 3 March 1969 interviewed Pasolini about the nature of the visitor, the director replied: ". . . The young man is not Christ. He has something of the divine, but he's not Christ. Maybe he's an angel, maybe the devil, maybe God . . . but God the Father, not God the Son." More specifically, Pasolini suggests that the visitor is the frightening God of the Old Testament. On BBC television he said he originally intended this character to be a type of "fertility god, the typical god of preindustrial religion, the Sun-god, the Biblical god, God the father."[61]

Georges Bataille's classic work *L'erotisme* (1957) discusses the link of religion and sexuality in ecstasy. This is certainly evident in tribal rituals in Africa, especially in preindustrial societies. In *Teorema*, Pasolini dares to handle the taboo subject of sex in a commercial film and infers that there is something sacred in the sexual relationships of the guest and the members of the bourgeois family. The relationships in the film create a rapport more among souls than bodies, believes Pasolini. For Alberto Moravia, sex in *Teorema* is a means and not an end, an instrument of bringing the five characters into reality.[62] This is not so according to Dominique Noguez in *Take One*. For Noguez, *Teorema* is primarily "a hymn of praise to sex—and even, a hymn to the phallus."[63] The Catholic priest, surgeon, and psychoanalyst Marc Oraison considered *Teorema* as effective for revealing love through a person. The results of each encounter are not catastrophic, he indicated, but demonstrate a growth of consciousness. Oraison himself felt that he closely identified with the father who sees the vanity of this world.[64] In his life and works such as *Teorema,* Pasolini continually cultivated the erotic, but at the same time criticized the use of sex as a commercial product of consumerism.

In the political realm, as the leftist cinema journal *Ombre rosse* of January 1969 indicates, Pasolini reveals a precise moment of bourgeois conscience/consciousness in *Teorema.* In essence the director opens a dialectical process on the screen. The "before" stage captures the sterility of the bourgeois family, asphyxiated by their tainted values. It is a veritable spiritual, aesthetic wasteland with no sense of salvation. In the "after" stage, once the prime mover passes through the ranks of the household, a startling metamorphosis takes place. John Bragin develops the "proof" of the disintegration of this bourgeois society:

> The film is far more of an assault on bourgeois morality than the superficial verbal attacks and gratuitous brutalities of Godard's *Weekend,* because it gets straight to the emotional roots of a civilization aberrated by centuries of sexual guilt, psychological suppression and socio-political dissolution.[65]

With sex as the intermediary, a metaphor for raising consciousness, the visitor transforms the lives of the family from superficiality to profound awareness of society. Thus Moravia aptly calls the young man a type of "Marxist psychoanalytical God."[66] The father and the maid are the keys to the political interpretation of the parable. The industrialist Paolo renounces materialism and offers his factory to the workers. This may have heightened his personal awareness of sociopolitical injustices, but it hinders the progress of revolution, a Marxist viewer would feel. The workers did not have to struggle for their rights. The gesture may appear too paternalistic, although Pasolini situates it in the spirit of good faith by the antimaterialistic father. Pasolini then canonizes the maid, Emilia. She is a peasant woman, a victim of the repressive bourgeois, and represents the proletariat from a preindustrialized era. She is sacred because she is not tainted by the bourgeois system.

As with most of his preceding films, Pasolini was challenged on all sides for making *Teorema.* Italian Marxists, for example, repudiated the film for its use of sex and the father's antirevolutionary gesture. By receiving the Catholic prize for the film at the 1968 Venice Film Festival, however, he became an international target. His treatment of sex was seen as provocative and immoral by a large Catholic and non-Catholic public. A small international committee under the presidency of Marc Gervais, a Canadian Jesuit and professor of cinema, gave the Catholic award to *Teorema* at the Venice festival, seeing it as a contemporary religious quest which is profoundly human and spiritual. The film, the committee reiterated, was not intended for the general public, but "aware" audiences. Two members of the jury resigned in protest. Monseigneur Jean Bernard, president of the Office Catholique International du Cinéma wrote to Pope Paul VI to apologize for the prize. The pontiff responded via Cardinal Cicognani that he understood the predicament of awarding a Catholic prize to a film that showed "obscenity." When Monseigneur Bernard issued a statement regretting the prize because the film did not respect the sentiments of the ordinary Christian, Pasolini immediately held a press conference in New York. He rejected the prize, "these mildewed laurels," for the film *Teorema,* and with it the award for *Gospel,* presented to him a short time earlier. He lashed out against the ecclesiastical establishment:

> And thus the old paternalistic spirit of the clerical Church, repressive and derogatory, is reborn after the brief parenthesis of Pope John but is reborn as an anachronism. Evidently the ancient bureaucrats want to enter their tombs as did their fathers, leaving behind them an unchanging world. Too bad for them, the world instead has changed and is changing. Industrial power has no further use for the old Church; it doesn't need it anymore. Only Franco and the Greek colonels still need it.[67]

Variety of 7 May 1969 reported that the National Catholic Office for Motion Pictures demonstrated its independence from the OCIC by displaying a rational, balanced view. "Pasolini's work is paradoxical in that, like Buñuel, he is an atheist passionately concerned with the sacred." Philip Hartung, one of the members of the Venice OCIC jury, perhaps best sums up the significance of *Teorema*. He accurately calls the film "a cry against the materialism of our times" and implies that it can offer a social, political, and spiritual message at the same time.[68] The tempest in the teapot died down.

Hawks and Sparrows: Marx Revisited

Pasolini once observed, "They tell me that I have three idols—Christ, Marx, and Freud. These are only formulae (*formules,* French). My only idol is reality."[69] After concentrating on neorealistic subjects in *Accattone* and *Mamma Roma,* Pasolini turned to a religious or sacral reality in *La ricotta, Gospel,* and *Teorema,* but with varying perspectives. A subproletarian martyr, a spiritual revolutionary, and a mysterious divinity became the protagonists. *Hawks and Sparrows (Uccellacci e uccellini,* 1966) reflects the forceful, direct political statements of the director, coming in the wake of his religious interpretation of Matthew's gospel.

In 1964, at the height of the success of *Gospel* and in the spirit of John XXIII, Pasolini experienced a thrilling openness to possible Marxist-Christian dialogue. Two years later he became almost totally disillusioned with Marxism. *Hawks and Sparrows* represented unfulfilled hopes and an unsettled political feeling. The critic Mino Argentieri referred to this political work as a tale, essay, confession, pamphlet, didactic representation, picaresque saga, as well as a refined figurative composition.[70] Pasolini originally called it an "ideo-comic film," but on completion considered it more a "sociopolitical allegory." As a type of fable in the spirit of the Latin poet Phaedrus or the French La Fontaine, it possesses a universal lesson that cuts through all civilizations and ages, as we will shortly see.

Sung credits in operatic style open the film. In journeying down la strada *of life, an elderly man (Totò) and his carefree son (Ninetto Davoli) chance upon a talking crow. The prattling bird lectures them on ideology, attempting to teach them about events which have some effect upon their lives. With a fable he transposes them to the thirteenth century where they become monk and friar with a mission to bring God's love to the birds. They are disillusioned following their evangelizing when a hawk suddenly swoops down and devours a sparrow. In the fable St. Francis also helps enlighten them. Back in the twentieth century they encounter one peculiar situation after another—flesh (a woman's charm), capitalism (trespassing on another's property), and ideology (Palmiro Togliatti's funeral). Slightly less naive, they continue down the road of life, but only after making a meal of their avicular mentor in a type of political communion.*

In *Hawks and Sparrows* Pasolini utilizes but also transcends the Gramscian principle of a "national-popular epic." The film itself is a contemporary, attractive vehicle for the director's ideology. At the same time, however, he appreciates the modification of Marxist ideology since Gramsci's time and even more over the past several years. Social classes are less distinct, for instance. Leftist Cuba, according to the sign, is 13,257 kilometers away. Into the mouth of the crow he places the dialogue about the age of Brecht and Rossellini being dead. The great ideological drama represented by Brecht no longer has any validity, and the era of neorealism has also waned, Pasolini proclaims. Ironically, in Pasolini's repertoire, this film is the most ideological in the pure sense of the word. Furthermore, with his characters—remnants of the neorealist period—the director is very much under the influence of Rossellini. He speaks of his indebtedness to De Sica (*Miracle in Milan*, 1956) and Rossellini (*Flowers of St. Francis*, 1949). On at least one occasion he referred to the film as homage to Rossellini.

Just a few years after the death of Communist party leader Palmiro Togliatti in 1963, Pasolini felt that an ideological era had come to an end. A radical change was taking place, as the director described it:

A historical epoch, the epoch of the Resistance, of great hopes for communism, of the class struggle, has finished. What we have now is the economic boom, the welfare state, and industrialization which is using the South as a reserve of cheap manpower and even beginning to industrialize it as well. There has been a real change which coincided more or less with Togliatti's death. It was a pure coincidence chronologically, but it worked symbolically.[71]

In making this film Pasolini wished to demonstrate that there was a brand of communism, born of antifascism, that had a purpose as well as a true intrinsic value for a specific period of time. In the mid-sixties it no longer served its original purpose; it had become irrelevant.

To have a universal application, an allegory must have component elements that reach beyond a certain time and place in history and yet are still situated in history. The allegorical *Hawks and Sparrows* includes characters and situations which have a bearing on contemporary society, be it French or Italian, North or South American. The crusty old gentleman, a type of Everyman, and his son walk down the highway of life. They could be Beckett's Vladimir and Estragon in *Waiting for Godot*, or Don Quixote and Sancho Panza, as Siciliano suggests, on the move and searching.[72] Innocent Totò with his Keaton visage and Chaplin gait cuts a tragic figure.[73] Reality has passed him by. The young son represents the budding generation, full of hopes. On the road they encounter all types of situations, not too different from Roman Polanski's two allegorical figures in *Two Men and a Wardrobe*. In the end father and son, these "two picaresque heroes of the subproletariat," in Bini's words, have passed through various stages of human development and have become conscious of another reality.[74]

In this political examination of conscience, Pasolini maintains that he and the crow are one. The voice of the autobiographical crow is that of Pasolini's friend since adolescence, Francesco Leonetti. The crow is the pre-1963 Italian leftist intellectual—perhaps just old poultry now—who preaches social consciousness. He urges his comrades to go beyond appearances to more profound truths. Once upon a time he was useful, but is no longer so, given societal transformations. The crow speaks personally and almost prophetically to the naive duo:

> All people have is God, country, and death. How much have I spoken against these things. Perhaps I shall just close my beak and say no more. It does no good anyway. Ideologies are past. You come along after me and can't convert the hawks. Maybe someone else will come along after me and say it better.

Pasolini is still anarchistic, independent, and lyrical in *Hawks and Sparrows*. In the final sequence the bird is eaten in an ambiguous type of destruction, assimilation, or communion. Before he dies, humorously and ideologically he says, "Teachers are made to be eaten with *salsa piccante.*"

In his appearance in the film, Saint Francis explains the class struggle to the two wanderers. Some critics felt that Pasolini inserted a preachy socialist discourse in the mouth of the saint. Ironically, the director used the actual words of Pope Paul VI before the United Nations in 1965, urging people to love not only one's own, but others as well.

Rossellini, both inspirer and target of Pasolini's symbolism and satire, appraised the film with long-range vision:

> I consider *Uccellacci e Uccellini* a rare example of the long-sought "new cinema," new in the substance of the times and which must correspond to the essential need of our times, namely the search for bearings in the turmoil of pressing progress. The film is the poignant expression of an author (Pasolini) who good-naturedly peers at the vast ranges of an horizon stretching above and beyond incidental, shifting and transitory events, in the hopes of finding, as a man, intelligent bearings in the immensity of time and history.[75]

Episodic Productions

The sixties saw a flurry of artistic collaboration in Italy and in France, as well as between both countries. Producers assembled leading cinéastes to make a series of short "sketches" with some thematic link, at times almost imperceptible. Pasolini was involved in several of these collaborative efforts as well as other similar minor projects that are little known or poorly distributed. Some reflect his political insights at the time, while others show his preoccupation with future major works. The latter are seminal ideas waiting to blossom at a later moment. Some of them never bloomed.

Not too long after Pasolini's first collaborative work with Godard, Rossellini, and Gregoretti in *RoGoPaG* with his contribution of *La ricotta,* and the success of *Hawks and Sparrows,* the director had an inspiration. He thought of shooting a trilogy of short films with the same duet of Totò and Ninetto Davoli. The first was *The Earth Seen from the Moon (La terra vista dalla luna,* 1966), the third episode of *The Witches (Le streghe,* 1966), with other sketches by Vittorio De Sica, Mauro Bolognini, Franco Rossi, and Luchino Visconti. Pasolini's short was a type of footnote to the more serious and heavy-handed *Hawks and Sparrows.* In the same spirit as its predecessor, *The Earth Seen from the Moon* shows the adventures of Ciancicato Miao (Totò) and his orange-haired son Basciù (Ninetto Davoli) in the poorer quarters of Ostia and Fiumicino. Totò is saddened by the death of his wife. His spirits are lifted when he encounters the deaf-mute Assurdina Caì (Silvano Mangano). Totò then rejoices with his new wife in their subproletarian home until his desire to buy a better home plunges them into tragedy. Assurdina stages a suicide attempt atop the Coliseum to get money, but accidentally falls. The light surrealistic fable concludes with the explicit moral: "To be dead or to be alive is the same thing." The implicit one, however, which causes Assurdina's death, is materialism. Of the several short films in *The Witches* dealing with marital problems and the position of women in society, Pasolini's film is the least "realistic" in style, but the most political in perspective.

The next Totò and Ninetto venture was *What Are the Clouds? (Che cosa sono le nuvole?),* the third episode of *Capriccio all' Italiana* (1967). Steno, Mauro Bolognini, Pino Zac, and Mario Monicelli provided the other segments. This twenty-two minute film, a popular fable with surrealistic overtones, used "live" marionettes to portray Iago (Totò), Othello (Ninetto Davoli), and Desdemona (Laura Betti). Under the direction of the marionette player (Francesco Leonetti), they play out the tragedy of *Othello* before a public of subproletarians. The performance concludes with audience participation—they intercede for Desdemona. A third part of the cinematic trilogy was not possible, for Totò died in 1969.

Filmed during the same period as *La ricotta* (1963) and *Comizi d'amore* (1964), *Rage* or *Hatred (La rabbia,* 1963) shows the same aggressiveness and sharp criticism of what Pasolini considered a "neocapitalist" society. Pasolini was responsible for the first part of the film, approximately fifty minutes. The producer Gastone Ferranti wanted something more commercial and invited Giovanni Guareschi—author of the Don Camillo series—to collaborate on the second half, but independently of Pasolini. With his selection of newsreels and television clips, Pasolini wished to document the anger felt by the Left. Guareschi was to present the other side of the ideological coin. Both attempted to furnish a reply to the question, "Why is our life dominated by dissatisfaction, anguish, and fear of war?" Their documentary montage of images from the pessimistic fifties (death of Lumumba, Algerian crisis, genocide, return to atomic panic, Cuban revolution, Hungarian crisis, and Suez problems) are contrasted with the more optimistic events of the space flight of Gagarin and Pope John XXIII's reign of

aggiornamento. Pasolini was displeased with this juxtaposition of the two segments, referring to his own footage as banal and reactionary. Only the sequence
of Marilyn Monroe's death did he highly value.

In 1969, Pasolini completed a twelve-minute film, *The Innocent Fig (Il fico inno-
cente)* later changed to *The Sequence of the Paper Flower (La sequenza del fiore di carta)*
from an idea of Puccio Pucci and Piero Badalassi. The title of the feature was
later changed to *Vangelo '70*, for it attempted to spell out in modern terms the
significance of certain biblical themes. Carlo Lizzani, Bernardo Bertolucci, Jean-
Luc Godard, and Marco Bellocchio also contributed to the work. Pasolini's short
is a reinterpretation of the parable of Jesus' cursing of the fig tree because it bore
no fruit. Pasolini had Ninetto Davoli symbolically walk along the Via Nazionale in
Rome. The young man, carrying his large paper flower, is struck by a flood of
images dealing with current events, from the Vietnam War to East-West relations. He is naive and does not fully comprehend their meaning, so God, in a
voice from on high, condemns him.

Also in 1969, approximately at the same time as Pasolini was preparing a short
television film on India, *Notes for a Film on India (Appunti per un film sull'India)*, he
found himself again obsessed with the classics. Almost ten years earlier he had
been asked to translate the *Oresteia* of Aeschylus for Vittorio Gassman's Teatro
Popolare Italiano. He finally had an opportunity to make this translation come
alive in *Notes on an African Oresteia*. In this fifty-minute, black-and-white film in
16mm., Pasolini is shown wandering through Tanzania and Uganda, scouting
locations and faces for a modern version of the Aeschylean trilogy. His newsreel
footage of the Biafran war reveals the tragedy of human suffering which takes
on a universal, eternal dimension. He thinks aloud, going back to the famine and
massacres of Troy. The Africa of today, like Greece of the *Oresteia*, evolves from
primitivism to a progressive democracy. The shadows of China and the U.S.,
however, still hover over the dark continent. Then he asks approximately twenty
African students at the University of Rome if they can identify with Orestes. In
some cases they can immediately see the parallels of their situation with that of
the Greek hero. In other instances, it appears that Pasolini imposes a western
European interpretation on the African situation. The film is roughly edited and
free-flowing. Haunting close-ups of possible characters such as Agamemnon and
the rich music save the film aesthetically.

Two other short films, both documentaries, reveal the creative and political
sensitivity of the director. In 1968–69, at the time of *Teorema*, Pasolini filmed a
series of documentary reportage for television. He first made a twelve-minute
documentary *The Walls of San'A (Le mura di Sana)* while he was filming *Decameron*.
His dialectical instinct heightened, he filmed the medieval city of San'A in Northern Yemen, cutting to the Italian city of Orte, slightly north of Rome, ruined
when once the industrial age struck. *The Walls of San'A* is a type of cautionary
message to UNESCO in documentary form. In the comparison and contrast
between the ancient and modern cities, Pasolini implies that if San'A is not careful, it, too, can find itself culturally destroyed.

Pasolini's last major short film emerged in 1971, *12 December (Dodici dicembre)*.
Once again a man of contradictions, Pasolini joins ranks with *Lotta continua*, the

extreme Left, after having condemned the Italian revolutionary youth just a short time earlier. This film differs from any other film in his repertoire insofar as it is an explicitly *militant* film. The original idea came from Giovanni Bonfanti and Goffredo Fofi, while Pasolini and Bonfanti assumed responsibility for the technical aspect of the film. For this collective work they gathered ex-partisans, workers from the Fiat plant, displaced persons of Naples, quarry workers from Carrara, among others. The filmmakers brought to light many aspects of the 12 December 1969 bombing of Piazza Fontana (Milan) and the "Pinelli Affair."

Although these shorts have not made a significant impact upon critic or public alike, they reflect some of the creative energy that Pasolini exhibited in the late sixties and early seventies.

Comizi d'amore, *Oedipus*, and *Medea:* From Freudian Psychology to Greek Tragedy

The unfavorable critics of Pasolini in the late sixties and early seventies condemned him to the hell of pornography. They criticized him for what they considered an obsession with sex, sensing that this gifted, lyrical artist was now turning his talent to commercialized pornography. Pasolini felt that his case was exactly the opposite. He saw sex as sacred and reverent, a ritual that had been distorted by Church and state alike. *Comizi d'amore* (1964), literally "forum of love," was the director's warning signal to society and his critics. With the two classics *Oedipus* and *Medea* the signals were getting stronger, and they would not cease until the artist was dead.

With *Comizi d'amore* Pasolini turned into an amateur sociologist and journalist. He used the reportage style of experimental cinema, already popular in Italy through the influence of cinéaste Jean Rouch's and sociologist Edgar Morin's *Chronicle of a Summer* (*Chronique d'un été*, 1961). Pasolini in his research sought to raise the taboo subject of sexuality in a cross section of milieux in Italy, on beaches and in cities, from southern Calabria to the industrial north. Microphone in hand, he interviews in the film a gamut of the Italian population, from students and soldiers to farmers and *petits bourgeois* about sex education, homosexuality, virginity, prostitution, and women's issues. Following the interviews he discussed the results with the novelist Alberto Moravia, who had written on this topic on many occasions; the psychoanalyst Cesare Musatti; and actress Antonella Lualdi.[76] Three women journalists also appeared in the film to discuss the topics—Adele Cambria, Oriana Fallaci, and Camilla Cederna.

The conclusions of Pasolini's interviews? Though Italian society has moved well into the twentieth century technologically, especially in the northern areas of Milan and Turin, it is still archaic in its attitudes toward sexuality. Hypocrisy and conformity mask the true feelings of love and sex. The Church influences Italian Catholics either explicitly or implicitly on sexual issues. The male, with a strong macho image, heads the power system, dictating attitudes for the family. Taboos still have their force in proletarian quarters and the Mezzogiorno region. In the professional and upper classes of society and in the northern industrial sectors, the people interviewed appear more enlightened about love and sexuality than their fellow citizens in the south, who belong to another age. Gervais approaches the film as Pasolini's "call for the demystification of sex and a rational effort at becoming more modern."[77] In *Le Monde* of 23 March 1977 the French socio-psychologist Michel Foucault noted that the predominant feeling in the film is the apprehension of a new era of tolerance in Italy, which in turn creates tension between people. The young, for example, approach this tolerance with gravity and distrust. In one way or another they relate sexual mores to the whole economic system of Italy. In *Comizi d'amore* Pasolini proves, therefore, as he did in *Teorema,* that sexuality, politics, and religion have strong, intertwined connections.

Playwrights or filmmakers who reinterpret myths for the stage or screen primarily trust that an ancient "sacred story" can communicate an eternal message. Although speaking originally in the past tense, a myth once modernized can dramatically convey some lesson to a contemporary audience. Such is the case with Sartre's *The Flies,* Anouilh's *Antigone,* and O'Neill's *Mourning Becomes Electra.* Pasolini, in *Oedipus Rex* and *Medea,* speaks in both tenses with a poignant communiqué.

A son's obsession with his mother and his hostility, bordering on hatred, toward his father gives way to the sexual phenomenon Freud terms the "oedipal complex." Both facets of this complex become integral parts of Pasolini's autobiographical adaptation of Sophocles' tragedy *Oedipus Rex* (*Edipo re,* 1967). In an interview with Jean Narboni for *Cahiers du cinéma* in 1967, the director reveals the origin of the adaptation:

> In *Oedipus* I am recounting the story of my own Oedipus complex. The little boy in the prologue is myself, his father is my father, a former infantry officer, and his mother the teacher, my own mother. I am narrating my life, mythologized, of course, made more epical via the legend of Oedipus.[78]

On Swiss television in October 1966, Pasolini discussed his relations with his father, Carlo Alberto, dead almost eight years. Throughout his youth Pier Paolo (and his mother) despised the father who was alcoholic, tyrannical, and authoritarian. Enzo Siciliano says, "Aristocratic vanity was one of Carlo Alberto's traits. . . ." The profascist officer had a set of values that were not attractive to Piero Paolo. In middle-class Italian society the son (especially the oldest) could be expected to *become* the father, pursuing his business, for example. That would have been the farthest from Pier Paolo's intentions. Pasolini's father died on 19 December 1958 of cirrhosis of the liver. In interviews in the late sixties and early seventies, Pasolini attempted to "white wash" or "recuperate" his relationship with his father, saying that his hatred was really a form of love, and that he had a positive rapport with him when Pier Paolo was at a very impressionable age.

His relationship with his mother, Susanna Colussi Pasolini, was tender. Through his life she was his most faithful companion, especially since their move to Rome from their native Friuli in 1949. For this reason he no doubt cast her as the mother of Jesus in *Gospel.*

Pasolini's rendition of the Oedipus myth, besides being classical and autobiographical, is uniquely inventive. It spans several different places and periods.

*Military music opens the first episode or prologue, set in the 1920s or 1930s. A mother is
very affectionate with her son. A father scowls at the child, feeling the baby is stealing the
mother's love from him. Cut. The next scene is a desert (filmed in Morocco). A peasant
carries a child, bound hand and foot to a pole, wailing like a captured animal. The third
and central part of the film is the adaptation from Sophocles' Oedipus the King and
Oedipus at Colonus. Following the devastating oracle, the young man Oedipus (Franco
Citti) is confronted in the desert by an elderly man with his cortege who cries out, "Get out of
my way, miserable wretch." Oedipus kills him (Laius, Luciano Bartoli) and his cohorts.
Upon entering Thebes he slays the sphinx, and then marries Queen Jocasta (Silvana Mangano). His reign, however, is befouled by the plague. The blind prophet Tiresias (Julian
Beck) sees that Oedipus' slaying of his father brought about this disaster. King Oedipus, in
his quest for truth, soon learns that he is the tragic victim of Destiny, the ultimate cause of
the plague. He unknowingly smote his own father and espoused his mother. Despondent, he
blinds himself while his wife/mother commits suicide. The final episode, a type of epilogue,
brings us back into the twentieth century. The blind Oedipus, with the assistance of Angelo
(Ninetto Davoli) walks past the factories of the town in the prologue, and out into the
country. In the field Oedipus remarks, "Life ends where it begins."*

Pasolini and his critics primarily concentrate on the Freudian side of the myth
depicted in the film, discussing in depth the double theme of parricide and incest.[79] Psychologists would certainly have the material at hand to analyze Pasolini's overt homosexuality in the late sixties and early seventies as stemming
from his relationship with his mother and father. In *Cinema nuovo*, Guido
Aristarco refers to the film as a type of "confession" more in the Catholic than
psychological sense.[80]

While being conscious of the Freudian aspects of *Oedipus*, the viewer should
also not forget the Jungian elements. There is throughout the film a sense of the
collective unconscious which prevails. Myth lends itself readily to a Jungian interpretation, almost giving the film an aura of "meta-history." The final hymn to
light by the blind Oedipus brings the spectator to the opening of the film, a type
of eternal return. Oedipus/Pasolini is the damned poet—a *"poète maudit"*—cursed
by Destiny and society.

Alberto Moravia, with whom the film was conceived on one of their visits to
Morocco, feels that the film is a perfect blend of realism, autobiography, and
ideology. Although Pasolini does not situate the film in the sphere of historical
consciousness but in the realm of myth, he manifests a double ideological thrust.
In one respect, this is Oedipus' struggle with the divinity. Even though he has
become a scapegoat of Fate, he emerges from the struggle into the light of truth.
In another, the confrontation of Oedipus with Creon reveals two opposing ideologies—idealistic and realistic respectively. In the end, Destiny will continue to
play its unrelenting, oppressive role, but it is up to the human being to challenge
it.

In discussing the Marxist and Freudian elements of the film, Pasolini states that ". . . Freud would seem to have come out with more points than Marx."[81] Assessing his psychological and political penchants, Pasolini proclaims: "I want to stress the fact that now, at forty-five years of age, I have emerged from the wilderness of Freudian and Marxist dogma."[82] In light of the remainder of his film repertoire this statement will have to be challenged.

For a second time, Pasolini taps the riches of Greek literature by his rein-terpretation of Euripides' tragedy *Medea*. With *Medea* (1969) he welcomes us into mythical and surrealistic worlds that are hostile, offering a psychological, eth-nological, and political reading of the classic narrative.

The young Jason (Giuseppe Gentili) receives his early training from the centaur (Laurent Terzeiff). In order to reclaim his rightful kingdom presently in the hands of his uncle Peleas, he must steal the Golden Fleece from Colchis. In the primitive civilization of sun-worship and cannibalism of Colchis, Jason encounters the high priestess and sorceress Medea (Maria Callas) who, through the assistance of her brother Absytros, helps steal the Golden Fleece.[83] Escaping, the duo kills the brother and strews his members along the way, assuring a delay. Ten years pass, with two sons showing the fruit of their love. Then one day Jason decides abruptly to end his covenant with Medea by marrying Glauce (Margareth Clementi), daughter of Creon (Massimo Girotti). Filled with revenge, Medea offers the bride-to-be a lethal robe, tenderly slays her two sons, then sets fire to the household. The blaze consumes her.

Pasolini's adaptation vividly reinterprets the intricate and emotional Euripi-dean play centering around the love of Medea for Jason which turns to jealousy and then destruction. Medea's sacrifice of her brother to aid Jason evolves into a cruel, inhuman, and passionate vendetta that concludes the film. To Euripides' drama Pasolini adds another dimension, the ethnological. Petraglia refers to the film as *"cinema anthropologico."*[84] Pasolini's camera, for example, without warning, enters the pre-Christian world at the opening of the film to document an eerie but profoundly religious ritual of cannibalism.

The sociopolitical dimension of *Medea* is equally complex. Pasolini contrasts the harmonious, primitive society of Colchis with the Corinthian kingdom, where machinations are the order of the day. Peleas holds the throne of Jason's father. He refuses to return it to the rightful heir, even after the young man obtains the Golden Fleece, indicating the hostile nature of the fickle state. Jason learns the harsh political lesson that kings do not always keep their promises.

Derek Elley refers to Pasolini's contemporary political perspective on the in-justice of the past as seen by Euripides: "Only the slant has changed—[there is] a greater emphasis on moral decline and an implicit condemnation of states-manship."[85] Pasolini also depicts Medea as an alienated woman who learns an-other political lesson in confrontation with her ambitious husband Jason. He wants to cast aside this albatross in order to marry the king's daughter. His love for Medea wanes as his interest in the power system grows. Medea, as a result, cries out for justice upon this xenophobic society, and for love from an un-faithful husband. She lashes out violently like a wounded panther.

Pasolini remarked that if he were to modernize totally this myth, Jason and the

Argonauts would become mercenaries from a western world (Corinth). They would arrive in the Third World (Colchis) and uproot a woman (Medea) from another race. As it stands, he has ingeniously blended the classical myth with modern sociopolitical issues in *Medea* as he had done with *Oedipus Rex*.

Decameron, Canterbury Tales, Arabian Nights: A Sexual, Literary Trilogy of Life

Three other adaptations followed in Pasolini's repertoire which would have greater continuity than his two unique renditions of Greek myths. These medieval worlds of Boccaccio and Chaucer and of an anonymous Arab represent three moments of a single film on life, or as he often said, three chapters of the same work. The trilogy was his declaration of a love for life. Through three period pieces he wished to play *"un gioco"* (a game), inserting his own personal vision of life into the films by way of his physical and aesthetic presence. In doing so he goes beyond the simple transferral of a piece of literature to celluloid. Bringing his philological and political background to his work, he opens the screen to a type of fourth dimension. These films are replete with nostalgia for a preindustrialized past, when the "noble savage" still roamed the earth. They exemplify a pan-sexual world where "Sex is the undisputed protagonist. . . ."[86] Sexuality is not a problem here, but an expression of freedom. The trilogy, although a hymn to Eros, possesses an aura of mystification and reverence for sex-without-guilt, which Ron Cohen astutely puts into perspective with regard to the cinematic triptych:

> Each tale attempts to remove the veil of self-conscious pretension and judgment, by confronting us without direct non-judgmental sex and by presenting us with a mystified picture of everyday life. Everyday life becomes mystified not only by the visual intensity of things but also because it merges with a view of fate which is not rational and based on cause and effect, but is mythological and based on forces beyond anticipation and control. Fate emerges as the structural force that connects, rotates, and interchanges people and their experiences, dreams, and fantasies. Pasolini looks at the world with reverence. This reverence is transferred to the screen and can be seen in the sets, the people, the costumes, and the objects which are brought to our attention with a power and richness that pushes them out of a zone of naturalism and into a zone of wonder and awe.[87]

This trilogy is the most ideological of his films, claims Pasolini.[88] This is certainly not obvious, especially in light of *Hawks and Sparrows* and *Teorema*. The cinéaste rejects a direct ideology and makes his political message more subtle and aesthetic than previously. With these three films he returns to the pure Gramscian ideal of making "popular" films without being "commercial." Sex, ideology, and the sacred are all graphically intertwined throughout these works. Siciliano also underlines Pasolini's implicit political intention in painting this multicolored medieval canvas: "To reconstruct the moments in which man—the new man, the juncture between peasant ideals and humanistic values—had discovered himself as the moral agent of his own destiny."[89]

Il decameron of Giovanni Boccaccio (1313–75) today furnishes the reader with the same powerful universal glimpse of the foibles and fantasies of society as it did six hundred years ago. His ribald tales, numbering 100, emerged over a ten-day period of storytelling during the plague in Florence.

For his 1971 version of Il decameron *Pasolini chose eight of the most representative and graphic tales, populated by peasants, priests, and purloiners. Variations on sexual relationships weave their way through the film from teenage love and the seduction of a supposedly mute youth by cloistered religious women to cuckolding a simple potter. The tradesman Ciappelletto (Franco Citti) holds the first few stories together, and a disciple of Giotto (Pasolini) the remainder.*

The *Decameron* is a blend of the scatalogical and the innocent. In a picaresque fashion the "heroes" make their way from one episode to another with a Commedia dell'arte style and humor. In personally assuming the role of the artist (after two actors refused it), Pasolini is able to discuss aesthetics and society through the mouth of the character. In this he approximates the fresco painter of *The Seventh Seal,* who conveys Bergman's apocalyptic vision of the world.

Pasolini changes the locale for the stories from bourgeois Florence to earthy, proletarian Naples. The Neapolitans in the film nostalgically represent a fun-

Pasolini's ***The Decameron.*** A ribald tale of cuckoldry. *(Courtesy of Movie Star News.)*

loving people of the preindustrialized age, filled with primitive innocence and absolute freedom. The characters have their misery but lack a political consciousness that would make the misery unbearable. He depicts the women, clergy, and bourgeois among them in a satirical manner. Richard Roud comments on the period in which Pasolini casts these individuals:

> For Pasolini, the world of Boccaccio was that of the breaking up of the Middle Ages: the ecclesiastical-feudal structure was giving way to the coming triumph of the bourgeoisie. And Pasolini sees in this period of transition the counterpart to what is happening today, with the dominant bourgeoisie now itself in a state of dissolution. "I sense all around me the possibility of a new explosion of freedom," says Pasolini. "I'm also pessimistic enough to think that perhaps it won't occur, but I want to depict it anyway."[90]

Although Pasolini shows his anticlerical hand at times by criticizing the institution of the Catholic Church and satirizing the foibles of the clergy, he still feels that religion and sensuality are two irrational yet necessary realities for humanity.

Throughout *Decameron,* Pasolini is faithful to the "street people." He has seduced his audiences with a colorful, and at times off-color, slice of Neapolitan life. (The majority of the fifty actors originated in Naples.) His sense of social realism thus prevails, concludes David Bevan:

> With utter honesty, bordering on brutality, Pasolini has torn off the tasteful and discreet finery in which Boccaccio clothed his Middle Ages and grasped the flesh and blood of reality. In so doing, it is not only the primeval instincts of mediaeval man that have been laid bare, but those, perhaps, of you and me.[91]

As he did with the Giotto disciple in Il decameron, *Pasolini becomes the keystone of the cinematic and architectural structure of* Canterbury Tales *(1972). He facilitates the taletelling in this crosscut of medieval society on pilgrimage to visit the tomb of Thomas à Becket at Canterbury. The seven tales include those told by the Cook, Summoner, Pardoner, Miller, Friar, Reeve, and Merchant, along with the Wife of Bath's prologue. The stories highlight the doings of vagabonds, thieves, and murderers on the one hand, and of the bourgeoisie, merchants, and students on the other. These characters first appear in frozen images as if in a Vermeer, Bosch, or Breughel painting and then suddenly spring to life. They speak with an assortment of accents to typify their origins—Cockney, Scottish, or Somerset. The music accompanying their adventures is folkloric, like the Neapolitan popular music in* Decameron.

The festivities along the way, interspersed with the tales, add refreshing entertainment but also reveal a pre-Eden atmosphere. The misty landscapes (with an occasional television antenna in sight), exotically lit halls, and a surrealistic hell à la Bosch in the final tale reflect the creative imagination of the director. We are also briefly prepared for *Salò* with whippings in the bordello, homosexual capers, urinating on the public, and vomiting following poisoning. The director did not ingratiate his own public with these activities.

On several occasions Pasolini said, "There is no aesthetic choice that is not also

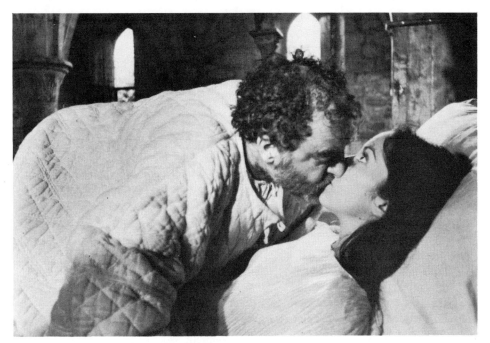

Pasolini's **Canterbury Tales.** Hugh Griffith as a lecherous old man springs upon his young bride (Josephine Chaplin). *(Courtesy of Movie Star News.)*

political." His dictum is certainly applicable to the trilogy, but more specifically to *Canterbury Tales.* In a quasi-documentary approach, Pasolini shows one half of the world to the other. He does it as usual in a Gramscian, popular framework. His heroes are the lowly people, the oppressed women and students. Pasolini also renders double homage to Charlie Chaplin, "the little man" of the silent film. He casts his daughter Josephine Chaplin as May in "The Merchant's Tale," and Ninetto Davoli as Peterkin, a chaplinesque "little man" who wins out against the forces of society, primarily bourgeois. Pasolini also describes the triumphs and losses of the bourgeoisie as well as their decadence. He also depicts the gradual rise of the middle class of which Chaucer is himself part. In sketching the transition of society in *Decameron*, Pasolini nostalgically bemoans the loss of this earthy, nontechnological milieu and era. He is disenchanted with contemporary society and finds delight in a momentary return to Chaucer's high-spirited world, much to the dismay of his cinematic colleague, Bernardo Bertolucci. The filmmaker of *The Last Tango in Paris* felt Pasolini had lost his political passion:

> The *Decameron* and *Canterbury Tales* are not really very inspired. Pasolini hates the world of today, so he keeps repeating to himself, "How beautiful the world was when poor people were really poor and innocent." This is the position of the reactionary poet.[92]

Pasolini had one more attempt to document this world of the "poor and innocent."

Pasolini's **Arabian Nights.** Exotic procession along the sea. *(Courtesy of Producer Alberto Grimaldi.)*

With *Arabian Nights* (*Il fiore delle mille e una notte*, 1974) Pasolini enters the timeless, mystical Arab world of folklore. In the beginning of the seventeenth century a French traveller and orientalist, Antoine Galland, presented this collection of oriental tales *Alf Laila Wa-Laïla* to Louis XIV, the Sun King. Most of the important tales were Egyptian, others were Persian or Indian. In general, they cut across several civilizations from the tenth to the fifteenth century.

Films of Hollywood and Cinecittà have colorfully recast for the screen similar stories of Scheherazade, Aladdin, Sinbad, and Ali-Baba, but none has done it with Pasolini's perspective. His vision offers a quasi-documentary kaleidoscope of medieval Islamic culture with controversial erotic and aesthetic emphases. From the anthology of tales Pasolini selects exotic and erotic (some critics say pornographic) stories that illustrate the lost past.

The film begins with the inscription, "The complete truth does not lie in one dream but in several dreams." As a framing device for his narrative dream, he uses the relationship of the clever slave girl Zumurrud (Ines Pellegrini) with the naive Nuredin (Franco Merli). After he is sexually initiated by Zummurud, Nuredin finds her missing. One tale flows into another as he desperately seeks her out. After many incidents of diverse sexual activity, mutilation, and castration, Nuredin finds his lost love. As in the nostalgic world of the fairy tale, they live happily ever after.

Underneath the carefree treatment of the joy of sex, there is a serious thrust to Pasolini's work. He set out to "proletaricize" the tales. This Third World is most

attractive, populated by rich and poor alike, but before they are awakened politically and economically. They have no sense of the horrible guilt and sin of the
western world. In *Arabian Nights* Pasolini also attacks capitalism and the corruption of present society, but in a brief glimpse of the past. Vincent Canby gives one
instance of Pasolini's approach:

> Most of the tales have to do with power, with the power of beautiful women
> to bewitch their lovers and power of the rich to control the poor. Pasolini
> clearly doesn't approve of this—the Marxist in him will out. Yet the manner of
> the film, in which Pasolini the movie director has so successfully purchased the
> favors of the poor, amateur actors, suggests that "The Arabian Nights" may be
> a demonstration of the very kind of corruption it condemns.[93]

It may appear that there are only kernels of ideology strewn throughout the
labyrinthine episodes. Pasolini, however, following the completion of *Arabian
Nights*, stated that his next film *(Salò)* would be ideological, but not as radically
ideological as his "Trilogy of Life," and especially *Arabian Nights*. Pasolini comments on the political-aesthetic rapport in the context of a Gramscian "national-
popular work of art":

> I wanted my cinematic "Trilogy of Life" *(The Decameron, The Canterbury Tales*
> and *The Arabian Nights)* to be seen and understood by all: that is why I chose to
> tackle the purest and plainest patterns of narration and to enter into those
> mysterious meshes of genuine tales which seem to me more fascinating and
> universal than any other moral ideological narrative form.[94]

The all-pervasive optimism, bordering on romanticism, that Pasolini radiated
during the filming of the cinematic triptych now disappears as he will move into
his final production in 1975. In the meantime, on 15 June 1975, almost four
months before his death, he wrote his repudiation of the trilogy in his article,
"Abiura della *Trilogia della vita*." Disenchanted with the evolution of society and
filled with anger at the inroads made by consumerism, he said he would never
again be able to show the youthful human bodies in the same positive way he did
in the trilogy. The sacredness of sexuality had become transformed into a consumer product. His further disavowal of sexual permissiveness, the subproletariat, and the Third World eliminated another segment of his critics and
public who stayed with him until now.

Pigsty and *Salò:* Fascism, Old and New

Sex and fascism have something very much in common—*power*, the power of
one person over another, demonstrated either explicitly or implicitly. Often
enough this power is perverted. *Salon Kitty, Night Porter, Seven Beauties,* and *The
Damned* all illustrate this. Wilhelm Reich in *The Mass Psychology of Fascism* describes the interrelationships of sexuality, politics, and religion which will lay the
ground work for our discussion of Bertolucci's *The Conformist:*

To comprehend the relation between sexual suppression and human exploitation, it is necessary to get an insight into the basic social institution in which the economic and sex-economic situations of patriarchal authoritarian society are interwoven. Without the inclusion of this institution, it is not possible to understand the sexual economy and the ideological process of a patriarchal society. The psychoanalysis of men and women of all ages, all countries, and every social class shows that: *The interlacing of the socio-economic structure with the sexual structure of society and the structural reproduction of society take place in the first four or five years and in the authoritarian family.* The church only continues this function later. Thus, the authoritarian state gains an enormous interest in the authoritarian family: *It becomes the factory in which the state's structure and ideology are molded.*[95]

Between *Teorema* and *Medea*, Pasolini filmed *Pigsty* (*Il porcile*, 1969), a most peculiar film, yet one which Marc Gervais called "un film-clef," a key work in his repertoire. The two panels of this diptych superficially differ as night from day. They were conceived and written separately. The first, a medieval allegory, was designed as a companion piece to Buñuel's Mexican film *Simon of the Desert*, a forty-minute story of Simeon Stylites'. temptations. The second part of the Pasolini work originated in a verse tragedy. The stylized juxtaposition of the Spanish, medieval, and apocalyptic fable *Orgy* and the contemporary one, also named *Pigsty*, is highly creative and revealing. Placed side by side, they indicate an aesthetic and political dialectical process in which one situation confronts the other. The first haunting, quasi-surrealistic section is supposedly inspired by Mizoguchi, and the second, more intellectual and meditative, by Jean-Marie Straub. The link to both is cannibalism as well as the type of *Hellzapoppin* character Maracchione, the observer/gardener, played by the ever-faithful Ninetto Davoli.

A strange, starving young man (Pierre Clementi) roaming about the volcanic desert of Etna, comes across a soldier, kills, and devours him. Around himself, the youth gathers others who take to cannibalism, one of whom is a timid young man (Franco Citti). After terrorizing the countryside with their cannibalism, they themselves are condemned to death. Staked in the desert, they are abandoned to the sun and the wild dogs.

This tale is followed by a second which takes place in modern-day Godesberg, near Cologne. Julian (Jean-Pierre Léaud) does not reciprocate the amorous sentiments of Ida (Anne Wiazemsky). She further tries to incite him to political activism, but she is unsuccessful. Julian's father, Krupp-like industrialist Herr Klotz (Alberto Lionello), does not get him interested in life at all. Julian falls catatonic and awakens one day to go forth to make love to the pigs. He is devoured (offstage) by them, as reported later, as in a Greek tragedy, by the gardener (Ninetto Davoli). Ida settles for a conventional marriage. Herr Klotz is obliged to merge with the ex-Nazi Herdhitze (Ugo Tognazzi) who blackmails Klotz about his son's porcophiliac tendencies.

Several of the *Pigsty* themes had already been represented in Pasolini's opus: pigs as peers *(Mamma Roma)*, desert and primordial regions *(Teorema)*, and the killing of the father *(Oedipus)*. *Pigsty* pushes these to their limits, at times barely tolerable. One has only to hear the words of the young cannibal to grasp the horror and yet the symbolism of his gesture: "I killed my father; I ate human flesh; I tremble with joy!" In *Medea*, as well as in *Pigsty*, cannibalism is considered a sacred ritual, a type of communion.[96]

The dual allegory depicts two individuals separated by centuries and cultures, both rebelling against society. No individualism is tolerated in society, insists Pasolini. Society, moreover, has remained anthropophagic but in a more subtle and sophisticated way today, as we see in the forced business merger. To remain independent, the cannibal in *Orgy* has enigmatically killed his father and gone off into the desert. In the second panel, Julian revolts against his father by lapsing into catatonia, then by making love with the pigs. This father-son relationship reflects an important theme throughout Italian political films, as we will see with Bellocchio's *In the Name of the Father*, and Bertolucci's *The Spider's Stratagem*.

Prominent in Pasolini's work here is his portrayal of neofascism, a modernized Nazism in an advanced German society. The second parable begins with a most melodic rendering of the Nazi anthem, the Horst Wessel song, but seen satirically, with pigs going about their daily business in a sty. Nazism has survived in luxury through the power of industry. Julian's father reflects an almost physical and psychological double of Hitler—wild-eyed, with a small black moustache and a desire to control. The rival Herdhitze manifests an anti-Semitic philosophy. He is a Nazi war criminal and has in his private collection Jewish skeletons. The conversation between the two businessmen reflects their racist and industrialist mentalities, not uncommon during the Third Reich.[97] The smoking factory stack recalls the concentration camps at a time when Germany became highly industrialized, sacrificing the bodies of six million Jews, as Alain Resnais's *Night and Fog* gruesomely points out. Why does Pasolini bring in Nazism, asks Moravia? The director replies that Nazism comes from a desire to save one's personal interests at all costs, even if it means becoming cannibals. The Nazi society fed on the cadavers of the camps, concludes the novelist.[98]

Student activism appears ineffective in the modern allegory. Pasolini is still in his antirevolutionary stage of the late sixties, during which he called the students "papa's boys." Ida, who plays a parallel role in Godard's *La Chinoise* (1967), pours out a flood of revolutionary verbiage in order to incite Julian to act. She urges Julian to accompany her to protest against the Berlin Wall and come out with slogans such as "Down with God!" Just as at the end of *La Chinoise* where the students close up their Maoist cell to resume courses at the university, Ida settles into the bourgeois life. Political activism of the young is doomed to failure. Julian stands his ground in his individualism and rebellion against society. In this venture he goes all the way.

Although allegorical, the feature *Pigsty* has a sharp, biting sting to it. Anti-German, antistudent, anti-Church, antisociety in general, *Pigsty* comes across as a sad nihilistic piece in the repertoire of Pasolini. All aspects of society appear to be sacrificed in the film to allow for individualism to survive.

Throughout the filming of the *Trilogy of Life*, Pasolini experienced a *joie de vivre* that he probably had not sensed since his early days in Friuli. At the completion of the trilogy in 1974 a dark cloud hung over him. He was a disenchanted revolutionary without hope. For the most part, he no longer had any political aspirations for society. His final production, *Salò or the 120 Days of Sodom* (*Salò o le 120 giornate di Sodoma,* 1975), would be marked by this psychological pessimism and political nihilism. The exotic sexual relationships he romantically portrayed in the trilogy, moreover, turned into cruel destructive ones. Pasolini's swan song became a funeral dirge.

Pasolini made *Salò* under the influence of a "drug"—the Marquis de Sade, libertine writer at the turn of the eighteenth century, canonized by the French Surrealists in the thirties. The director's battles through the years were not unlike Sade's—against religion, contemporary repressive morality, hypocrisy, and puritanism. Both were members of a counterculture fighting for the liberation of language and custom. From 22 October to 27 November 1788, Donatien Alphonse François de Sade (1740–1814), imprisoned in the Bastille near the end of the Ancien Regime, wrote about the four-month-long sexual exploits of four libertines with their wives in the Chateau de Silling. This material comprised the four-volume work *120 Days of Sodom* (published posthumously in 1914), a type of compendium of sexuality.

The moralizing Pasolini turned Sade's quasi-scientific study of sexual perversions and anomolies into a most graphic and disturbing political allegory. He updates it to World War II and situates it in the decadent atmosphere of the Republic of Salò in northern Italy. The Italian Social Republic was the political state set up by Hitler from September 1943 to April 1945 following Mussolini's liberation by the SS parachutists of Otto Skorzeny. It was here that Pasolini's younger brother Guido died in the Resistance and that Pasolini was evacuated during his studies at the University of Bologna.

In assessing the various types of films made on fascist themes, Joan Mellen has discovered that they primarily deal with three areas—the *social dynamic,* the means by which fascism functions; the *political* nature of resistance, the physical and ideological struggle against fascism; and the *psychological* dimension, the dissection of the personality susceptible to fascism with its configuration of homosexual anxiety and sadomasochism.[99] There are threads of this triple aspect of fascism in Pasolini's *Salò.*

As if it were a literary work, the film opens with a selected bibliography in the credits:
   Roland Barthes: Sade, Fourier, Loyola
   Maurice Blanchot: Lautréamont et Sade
   Simone de Beauvoir: Faut-il brûler Sade?
   Pierre Klossowski: Sade mon prochain, Le philosophe scélérat
   Philippe Sollers: L'écriture et l'expérience des limites[100]
In 1944–45, the fascists round up young peasant boys and girls, nine each, and take them to a chateau at Marzabotto. There they are held captive by four dignitaries—a duke (Paolo Bonacelli), an ecclesiastic (Giorgio Cataldi), a president (Aldo Valletti), and a magistrate (Uberto Paolo Quintavalle). While a woman pianist accompanies the ribald stories of the women (Elsa De Giorgi, Caterina Boratto, Hélène Surgère), the men engage in their perversions. In a Dantesque manner, the young victims pass from the vestibule of hell through the "Circle of Passion," the "Circle of Excrement," and the "Circle of Blood." For

three days their lecherous captors use them as objects of rituals of homosexuality, sadomasochism, voyeurism, proctophilia, caprophagia, as well as the more graphic and violent head-scalping, eye-gouging, nipple-burning. Finally some of the young victims switch allegiances and become fascist torturers.

The complex forces of power, sex, and fascism are once again intricately inter-twined in *Salò* as in *Pigsty*. Pasolini, always obsessed with the contemporary man-ifestations of Evil, believes Sade to be "the great poet of the anarchy of power." Like Rosi in Italy and Costa-Gavras in France, the director uses cinema as a vehi-cle to combat the oppressive power forces in society. Certain elements in society make laws to create power plays and then apply them rigidly. In the realm of allegory, the parallels of the Salò government and today's political-economic culture may be obvious, but in the film they are displayed in their bestial ex-tremes. Luigi Bini observes this application: "The fascism of Salò constitutes for him [Pasolini] the ready basis of a metaphorical discourse on Power, which he identifies with the true fascism of today."[101] The victims of the manipulation come from the lower class, while the perverted perpetrators of evil are universal types from the upper class—state, law, Church, and business. Their culture is elitist in nature. The fascist power eliminates individualism, as in the case of the young leftist Ezio who is caught making love to the Black maid. He is shot for deviation from perversion and racial purity, but valiantly dies naked, raising his clenched fist in a defiant salute.

When novelist and cinéaste Alain Robbe-Grillet made *Glissements progressifs du plaisir* (1973) blending Michelet, Barthes, and Sade, the critics did not hesitate to call it aesthetic soft-core pornography, perhaps one cut above *Emmanuelle*. The French filmmaker stated that his was a deliberate and serious attack against the commercialization of sex. His intention was nonetheless somewhat ambiguous, for it cultivated the sensual images of naked girls in a Sadian prison, while lash-ing out against the cover-model exhibition of women. Dubious indeed, claimed his critics. Pasolini's treatment of sex may fall into the same domain. He himself calls *Salò* an erotic but not pornographic film. Eros in his films, he believes, is always a dramatic, metaphorical relationship. Using young male and female naked bodies he tries to make a sociopolitical statement about contemporary hedonist attitudes toward sexuality, while simultaneously suggesting a type of collective memory of stripped bodies prepared for the crematoria.

With this graphic and extremist film, Pasolini demonstrates how the power structure destroys the soul. It transforms human bodies into objects. Here Pas-olini recalls Marx's caution against "the commercialization of Man" *(la mer-cificazione dell'uomo)*. Sex has become a commodity in a consumer society. The sexual subjugation that the director describes in *Salò* parallels the boss-worker relationship as well as the class struggle that he observes in a neocapitalist system. The abusive use of sex becomes the metaphor for this manipulation by the sys-tem. Bertolucci symbolically saw the director's face on the screen during the projection of the film. He felt that the work in essence dealt with the relationship of his friend to today's youth, completely transformed by the consumer society. He adds:

The movie is a metaphor of our reality—on the power of brainwashing by the media. Because the year before he died Pier Paolo made a crusade against this thing that he called "the genocide of culture by the consumer society."[102]

Gideon Bachmann kept a diary of his contacts with Pasolini during the filming of *Salò*. The critic wanted to make a film on Pasolini showing a man who loses his identity and no longer feels useful to society. Bachman reflects on the lower depths of the director's soul at the time:

> Pasolini was making a film against fascism, maybe, but he was also making a film that showed how deeply anchored in our souls cruelty and destructiveness really are. A film that was both ethological and Marxist, surely an operation of major tactical *raffinesse*.[103]

Salò was not meant to be a historically accurate depiction of fascism but a stylized, allegorical one as noted earlier. It did, however, have something to say about old and new forms of fascism. By filming *Salò* in 1975, Pasolini wished to reiterate that the *"padroni fascisti"* of the film are still around. This type of fascism did not die in Hitler's bunker but lives on today in the vehement defenders of law and order in contemporary Italy, he believes. As in the days of the camps, the Fascists can readily transcend the pain and anguish of the tortured victims of society. In the film the oppressed sense their helplessness. Enzo Siciliano discusses their "passivity," while Richard Roud implies "complicity."[104] To recall aesthetically the fascism of old, Pasolini includes the works of the Italian Bauhaus and period wall ornamentations. He had reproduced and enlarged paintings of Feininger, Severini, and Duchamp. For musical accompaniment he inserted into the score what he sees as typical fascist music, "Veris leta facies" (The Bright Face of Spring) from Carl Orff's *Carmina Burana*.

The censors and critics pounced upon *Salò* in the wake of Pasolini's death. As Louise Barnett points out, the film was "an exercise in self-degradation," bleak and empty.[105] Others saw it as a camouflage for pornography with no redeeming social value. Even critics sympathetic to Pasolini's earlier works felt it sexually excessive. Roland Barthes, who is also quoted in the film, wrote in *Le Monde* of 16 June 1976 that *Salò* had a double weakness—an unrealistic side of fascism, and an overly realistic side of Sade. The film reflected all too poignantly perhaps the complete despair over the civilization that Pasolini witnessed about him. The producer Alberto Grimaldi appealed the censorship case, admitting to the highly provocative nature of the film but underlining its superior political and intellectual, as well as its expressive and formal qualities. When *Salò* was eventually screened in Italy, France, and the United States, critics and public saw the film as a prophetic work, a final metaphor for Pasolini's own tragic demise in November 1975.

Conclusions

From *Accattone* (1961) to *Salò* (1975), Pasolini traveled light years in his aesthetic and political development. He oscillated from the profoundly sacred to the highly erotic, believing that both have something very human and spiritual in common. A man of paradox! He tells Georges Moraux, "I am one of the many marxist intellectuals who do their best to keep an open mind, to retain their critical faculties alert and to assume without fear their own contradictions."

At the heart of Pasolini's films are his politics and his characters. Ordinarily his hero is the chaplinesque underdog—prostitute, blue-collar worker, drifter, or peasant, all from the lower echelon of society. He presents them in a political manner in his fiction films, yet he cannot accept some of the other types of political fiction film which will be treated in this study. In principle he opposes political fiction in which politicians, lawyers, or police are inaccurately characterized and the drama romanticized. This commercial treatment of the characters cannot possibly tell the truth, believed Pasolini.[106] He considered this type of political film an incestuous ball-catching game where creator and audience both play with supposed conviction. He confessed to Gideon Bachmann during the filming of *Arabian Nights:*

> One of the least appetizing things of the past few years are precisely those fashionable political films, these fictional political films, which are the films of half-truths, of reality-unreality, of consolation and of falseness. They are made to pacify the consciousness. Instead of arousing polemics, they suffocate it. . . . I avoid fiction in my films. I do nothing to console, nothing to embellish reality, nothing to sell the goods.[107]

The sympathetic characters of Pasolini are not fictional, but make up the fiber of Italian society. They convey Pasolini's ideology. Gillo Pontecorvo remarked in our interview of January 1982 that he considered Pasolini's *Accattone* the most political of the contemporary political fiction films.

Pasolini's works, deliberately provocative, challenged the Communist party, the Catholic Church, the public and the critics to reconsider another deliberately ignored side of life. He did this in his films by assuming the role of a present-day Socrates, whom he saw as the prime analogue for the societal rebel.[108] As a result he was charged with corrupting the youth and introducing new gods. Society has had a difficult time tolerating this *"ragazzo di vita,"* but will not find it easy to forget the blood of a poet spilled in the sacred name of sexual and political nonconformity. His own poem, "A Desperate Vitality," will serve as a haunting reminder and a succinct epitaph:

> You shall go down into the world,
> and you shall be candid and gentle, well-balanced and faithful,
> and you shall have an infinite capacity to obey
> and an infinite capacity to rebel.
> You shall be pure.
> Therefore I curse you.[109]

3

BERNARDO BERTOLUCCI: The Strategy of a Freudian Marxist

> I hope there is just as much need for political consciousness
> in me as there is for aestheticism. Perhaps I shall make my
> best films dealing with politics without talking about pol-
> itics.
>
> —Bernardo Bertolucci, 1971

A curious encounter lies at the heart of Bernardo Bertolucci's professional film career. One Sunday afternoon at the Bertolucci apartment on the Via Giacinto Carino in Rome, the teenage Bernardo, in the big city for less than two years, cautiously answered the door. A young man in blue with a large crop of black hair asked to see the boy's father Attilio Bertolucci. Suspecting the person to be an unwanted visitor, Bertolucci closed the door in the man's face and went to call his father. Despite the suspicion, Bertolucci sensed on that occasion that there was something very forceful and even exceptional about this character. It was none other than the poet Pier Paolo Pasolini. Bertolucci felt the same way after twenty years of friendship, sometimes stormy in the early seventies. He would be emotionally devastated at the death of the controversial filmmaker in 1975.

The link between Bertolucci and Pasolini was initially the medium of poetry. Both would turn to cinema when they felt a creative urge to express themselves in a medium other than poetry. It was Pasolini who encouraged the budding poet, young Bertolucci, to publish his poetry. It was the same role that the senior Bertolucci played when he facilitated the publication of Pasolini's *Ragazzi di vita*. Attilio Bertolucci was the one responsible for bringing the two poets together. He himself was an established poet, critic, and translator, holding a position of importance in the ranks of other Italian poets such as Montale, Ungaretti, and Penna.

Pasolini invited the young and extremely cultured *cinéphile* to be his assistant on *Accattone* (1961) and furnished the subject for his disciple's first film, *The Grim Reaper* (1962). In his volume of poetry *In Search of Mystery*, the young Bertolucci reciprocated and wrote a poem, "A Pasolini." For the next thirteen years their careers overlapped as they shared a Marxist dialectic and Freudian perspective in their filmmaking. For these tendencies both were taken to task by Left and Right alike, and usually had to settle for censorship, trials, or suspended jail sentences. The two nonconformists had touched the raw nerves of society.

Bertolucci's life is further marked by an odyssey, serpentine in form, exhausting in length. It takes him from the countryside of Emilia in northern Italy to the heart of Rome, from poetry to cinema, and from the revolutionary politics of Marx to the sexual insights of Freud. In a highly complex and eclectic manner, he allows himself and his film characters to be marked by the countless experiences on this very personal itinerary.[1] His film repertoire—eight features as well as shorts, and television productions—capitalizes on these experiences and reflects the complex sociopolitical philosophy of the director:

> My films are built according to so mysterious a stratification that there is no separation of politics, psychoanalysis, language, means of production, etc. It seems that everything is mixed together in my films, and that making them is my way of trying to get out of that labyrinth, that chaos.[2]

Our challenge is to follow Bertolucci out of his labyrinth.

The northern province of Emilia is to Bertolucci what Friuli was for Pasolini— an early encounter with land, poetry, and budding socialist contacts. Situated between Florence and Milan, with Bologna and Parma the two leading centers of culture, Emilia has deeply marked the personal character and the films of Bertolucci. Poor and "red" could best describe the Emilia of Bertolucci's childhood and the region of today. It has been a privileged place for him, the political and cultural stage upon which he could play out his cinematic dramas from *Before the Revolution* (1964) through *Tragedy of a Ridiculous Man* (1981). Psychologically for him, it is a return to the womb; nostalgically, it is a desire to recapture a utopia, blissfully filled with childhood memories. His early years in the Po Valley were "golden, a house in the country, understanding parents and a pursuit of intellectualism," as he often described this period.[3] His filming of *1900* on location in Emilia provided the major opportunity to assess his attraction to the region and to account for the uniqueness of the province:

> Emilia seemed like a miracle within the context of Italy. How did this miracle happen? How come this island exists where the peasant world is still almost completely intact in its identity? I think there's only one explanation. Emilia is the region that's been socialist ever since socialism has existed and communist ever since communism has existed. It's been through socialism and communism that the Emilian peasants have become conscious of their culture and have understood that it's something to defend.[4]

He lyrically describes his relation to the peasants and the earth, so obvious in *1900:*

> But this is my land. This is the juice of my own. Here I recognize and understand the different smells of summer and fall, the stones of the river, the breeze of the wind, the gradation of the wines, as well as the people and their way of seeing things.[5]

Within the sphere of Emilia, Parma for Bertolucci has a noble, almost mythical position. It represented for him a cultural heritage, his paternal homestead, the bourgeoisie, and cinema. His father often told the young Bernardo that under fascism, Parma was a separate province, extremely refined, and linked directly with the French world. It was not surprising that Bertolucci's first feature, *Before the Revolution,* based on Stendhal's *Chartreuse de Parme,* dealt with a young man's oscillation between the bourgeois, cultured tradition, and an alluring Marxist philosophy.

Bertolucci was born in Parma on 16 March 1941. He specifies and says that it was a hamlet of four or five houses called Bacchanelli, six kilometers from Parma, and just a few hundred yards from "Le Piacentine", where *1900* was filmed. Bertolucci's grandparents were landowners in the region. His mother, Ninetta Giovanardi Bertolucci was Australian, daughter of a Parmesan father, who emigrated there for political reasons, and an Irish mother. Ninetta Bertolucci was an educated woman who wrote a dissertation on Catullus at the University of Bologna. The influence of Bertolucci's father Attilio upon him over-shadowed that of his mother until recently. One has only to compare *The Spider's Stratagem* (1970) with *Luna* (1979). Attilio Bertolucci, a highly cultivated man, was a poet, devotee of Conrad and Proust, and film reviewer for the local *Gazetta di Parma.* The father linked his literary and cinematic interests in his editorial work on a May 1950 special issue of *Sequenze: Quaderni di cinema* dealing with literature and cinema. He gathered the articles of poet Eugenio Montale, playwright Luigi Pirandello, novelist Alberto Moravia, and scriptwriter Cesare Zavattini, among others. Father and son would see two or three films on a single trip to Parma, often Westerns. For the young Bernardo, Parma meant the dream world of cinema. In those early years, the father was instrumental in the son's aesthetic, cinematic formation:

> My father taught me to see, grasp, and love the cinema. To a great extent, my passion for cinema derives from his passion for it, just as his love of the countryside sprung from my grandfather's love of the land. I was fortunate enough in being able to experience a culture which preceded me, even a cinematic one, to have had roots, if only to liberate myself from them.[6]

In 1952, at the age of eleven, Bernardo's utopia vanished. For his work his father was obliged to move to Rome where he would continue his writing, film reviews for the predecessor of *L'Espresso,* for the radio, and more recently for the newspaper *La Repubblica.* For Bernardo this was one of the major ruptures in his life. On one hand it cut him off from his pastoral heritage, and on the other it led him on a search for self-identity. Like Joe in *Luna* he descended upon Rome as if it were another planet. In the bustling capital he was uprooted. His nostalgia for his native Emilia would not readily leave him. His contacts with his father's poet-friends, his classical and aesthetic education in secondary school and the University of Rome, and his access to the cinema world of Rome compensated for this loss.

Like Pasolini with his early verses and Friulian poems, Bertolucci began to express himself poetically at the age of seven, no doubt under his father's tutelage.[7] The poems written from age fifteen to twenty were gathered together in 1962 and published in the small volume *In Search of Mystery,* the title of which came from a verse by Giovanni Pascoli. This volume won the Premio Viareggio, an Italian literary award for a first work. The prize, awarded just a few days before *The Grim Reaper* (1962) went to the Venice Film Festival, marked the end of one stage of his life and the beginning of another. The book of poetry became a "tomb" for his verse, he jokingly observed, for he did not pursue the literary avocation any further. Bertolucci acknowledges the creative impulse to move on:

> I first began to want to make films in the desire, the need, to do something different from what my father did. He was a poet, and I wanted to compete with him, but not by doing the same thing. I used to write poetry myself, but I realized that I would lose that battle, so I had to find a different terrain on which to compete.[8]

The break was only superficial. The poetry was not left behind. Bertolucci simply said he now preferred to write poems with his camera. Into his filming Bertolucci poured his poetic spirit, with an acute sensitivity to color, sound, and composition.

The image of his father was not abandoned either. Although Bernardo left home at the age of nineteen—"a personal revolution to deal with my father-image difficulties"—the paternal figure haunts all of his feature films.[9] It can be detected in the quest of Athos, Jr. for the true story of his father in *The Spider's Stratagem,* the master-disciple relationship of Cesare-Fabrizio in *Before the Revolution* and of Quadri-Clerici in *The Conformist.* In *Last Tango in Paris,* Paul (Marlon Brando), the father figure, is shot with Jeanne's father's kepi on his head, while in *1900* a peasant announces that "the *padrone* is dead!" These last two cases take on an aura of symbolism. Actress and friend of Bertolucci and Pasolini, Laura Betti told critic Gideon Bachmann: "Bernardo is fighting, all the time, to liberate himself from his many fathers. Pasolini is the most important of these, of course. And Bernardo's real father, a great poet and critic. But he is a true talent, a fighter. All his neuroses, his analyses, his girlfriends won't deter him."[10]

Constants

Besides the poetic, paternal, political, and psychological factors intricately at work in Bertolucci's films, there are several constants that are also visible. Structurally, these thematic and technical aspects of his work serve as elaborate architectural supports.

Into the setting of Emilia (on occasion Paris or Rome), he situates the young male protagonist seeking an identity—Fabrizio, Giacobbe, Olmo, Athos, Jr., Joe. Often enough he is a complex antihero, betraying the party, the movement, friends, the past, or, more seriously, himself. Bertolucci feels he interrogates himself through this type of character, reflecting his own concerns, fears, and quests. The world of the young hero is fraught with ambiguity, double vision, and schizophrenia. Drama teacher Giacobbe (Pierre Clementi) in *Partner* moves in and out of a dreamlike world, haunted by his revolutionary double. In *The Spider's Stratagem* Giulio Brogi plays Athos Magnani—father and son—in the young man's search for the truth surrounding the father's death. Dominique Sanda in *The Conformist* is the exotic prostitute in the Ventimilia bordello as well as Anna the lesbian wife of Professor Quadri. Paul (Marlon Brando) and Marcel (Massimo Girotti) in *Last Tango* discover that the dead Rosa set them up as twins with the same robes, wall paper, and so on. Bertolucci considers Olmo and Alfredo as two halves of the same soul, his own. The coming together of the two fathers of *Luna*, finally, shows a merging of the paternal theme with that of the perpetual double.

Death stalks the characters of this Bertoluccian universe, starting with *The Grim Reaper*. When it strikes, it abruptly terminates relationships and creates ambiguity in the survivors. Rarely does death show its face naturally. Suicide *(Before the Revolution)*, homicide *(Conformist)*, torture *(1900)*, political execution *(Stratagem)* bring into play most complex forces.

Music, lush and at times romantic, surrounds Bertolucci's characters in their quest. Born in Parma—the birthplace of Giuseppe Verdi, Arturo Toscanini, and Renata Tebaldi—Bertolucci fills his films with regional opera, song, and dance. Fabrizio attends Verdi's *Macbeth* and Caterina performs in his *Il trovatore* and *Masked Ball*. The performance of Verdi's *Rigoletto* marks the death of Athos Magnani, Sr. as well as the moment of his son's comprehension thirty years later. Curiously enough, a character named Rigoletto enters upon the scene in *1900* to announce the death of Verdi, just as the two boys Alfredo and Olmo are born. In music Bertolucci thus finds solace, clever symbolism, and a pleasurable aesthetic experience. His choice of film music, primarily with the assistance of Ennio Morricone, radiates this aesthetic love.

In the same musical context, dancing has become his cinematic signature. " 'It's a privileged moment,' the director said, explaining the recurrent image. 'It's like being drunk. All the films I love have moments of dance—films of von Sternberg, Renoir, Ophuls. You can do anything with dance. You can be comic and tragic.' "[11] The seductive dance of aunt and nephew in *Before the Revolution* becomes the first step to an incestuous relationship. The tango is an obsession of Bertolucci, the director acknowledges. This dance of death, sometimes very frigid, at other times very sensual, takes on a more erotic air in *The Conformist* with Anna and Giulia than in *Last Tango* with the various couples. The folk dance of *1900* is a momentary return to the carefree, joy-filled world of the lower classes. Joe's rock dance for onlooker Mario (Franco Citti) in *Luna* has strong homosexual overtones. The film opens with Caterina's dance with a mysterious man while the baby plays at their feet with the ball of yarn, a symbolic umbilical cord. Primo in *Tragedy of a Ridiculous Man* comes across his maids dancing to rock and roll and is amused.

In Bertolucci's early films the spectre of sex remained closeted, for the most part, for society with its laws and taboos prevented it from coming to the fore. With the supposed newly discovered freedom of society and Bertolucci's personal liberated attitude toward sexuality on screen after beginning psychoanalysis, sexual images were not implied but made deliberately more explicit.

The Communist party, the Catholic Church, and the traditional group of censors (magistrates, psychologists, and filmmakers) in one form or other challenged Bertolucci's depiction of sexuality as they did Pasolini's. The scenes of incest in *Before the Revolution* and *Luna*, sodomy in *Last Tango* and *1900*, homosexuality in *The Conformist* and *Luna* illustrate a blend of lyricism and sexual reality. Bertolucci, the iconoclast, purposely set out to provoke the Establishment with explicit images from *Last Tango* on, forcing it to reconsider its puritanical attitude toward human sexuality.

Certain technical aspects of Bertolucci's work are consistent throughout his repertoire and distinguish it from that of his predecessors as well as his contemporaries. For his subjects he would on occasion turn to a literary work—a short story such as Jorge-Luis Borges's "The Theme of the Traitor and the Hero," Moravia's novel *The Conformist,* or Dostoevski's short story, "The Double." Bertolucci feels absolutely free to alter the litterateur's work, almost to the point of nonrecognition, as did Rosi with Platonov's "The Third Son" for *Three Brothers.* Bertolucci's wish is that the cinematic adaptation have a creative, aesthetic life of its own, distinct from its source.

The filmed adaptations as well as the original scripts are filled with cinematic and artistic references that color the results with an aura of intellectualism. Bertolucci toils over these original scripts alongside Gianni Amico or Franco Arcalli.[12] The final literary product is meant to please the eye of the producer and serve as a point of departure for the actual filming. It is but a necessary evil, believes Bertolucci. Once the collaborators are beyond the script, spontaneity in the production becomes uppermost in Bertolucci's mind. Brando's autobiographical improvisations in *Last Tango* represent the epitome of this risk. Bertolucci, like Rosi, basically followed the advice of his idol Jean Renoir, "You must always leave a door open on the set."

The cinematographer Vittorio Storaro has been to Bertolucci what Pasquale De Santis has been to Rosi and Tonino Delli Colli to Pasolini—a creative artist and technician who collaborates fully in designing lush, exotic images. Storaro's international reputation, earned from his work with Francis Ford Coppola *(Apocalypse Now),* Warren Beatty *(Reds),* and Michael Apted *(Agatha),* is based on his precise, meditative, and artistic manner of creating a play of light in a film.[13] From *Stratagem* and *Conformist* to *Luna*, Storaro has provided Bertolucci with highly stylized sets and lighting, criticized by some reviewers for their recherché, artificial, and exotic flavor. Manifesting a penchant for golds and ochres, Bertolucci and Storaro paint the canvases of *The Conformist* and *Last Tango* with memorable images. Before shooting, Bertolucci often shows his director of photography paintings or films that would help create the aesthetic and historical ambience. The fascist settings in white marble and art deco of *Conformist* vie with the splendor of soft, backlit compositions in *Last Tango*. With a blend of politics and aesthetics, Bertolucci and Storaro fill the screen of *1900* with a flurry of red flags, appreciated neither by the Russians nor the Americans.

Besides their carefully framed shots, Bertolucci and Storaro coordinate their shots with a constantly moving camera, sometimes gazing, sometimes participating. Bertolucci aspires to use the camera in confrontation with reality as in a dialectical process. His long and short tracking shots are as characteristic of his work as the travelling shots of Resnais in *Last Year at Marienbad* or *Hiroshima, mon amour*. Of the footage shot in this manner, Bertolucci only makes use of ten percent, carefully editing it with Franco "Kim" Arcalli, collaborator of Louis Malle, Franco Brusati, Vittorio De Sica, Marco Bellocchio, and Michelangelo Antonioni, among others. Here the raw material begins to take on new life. Working with Arcalli from the script to the editing stage of the production, Bertolucci is able to control better the continuity of the work. It was first with *Stratagem* that Bertolucci discovered alongside Arcalli a fresh perspective on creating through editing.

The political vision of Bertolucci cannot be separated from the aesthetic or thematic aspect of his work. His ideological evolution is lengthy and filled with many contradictions that he recognizes. His bourgeois background and present lifestyle, for example, may on the surface conflict with his leftist political leanings. The political tension within him—seen as a personal dialectic—has given birth to many of his earlier films, prior to his concentration on the psychological bearing of his characters.

As a child, Bertolucci had breathed in the socialist atmosphere of Emilia, one of the earliest socialist and communist sectors of Italy. He first heard the word "communist" in 1949–50 coming from the mouths of the farmers he used to visit. For them it meant "hero."[14] They spoke of a demonstration surrounding the death of the Communist Alberti at the hands of the police. With hindsight, Bertolucci felt that in his heart he became a Communist from that time on, even though he did not yet officially enter the Communist party.

Bertolucci once had doubts about the party which he tried to capture in *Before the Revolution*. Within himself he felt the ideological turmoil of being of bourgeois origin, stifled by a conformist, traditional past, and tempted by the Left, not unlike his protagonist Fabrizio. In the sixties, felt Bertolucci, the Communist party had no style, no vision. Then things suddenly changed. It was the events of 1968 in Europe and then in the United States that created many radicals, or at least allowed latent militants to come to the fore. Bertolucci recalls:

> What happened to me politically? The anti-communist wave of the extreme left, born in '68, actually pushed me to the PCI, the Italian Communist Party. In a certain way, I saw my own criticisms in those of the young, I saw they were embittered by bourgeois and petit-bourgeois necessities. And this is why I joined the PCI in '69.[15]

Yet there is some ambiguity in his joining the party in the late sixties, and this continues on today, when he spoke of the party as floating, not having a real identity, in the course of our January 1982 interview. In *Sight and Sound*, following his success with *The Conformist* (1970), he confesses to Marilyn Goldin:

> I think that the most important discovery I made after the events of May, 1968, was that I wanted the revolution not to help the poor but for myself. I wanted the world to change for me. I discovered the individual level in political revolution. . . . I find that the great foolishness of young Maoists in Italy is their slogan, "Serve the People." My slogan is "Serve Myself," because only by

serving myself am I able to serve the people—that is, to be a part of the people, not serve them.[16]

To the Left this may sound as if Bertolucci were rationalizing his egocentric position. Like other European Communist intellectuals, he states, he is divided; he has a split personality. The real contradiction within him is perhaps that he may be unable to synchronize his heart and his brain.

In the midst of the social revolution of the late sixties Bertolucci filmed *Partner,* a film which suggests the schizophrenia of culture and revolution. At that time he was still under the influence of Brecht and Godard. His statements also reveal a sharp antagonism toward America, the CIA, and President Johnson. He calls Italy an immense aircraft carrier for the U.S. With *Last Tango*'s international success in 1972, he entered a loftier financial bracket; his tone changed. His critics of the Left bemoaned this, sensing that his monetary situation would color his political vision.

Following *Last Tango* Bertolucci entered upon the greatest contradiction of his cinematic career—*1900,* a pro-Communist film financed by capitalist dollars. What may appear as hypocrisy to these critics is for Bertolucci the epitome of the Gramscian principle of reaching the masses with an ideological message. In *Luna* he even satirized his own bourgeois-leftist contradictions by casting Renato Salvatori as the rich Communist.

Although a longtime supporter of the Communist party's youth federation, he spoke out against what he called the "agitprop kids," those who believed we must start from zero in the rebuilding of society and culture. He finds this idiotic, anti-Leninist, and somewhat fascist. To start from a prehistorical position is alien to his ideology and aesthetics, he mentioned to Amos Vogel.[17] With *1900,* Bertolucci showed that he was in favor of the "historical compromise," the attempt by the Italian Communist party in the mid-seventies to shy away from a Soviet-dominated ideology and move toward a government coalition. According to Aggeo Savioli of *L'Unità,* Bertolucci is a member in good standing of the Communist party and has used his talents on behalf of the party, especially in the short documentary *The Poor Die First,* on the hospital situation in Rome. The party has backed him in the struggle against censorship, although, as in Pasolini's case, the liberal treatment of sex in his films may not be conducive to party ideology. In our interview of January 1982 he maintained that the party does not take an official position with respect to his films. In certain cases such as *1900* or *Luna* the ranks are obviously divided.

Finally, to set the stage for an aesthetic, political discussion of Bertolucci's opus, it is important to understand his philosophy of the political film. Aside from *The Poor Die First,* a militant film made for a noncommercial circuit, the films of the director are primarily political fiction. His later films manifest a proliferation of complex psychological themes. His works nonetheless ordinarily deal with politics and demonstrate a leftist, nonmilitant orientation. Until *Stratagem* and *Conformist* in 1970, he was in the shadow of the leftist filmmakers of the Godardian school who aimed at an intellectual elite or the student film ghetto. He wanted to use the camera as a political instrument or weapon. With *Stratagem* he broke into mass distribution, provided by television, and with *Conformist* aimed at a large international, commercial audience. Like other young filmmakers in 1968, Bertolucci felt you could make a revolution with a film. This was an illusion of the *petit bourgeois*, he stated, adding, "I was naive. You cannot make political films in a commercial situation. The more revolutionary the film, the less the public would accept it."[18] Now he sees that film can only be *at the service of the revolution*, and *1900* contains his proof that this is feasible. His ideal in this political fiction world? "Since I am of bourgeois origins, my effort is in finding a dialectical union between Marx and Freud."[19]

From Cinematic Prehistory to Ideological Debut

In 1959, Bertolucci went to Paris for the first time. There he soon had what was almost a mystical experience. He witnessed Godard's *Breathless*. From then on he would make constant pilgrimages to the Cinémathèque under the patronage of Henri Langlois. Bertolucci canonized him, for he shaped a new world of cinema by the projection of international classics. At the Cinémathèque he encountered new idols and renewed his allegiance to the old, those filmmakers whose works he first marvelled at with his father in Parma. These classics were primarily American movies filmed from the twenties to the fifties; then there were the works of Mizoguchi, Dovzhenko, Max Ophuls, Renoir, and von Sternberg. It appears that from among these filmmakers there were three major influential directors who contributed to Bertolucci's formation before he loosed his ties with his cinematic heritage. Rossellini, Pasolini, and Godard have definitely left their mark upon the early cinema of Bertolucci.

In the postwar Italian film world, Rossellini represented the renaissance of spirit, as we noted earlier. Bertolucci considered him everyone's master, especially in light of *Open City* and *Voyage to Italy.* Freshness of vision, a sharp eye for ethical problems, and a keen political perspective characterized this area of influence on Bertolucci. This influence soon waned. He later felt that Rossellini the innovator became too didactic with his documentaries and television productions in the seventies. Pasolini's impact upon the young Bertolucci would be different. This was a true master-disciple relationship that extended through the rich fields of literature, art, and cinema. Bertolucci's reading had drawn him into the worlds of Pascal, Melville, Stendhal, Wilde, and Marx. Then he would acquire an interest in the Americans—Fitzgerald, Chandler, and Hammett. At this stage, Pasolini encouraged him to write. The art world was not new to Bertolucci since his father taught art in Parma. Pasolini sharpened his interest in it when he invited Bertolucci to be his apprentice for *Accattone.* The language of art became the language of cinema during the production, as noted in the previous chapter. Although Bertolucci could not appreciate Pasolini's nostalgic tendency in the *Trilogy of Life,* calling it unreal and unhealthy, he felt that his mentor redeemed himself by capturing the excruciating reality of the fascist present in his ultimate work, *Salò.* With his third influence, Godard, the situation was still different, Godard broke open the vistas of cinema with his experimentation in unconventional language, irrational content, and a revolutionary political perspective. Bertolucci was under his tutelage during his formative years. As happened with Pasolini, Bertolucci's career took another turn, especially with his desire to reach the masses instead of the miniscule ghetto of the elite. Their relationship dissolved when Godard walked out of *Last Tango* after ten minutes. The New Wave director also felt Bertolucci was a revisionist and a sellout to the Establishment. In 1973, Bertolucci referred to Godard as "a left-wing anarchist." Through the next several years Bertolucci exorcized these three spirits who inhabited his house of cinema.

Bertolucci's first steps in the cinema world were shaky but promising. For a high school graduation gift he received a movie camera. In the summer of 1956 with his brother and two cousins as actors, he filmed *The Cable Car (La teleferica)*. He reminisces about this first venture:

> And when I was fifteen I was visiting in the mountains and someone gave me a 16-mm camera. I made a ten-minute film about kids that was called *The Cable Car*. I wrote it and shot it and edited it. I showed it to the farmers in the little place where we were staying. They were interested, since it was only the second film they had ever seen—the other being a United States Information Agency film about agriculture in Vermont.[20]

Bertolucci's father commemorated this historic moment in filmmaking for his son in a poem, mentioning that it was an 8-mm camera:

> Hasten, the cable car is afar
> and Bernardo, who has the long legs
> of a fourteen year old, the stirrings
> of a story-teller,
> insists upon real time, and longs
> that you stray among chestnuts and fern
> to seek, by the light which diminishes
> little by little—hasten
> the night is frightful in the mountains—
> the metallic wires that slash the hands
> and take away the timber . . .[21]

Bertolucci referred to his *Cable Car* as a type of home movie; nonetheless, it already showed his love for cinema and desire to create. He followed this up at the age of sixteen with *The Death of the Pig (La morte del maile)*. In the winter of 1956 Bertolucci was at Parma. Here he did this short film on how the local farmers slaughter pigs for the Christmas festivities. A peasant child, hidden, watches the pig-slaughtering which was something mystical for him. It was "a kind of cinéma-vérité, a film about the snow, and the pig's blood falling upon it, the pig shrieking at death, and at dawn, the peasants hoisting three stakes resembling a pitchfork; it was a simple film, formally attractive, that I have appreciated."[22] The pig butchering of *1900* brings him back in time to this early film.

In the late fifties Bertolucci's rapport with Pasolini became ever stronger. The literary relationship soon had a fraternal and cinematic basis to it. It enriched the lives of both poets. It deepened on the set of *Accattone*. Neither Bertolucci nor Pasolini had a technical background in cinema, nor had either been exposed to a theoretical training. The master came immediately from poetry and the novel, and the disciple half his age came from the enthusiastic world of "cinéphilia." Bertolucci told Joseph Gelmis: "Working with Pasolini was a very important experience. He was just as virgin to the cinema as I was. So I didn't watch a director at work; I watched a director being born."[23] For the disciple, thus, it was like witnessing the reinvention of cinema and a new language, a language Bertolucci would later call "un faux naïf" one that was slightly artificial and not really thought through yet.[24] On the set of *Accattone* Bertolucci worked closely with the actors, while handling the normal all-encompasssing duties of assistant. He taught the nonprofessionals the dialogue, for they had little ability to read or write.

Still under the tutelage of Pasolini, Bertolucci had the opportunity to undertake his own production. The producer Antonio Cerni had asked Pasolini for a script that had something to do with the subproletarian theme now in vogue after *The Ragazzi* and *Accattone*. Pasolini came up with a subject that Sergio Citti and Bertolucci developed into a script. Pasolini was unable to commit himself to the production because of his work on *Mamma Roma*, so Cerni offered Bertolucci the chance to make his first feature film. Since the script was drawn up for another director, Bertolucci had to modify it according to his own vision, a principle that he would always follow in his work.

The Grim Reaper and *Before the Revolution:* A Prodigy at Work

The Grim Reaper (*La commare secca*, 1962), a euphemism for death in the Roman dialect, is the hiatus between the two directors.[25] The film penetrated the same lower depths which *Accattone* did with prostitutes, thieves, and vagrants. In some ways, however, it went beyond the Pasolinian world. Bertolucci mentioned to Gordon Gow that the structure of the film had some basis in Kurosawa's *Roshamon,* and reflected some of the tragic atmosphere of Pasolini's works, but it still had a very personal style to it.[26]

In this film—half-interview, half-detective story—Bertolucci situates the action in the area of Parco Paolini, near St. Paul-Outside-the-Walls, along the Tiber. The body of a prostitute is discovered and the spiraling search for the murderer begins. Through flashbacks creating a tension between hypothesis and eyewitness report, between lie and reality, the circumstances surrounding the woman's death are reconstructed. The suspects give their own subjective interpretations of their activities that day. There is the purse-snatching "Canticchia" (Francesco Ruiu), the Calabrian soldier Teodoro (Allen Midgette), two youths Francolicchio (Alvaro D'Ercole) and Pipito (Romano Labate), and the gigolo. Ambiguity and suspense escalate. A passerby had witnessed a northern blond young man with clogs beating the prostitute to death. The police apprehend Natalino (Renato Troiani) at a dance on a barge reminiscent of the Accattone *set.*

Bertolucci's *The Grim Reaper.* A lonely Calabrian soldier is one of the suspects in the homicide of a prostitute. *(Courtesy of National Film Archive, British Film Institute.)*

Godard's presence cannot be overlooked. The probing questions of the detective (voice-off), the technique of cinéma-vérité in general, and in particular the jump cuts in the reconstruction of the homicide, are not too distant from the New Wave director's radical cinema language at the time. Yet the overall influence of Pasolini is most noticeable. The screen is peopled with subproletarians haunted by death and violence. They speak the Roman dialect which spices up the dialogue. The scene of the three bald-headed young men in the park offers a surrealistic and Pasolinian twist to the film. Implicit here is the homosexual rape of the young man who ventures into their terrain. The film also contains the poetry of the master with a rhythm that is musical. Bertolucci was interested in creating a lyrical language to show the passage of time and a reaction to the weather. In essence, what had been Pasolini's insight into the subproletarian world of Rome—not Bertolucci's pastoral world of the outskirts of Parma—became transformed through the camera of the young twenty-year-old director. It is a moving, participating camera that attempts a vision other than the master's aesthetic compositions à la Masaccio. Bertolucci's paradoxical dependence upon and independence from Pasolini was immediately perceived at the Venice Film Festival in 1962 where Frank Perry's *David and Lisa*, Roman Polanski's *Knife in the Water*, and Andrei Tarkovsky's *Childhood of Ivan* were screened that year. The reservations that certain Italian critics had about the film of this neophyte, a literary cinéaste, revealed the inbred conformism that would still be rampant when *1900* would be screened almost fifteen years later.

Two years after Bertolucci completed his cinematic rite of passage with *The Grim Reaper*, he analyzed the political rite of passage of Fabrizio in *Before the Revolution* (*Prima della rivoluzione*, 1964). The young protagonist was roughly of Bertolucci's age, cultural milieu, and geographical origin. Autobiography, literature, and cinema coalesce. Intermingled with his own internal questioning about his bourgeois roots and his political future, Bertolucci develops the Stendhalian hero Fabrice del Dongo. In Stendhal's chronicle *The Charterhouse of Parma* (*La Chartreuse de Parme*, 1839), the passionate Duchess Sanseverina, Fabrice's aunt, is anxious for the young nephew to succeed. She pushes him toward religion, a profession he does not love any more or less than he does the chaste, devout, and tender Clelia Conti. In this artistocratic family described by Stendhal, hypocrisy has certainly made its inroads. Bertolucci will contemporize and illustrate this milieu.[27] If the surface of this sociopolitical film were scratched, some of the relationships, tone, and milieu of the nineteenth century world of bourgeois Milan would come into view.

A quote from the French statesman Talleyrand introduces the film: "Whoever has not known life before the Revolution does not know the sweetness of life." This sets the tone for the film, implying that even with the radical desire to recreate the world with new values, the revolutionary is still inextricably wedded to his past.

It is Easter 1962. Fabrizio (Francesco Barilli) is quasi-emotionally involved with the simple, cultured, and pious Clelia (Cristina Pariset) and politically aligned with his peer Agostino (Allen Midgette) and his mentor Cesare (Morando Morandini). The arrival in Parma of his young attractive aunt Gina (Adriana Asti) wreaks havoc with these once

stable relationships. She seduces him and causes deep sexual tension within him. His en-
gagement with Clelia passes through a cooling-off stage. Agostino commits suicide, for not
even Fabrizio could help him. Fabrizio becomes disenchanted with Cesare's political philoso-
phy. Gina returns to Milan. At the Communist L'Unità celebration several months later
Fabrizio admits he cannot follow the party ideology. Returning to a bourgeois past, he
marries Clelia at a wedding that has the aura of a funeral. It marks the death of political
consciousness.

With its vast stratification of worlds, *Before the Revolution* touches upon the
aesthetic, musical, literary, technical, and political interests of Bertolucci in his
early twenties. The composition in each frame depends upon the camera technique as well as the aesthetic vision of the young director. In the realm of art,
Bertolucci chides Pasolini at times for his contrived staging of shots with particular canvases in mind. This will soon, however, become characteristic of Bertolucci's own filming. Wilde, Talleyrand, Melville, along with excerpts from Pasolini's poetry, are juxtaposed with references to Howard Hawks's *Red River* and
Jean-Luc Godard's *A Woman Is a Woman*. Resnais's shadow appears in Gina's pon-
dering of the photos on her bed, harking back to a similar action with similar
lighting in *Last Year at Marienbad*. The voice-off and travelling camera also recall
Resnais's techniques. There is a newsreel effect of filming the opera house,
where Verdi's presence can be felt. In Fabrizio's discussion with his filmbuff
friend, the latter admits, "One cannot live without Rossellini," a nod of Bertolucci
to Italy's neorealistic roots. Into his quasi-neorealistic atmosphere of the black
and white film he cleverly inserts a series of color movie clips. All of the above
threads are carefully, but at times artificially, stitched together. The political,
nonetheless, predominates.

The Bertoluccian Fabrizio, erstwhile antihero, deeply sensing culpability for
his class origins, is revolted by the bourgeoisie of Parma. Here the river cuts the
city in two definitely distinct classes. A crippling lassitude permeates the upper
class atmosphere wherein Fabrizio uncomfortably finds himself. Family, Catholic
Church, and even art suffocate him. His sophisticated family is conformist by
nature, pious in religion. Aunt Gina, representing the Milan "big-city spirit," is a
dangerous breath of fresh air at Easter time. She will be the competition for
fiancée Clelia, who was destined to continue the bourgeois experience for
Fabrizio. In voice-off he recites from Pasolini's *The Religion of My Time*, where the
Church is "the merciless heart of the state." The theatre at Parma where Verdi's
Macbeth is performed represents for Bertolucci the grandiose but ridiculous temple of bourgeois culture, and opera the funeral chant of the bourgeoisie. All of
this is very repulsive to the unsettled Fabrizio.

Fabrizio is simultaneously attracted to the Marxist ideology of Cesare, his
Garibaldi whom he has placed on a supposedly unshakable pedestal. During a
visit to his mentor's home, Fabrizio admits to Gina that here he truly feels in his
"niche." At the outset of the film he shares Cesare's high moral and political
ideals, always rejecting the externals of his bourgeois upbringing. Cesare's ideals,
however, had not been totally internalized by Fabrizio. Instead, Fabrizio is only a
highly theoretical, political book from which leap forth fine sounding ideologies.

Gina recognizes this and challenges her nephew. At Cesare's she says, "What do you want to change? You can't change anyone! Not one single person!" Her words will soon be very prophetic.

The catalytic events of Fabrizio's incestuous relationship with his mother's sister and the death of his companion stir within him strong but confused feelings. He struggles to orient himself with the contemporary issues and ideologies of 1962. To situate him in time, Bertolucci eclectically cites the current events of the Algerian War, the death of Marilyn Monroe, the Angolan crisis, Italian elections, Godard's film *A Woman Is a Woman,* and the trial of French General Raoul Salan for his participation in the Algerian revolt. Fabrizio senses more and more internal conflicts, which are only increased by his encounter with Gina's friend, Puck (Crecrope Barilli). This genteel aristocrat has been destroyed by progress. Fabrizio despises Puck for being a representative of the landed gentry, a type of hangover from the Old Regime. He is nonetheless attracted by Puck's sensitive view of life, leisure, nature, and people.

The apex of Fabrizio's political evolution occurs toward the end of the film, during the September Communist party festivities. After his "red vacation"—a summer in which he was closely attuned to the party's ideology—Fabrizio confesses to Cesare that he is abandoning the party. His values and those of the party are no longer compatible. He has a type of "nostalgia for the present" and cannot join the revolution. Bertolucci reflects on this ideological switch in Fabrizio: "His impotence was the result of his social and cultural growth. It was the story of a lost fight."[28] Cesare tells Fabrizio that he has thus failed the party. Fabrizio left because he was disillusioned. He feels that no one, not even the party, says anything about the struggle in Angola, indicates concern about Algeria and the colonial problem, or shows alarm if a Black is killed in Alabama. Fabrizio realizes that Cesare tried to transform him ideologically, but it was not possible, thus confirming Gina's astute observation about the impossibility of changing anyone or anything in society. Instead of being Cesare's comrade in the revolution, Fabrizio opts for another niche in life, the secure, bourgeois marriage with Clelia, long expected of him.

Before the Revolution, a pessimisstic tale of the defeat of a young idealist, represented not only the young Bertolucci's situation, but that of many European youth and intellectuals alike in the sixties. It thus became simultaneously a type of self-portrait and collective composition, or group picture. For him personally, the film was an exorcism of strong, internal feelings and contradictions. For the director it would not be an ambiguous film but a film on ambiguity, and more specifically, on political and cultural ambiguity.[29] The Italian Communist party was not pleased with *Before the Revolution,* for the film appeared diametrically opposed to the process of political consciousness that it preached.

Television and the Documentary

It would be several years before Bertolucci would undertake his next feature-length film, *Partner* (1968). During the interim he tried his hand at the documentary film for television and a short for a collective film. His first television venture was a series of three films from forty to forty-eight minutes in length. The Italian oil company AGIP sponsored the documentary triptych *The Petroleum Route (La via del petrolio,* 1965) less than a decade before the oil crisis and just a few years after the death of the petroleum czar Enrico Mattei. With a crew of four he shot twelve hours of material "in synch" (not dubbed) for the two-and-a-half hour television production broadcast in January and February 1967. He had great freedom to shoot what he felt was best, relying upon his aesthetic and technical experience from his first two features. It was during the four-month editing period that he created the real style and tone of the work.

The first episode, "Origins" *(Le origini),* introduces the real protagonist, oil, "black gold," that is imported into Italy. Although most instructive in content, this segment of the documentary is not devoid of lyricism. The second installment, "The Voyage," *(Il viaggio),* traces the shipment of oil from the Near East to Genoa aboard an oil tanker.[30] A few literary and cinematic quotations ranging from the dark poet Rimbaud ("Le bateau ivre") to war films make their way onto the soundtrack. "Across Europe" *(Attraverso l'Europa)* concludes the work, showing the pipeline travelling from Genoa to Ingolstadt, Germany. As in *Before the Revolution,* aesthetics and literature merge in *The Petroleum Route.* This time Bertolucci charts a financial, commercial itinerary instead of an ideological one.

Antonin Artaud *(The Theatre and Its Double)* and Julian Beck of the twenty-year-old Living Theatre left their mark on Pasolini and Bertolucci. From Artaud's theatre of cruelty and black humor comes a more contemporary vision of corporeal expression, guerrilla theatre, the happening, and other forms of radical theatre. For the twenty-eight minute episode of the collective film *Love and Hate* *(Amore e rabbia,* 1967)—a collaboration of Godard, Bellocchio (replacing Zurlini), Lizzani, and Pasolini—Bertolucci invited Beck and his troupe to film a type of experimental sketch. This episode, *Agony (Agonia),* at first entitled *The Barren Fig Tree(Il fico infruttuoso),* followed the original intentions of the two journalists Puccio Pucci and Piero Badalassi who wanted to show unusual contemporary parallels with the gospel. For twelve or thirteen days at Cinecittà, Bertolucci rehearsed and filmed with the troupe, days filled with creative birth pangs as well as intense joy. The ritualized drama resulted from the intricate play of cinematic and theatrical elements.

Agony is the nightmarish, hesitant step of an old man (Julian Beck) on the threshold of death. His bedside visitors (members of the Living Theatre) question him on what good he had done during his lifetime. The revelation is tragic. As he dies, it is learned that he was a corrupt prince of the Church.

The theme of an assessment of life as it comes to a close for an elderly person is not original or unique. De Sica's *Umberto D,* Petri's *Numbered Days,* Kurosawa's *Ikiru,* and Resnais's *Providence* depict the anguish, doubts, and concerns of individuals who are about to shake off this mortal coil. From a political standpoint, in the late sixties it was most fashionable to attack the Establishment, criticizing it for its hypocrisy, self-interest, and bourgeois attitudes. With *Agony,* Bertolucci attempts to show that a head of the Catholic Church is not only not free of sin, but is one of the biggest sinners in the world. Dante's influence from the *Inferno* is readily perceptible. For the director this short film was meant to be an indictment, a cinematic act of terrorism.

As in the case of his other short films destined for television, Bertolucci rose to the occasion when asked to make a documentary film for the Communist party. *The Poor Die First (I poveri muoiono prima, 1971)*, a noncommercial film created for the Unitelfilm cooperative, was part of the "parallel cinema" that interested Bertolucci in the late sixties and early seventies. This thirty-five-minute film in black and white discloses the abominable health conditions in the Rome hospitals. To document these abuses of the poor, the leaders of the labor union C.G.I.L. procured permission from city officials for Bertolucci to film in the hospitals. With a miniscule crew he entered one hospital and filmed the tragic accumulation of sick patients in the corridors and toilets. Some hospital aides assisted him in pointing out the abuses. The poorer patients were especially badly off and discriminated against by the hospital administration. They were the neglected of the earth. After a half-hour or so of this exposure of the pathetic conditions, Bertolucci was evicted, but not without his incriminating footage.

The next phase, the traditional agitprop action, brought this film "of witness" (says Bertolucci) to the attention of the Italian public. It was used explicitly to confront social issues during the administrative municipal elections of 1971 in Rome. As with the Soviet propaganda films of the 1920s *The Poor Die First* was screened on the city walls for the masses. The militants then followed up the projection by distributing tracts on health problems. *The Poor Die First* would be Bertolucci's only true militant film, designed for immediate political (and propagandistic) effect. The second militant project that he attempted, *Work at Home (Lavoro a domicile)*, a study of women working at home without contracts, laws, and benefits, never got beyond the script stage.

Partner and *The Spider's Stratagem:* Radical Doubles

In 1968, still under the influence of the iconoclast Artaud, Bertolucci filmed *Partner*, loosely based on Dostoevski's short story, "The Double." The air was still filled with the revolutionary mist of Brecht and Beck's Living Theatre. In fact, *Partner* would not have been made if he had not encountered Beck and company. From his earlier experiences with the troupe he learned much more about the new theatre. At this time Bertolucci had still felt an attraction to the cinema for an elite, whose practitioners were Rocha, Straub, and, more and more, Godard. Bertolucci and his fellow conspirators took the revolutionary position of striking out against all traditional, preexisting forms of cinema, with the intention of spreading the revolution. Their recherché films paradoxically could hardly be meant for the masses. Instead only an elite of elites would see them—university students, film technicians, frequenters of the Latin Quarter cinema houses, and cinéphiles in general. Strong leftist political ideologies and radical cinema techniques prevented their films from travelling beyond these circles. *Partner* could be considered a microcosm of this closed world.

> *Giacobbe (Pierre Clementi), a French drama teacher at the Academy of Dramatic Art in Rome, has divinized Artaud in the light of his revolutionary theatre. For Giacobbe life and art are one. Pushing this precept to its logical conclusion, the frail, gentle professor would like to bring about the revolution through the theatre of cruelty. Suddenly encountering his double, Giacobbe begins a new life with a split ego. Reality cannot be distinguished from the dream world as Giacobbe I becomes more revolutionary and fiery Giacobbe II toned down. The doubles merge, but one must be eliminated for survival. Giacobbe terminates his alter ego and conforms.*

Once again the complex edifice designed by Bertolucci must be approached with total vision. The multi-levelled structure uses cinema, psychology, drama, literature, and politics for support. Although the film may be an eclectic opus, its keystone is the relationship of art and revolution to life. Bertolucci identifies closely with the divided Giacobbe and puts into his character what he reads and feels in 1968. In a surrealistic fashion he includes literary and cinematic references from Cocteau, Rimbaud, Brecht, Artaud, Sade, Eisenstein, and others. He follows the same principles of citation as he did with Cesare and Fabrizio in *Before the Revolution.*

Bertolucci's *Partner.* Drama teacher Giacobbe (Pierre Clementi) discovers a revolutionary character as his own alter ego.*(Courtesy of National Film Archive, British Film Institute.)*

Ambiguity permeates *Partner*: schizophrenia, Bertolucci's inner political tension, a struggle with the biblical angel—or the theatre's double? One is never certain. In political terms the film primarily concentrates on the quest of a young man for liberation from his suffocating past, his current milieu, and himself by engaging in a personal revolution. In this sense, Giacobbe is an extension of Fabrizio and meets the same fate as the earlier protagonist. The lofty ideals of rebellion are held in check by a string of bourgeois values from which the antihero has a difficult time escaping. His double prods him to be more aggressive in society. When he does so it is done violently, as against the Establishment or his girlfriend Clara (Stefania Sandrelli). He might like to see the death of American imperialism, but he is too much a product of his environment.

Bertolucci—via Giacobbe—states at the conclusion of the film that this was all a parable about American imperialism and syphilitic marines. When asked by Gelmis what he achieved in tacking on this "Marxist sermon," Bertolucci replied:

> It's because it comes so suddenly that it has an impact, because it isn't expected. If we had spoken about American imperialism during the whole film, people wouldn't have remembered the film so clearly. In the first scenes of the film there is a North Vietnamese flag. The titles are on a North Vietnamese flag, red and blue and a white star in the middle. So from the very beginning, whoever is receptive enough and wants to understand it, it's clear that it's about imperialism.[31]

Partner can be situated between Godard's *La Chinoise* (1967) and the 1968 Paris student demonstrations, although "les événements," the political events, are included in the conclusion of the production. Bertolucci said that the film perfectly reflected the spirit of the times. It represented an imaginative phase of international cinema, despite its sometimes partisan and artificial ideological thrust. Bertolucci's contribution to this period, however, demonstrates a fertile imagination, together with a critical questioning of how the revolution could really come about. Directly following his personal reflections in the course of the filming and his exposure to the political events of 1968, the director entered the ranks of the Communist party.

The television industry and the cinema world in most countries are separate and distinct entities, and ne'er the twain shall meet. Not true in Italy, however. RAI, Italian Radio and Television, has taken ambitious steps over the past decade to attract well-known directors to produce for the small screen. The directors themselves profit from this, for their products have a double life—before the millions of the television public, and in countless cinema houses in normal film distribution. Bellocchio, Rossellini, Fellini, and Bertolucci have been among the more celebrated artists who have bridged the two media.

For his preceding works Bertolucci often turned to literature, at least as a point of departure—Stendhal for *Before the Revolution* and Dostoevski for *Partner*. Autobiographical elements nonetheless were hardly lacking in both films. In *The Spider's Stratagem* the same holds true.

Bertolucci explains the origins of the film:

The idea for the film came to me while reflecting on a famous quote from Bertold Brecht: 'Happy the country which has no need of heroes.' And this is precisely the key, the pivot of this story.[32]

Bertolucci takes Jorge-Luis Borges's four-page short story, "The Theme of the Traitor and the Hero," and transposes it in a quasi-surrealistic fashion.[33] Nineteenth-century Ireland becomes twentieth-century Italy; the insurrection against the English, the resistance against fascism; and the protagonist (Ryan), Athos, Jr. The universalized story of Borges could have taken place in any oppressed state, whether it be Ireland, Poland, or the Republic of Venice. For convenience's sake, says Borges, it is set in Ireland in 1824. The novelist and short story writer draws from the last line of Jean-Paul Sartre's *The Words (Les mots):* "A man is made by all men . . . he is all the people and all the people are he. . . ."

A young man, Athos Magnani, Jr. (Giulio Brogi) descends from the train at Tara, in the Po Valley.[34] His father (also played by Brogi) has become a myth in this small town since his death on 15 June 1936, supposedly at the hands of the Fascists. In the son's enigmatic contacts with his father's mistress Draifa (Alida Valli) and antifascist comrades Costa (Tino Scotti), Gaibazzi (Pippo Campanini), and Rasori (Franco Giovanelli), he gradually discovers that his father, who was involved in an assassination plot against Mussolini, turned traitor and was killed by his fellow conspirators. Since the movement needed a hero more than a traitor, the execution was attributed to the Fascists. Athos, Jr., in bad conscience, continues propagating this myth by his commemorative words to the assembled townspeople. When he tries to leave Tara, however, he finds that the train does not arrive. In this quasi-Twilight Zone, the track is already overgrown with weeds.

With *Stratagem*, Bertolucci initiated a new phase of his career. In a sudden change of conscience, he began directing his films not toward an elite but a vast public. He wished to communicate with a large segment of society, holding up a mirror to it in one way, but also baring his soul in a representative self-examination. He had begun psychoanalysis four months prior to filming *Stratagem*. Gradually he was coming to grips with his relationship with his father. At times he felt that he was living in the shadow of the senior Bertolucci in the area of poetry and knew now that he had to compete with him on his own terms—cinema. In his interview with Joan Mellen for *Cinéaste*, Bertolucci indicated that "The relation between the father and son is the real point of the film." Their conversation continued:

Q. The son wants to become the father?
A. Yes, all the great problems between father and son are the basis of the film.
Q. Even the incestuous relation, with Dreyfa, is present.
A. Yes, with Dreyfa.[35]

The young Bertolucci/Athos, Jr. makes a psychoanalytic journey through the realm of preconscious memory, gathering data about his father so that he can

Bertolucci's *The Spider's Strategem.* The young Athos (Giulio Brogi) watches his father's wartime mistress Draifa (Alida Valli). *(Courtesy of Movie Star News.)*

exorcise this spirit. Bertolucci himself felt that even though his own father was antifascist, he still represented the bourgeoisie, and it was the *petite bourgeoisie* that invented fascism. In the desecration of his father's memorial, Athos, Jr. finally rids himself of his father's ghost. Like Aunt Gina of *Before the Revolution,* Draifa (named for her father's political hero, Dreyfus) also trespasses on sexual territory with the young Athos. She is the catalyst and link with the past. In Athos's journey to his father's town, his peculiar encounters, and the desecration of the monument, he has gained self-knowledge.[36] The tragic flaw in his character is his ultimate conformity. He had the opportunity to demythologize the hero for the sake of truth—in the style of post-1968 political consciousness— but instead upholds the status quo. In Fabrizio, Giacobbe, and now Athos, Jr., the Bertoluccian conforming antihero lives on.

Stratagem is replete with aesthetic and literary images, starting with the credits themselves. The title alludes to Book 6 of Ovid's *Metamorphoses,* the story of Arachne changed into a spider by Athena. Bertolucci explained his usage in the biological terms of self-preservation. The clever strategy of the male spider is to fecundate the female without being devoured. T. Jefferson Kline refers to Draifa as a mythical Ariadne and Arachne.[37] Verdi's *Rigoletto,* full of conspiracy and duplicity, provides the musical accompaniment for the crucial moment of the father's execution in June 1936 and the son's discovery of the father's treachery.[38] The Italian poet who greatly influenced Pasolini and Bertolucci, Giovanni

Pascoli (1855–1912), appears in verse here in "La cavalla storna" (The Grey Horse) read by the mysterious boy/girl.[39] The surrealism of Magritte *(La repro-duction interdite)*, the brightly colored and shadowed zones of De Chirico, the credits superimposed (with the back of the character's head in full view) on the animal paintings of the local painter Ligabue, serve as aesthetic references to guide the spectator through the eerie village. Once in Tara, Athos, Jr. enters a type of psychological and political labyrinth from which he cannot escape, a worthy parallel to Robbe-Grillet's *The Man Who Lies (L'homme qui ment,* 1968), set around a supposed legendary Resistance hero Jean Robin. The younger Athos may also have unwittingly been caught in the political web spun by Draifa and his father's co-conspirators.

A string of subtle and not too subtle themes weaves through *Stratagem*—the need for a hero, the Oedipal search for the father's murderers, and the quest for adulthood. Bertolucci also is preoccupied with the subjectivity of history, the conflict of myth and truth, and the dreamlike quality of reality. Despite the heavy emphasis on the sociopsychological aspect of the content, Bertolucci does not hesitate to acknowledge the political side of the work. He compares the father-son relationship to that of the heads of the Italian Communist party:

> I find that this is a very Berlinguerian film. It could very well be a cinematic manifesto of Berlinguer, because the rapport between Athos father and Athos son is the same as between Berlinguer and Togliatti: the mythomaniacal son's discovery of the father's treason is a bit like Berlinguer's discovery of Togliatti's Stalinism. Just as Togliatti's Stalinism was necessary in postwar Italy, the treason of Athos's father in *Stratagem* was necessary. . . . But perhaps I am going a bit far?[40]

Bertolucci proposes that the individual counts precious little in the course of revolutionary struggle and that the weight of one person's action is relative. Appearances count more than reality and the hero is more useful than the traitor for the collective movement. The politicized use of heroism in society at a specific moment is expedient. In *Stratagem* a cowardly character thus gets to become a political martyr. The tragedy of this realization by the son is that, in spite of his own self-knowledge and growth, he, too, collaborates in the lie.

Stratagem, televised on 25 and 30 October 1970, advanced the reputation of the trio of Bertolucci, his brother Giuseppe, and the cinematographer Vittorio Storaro.[41] Although Bertolucci considered it a film aesthetically made "in a minor key," in his repertoire it can be viewed as a major work.

The Conformist: At the Heart of Psychological Fascism

Bertolucci was not yet born when the primary action of the film *The Conformist* (*Il conformista,* 1970) took place. Through his family's recollections, his father's stories, personal reading, and above all the "collective memory" of film, he was able to reconstruct this period in a powerful tableau of fascism. Drawing upon the wealth of Alberto Moravia's novel *Il conformista* (1951), and modifying certain details, he could capture the politics but especially the psychology of Italian fascism in the thirties and forties. Desiring to portray adequately this milieu and time, he had his assistants see miles and miles of films from the thirties, he said. This predisposed him to recreate a disturbing, bizarre world.

In Paris of the Popular Front, 1938, Marcello Clerici (Jean-Louis Trintignant) receives the phone call that sets in motion a political assassination. He leaves his newly married bride Giulia (Stefania Sandrelli) to go off on his mission with his fascist aide de campe Manganiello (Gastone Moschin). The voyage sets off a chain of reminiscences: as a child he shot the chauffeur Lino (Pierre Clementi), who was making sexual advances on him. Later, wishing to be "normal," he joins the ranks of the fascists, confesses his childhood crime to a priest, and marries into a fine bourgeois family.

Clerici's honeymoon to Paris provides him with the cover to plan the elimination of his former university teacher Professor Quadri (Enzo Tarascio) who has been a rabid antifascist in exile. Clerici becomes enamoured of Quadri's exotic, enigmatic wife Anna (Dominique Sanda), who prefers a sexual rapport with his wife Giulia. On the day of Quadri's execution in the countryside, Clerici watches as the fascist henchmen knife the antifascist professor à la Julius Caesar and then bloodily gun down Anna. Ironically, on 25 July 1943, as Rome is liberated, Clerici chances upon Lino the chauffeur whom he thought he killed. It is the moment of realization—he conformed, he killed, but for nought.

The modifications from Moravia's novel made the film an intense political and psychological experience that differed from the original work. The director's greater political consciousness since his entrance into the Communist party and his growing psychological awareness because of his initiation into psychoanalysis could also account for the brilliant reinterpretation of the Moravia novel. Bertolucci makes of Quadri's wife Anna a more complex and sexual creature. He adds the personage of the blind fascist propagandist Italo, perhaps a symbolic representative of Italy, who takes on some of the interior monologue of the original Clerici. The director alters the climax of Moravia's linear chronicle. In the novel the hand of Fate—or God's justice—strikes Marcello Clerici and his family. As they leave Rome together they meet their death, strafed by an overhead plane.

Although the novel and film share a symbiotic relationship, they are autonomous. Moravia for the most part assesses the adaptation in most favorable terms, believing it to be Bertolucci's best film. He believes that Bertolucci was not absolutely faithful to the original literary piece but that this was not necessary, given his different purpose. Nonetheless, Moravia did not appreciate the ending of the film, and also felt that the director gave the entire work an overly Freudian interpretation. The novelist discussed his own work more as a Faustian novel wherein the Faustian protagonist sells his soul to the state, which in turn offers protection and security.[42]

At the New York Film Festival of 1970, Bertolucci referred to *The Conformist* as a "commercial film," "a bit of whoring" on his part. Following *Partner* he had begun to change from the hermetic, Brechtian style for an elite to a "popular" one whereby he could touch the masses, as well as readily procure international funding. With *The Conformist* he entered the world market, taking the first major step by inviting Dominique Sanda, Pierre Clementi, and Jean-Louis Trintignant to work with him. He structured the action of the novel into a suspenseful dramatic and ideological adventure. Then he added a lush visual tone to the film, carefully composed shots sometimes veering toward the self-conscious or artificial—for example, in a type of De Chirico style, the enormous neoclassical architecture dwarfs the characters in the Italian fascist minister's office. This alternates with the exuberant *art nouveau* style in Paris in the Hotel d'Orsay and the dance hall, and along the gaslit streets. Much of this atmosphere Bertolucci restylized from the films of Ophuls, von Sternberg, and Renoir.[43] The result is a period piece par excellence. Bertolucci's continuously tracking camera sweeps along with the action, while the hand-held camera at the slaying of Anna in the forest participates in the execution. The sumptuous and at times humorous background music of Georges Delerue, as well as the period dance tunes, create an unusual but harmonious atmosphere in the film. Aside from the elaborate flashbacks within flashbacks, *The Conformist* was thus able to speak directly and clearly to a large, international audience that Bertolucci envisioned as part of his latent Gramscian desire.

Bertolucci told Joan Mellen, "*The Conformist* is also in the present, but it's the present dressed as the past."[44] The director has often pointed out, as his French and Italian colleagues have done, that fascism lives on, whether it be in the mili-

Bertolucci's *The Conformist*. Marcello (Jean-Louis Trintignant) becomes the focal point for the frenetic line dance led by Giulia (Stefania Sandrelli). *(Courtesy of Movie Star News.)*

tary, the Catholic Church, or the Italian government. Like a malevolent phoenix resurrected in the seventies and gathering momentum in the eighties, neo-fascism manifests itself in a law-and-order philosophy or armed aggression against the Left and has become more and more perceptible in European and American society. In one respect it is violent reaction aimed at international ter-rorism. This neofascist current in contemporary culture, plus a certain nostalgia for or curiosity about fascism, have added to the popularity of *The Conformist*. Most European films depicting fascism of the thirties and forties have concen-trated on the glamor, adventure, or sheer heroics of the antifascists on the one hand, or the perversions of the fascists on the other. Few have captured the politics and psychology of fascism as clearly and dramatically as Visconti's *The Damned* in 1969 and Bertolucci's *The Conformist* the following year.

To set the atmosphere for fascism, Bertolucci uses the stylized aesthetics result-ing from the photography and lighting of Vittorio Storaro and the lavish sets of Nedo Azzini, who later did the sets for Liliana Cavani's *Night Porter*—also about fascism. The white marble seats in perfect geometric layout in the mental hospi-tal, the large offices with extensive unused space, and the fascist radio program of entertainment and propaganda cast the spectator right into the thirties. Il Duce's specter haunts these places, for the action covers the period of 1928 (the attempted seduction of the young Marcello) to 1943 (the fall of Mussolini).

In terms of ideology, Italian fascism developed out of a desire of certain indi-viduals and groups to create a society with law and order, designed to conserve goods already gained or to amass further wealth and power. The bourgeois and petit bourgeois had everything to lose by political chaos; the poor, nothing. The upper class always left itself open to change, accepting the ideology of the domi-nant political party, giving or selling one's political soul outright.

The state and Church play out their roles in this ideology. The government wishes an antifascist, Prof. Quadri, to be eliminated by Clerici. In the meantime, the priest in confession treats lightly and forgives Marcello Clerici's "murder" of the chauffeur Lino, once he learns that the penitent belongs to the fascist organi-zation. Clerici has the blessing of both institutions as he "normalizes" his con-science.

A collective psychosis at the basis of fascism pushes an individual with a weak ego to join strong, repressive organizations. In this type of character there is a heightened sense of honor and duty, coupled with a great desire for respec-tability. The latent fascist needs a strong paternal figure to obey and respect, often personified in an authoritarian regime. The loss of a personal, ethical sense and the emergence of a decadent spirit are usually not far behind, represented in the film by the activities in the fascists' office and the haunting Ventimilia brothel.

Marcello Clerici is a complex character: he marries without love, involves him-self without ideology, and confesses without belief. He is perfect material for the fascist movement he throws himself into, albeit with inauthentic motivation. He assimilates the dominant ideology in order to be respected as "normal." His fa-ther's madness and his "crime" hover over him, haunt him. To escape his interior disquiet, he joins a new order but is equally ready to switch allegiances to the next regime when it is expedient. He must conform, which means to be a Communist or Socialist during the Popular Front, a Gaullist under de Gaulle, or a rabid anticommunist in the age of McCarthy. Through it all, Clerici's real intentions are masked by his external gestures. He behaves as he is required to behave; he is impulsive, "macho," aggressive, abrupt, and dominating. His hat and gloves become iconographical trademarks of the fascist, while his rigid, jerky walk also gives him away. Sexually, a repressed homosexual inclination gnaws at his innards, perhaps born in his encounter with the chauffeur. It is more enigmatic and less explicit in the final sequence with the male prostitute. His relationships with Giulia and Anna are superficial and/or frigid, as if programmed.

Clerici's initial encounter with Prof. Quadri in exile in Paris links the political and psychological faces of fascism. Quadri, Clerici's former philosophy teacher, now a bourgeois antifascist leader in Paris, discusses with his disciple the latter's interest in Plato's *Republic*. Through a very artistic dramatization of the cave allegory of Book 7, Marcel and Quadri point out the shadow-image/reality dilemma occurring in fascist Italy. The nation believes that fascism is the only viable reality. With the manipulation of the window-shutter's light, creating shadows, the point is made. Though Quadri is still Clerici's quarry, the disciple still feels great respect for him. Once again, Marcello's need for a strong paternal figure to replace the negative one he has in his demented father is manifest. The teacher was the surrogate father for this conformist in the same way as the fascist organization will become for him. In the end, however, this paternal image must be destroyed in order to find personal redemption. Clerici is instrumental in the assassination, fulfilling—without feeling—his fascist duty.

The Clerici-Quadri relationship must also be read on a personal level for Bertolucci. From the death of the father emerges new life in the son. This was already discussed in terms of Bertolucci's own competition with his father. Here it takes on cinematic overtones. Tongue in cheek, Bertolucci gives Quadri Jean-Luc Godard's Paris address and phone number. Into Quadri's mouth he also puts the words from *Le petit soldat:* "The time for reflection is ended, and it's now time for action." Done in humor, this pleasantry also suggests Bertolucci's "elmination" of Godard from his paternal pantheon. Bertolucci had originally intended to have Godard's wife Anna Wiazemsky play Quadri's wife Anna. The message went out to Godard: an Italian fascist will remove his teacher and lay claim to his wife. The New Wave director did not receive it well, Bertolucci remarked. The director interpreted the relationship with his cinematic mentor in political terms:

> But I also wanted to tell Godard at the same time that—hypothetically—if I were a fascist and Godard were an anti-fascist, we were both of us still bourgeois. Professor Quadri is a bourgeois anti-fascist, but there is a kind of anti-fascism that isn't based only on the idea of freedom, but also on mass struggle and on scientific fact.[45]

With *The Conformist* Bertolucci thus breaks his ties with the old household gods and introduces new ones, not the least important of which is the Communist party. This is his first major commercial feature as a member of the party. He

salutes his comrades in song with the flower girl in Paris singing the International in chorus with the street urchins and the jubilant masses chanting the
Bandiera Rossa at the moment of Liberation. At the same time, Bertolucci proclaimed, Communism is "the wave of the future."

Last Tango in Paris: A Tragic American in Paris

To get at the essence of *Last Tango in Paris* (*Ultimo tango a Parigi,* 1972) requires
stripping away all the paraphernalia that surrounded the film in 1972. This
"succès de scandale" became immediately encrusted with elements that detracted
from the aesthetic and psychological intentions of the director. At the outset of
the production, nonetheless, Bertolucci realized the risks he was taking with the
sizzling subject of sex and, more specifically, an oasis of free and unadulterated
sex. He went ahead. Pauline Kael subsequently announced in the *New Yorker* for
14 October 1972, at the time of the first American screening at the New York
Film Festival, that the film would be a landmark in cinema. The publicity in the
U.S., quasi-erotic, drew film viewers who were more curious than serious. In the
meantime other critics saw both the brilliance and the daring of the director, but
played up the brutal sexual scenes. The flashy cover stories in *Time* and *Newsweek*
did not help get at the core of the film. Italian authorities seized the film. As a
result of the court case, Bertolucci was given a two-month suspended sentence
and supposedly denied the right to vote until 1981. It was classed with such works
as *Deep Throat, I am Curious Yellow, A Clockwork Orange, Women in Love,* and *Lady
Chatterly's Lover.* The superficial critics had an assortment of labels for the X-
rated film—eroticism, obscenity, pornography, trash. Even his faithful colleague
Pasolini spoke harshly of the work. Those in league with Kael who seriously
studied the film as a Strindbergian "dance of death" guided the most concerned
filmgoers through a labyrinth of first impressions and possible distortions.

*In an unfurnished Paris apartment, for three days following the suicide of his wife, the
haggard-looking American Paul (Marlon Brando) engages the frisky Jeanne (Maria
Schneider) in a ritual of anonymous sex ranging from an animalistic tussle on the floor to
masturbation and then sodomy. In the meantime Jeanne continues her relationship with her
fiancé Tom (Jean-Pierre Léaud), filmmaker, while Paul mourns over his wife Rosa's bier.
Abruptly Paul breaks off visiting of the apartment. Jeanne, frustrated, plans to marry Tom.
A changed Paul discovers Jeanne a short time later, but she is no longer interested, as is
obvious at the tango marathon which they watch. Paul pursues Jeanne to her family's
apartment where she shoots him with her father's pistol, ready to inform the police, "I don't
know who he is . . . I didn't know his name . . ."*[46]

Bertolucci places these tragic characters into a setting that may appear artificial
in the light of the film's aesthetic beauty (rust colors, exotically framed shots, soft
backlighting) and its logic (an agreement of two strangers to meet anonymously
for sex). The spectator is invited into this world, a microcosm of human suffering
and pleasure, as a type of observer or even voyeur. Once he or she enters

through the door of suspended belief, the drama becomes intensified. It does not let up until the pistol shot ultimately destroys the relationship.

The power of the film derives from Bertolucci's characterization of Paul and Jeanne, who are most complex and unpredictable. In Paul, Bertolucci wanted to recreate a character who could represent an American in exile, lost and depressed—a Henry Miller, F. Scott Fitzgerald, or Ernest Hemingway. At the same time he wanted an archetype of the *homo eroticus,* someone caught between *Eros* and *Thanatos,* as Moravia puts it.[47] Through the coaching of Bertolucci, an allowance for improvisation, and the talent of Brando, Paul dramatically took on the vestiges of a psychologicaly shipwrecked individual, groping about for anything that would keep him afloat. His one hope for survival was the neo-Lolita Jeanne. Maria Schneider convincingly plays out this role for a young sexually manipulated nymphomaniac. The juxtaposition of these two individuals results in a tense, tender, and erotic relationship where impersonal sex is the catalytic agent. It is the *amour fou* of surrealist Breton pushed to its extreme.

The sexual aspect of the film in reality is only the tip of the iceberg, a small part of the total psychological picture. Sexuality is nevertheless a medium of communication in a world where the characters have lost the ability to communicate. Exposed to readings in Freud, and still undergoing psychoanalysis, Bertolucci was able to draw upon these two factors to construct this intense physical

Bertolucci's *Last Tango in Paris.* Paul (Marlon Brando) makes a futile effort to win back Jeanne (Maria Schneider) in the dance hall. *(Courtesy of Movie Star News.)*

and psychological relationship between Jeanne and Paul. Jeanne appears to be struggling with the remnants of an Oedipal complex with her late father. Paul, in a sense, represents her father, killed in Algeria in 1958. She symbolically eliminates this obsession as she shoots Paul with her father's pistol as he dons her father's kepi. Paul regresses from an emotionally distraught middle-aged man, through childhood with the Little Red Riding Hood tale, through the anal stage with his grotesque demands on Jeanne for anal penetration, finally to the fetal position when he collapses on the floor after being shot. Bertolucci illustrated this type of pathetic character dissolution for Brando by taking him to see the paintings of the Anglo-Irish painter Francis Bacon at the Grand Palais in Paris. Bacon's canvases are ordinarily filled with distraught characters suffering from existential anguish. The paintings that director and actor saw possessed an aroma of despair and tragedy. The credits for *Last Tango in Paris* appear above Bacon's paintings, with the twisted features of the male smeared with colorful splotches of painted flesh.

Sexuality as an instrument of rekindling human feeling, noncommunication as a potential hazard in a marital situation, and unhappiness as an epidemic disease due to mass media reflect several leitmotifs discernible in the film. A predominant one that links many of them is death; it can be read in political and psychological terms. Its odor prevades the entire film from the outset—the inexplicable suicide of Paul's wife, the death of Jeanne's father in the Algerian War, and eventually Paul's own death. Bertolucci politically paints his own picture of bourgeois death, perhaps a figure of walking death. The director reflects, "*Tango* is my own fantasy about death—and capitalism, too."[48] Bertolucci chose Paris for this setting because he sees it as one of the most bourgeois capitals of the world. Ironically it is reactionary and progressive at the same time. Jeanne's mother's Paris apartment reveals the skeletons of the past—for instance, the father's clothing, his weapon, and the darker, heavier atmosphere that lingers over the residence. In terms of traditional religious values, Rosa's mother is more concerned about a religious funeral for her dead daughter than about Paul's shattering experience of the loss of his wife. The pious mother continually forced her daughter to repress her feelings, says Paul accusingly.

As Paul sodomizes the humiliated Jeanne, he extracts from her a type of anarchistic litany in which she is forced to reject all traditional, bourgeois values—family, Church, love. It is a didactic lesson on the apparently moribund institutions in Bertolucci's eyes. Jeanne is a continuation of the upper-class social structure—which adds a further edge to their relationship. The contrast in origins of Jeanne and Paul comes out in their disjointed dialogues—she is from an established military family, he from a small-town farming milieu. His confessional remarks to Jeanne about being embarrassed going to the high school dance with cow dung on his shoes accentuate class divisions. At the close of the film Jeanne will probably settle down to a bourgeois marriage with the Godardian pseudo-revolutionary filmmaker Tom and name their children Fidel (Castro) and Rosa (Luxemburg).

Sex, although the vehicle for social communication and instruction in *Last Tango*, is itself political. The sexual relationship of Jeanne and Paul depends upon power and male supremacy, factors which provoked the wrath of many feminists. Bertolucci sees the sexual encounter as having a strong political thrust to it, for he links it with power and death. "It's about a human relationship between a man and a woman in the present. I think it's the most political film I've ever done, but the characters never speak about politics."[49] The absent father of Jeanne, who died when she was six, haunts the film. He was the colonizer, the civilizer, who linked himself with the power struggle. His racist attitude, especially toward women, becomes manifest as mother and daughter examine his souvenirs of war. Paul becomes a prolongation of the paternal figure for Jeanne, and meets his death wearing her father's kepi.

Of all the critics reviewing the film, Joan Mellen best perceives its sociopolitical implications. She underlines the impact of bourgeois standards upon society. *Last Tango* is "a paean to the damage inflicted on us all by bourgeois values, and on the inability of even pure sex to rescue us from bondage to the family and its lifelong hold on our sensibilities."[50]

The censorshp case following the completion of the film took on an aura of the political nature of the film itself, according to Bertolucci. Touching upon the taboo subject of uninhibited sex on the screen created problems for the producer Alberto Grimaldi and the director. Censorship always has a political basis to it, noted Bertolucci. It is a manifestation of political oppression. Paradoxically, this "oppression" seemed to be more widespread than first imagined, for the Russian critics were as vehemently opposed to the film as the Italian unions, both representing Marxist ideology. The censorship case, however, did contribute to the box office receipts.

1900: **Hollywood Epic and Soviet Ideology—A Marriage of Convenience**

Bertolucci laid out his objectives clearly:

> I did not want to make of this film a work simply destined for the elite. It is a "popular" film. Not only a film which pleases the public, it is a work rooted in the culture of the people.[51]

Bertolucci's intentions reconcile the commercial and ideological market. Making use of an aura of glamor, superstars, an epic form, as well as financing with American dollars, he was able to disseminate a socialist ideology in a manner befitting Antonio Gramsci's national-popular ideal. In one respect *1900* (*Novecento,* 1976) has all the earmarks of a *Gone with the Wind, Intolerance, War and Peace,* or *Napoleon,* epics that drew and amazed the public. In another, the film historically and dramatically lays out the origins and evolution of socialism in the region of Bertolucci's native Emilia. One could sense here the powerful surge of nature and the ideology of Dovzhenko's *Earth.* Bertolucci's vision here is simultaneously Marxist and commercial, resulting from his desire to uncover this history of the masses for the masses.

Bertolucci describes this two-act epic as the history of the twentieth century symbolically seen over the four seasons, and in the framework of a flashback from April 1945.

Act One: *Summer—In 1901, the* padrone *Berlinghieri (Burt Lancaster) celebrates the birth of grandson Alfredo (Paolo Pavsi, later Robert de Niro) at the same time as the bastard Olmo (Roberto Maccanti, later Gérard Depardieu) enlivens the peasant homestead of the tough grandfather Leo Dalco (Sterling Hayden). As the two boys grow up side by side, socialism makes its inroads. These historical events, perceived through the eyes of the youths, are golden. The peasants develop "La Casa del Popolo" to help in their education. Enlightened, they confront their feudal* padroni *as well as the law, attempting to show their need for a socialized culture.*

Fall—a chill fills the air shortly after World War I. The veteran Alfredo assumes his bourgeois life while Olmo returns to the hard work of the peasantry. Class divisions cry out for reconciliation; the friendship of Olmo and Alfredo bridges the gap for them. The fascists begin to organize during a meeting at church. In the course of a funeral procession for four victims of the fascists' burning of "La Casa del Popolo," the ambitious Attila (Donald Sutherland) emerges as a leading Black Shirt.

Act Two: *Winter—The Fascist chill turns into a political freeze, dominating Italy's history in the twenties and thirties. Following class lines, Olmo marries the leftist teacher Anita Foschi (Stefania Sandrelli) while Alfredo takes the wealthy Ada Fiastri Paulham (Dominique Sanda) for his wife. Olmo becomes a Communist, Alfredo a liberal, renouncing his bourgeois class origins. Yet at the death of his father, Alfredo becomes the* padrone. *Fascism spreads like an incendiary caught by the wind. War breaks out again.*

Spring: On 25 April 1945, the Liberation of Italy takes place. Vengeance becomes the modus operandi *of the peasants. The women track down Attila and his wife Regina (Laura Betti) with their pitchforks. Alfredo is tried by a people's court, found guilty of being* a padrone, *but allowed to remain free.*

Epilogue: A moment in the future shows the same class struggle between friends Olmo and Alfredo, now elderly and almost senile.

This kaleidoscopic fresco, primarily colored in ideological crimson, represents for Bertolucci a nostalgic and historical return to his youth and the years preceding it. As in the years of *The Conformist*'s action—the rise of fascism—Bertolucci was not yet born. He does, however, recall seeing Nazi soldiers during a search, perhaps the closest he got to flesh and blood fascism. His sources for *1900* and *The Conformist* would therefore have to be the collective memory of his family and those interviewed who lived through these harrowing experiences. Films such as *La Marseillaise* and *Rules of the Game* helped give him the *Gestalt* of the period. As a child somewhat like Alfredo he often visited the local peasants to listen to them talk of socialism as well as of the problems and joys of earthy farm life. In retrospect, Bertolucci implied that he used *Stratagem* as a type of dry run for *1900*, studying the people of Emilia and scouting locations even before he conceived the film. He would shoot *1900* approximately twenty miles from Parma, an area he knew in great depth.

Emilia is traditionally a socialist and communist region. I reconstructed all the characters based on my childhood memories. The peasant class—which differs from the working class—has a long-standing tradition of popular culture. When I began to prepare the film, I thought I was going to film the agony of this peasant culture. From our first studies (*répérages*) we became aware that in Emilia the bombardment by television and the mass media has not destroyed the peasant culture. It is a miracle due to the peasants' spirit of resistance rooted in socialism.[52]

Instead of the death of a culture, Bertolucci documented the rebirth of a sociopolitical spirit among the peasants. This was diametrically opposed to Pasolini's apocalyptic vision of the rigor mortis of the peasant culture.[53] Bertolucci's sensitivity for the peasants returned to him as he filmed there on location for almost one year, following the two-year preparation of the script with his brother Giuseppe and Kim Arcalli, during which time he visited the region often.[54] Bertolucci's *1900* would be a type of nostalgic *anti-destin* à la Malraux, a creative artwork like a Michelangelo sculpture or Van Gogh painting that would stave off the blind force of Destiny. Bertolucci offers his historical perspective: "Over the last 20 or 30 years, we have suffered a kind of amnesia; we have forgotten our roots. We have forgotten that our grandfather was an oak, and that we all grew around him."[55] Generally speaking, he believes, consumerism is responsible for this phenomenon. He feels that *1900* will fill up the lacunae in our collective memories caused by our contemporary amnesia.

The results of Bertolucci's ultimate desire to fill in these gaps in our memory is a five-and-a-half hour epic in which the aesthetic beauty of the work is in conscious support of the political content. The sun-filled compositions of the summer period reflect childhood impressions of the birth of a glorious, romantic period of socialism. The tightly compressed, darker compositions of the bourgeois home of the *padrone* provide a strong contrast with the open, natural images of peasant life in Leo Dalco's quarters. The same principle applies to the contrast of socialist and fascist gatherings. The train covered with furling red banners or the funeral cortège of the four socialist martyrs decorated in crimson does not camouflage the ideology of Bertolucci. The scene of the peasant dance in the forest could come directly from an Impressionistic painting. Music also plays the same supportive role as in Bertolucci's other films: folk music accompanies the peasant dance, a Russian-clad musician plays the International, and mourners at the socialist funeral reverently process to the rhythm of the political music.

Bertolucci's purpose in making this political film, which he prefers to call ideological, was to bridge the existing gap between the city-dwellers who go to the cinema and the flesh-and-blood peasants. The film medium was to serve as an instrument of communication, education, and enlightenment, perhaps in the tradition of Eisenstein, Pudovkin, or Dovzhenko. To do so he had to create a "popular" film in the Gramscian sense, but without going to the full extreme of the Communist party line. He specifies:

'Popular' for me means talking about a system of ideas, about the class struggle, about communism, in order to give a face, many faces, to the word 'communism,' which has always been abstractly connected to monstrous images in America, due to all the anti-communist propaganda there. I wanted to make a film that would get everywhere, even to places where communism is considered to be the end of liberty, of humankind, of the individual. For the distributors, 'popular' means tearing off a lot of tickets and taking in a lot of money; so there is a sort of convergence in our intentions in the sense that we both want a lot of people to see the film.[56]

Continuing to apply basic Marxist principles to his work, Bertolucci schematized *1900* with a constant positive dialectic. For the director this was a progression from what he considered previously in his films as a type of occasional "schizophrenia." Olmo and Alfredo represent two sides of his personality trying to come together, a sentiment he already had in *Partner*. In this dynamic dialectic, there is tension (and at times growth) resulting from the encounters or confrontations of various forces—the peasants with the bourgeois landowners, the American and French actors with the non-professional actors among the Italian peasants, fascism with socialism, Hollywood finances with Marxist ideology, and fiction with documentary. The dual opposing forces create a healthy phenomenon, but, as seen by the French critics, they are Manichean in essence, reinforcing the stereotype of good and evil or black-and-white opposition.

The strongest sociohistorical forces in *1900* are communism and fascism. From the outset of the film Bertolucci sympathetically presents the simple peasant class, attractive but unaware of their political potential. In his manifesto or profession of faith in Marxism, Bertolucci depicts them as struggling for their rights against oppressive forces especially with the aid of the socialist teacher Anita Foschi at "La Casa del Popolo." We cannot help but side with the underdogs as these peasants are threatened, tortured, or executed by the Fascists. The ritual of the funeral of the four dead socialists concretely draws the sympathy of the spectator. The human dignity of the peasants all but disappears in the onslaught by the Fascists. When the strong-willed women hold back the cavalry by peaceful resistance, the spectator is elated at the victory of the minority. Gradually we see the positive, heroic transition from socialism to communism, then, during World War II, to a ferocious antifascism. Throughout Act One the utopian dream of an all-pervasive socialism still seems a possibility. In the last part of Act Two there is a type of historical compromise. The weapons of the partisans are handed over to the provisional government force. Symbolically dramatized, the continual struggle of one class with the other—Olmo versus Alfredo—comes to a draw at the close of the film.

Fascism is exposed in *1900* as the dark side of the human soul. Although Bertolucci presents fascism historically, he wishes to make certain it also mirrors its current manifestation. As opposed to the healthy, normal, committed peasants, the Fascists appear as inhuman villains. Attila and Regina are the fascist Lord and Lady Macbeth, political and social climbers, constantly plotting for a piece of power. Like Marcello Clerici, they will conform to the dominant class's ideology in order to prosper. They are ugly, vulgar, and decadent, lusting to control others. Their lust is manifested sexually in a sadistic act of sodomy as well as the slaying of a young boy.

Gideon Bachmann records Bertolucci's description of Attila. For the director this cunning Fascist is:

. . . the materialization of the aggression dormant in all the characters around him, which they suppress or choose not to express. He represents all destructive forces. His ferocity is as senseless and absurd as that of the fascists in our days, who claim to be motivated historically. But in Italy we have a working class that will forever hinder the return of fascism.[57]

As Attila kills a dangling cat by ramming it with his head and then leads a disruption of the funeral procession of the socialists, he simply proves that he is a survivor of the race of his namesake, "The Hun."

The critical reactions to *1900* covered a full gamut of observations and insights. Most appreciate the film's epic proportions, the amount of psychic energy necessary to produce this lengthy work, and the powerful images that pervade it. Bertolucci stated that the Communist party leaders opposed the film, while its youth—to whom Bertolucci said it was primarily directed—loved it. Beside the political generation gap the film indicated another, between politician and artist. Harsher criticism came from the European Left; the radical critics underlined the irony of Bertolucci's protagonist in *Partner*, saying that "American imperialism is the number one problem today." Later, the critics point out, the director accepts financing from several major American studios. Bertolucci rationalized this financing by stating, "I'm a filmmaker not a militant." The reaction therefore of the purist Left was to say that the production was polluted by American capital. Other critics of the Left felt that Act Two had certain historical errors.

The other camp was equally critical. American critics referred to the film as

Bertolucci's *1900*. Olmo (Gérard Depardieu), an aggressive farm hand, struggles in the growth of socialism. *(Courtesy of National Film Archive, British Film Institute.)*

"Marxist opera," "dosed with propaganda," or Bertolucci's "apology to the Communist party for having made so much money on *Last Tango in Paris*." There appears to be no clear line between the propagandistic effect of the film and its enlightening or educational purpose. In propaganda analysis, nonetheless, the sympathy for the underdog (Socialists), hatred for the oppressor (Fascists), and a more positive, almost romantic interpretation of one historical movement as opposed to another, may seem overtly propagandistic. Bertolucci's dual intention reinforces this interpretation. He wished *1900* to be directed toward the young to attract them to their own socialist roots, and secondly, he wanted to complete the film as soon as possible so he could sway the 1976 elections toward the Left.

In the end, entanglements with the court which criticized the violence and sex in the film, the turmoil with the producer Alberto Grimaldi who wanted to make it a marketable product, and the public who did not wish to see the colossal work of five hours and twenty minutes in two lengthy sittings left Bertolucci weary. Four years of his life went into the production, which he considered a wager. The film *1900* may in essence be a Marxist tract with capitalist backing, but it is also a cinematic feat that will be a landmark in epic cinema.

Luna: Freud Revisited

The problems with the producer and distributors of *1900* tapered off, and the scars were almost healed when Bertolucci attacked his next project. It would, however, be a film which would stir up almost as much controversy as *Last Tango in Paris* and *1900*. *Peyton Place* and *Murmur of the Heart* had already touched upon the topic of incest, but neither was as ostentatious as Bertolucci's psychodrama *Luna* (*La luna*, 1979). With this topic Bertolucci saw himself as "a child playing with fire, the universal taboo of incest."[58] As with his other films, the publicity distorted the reality. On occasion the voyeur rather than the aesthete would be seduced into seeing the film.

For almost ten years Bertolucci had been in psychoanalysis. Throughout these most revealing sessions he constantly addressed the question of his father's role in his life. Then one day he realized he began to speak about his mother. It was a radical change. He recalled riding on the handlebars of a bicycle with his mother when he suddenly confused his mother's face with the moon. From this distant memory the film was born. The image of the moon was reinforced by the memory he had of a movie theatre whose roof opened to reveal a sky, at times with a moon, at intermission. He jokingly referred to it as "Italian air conditioning" in our interview. The idea of the film was also a return to his native haunts, for example, the birthplace of Verdi. All of these autobiographical elements would find their way into the film.

As he began to work on the scenario of *Luna* with Franco Arcalli, he had thought of casting Liv Ullman for the major role. This did not work out, and Jill Clayburgh assumed the part, still glorying in her success with *Unmarried Woman*. Bertolucci never regretted the choice or the outcome. Franco Arcalli, who had given a new vision to Bertolucci over the past few years through his avant-garde editing, died before they completed the script. Giuseppe Bertolucci assisted in reworking the material with Bertolucci, while Clare Peploe took care of the dialogue. Twentieth Century Fox, under President Alan Ladd, Jr., underwrote the film, as Giovanni and Bernardo Bertolucci formed their own film company under the name of Fiction Cinematografica. The result of this extensive collaboration was unique.

A little boy plays with a ball of yarn at a Mediterranean villa while his mother dances with an enigmatic man. At night the child rides the handlebars of the bicycle, gazing at his mother and the haunting face of the moon behind her. Almost ten years later, the mother Caterina (Jill Clayburgh) and her son Joe (Matthew Barry) are living in New York with her husband Douglas (Fred Gwinn). The couple is about to go off to Europe when Douglas suddenly dies of a heart attack.

Caterina takes Joe to Rome where she will perform in the opera houses of the Italian capital. Joe, awkward, restless, and uneasy, succumbs to drugs in order to find both comfort and escape. This shocks his mother who attempts to help him through the crisis. In an intimate moment Caterina tells Joe that his real father is still alive. Joe sets out in search of the absent father, locates him, and dramatically unites the trio at a rehearsal of Verdi's Masked Ball *at the Baths of Caracalla.*

Where *1900* is laced with Marxist ideology, *Luna* favors Freudian psychology:

> With *1900*, I had satisfied a need for omnipresent politics, for materialization of the utopia of a Berlinguerian "historical compromise." In *La Luna*, my approach is more secretive and sombre. My phantasms are cleared up by the light of the moon. I have found it exciting to hide no longer behind certain social and political facades *(alibis)* but to move more fundamentally toward the object of desire.[59]

Bertolucci explained in an interview for *Le Monde* of 4 October 1979 that he wanted the film to appeal to the spectator on the sensual level. His camerawork was sketched out so that the camera would move toward this object of desire. The political tone and purpose of Bertolucci's opus are noticeably absent, yet it is important not to cast the director into a preconceived mold. His thematic interests are now more sociopsychological, revealing a fresh twist in his cinematic orientation.

Throughout *Luna* Bertolucci draws up a commentary on the decadence of modern society and the failure of the family, set in the context of the upheaval of values. This is most evident in Joe and his surroundings. He is uprooted from his normal support systems as a teenager in America. A new language, culture, and friends force him to adapt or turn inward.[60] To a large extent Joe chooses the latter. The drug culture has made crippling inroads here. Ironically his source is a devout Arab, Mustafa, who sees no tension between his destruction of Joe's life and his personal morality and belief.

With Caterina's marital relations shattered by the abrupt death of her husband Douglas and with Joe's solitary feelings emerging from his severed ties with a familiar world, it is somewhat comprehensible that an incestuous relationship

Bertolucci's *Luna.* A tender relationship develops between the recently widowed Caterina (Jill Clayburgh) and her only son Joe (Matthew Barry). *(Courtesy of Movie Star News.)*

could develop. Bertolucci, however, does not graphically describe the sexual rapport as he did with *Last Tango in Paris,* but subtly and tenderly builds up motivation for the relationship. The nude lesbian scene between Caterina and her friend in the shower is more explicit than the incestual rapport. Both sexual relationships appear ephemeral, important to help the characters survive momentary traumatic experiences.

The contrast between the poorer sections of Rome and Caterina's apartments in New York and Rome is striking. Her lavish quarters go with her profession, and when she follows Mustafa to his home in a poverty-ridden area, she finds herself in another world. The abandoned factory where Joe laments the firing of the New York Yankees coach Billy Martin—his father figure—reinforces the emotional state of the distraught and isolated youth.

Bertolucci jokingly inserts the character of the rich Communist played by Renato Salvatori as a type of self-portrait. The director realizes that his fortune was made by a nonideological film, *Last Tango,* hardly approved by the Communist party. He reacts to the negative view by some vocal members of the party:

I have proved that I was a Communist with *1900* whose ideological color is obvious. Crap! I have the right to step back and laugh at my political affiliations! The Italian Communist party is comprised of peasants, workers, prostitutes, thieves, industrialists, and wealthy Emilians like myself. *L'Unità* wrote about *La Luna* saying that they would not want a comrade like Bertolucci! Ah, well! They are clods and racists. I am a wealthy Communist and I have the right to create a bit of self-irony.[61]

Apart from these few passing references to the social, psychological, or political situation of Caterina and Joe, Bertolucci tends to develop a more Freudian perspective, as he had already done, especially in *Last Tango*. He does not hesitate, however, to refer thematically to his other films. The search for the father continues in *Luna* as in *Stratagem*. The return to native Emilia also recurs as Caterina visits her former voice teacher and also points out to Joe the home of Verdi. Bertolucci's favorite composer provides a musical ambience, as well as a father-figure for Caterina. The homosexuality theme recurring between Olmo and Alfredo, and the uncle of Alfredo, appears in a lesbian sequence between Caterina and her friend. Although Bertolucci dropped a sequence specifically in honor of Pasolini, he kept two that recall the controversial filmmaker. Mario (Franco Citti) makes subtle homosexual advances on Joe at the café. Mustafa reflects the oriental innocence of instinct in *Arabian Nights*. *Luna*, with *Last Tango* another hiatus in Bertolucci's sociopolitical opus, captures the originality and daring of an artist who sets out to challenge, provoke, but especially entertain the masses.

The Tragedy of a Ridiculous Man: A Voyage into Ambiguity

During the lively press conference of 24 May 1981 at the Cannes Film Festival where *Tragedy of a Ridiculous Man* (*La tragedia di un uomo ridicolo*, 1981) represented Italy with Liliana Cavani's *The Flesh* (*La pelle*) and Ettore Scola's *Passion of Love* (*Passione d'amore*), Bertolucci elucidated some of the cryptic elements of the film deliberately left hermetic. He first stated that, whereas *1900* was a film on the past and the future, *Tragedy* was a film on the present. The events of the film make up the fabric of everyday life in Italy, which is both disconcerting and mysterious. He reiterates this in his interview for *Le Matin:* "I have never made a film so closely related to the present . . . but it is not contrived. It is simply a fact that history adapts itself to the present reality."[62] The title, explained the director, emanates from his own reflections on the contemporary scene—a "tragedy" among "ridiculous" characters. Ugo Tognazzi, who plays the protagonist, suggests that it is more the situation than the character that is ridiculous.[63] No one escapes the tragedy and the ridiculousness of the circumstances of Italian society. The director remarked, "I realized when I began shooting the film that I was surrounded by ridiculous people, and when I looked into the mirror, I saw one."[64]

The year is 1976. Giovanni (Riccardo Tognazzi), son of a wealthy cheese manufacturer, Primo Spaggiari (Ugo Tognazzi) and his French wife Barbara (Anouk Aimée), is abducted as his father watches helplessly through binoculars. The tough ex-partisan is pained, for he may have to sell the plant, which is as old as the son, in order to meet the ransom. Primo does not cooperate with the police and decides to work things out by himself. He even suspects Giovanni of having a hand in the kidnapping. It appears that his son's young friend Laura (Laura Morante) and the priest-worker Adelfo (Victor Cavallo), both Spaggiaro employees, are somehow involved in the abduction. The situation changes when Primo takes control by having Laura fabricate a letter to obtain the ransom money from local money lenders. He then recovers the money from Laura and Adelfo. Some time later Adelfo leads Primo to a dance hall where the prodigal son Giovanni mysteriously arrives on the scene.

As with Dino Risi's *Dear Father (Caro Papa . . .)* and Rosi's *Three Brothers,* Bertolucci's *Tragedy* pursues the current impact of terrorism on Italian society. Terrorism touches almost every aspect of society, commented Bertolucci during his Cannes press conference. It has transformed society radically, primarily filling it with fear and uncertainty. Yet, Bertolucci suggests, *Tragedy* is not primarily a film on terrorism as such, but on private life, which nonetheless cannot be sheltered from this spreading phenomenon. Terrorism is omnipresent and the media have popularized it. It is a war waged on many fronts, yet Bertolucci feels that the terrorists have lost it. They do not have the support of the masses. In his interview with *Le Matin,* he discusses the effects of terrorism: "With this story of kidnapping I have tried to communicate to the public the emergence of a psychological attitude created by terrorism which is manifest in aggression and an increasing distrust in relationships."[65]

At the end of *1900* a peasant dramatically proclaims the death of the *padrone.* This was wishful, utopian thinking, for Primo Spaggiari and his race of ambitious climbers still populate the earth. Bertolucci describes this self-made man and former peasant in socioeconomic terms:

> He is a type I know very well. . . . He's used a degree of cunning, a certain commercial flair, perhaps even a touch of dishonesty to build up his business— a Parmesan cheese factory—and run it. He is a typical Italian. Even though he will never appear on the cover of *Fortune* magazine, it is his kind of small entrepreneur who keeps Italy's economy running in the midst of anarchy.[66]

Tragedy depicts the life struggles of this *padrone* whose upper-class tranquillity is dramatically upset by terrorism. The kidnapping offers him the opportunity to reevaluate his origins, his ascent to power, and his contacts with his employees. He directs the enterprise with skill and hard work. His employees may criticize him, but they respect him. A gulf, nonetheless, separates them, despite Primo's birth into the peasant class. When Primo searches out the two young employees Adelfo and Laura, he admits that he no longer recognizes his employees and has forgotten their smells. He also realizes all too late that in his upward climb he never knew his own son. During his conversations with the employees, Laura suggests that Primo give the factory to the workers and establish a type of cooperative along the lines of the Kolmuz in Russia.

Bertolucci also wished to underline the morality of this industrial figure. At the press conference he described Primo as a person who would use his own son much in the same way he would fertilizer. His rationality overcomes his sentimentality. This is in contrast to his spouse Barbara who would do anything, sell anything, just to have her son returned. Filial love to her matters more than a cheese plant. Coldly, logically, almost heartlessly Primo tries to manipulate the situation. Bertolucci describes him at this point as a materialist full of contradictions. In the end, the wealthy industrialist learns the importance of a father-son relationship, a recurrent leitmotif in Bertolucci's opus.[67]

In *Before the Revolution* Bertolucci first approached the subject of youth, revealing the shallowness and the lack of political commitment in the young, bourgeois-bred Fabrizio. Bertolucci is still perhaps just as critical of youth, and his characters convey this. Lt. Col. Macchi (Renato Salvatori) of the Milan antiterrorist brigade suspects the son's complicity in the kidnapping. Giovanni would be excellent material for a terrorist, says Macchi, for he is the son of a wealthy father, opposed to bourgeois values, and has a rebellious streak. Laura mentioned to Primo that indeed Giovanni did consider kidnapping the father. Riccardo's birthday card to his patriarchal father showed that he still considered him "a bourgeois pig."[68]

Primo Spaggiari harshly sizes up the youth of today: "They talk less than my generation did, and from their silence you can't figure out if they are asking for help or getting ready to shoot you. To me, our children represent the dreadful ambiguity of our life today." These words, observed Bertolucci in the Cannes conference, came almost word for word from Pasolini's prophetic writings for *Corriere della Sera* a year before he was brutally killed by a seventeen-year-old youth. The director commented further on Pasolini's critical observations to Eric de Saint Angel:

> Pier Paolo Pasolini thought that the consumer culture was responsible for the loss of innocence among the youth. In saying that, he was especially alluding to the young proletarians. More generally speaking . . . I think young people reflect the sad confusion of contemporary life such as we have created it, and that they evolve better in the more mysterious aspects of life.[69]

Bertolucci, concretizing his own position on youth, said that he personally falls in between these two generations of Barbara-Primo and Laura-Adolfo, perhaps making him an acute observer. In the film neither the youth nor the elders—save Barbara—come across as heroic. They ordinarily have more faults than virtues. They are all, nonetheless, ordinary people struggling to find some type of meaning in the chaos of their existence.

Against the background of assorted paintings (some reflecting dubious taste), pig-slaughtering, dance hall music, and Parmesan cheeses, Bertolucci has set a poignant psychodrama with terrorism as the core.[70] Although he says it is not a social document as such, it can hardly be taken as other than that, given the intricate discussion of terrorism, bourgeois morality, youth and their confusion, and the *padrone* mentality. In our interview he calls it a political film which speaks only indirectly about politics. Vincent Canby assesses the political as well as the psychological perspective of *Tragedy:*

> "Tragedy of a Ridiculous Man" is a distant meditation on Italian politics. It sees politics defined by the generation gap, reduced—or expanded—to the

dimensions of an Oedipal conflict, to the fears of a father that his son might be a murderous stranger. The mystery ends, though it's not truly resolved, by the suggestion that we, in the audience, must solve "the enigma of a son who dies and is reborn."[71]

Bertolucci's genius with *Tragedy* lies in his ability to address cryptically these many complicated levels of contemporary human existence through universal and yet very particular Italian characters and crises.

Conclusions

In two decades Bertolucci has made his way from modest, Italian productions to large-scale commercial epics and dramas. The political perspective that once permeated his work disappeared on occasion, being replaced by a psychoanalytic penetration of the human psyche as well as a sensual depiction of complex sexual relationships. This transformation may have come about since he has seen an overdose of political films within recent years. He and the public have perhaps grown weary of pure politics in the cinema. This development has paralleled to a certain extent the career of Pasolini, his onetime master. Only after Pasolini can Bertolucci be considered the most controversial Italian filmmaker in recent cinema history for his films and his radical ideas. Joseph Gelmis inquired of Bertolucci, "What are you trying to do with your films: entertain, educate, propagandize?" Bertolucci succinctly replied, "To know. I want to know."[72]

4

MARCO BELLOCCHIO:
An Autobiographical Leap into the Political Beyond

> I don't stand there with the Bible in my hands or the Little Red Book. I speak through feelings, proposing as a starting point my personal experience.
>
> —Marco Bellocchio, 1980

Bernardo Bertolucci and Marco Bellocchio were child prodigies in the Italian cinema world. They established themselves quickly with several profound and innovative feature films while still in their twenties. They immediately received a national and then international reputation for their nonconformist films. Both were born approximately the same time, Bertolucci in 1941 in the area of Parma, and Bellocchio in 1939 in Piacenza. The Emilia region marked their early films, as both dealt with youth in confrontation with a provincial bourgeois environment. In the late fifties the two young men discovered the novelty of Roman culture and experienced a greater exposure to cinema. As they began to direct one film after another, the similarities continued; their works were autobiographical, anti-Establishment, political, and then psychological, imbued with the music of their neighbor, Verdi. Two peas in a cinematic pod. At the release of *Last Tango in Paris* Bellocchio considered Bertolucci as having sold out to the Establishment. Bertolucci criticized Bellocchio for his tedious penchant for the naturalistic. They appreciated each other's radical works, yet did not lose an opportunity to chide each other when their respective productions did not meet the other's expectations. This became a healthy, friendly rivalry of two young film artists, now in their mature years.

Bellocchio's films are complicated; so, too, his character, biography, and politics. He lucidly recounts the relationship of these elements to each other:

> The rapport between my personal life and my three films *(Fists in the Pocket, China is Near,* and *In the Name of the Father)*—I exclude *Rape on the Front Page*—is significant if not direct. My biography, lifestyle, and political views determine the type of film I make. This does not mean that I must describe and report in

the films everything that I have experienced, but in a greater moral sense it is a problem of conscience.[1]

For Bellocchio, thus, life and art are inextricably intertwined, and at the same time reflect the society in which they are situated.

The northern provinces differ significantly from Rome or from the Neapolitan region so dear to Rosi. Greater wealth, a higher standard of living, more industry such as Fiat and Pirelli, and a closer relationship with some of the bourgeois traditions of France, characterize this northern sector. Marco Bellocchio grew up in the industrial north. His family was above all Catholic, conformist, and anti-Communist. This world was not unlike the Catholic, provincial world of François Mauriac. Bellocchio's bourgeois childhood and adolescence had left a mark on him; in our intervierw of 24 April 1981 in Rome he went on to say that it was a *scar*. He describes the related political and religious temper of the times:

> We were in the immediate postwar period and Communism and anti-Communism were strongly opposed to one another. It was particularly noticeable in a country like Italy where there were 8 million Communists and in those days Communism was frightening to the Catholics, although it is no longer so, or at least much less so. In 1948 many Italians sold everything and literally fled the country because they were sure of the advent of Communism. Therefore Catholicism *faceva quadrato* (formed a square) around the Vatican and often took up extremely reactionary positions. It was in this climate of rabid anti-Communism that my generation grew up. Young Catholics today are very different.[2]

Bellocchio's father was an attorney, his mother a teacher. He grew up in this cultured climate with few material needs. There were six other children in the family, some of whom would later help Marco write or produce his films. He enjoyed his childhood days, today gleaning from them his own understanding of his personal growth, consciousness, and intellectual formation. His adolescence put an end to those idyllic years. Sandro Bernardi points out that Bellocchio passed through a sad and solitary adolescence spent in a nervous state in religious boarding schools. He attended all private schools—San Vincenzo Grammar School, directed by the Christian Brothers, and San Francesco High School in Lodi, run by the Barnabite Fathers. These religious teachers, he felt, imposed on him the value of perpetuating the same system. His rebellion against them was somewhat mild and without ideological basis. It was at the beginning of secondary school, he said, that he lost his faith. Upon graduation he enrolled at Milan's Catholic University of the Sacred Heart, primarily interested in the philosophy program. He divided his time between his philosophy at the university and drama courses in the Accademica dei Filodrammatici.

Unlike Rosi, Pasolini, and Bertolucci, Bellocchio engaged in formal preparation for a career in cinema. In 1959, at the age of twenty, he moved to Rome where he enrolled in the film school Centro Sperimentale di Cinema. In his first year there he concentrated on acting, but the following year transferred into the two-year program in film directing. In the course of the academic program and during the intervening summer vacation he fulfilled his directing requirements by making short films, his first technical exposure to film production. He received his diploma in 1962.

Bellocchio's one year in England in 1964–65 made him cosmopolitan in outlook and culture. It also opened his eyes to another world of cinema. At the Slade School of Art in London he studied theory under director Thorold Dickinson *(Spanish ABC, The Queen of Spades, Secret People)*. He also completed a thesis on Michelangelo Antonioni and Robert Bresson. Bellocchio admits to a major influence from the French director. Bresson *invents* his style, Bellocchio remarked. Consequently, the early films of Bellocchio will bear some of the darker imprint of the director of *Mouchette*.

During his stay in London, Bellocchio had occasion to come into contact with the fresh wave of British filmmakers. He greatly appreciated the cinema of Tony Richardson, Karel Reisz, and John Schlesinger, following closely the various developments of the Angry Young Man movement of British filmmakers, also known as directors of the Free Cinema. Their disturbing slice of daily life, black and white photography, quasi-documentary depiction of social problems, and nonprofessional actors, are all factors which can also be witnessed in the first few works of Bellocchio.

While in the British capital the young graduate of the Centro Sperimentale struggled with his own film script. From his scribblings and his search for funding in 1965 emerged his first film, *Fists in the Pocket (I pugni in tasca)*, bearing an autobiographical stamp. His next film, two years later, was more political in nature. *China Is Near (La Cina è vicina)* caused tremors equal to the first cinematic quake. In between these two works he played Piero di Stacia in Liliana Cavani's *Francis of Assisi*.

Then came a political hiatus that many French and Italian directors experienced around 1968. Political outbreaks upset the film festivals at Cannes and Venice. Directors considered using the film medium as a weapon against the Establishment. Bellocchio joined forces with the revolutionaries in 1969. He offered his services to Carlo Lizzani in the collaborative work *Let's Discuss, Discuss (Discutiamo, discutiamo)*. In the same year he directed two militant films *Paola* and *Long Live Red May Day (Viva il primo maggio rosso)*. These commitments terminated his direct political activity.

Returning once again to biographical sources, he made a brutal film on the oppressive milieu of a Catholic boarding school for boys, *In the Name of the Father (Nel nome del padre, 1972)*. The following year he took on another institution, the press. He accepted an offer to complete a project started by another director, *Rape on the Front Page/ Slap the Monster on Page One (Sbatti il mostro in prima pagina)*.

In 1974, Bellochio was commissioned to make a film on the physical, social, and psychological conditions of mental institutions in the area of Parma. *Fit to be Untied (Matti da slegare)* was the result. Two years later, in 1976, the military became the next target in *Victory March (Marcia trionfale)*.

Film, television, and theatre merge in the director's life in 1977. From Chekhov's *Seagull* came a brilliant but difficult film for television, *Il gabbiano;*it was given an unusually warm reception in the U.S. four years later in the presence of the director. Coming almost full circle in 1979, Bellocchio took up the theme of his first film, family madness, with his Cannes film entry *Leap into the Void (Salto nel vuoto)*. He then filmed five programs for Italian television entitled *The Cinema Machine (La macchina cinema)*. His most recent works are *The Eyes, the Mouth (Gli occhi, la bocca, 1983)* and *Henry IV (Enrico IV, 1984)*.

The director has often referred to his work as *"uno zigzagare continuo,"* which characterizes his dabbling in short and long feature films, documentaries, television plays and series, theatre, acting, militant films, as well as poetry. He often attributed this creative oscillation to a desire on the one hand to be free—not chained to one form or genre—and on the other to live out a healthy dilettantism. In our April 1981 interview in Rome he mentioned that he preferred to be "elastic," stretching for available opportunities as well as discovering work that fulfilled his creative needs at the particular moment. There is, nonetheless, a consistency and pattern to his work, for he believes that, in reiterating some of the same major themes, he can explore them deeper and deeper at each turn in the road. *Leap into the Void* certainly bears this out.

In the "auteur theory," consistent technique, tone, and theme are said to pervade a director's work in the span of his career. This is most obvious in the repertoire of Marco Bellocchio. The atmosphere he creates in a film is dense, hermetic, and at times suffocating, especially noticeable in his early black and white films. In the footsteps of his idol, Luis Buñuel, Bellocchio exhibits a penchant for sadism, violence, cruelty, and scandal, with the conservative and Catholic bourgeoisie as his prime target. He paints a dark picture of provincial life, concentrating on death, oppression, and madness. His films, streaked with cynicism, hostility, and black humor, reveal the sombre side of his own life. With these sometimes unwieldy instruments, he attacks one institution after another. His inherent violence is designed to shock, intimidate, and eventually, if possible, enlighten the viewer. His desire, as he made perfectly clear in our session, is to make the institution feel culpable for its misuse of power in the destruction of the individual and society. He does this in some of his films, especially documentaries, in a didactic fashion. He ordinarily intends to set up a dialectic that will encourage further questioning of society's problems. In other films, like *China Is Near* or *In the Name of the Father,* he assumes the role of anarchist or iconoclast.

The venom of Bellocchio is often diluted by the use of metaphor. Family meals mark a ritual moment of exchange of ideology, usually of the status quo. The humorous names, such as Padre Corazza (cuirass), shed some light on characters. To prove one's existence or to show narcissistic self-love, Bellocchio uses mirrors. Epilepsy represents a decaying element in society. In general, the institutions he studies are meant to be microcosms of a sick society that needs healing.[4]

Some critics have accused the director of being heavy-handed or doctrinaire. In certain instances, as in *In the Name of the Father,* they say he speaks with the rancor of an Italian defrocked priest. He strikes out at many targets—family, Catholic Church, state, military, psychiatric hospitals, boarding schools. His overall perspective is leftist, militant, anti-Establishment, and derives from his personal experiences, both social and political.

Like his cinematic colleague Bertolucci, Marco Bellocchio grew up in a bourgeois environment and grew to despise it. Seeing the seeds of guilt planted in him and his generation by the Catholic Church, the family with its meaningless rituals, and the private boarding schools with their repressive mentality, he adamantly turned against them. He became a rebel with a specific cause—to attack and, if possible, modify these institutions.

The year 1968 was for Bellocchio a moment of enlightenment. For the first time, he reminisced in 1980, he was able to verify, but without daring to shatter, the frailty of his father's generation, with their overpowering hypocrisy. He understood that they were not omnipotent. The thirty-year-old Bellochio further saw that it was no longer necessary to live his life according to the examples of his predecessors and to identify himself with them.[5]

In the wake of the student unrest of 1968, Bellocchio became fully *engagé*, politically committed to reform society in a revolutionary manner.

> In late 1968 I joined the Communist Union [Unione dei Communisti], simply in order to fulfill completely my political commitment, and because I recognized the necessity of a political, revolutionary organization. At the heart of the Union I worked as a film director in the press and propaganda sector.[6]

Bellocchio specified that his primary reasons for joining the U.C.I. were first moral and ethical, and only then political. In 1968, his conscience dictated this to him. This logically led him to offer advice to the youth, as can be seen in his interview with *Cinéaste* in June 1969:

> As the students today in Italy have understood—and not only the students but every sincere revolutionary—the thing to do today is not to demonstrate and get beaten by the police but to get organized in a party with, of course, the proper kind of principles. The director, too, as a revolutionary artist—if we want to define him this way and he wants to be one, for this involves a certain amount of sacrifice for him—has to work for that political organization. That's all.[7]

His political militancy only lasted a little more than a year, during which he filmed *Paola* and *Long Live Red May Day*. Although he diligently attended the political rallies, he was not totally committed to all of the ideology of the Union. Bellocchio noted that the cinéastes in the party had strong guilt feelings over their past and were also considered the more reactionary members of the organization. In retrospect he felt that this was a positive experience, even though he is critical about the party and the period:

> I have often failed, but I've never given in. At the time of the union of Marxist-Leninist Communists, the conjecture was that in order to change, the bourgeois intellectuals should serve the people, live among the people, for the people have the right ideas, etc., etc. But actually the people one set up did not exist, were nowhere to be found. It was a myth, an infallible abstraction and all that came to nothing. Once again desire was frustrated.[8]

He left the Union of Communists when he discovered that these Marxist-Leninist ideologies were superimposed upon reality. The group was condemned to running up against a wall, to use his own expression.

Today Bellocchio seems to be politically independent, belonging to no established party. His concern for society is political, but in a more diffuse, general sense. He cannot escape witnessing the growing social maladies around him and hopes that his films will help alleviate them. At the same time he feels that there is less a call for political films such as were fabricated in the late sixties and early seventies, given the parliamentary procedures in government. For himself, he prefers to be more humanitarian than political, and more psychological than militant. His emphasis is more on *researching* and *understanding*—words he constantly used in our April 1981 interview in Rome—than on striking out blindly in a propagandistic fashion.

Crime and Punishment, Down with Uncle, Ginepro Becomes a Man: Film School Projects

The first year of Marco Bellocchio's course work at Rome's Centro Sperimentale di Cinematografia was devoted to acting, before he decided upon a career in film direction. As part of the requirements of the first year in film production he made a short fifteen minute film, *Crime and Punishment (La colpa e la pena).* He called upon the first- and second-year students of the Centro to collaborate with him. Already his work reflects an interest in politics, religion, and psychology. Imitating many of the stereotypes of the American film noir, he shows the interrogation/confession of a victim (Alberto Maravalle) in the presence of the gang leader Stefano (Satta Flores). It has Kafkaesque overtones to it.

Between the first and second years of the program, in the summer of 1961, Bellocchio and his companions, such as Gustavo Dahl and Sandro Franchina, made *Down with Uncle (Abbasso il zio).* They filmed the short work in Bellocchio's native Emilia. The simple film, recalling René Clement's *Forbidden Games,* deals with the macabre subject of cemeteries. Some children play in a cemetery, become terribly frightened, and then return home. Sandro Bernardi refers to it as documentary in style and mentions that an excerpt of it was included in the next short film made by Bellocchio at the Centro. From this cinematic essay right through his most recent works, Bellocchio will manifest a preoccupation with death.

The second required project Bellocchio filmed at the Centro was *Ginepro Becomes a Man (Ginepro fatto uomo,* 1962). As with his two earlier films, he invited his colleagues to play various roles in the film as well as to take care of the technical aspects of the work. The approximately thirty-five minute film is an elaboration of the earlier study *Crime and Punishment* with Ginepro played by Stefano Setta. Ginepro's friend, Maddalena (Kerstin Wartel), deserts him. He finds himself alone and abandoned. He is finally liberated by throwing down the statue of Minerva, a type of mother figure.

These short films, especially *Ginepro,* introduce the intricacies of Bellocchio's technique and hint at inherent structures, relationships, and symbols which will occur in his first three feature films. The poor sound and lighting of the Cineteca copy in Rome, however, detract from the original work of *Ginepro*. The overly long meditative shots, alternating with chatty dialogues and little action, moreover, make the short a tedious but original closet drama. Its major redeeming value lies in its low-keyed and existential development of relationships.

Fists in the Pocket, China Is Near, In the Name of the Father: **Autobiographical Triptych**

Within a year of Bertolucci's provincial study of family, incest, and politics in *Before the Revolution* (1964), Bellocchio undertook some of the same major themes, but with them created a more hermetic, cynical, and somber work. *Fists in the Pocket* (*I pugni in tasca*, 1965) would be Bellocchio's first panel of a cinematic, autobiographical triptych, a sketch of family life in the northern provinces. The second, *China Is Near* (*La Cina è vicina*, 1967), has as its subject the political institution, while the third, *In the Name of the Father* (*Nel nome del padre*, 1971), describes the tumultuous life of a Catholic boarding school for boys. All three spring from his personal experiences and reflect his own hostility, and at times ambiguity, with respect to these social organisms.

French novelist André Gide once wrote, "Families, I despise you" (*Familles, je vous haïe!*). Marco Bellocchio reproduces some of the same antagonism of Gide for this smallest sector of society, showing its decadence and impotence. Ironically, it was his family who helped to make the script of *Fists in the Pocket*, which he wrote in England, become a reality. His brother Tonino, an attorney, financed the project in great part. The production cost approximately $50,000. His mother made available the family villa at Bobbio, about twenty miles from his native Piacenza. Here Bellocchio was able to shoot all the interiors without the added expense of a studio. The rest of the production was organized and supervised by Enzo Doria. His friends from the Centro assumed many of the responsibilities of the production—Lou Castel, acting; Alberto Marrama, photography; Elda Tattoli, dubbing. With the assistance of these friends and family, the film took shape.

In a small provincial town of northern Italy, an upper class Catholic family struggles to survive psychologically and financially. The mother and three brothers and a sister live in anxiety, tension, and frustration. The financial burden falls on the shoulders of the eldest brother Augusto (Marino Mase), apparently the only stable member of the family. The mother (Liliana Gerace) is blind, and Alessandro or Ale (Lou Castel), epileptic. Leone (Pierluigi Troglio) suffers from a mental disorder, and the sister Giulia (Paola Pitagora) from hypertension. To alleviate the pecuniary problems of Augusto, who would like to marry, Ale decides to push his mother off a cliff. He then tranquilly drowns his brother Leone in the bath and is about to suffocate his sister, but hesitates. Giulia is traumatized when Ale reveals his actions. While listening to the aria "Sempre Libera" from Verdi's La Traviata, *Ale has an epileptic fit and gasps his last breath, writhing on the floor. "How sad I am, Mamma!", he mutters. Giula ignores him.*

The influence of Bresson on the film's tone and technique is readily perceptible. Strong black-and-white contrasts, concentration on interiors, and taut, claustrophobic shots of family gatherings—all create a confining, depressing atmosphere such as one finds in *Diary of a Country Priest* or *Mouchette*. Sickness,
mental disorder, and physical disability pervade the life of the family. Bellocchio
speaks here in metaphorical terms. Epilepsy is a sign of decadence.[9] For the
director it represents all the troubles and weaknesses found in the young. In
social and psychological terms, Bellocchio believes that epilepsy is a categorical
refusal of an order founded on bourgeois values of family, work, and religion.

The family decays physically and socially at the same rapid rate as the villa.
The ambiguous quasi-incestuous relationship between Ale and Giulia, like Cocteau's *enfants terribles* Paul and Elisabeth, further erodes the stability of the family,
yet momentarily provides solace in a frustrated existence. Bellocchio clinically
observes this disintegration taking place before the spectator's eyes.

The cruel glimpse of the family has its autobiographical roots in the director's
adolescence spent in the Milan area. He elaborates:

> The boy in *I Pugni in Tasca* is destroyed because he will not accept reality. His
> attempt to escape reveals not only decadent but semi-fascist traits. I was
> brought up in a large family which was founded in the Fascist period in Italy,
> and though my father was not a member of the Fascist party, I suppose he was
> emotionally linked to its policy. *I Pugni in Tasca* is autobiographical in its de-
> scription of a milieu which I had to get away from in order to survive.[10]

When asked by Mimmina Quirico for *Amica* why he is so fascinated by the family
as a potential subject for his films, he replied:

> Whatever I do, the family concerns me. Current affairs don't interest me (in
> the journalistic sense of the term). As with Pasolini, family ghosts will accom-
> pany me all my life. With this difference: I do not renounce life and I don't
> want to be possessed by ghosts.[11]

The emotionally crippled members of the family cannot bring themselves to
work, which cuts them off from a real and important segment of society. Their
stagnancy prevents Augusto from marrying Lucia. The only way for Ale and
Giulia to survive in this repressive and unhealthy climate is to eliminate their
bourgeois past, and with it the outdated values that have stunted their psychological growth. Following the mother's death, the brother and sister systematically
remove and destroy the remnants of this archaic past. They tear up the vast
collection of the Catholic magazine *Pro familia* stored in the attic. It supposedly
represents all that is good and pure in Italian society, but the brother and sister
deliberately reject these worn-out values. By their anarchistic behavior they pu-
rify themselves.

With *Fists in the Pocket* Bellocchio drew the wrath of Italian society because he
dared to criticize the "sacred ark" of the family. Luigi Barzini in *The Italians*
rhetorically raises many sociopolitical questions about this prime institution,
which Bellocchio also does, but more brutally and symbolically:

Bellocchio's ***Fists in the Pocket.*** *Left,* Alessandro (Lou Castel), finding himself stifled by conformist family and societal values, finally rebels. *(Courtesy of National Film Archive, British Film Institute.)*

The family was also invincible because it was the sacred ark in which Italians deposited and preserved against alien influences all their ancient ideals. It clearly preserved the national character from contamination. The Italy of the families is definitely the real Italy, the quintessential Italy, distilled from the experiences of centuries, while the Italy of the laws and institutions is partly make-believe, the country Italians would like to believe was or will be but know is not. Will all this continue? Will all regimes the Italians give themselves in the future be inevitably corroded and destroyed by the family? Is this belief the reason why Italians are always compliantly ready to experiment with new political ways and why so many of them do not fear revolutions? Will anarchy ever end in this country? Will the family always predominate? This is, of course, the central riddle of Italian history and political life.[12]

In its suspense and drama *Fists in the Pocket* is closely akin to Hitchcock's *Psycho* and Clouzot's *Diaboliques.* Goffredo Fofi goes further in referring to it as "a shock film."[13] How apt he is in describing the effect that the film had on the public of 1965. The taboo of incest, the dissolution of the family, the destruction of the sacred maternal figure, the jaundiced view of religion, and the negative attitude toward provincial, bourgeois life, did not appeal, mildly speaking, to those who cherished these traditional values. Bellocchio recounts the reaction that the government had toward the film:

Forty-one members of the Christian Democratic Party wanted to have the film banned because they found it an offence against the Italian family, and especially against the role of the mother in the family. In Italy the family is an almost holy institution, a pillar of society, and to criticise it is considered outrageous. Italian films receive financial aid from the State, and special prizes are given to films which have been artistic but not commercial successes. The politicians tried to prevent me from getting the money.[14]

In spite of the reactionary attitude of the members of the Parliament, *Fists in the Pocket* merited the *Nastro d'argento* (Silver Ribbon) for the most original screenplay of the year.

In the summer of 1966, Bellocchio filmed his second work, *China Is Near*, several months prior to Godard's celebrated *La Chinoise*. A remarkable coincidence. Prophetic in nature, both films revealed the Maoist undercurrents among the budding Italian and French radicals. Although tone, technique, and theme differ in both films, each has become a landmark in political fiction film.

China Is Near plays on two levels simultaneously—private social life and public political life. The film may thus be appropriately considered a political melodrama. In its whimsical and at times biting presentation, *China* could also be viewed as a sociopolitical farce. Without warning, Bellocchio's subtle humor quickly changes to cynicism, a caustic view of all of his characters.

> *Middle-aged Vittorio Gordini (Glauco Mauri), professor at the local school in Imola, lives in wealth and comfort with his sister Elena (Elda Tattoli). Their blissful existence is interrupted by representatives of the Socialist party who solicit Vittorio's candidacy for a councilman position. This would help attract the bourgeois vote. Vittorio, an opportunist at heart, agrees, much to the displeasure of his younger brother Camillo (Pierluigi Apra) who runs a three-man Maoist cell. For assistance in his political campaign Vittorio acquires the services of Carlo (Paolo Graziosi), who falls out of love with Vittorio's secretary Giovanna (Daniela Surina) and into love with Elena. Giovanna and Elena both become pregnant by Carlo during Vittorio's campaign.*
>
> *Camillo and his comrades disrupt the Socialists' campaign by bombing their headquarters and then setting German Shepherd dogs loose during Vittorio's campaign speech. Life eventually settles down as Vittorio will marry Giovanna, and Elena, Carlo.*

Elda Tattoli, Bellocchio's colleague at the film school, helped design the complicated script. Together they sculpted the quintet of characters in *China Is Near* with clever and intricate detail. Vittorio is a buffoonish aristocrat who has never grown up. His political commitment is never sincere, changing parties as he does ties. Elena, a sexually promiscuous middle-aged woman, commits herself to various lovers and to caring for the family inheritance. Her moral conscience is as dulled as her brother's political conscience when she decides to have an abortion to save face. Their brother Camillo is a despotic Maoist and submissive seminarian. Of these three family members Bellocchio says he recognizes himself above all in some of the traits, dilemmas, and contradictions of Camillo. From the lower class come the Socialist Carlo and his girlfriend Giovanna. Their work for the rich couple is self-serving. Both are opportunistic and parasitic. In the group of five characters, no attractive hero or heroine can be found.

Bellocchio satirically plays with religion, morality, and politics in order to point an accusing finger at the promoters of bourgeois values. The characters who embody these values appear to be ridiculous reactionaries trying to hold onto an archaic past. Religion is one whipping boy. Having been exposed to religious teachers in his elementary and secondary school education, Bellocchio knows the inner sanctum of established religion. With an anticlerical verve he caricatures the rector as an insensitive martinet. During the bombing episode, the babbling Capuchin friar who prays for the safety of the Socialists at party headquarters comes across as a simple-minded fool. The bed-ridden Father Comotti, to whom Camillo and the younger boarding students cater, has his moments of lucidity as well as moments of senility. He is unaware of the boys' deliberate singing of false notes in their song "A Ray of Love Appeared." The young clerical friend of Carlo who helps prevent Elena from having an abortion plays a bit too amicably with the young boys and then becomes religiously hysterical in the doctor's office. Roman Catholicism for Bellocchio resembles the relics that the youngsters hesitatingly kiss—dusty, archaic, meaningless—and the priests who continue to promote the religion are inept victims of it.

In his study of the provincial, Roman Catholic, bourgeois mores, Bellocchio designs characters in whom there is no profound sense of ethical behavior. The moral guide for decision-making is pragmatism. Vittorio uses Giovanna for free, casual love as she uses him for material security. Giovanna wants to retain her grip on Vittorio, so she has Carlo make her pregnant, claiming the child to be Vittorio's. Carlo manipulates Elena into not having an abortion because he would like to marry her. Elena in the meantime would like to arrange for an abortion so she could be free once again. Her brother, the count, agrees with her decision, since it would not look good for the Socialist candidate to have an illegitimate child.

Camillo appears no better. After he calmly serves Mass and attends to the needs of the senile Father Comotti, he engages in other activities. Political and sexual curiosity lead him and his peers to experiment in eroticism with a prostitute from the working class. They use terrorist tactics against the Socialist party, deface city property with Maoist slogans, and disrupt the party rally with their vicious dogs. On the moral, developmental level, all of these characters rate very poorly.

It is in the political realm that Bellocchio strikes the hardest. The title sets the tone—China is near! Bellocchio ideally hoped that China would be nearer to Italy in ideology, but he understands paradoxically that it is distant for those who think it is near and very near for those who believe it is still far away. Tommaso Chiaretti comments on Bellocchio's political sentiments:

> China, therefore, is anything but near. Here there's no talk of socialism and revolution, of strikes and of more or less enlightened neocapitalism. Here we have palace intrigues as dingy as their protagonists. Who, after all, are not

always silly, nor always base; they even have moments of chilling good-fel-lowship in their decision to climb together toward the modest summit.[15]

Those who were trying to bring China closer were the political Sinophiles, those in total opposition to neocapitalist society. In Italy, Marxist-Leninist and leftist Catholic action cells and study groups comprised these sympathizers at the time.

The director means *Fists in the Pocket* to be "didactic" but not in the Zhdanovian sense of having a positive hero, or with a Rossellinian focus on education. Belloc-chio tries to show how *not* to be, how *not* to live. He does this by first considering the class struggle. He states:

> The film tries to show an example of how the classes only apparently tend toward unification, integration, and disappearance, but how on the contrary, for everyone who wins there's always someone who loses, for everyone who gets richer there's always someone who gets poorer, for everyone who frees himself from his own material enslavement, there's something waiting to take his place.[16]

Vittorio follows the Socialist line to bring the bourgeois closer to the proletariat. On the campaign trail Vittorio encounters a concrete example of class struggle in a violent, physical episode. Despite his Socialist ticket and platform, Vittorio is condescending toward the working class as he prepares to address them. They sense this, and after he harasses a young village boy, they descend upon him and destroy his luxury automobile. To unite the two classes, he triumphantly an-nounces in the final campaign speech that he will marry Giovanna, a member of the working class. His political commitment is a farce, and his interest in uniting the classes is shallow and opportunistic. Camillo succeeds more readily in creat-ing a coalition of working and bourgeois classes by his experimentation with the working class prostitute—for the sake of consciousness, confesses Camillo.

The two classes remain as far apart as China is from Italy. The bourgeois, represented especially by Elena and Vittorio, are tragic figures. Appearances mean more to them than reality. They are chained to their wealth; they feel it can buy relationships as well as political power. Bellocchio uses a metaphorical scene at a rifle club to show the need for power and violence in such characters as Vittorio. He and his colleagues gather there to plan their political strategy. They use live sparrows for their targets. Later on we see that if the contemporary bourgeois are not careful they will become like the ancestors in the decrepit portraits under which Carlo and Elena amorously embrace.

In Italian political films like *1900*, the members of the working class are he-roes, saints, and idols. Bellocchio, however, treats the proletariat just as harshly as he does the wealthy. Giovanna and Carlo, both social climbers, manipulate their employers. By osmosis they absorb the bourgeois values they once crit-icized. Chiaretti therefore considers Carlo "a proletarian corrupted by the action of systematic integration by the bourgeoisie."[17]

Bellocchio caricatures the political parties, especially the United Socialist Party (PSU) and the Maoist cell. He portrays the PSU as disorganized, ineffective, and opportunistic. The strategy of the adherents indicates they prefer compromise to maintaining strong, purist principles of socialism. The party is willing to sponsor a political chameleon as candidate. Vittorio, for the sake of political and financial convenience, passed through the ranks of the Christian Democrats, the Social Democrats, the Communists, the Radical Republicans, and is on the verge of becoming a Sinophile like his brother Camillo when the Socialists woo him to their party. The PSU has certainly lowered its standards.

In the mid-sixties there was a keen desire in Italian political life for ideological unification. The sentiment resulted in this "historical compromise," as noted earlier, a Center-Left government that brought together the Christian Democrats and the Left. *China Is Near* offers some insight into the mentality of political compromise.

Bellocchio refers to Camillo as an "esthete of a revolutionary," and an anarchist. His Maoist cell is politically impotent. Their major "actions" are lamentable: painting "China is Near" on the wall facing Socialist party headquarters, and harassing the elderly Socialists with a bomb threat. The stubborn idealism of Camillo and his Sinophile comrades directly opposes the compromising realism or opportunism of Vittorio and the Socialists.

With his critical presentation of the foibles of the social, religious, and political sectors of Italian provincial society, the director deliberately sought to provoke and irritate his viewers. His cynical attitude immediately stirred up the political waters, as John Francis Lane observes:

Bellocchio's ***China Is Near.*** A campaign setting for Vittorio (Glauco Mauri). *(Courtesy of National Film Archive, British Film Institute.)*

. . . The film certainly caused a lot of unease in the Socialist Party, which at the time was in the government Centre-Left coalition. To say that Bellocchio's film had an actual influence on the fortunes of that party, which had to withdraw from the government after the 1968 elections (in which the Communists increased their votes at the expense of the Socialists), would perhaps be an exaggeration. But there is no doubt that Bellocchio and his co-scriptwriter Elda Tattoli put their fingertips on the weaknesses of that party's place in Italian life, thus anticipating the electoral debacle of May, 1968. . . .[18]

Even the young student radicals did not appreciate the film, as could be expected. Bellocchio's objective may be considered totally anarchistic, for his desire was to demolish completely a certain world and not create another from it, he told Marisa Rusconi in 1967.[19] In essence, *China Is Near* reflects what Bellocchio does *not* want politically; hence no individual is a standard-bearer of his ideology in the film.

Just a few years after the release of the film, Bellocchio honestly appraised the ideology put forth in *China Is Near*. When he made the film he was skeptical about the historical compromise and felt the coalition would hinder an already fruitful dialectic among the various parties of the Left and Right.

But I was very, very wrong, because I realize now I did not have a complete view of reality. Today I believe that even if these political forces have, in a certain sense, sold themselves to the bourgeoisie, there will be new forces, new ones are being born right now, and they are ready to fight. So the game is far from being over. *La Cina è vicina* is a film with important political errors.[20]

The second *mea culpa* which Bellocchio made in the early seventies—after having joined a group of Marxists-Leninists—was that he did not fully comprehend the importance of a small cell like Camillo's. From such tiny seeds an entire movement developed in Europe over the next few years. Although the movement was short-lived, it did foster both radical political and imaginative artistic activity. Bellocchio's militant films would soon spring from his affiliation with the organization.

To complete his autobiographical trilogy, Bellocchio dramatized his own Catholic boarding school experiences in his film *In the Name of the Father*. He looked at this undertaking as a final settling of accounts with his past. Aside from isolated courses here and there, Bellocchio's formal education primarily took place in private Catholic boarding schools in the northern provinces. His secondary school promoted the same type of mediocrity, stagnation, and total passivity as exhibited in the film, Bellocchio stated. At the time of the action of the film—scholastic year 1958–59—Bellocchio was eighteen and in a Catholic high school in Lodi run by the Barnabite Fathers. His precise, personal recollections nourish the script, which he wrote with his brother Pier Giorgio:

. . . Boredom, sleep, interminable lapses of time, schedules which fragmented the day, heat, cold, etc. These were all physical, material memories. I entered high school at an age when my relationship with religion already ended. Religion for me was Masses, sermons, diverse services, rituals, novenas, Communions, and the rules which governed them: fast, God's grace, repentance, seriousness of sins, kneeling, sitting, standing, genuflecting, blessing oneself, one, two, three times, a scheduled time for this or that, confessions, colloquia. . . . All of this had its precise place in high school life. These were obligations which were fulfilled lazily, without a rebellious spirit; they were compulsory exercises which did not engage the mind, and which one felt were a waste of time.[21]

Bellocchio moved from the didactic realism of *Fists* and *China* to eerie expressionism and humorous surrealism in this recent work. *In the Name of the Father*, a biting allegory replete with fantasy, ambiguity, and blasphemy, was designed to shock and alert the audience. Bellocchio, chronicling the events of more than a decade prior to the production, purports to show why Italian society is as it currently is in 1971—for better or for worse, but mostly for worse, he feels. The director chooses the institution of the school, as does Vigo *(Zero for Conduct)*, Volker Schlöndorff *(The Young Törless)*, and Lindsay Anderson *(If . . .)*, because it is a privileged place of social change as well as value orientation. The intricate rites of passage in each film make of the boy a young man. Bellocchio, however, puts into the minds of his protagonists Angelo and Franc the idea that their education is simply intellectual castration.

The Dantesque descent into an academic hell begins enigmatically. In the shadows, a hostile father strikes his son and commands, "Obey me!" The young boy—Angelo (Yves Beneyton), we later learn—defiantly strikes back twice. Then we pass over the threshold. In the first circle reside the eccentric and semifascist priests. The students, initiated and novice, occupy the next few circles. Then in the depths of the underworld we discover the servants— misfits, madmen, orphans, all rejects of society.

The intelligent and rebellious Angelo arrives on the scene and disturbs the status quo. He and his comrade Franc (Aldo Sassi) confront the powers to be, such as the Vice Rector, Padre Corazza (Renato Scarpa), and the other teachers. Two major events stir up the docile populace and oblige them to call into question the "divine" authority of their masters. Angelo and company terrorize the audience of priests, parents, and classmates with a shocking and violent Faustian play. Then, the servant Salvatore (Lou Castel) leads a revolt against the administration, for which he is dismissed. In the end, Angelo and the youth Tino, who is in interplanetary communication, cut down the sacred pear tree and travel in a car toward an unknown destination. Angelo tells Tino, "You are free now. Go work in a factory."

The title, *In the Name of the Father*, conjures up allusions to several levels of thought on which the film is based. Catholics will immediately recognize it as the beginning of the Sign of the Cross. It invokes the presence of a paternal God. The religious priests, the fathers who act *in loco parentis*, also share in the divine authority coming from on high. Bellocchio says they are a composite of Salesians, Barnabites, Jesuits, and Christian Brothers, religious orders that ordinarily direct schools for wealthy boys. The third level can be seen at the mysterious opening of the film as well as in the parent-child relationships alluded to in the film. A generation gap—cultural and psychological—separates father from son, sets them off in alienation one from the other.

Bellocchio first aims his weapons at the target of the Catholic Church. He specifically dates his work in the year 1958–59, and explains his rationale for selecting this period:

> I didn't think it was worthwhile to attack the Church directly—oh, maybe to satirize certain aspects, of course, but basically the film was meant to interpret the Catholic Church in a moment of transition, through one of its institutions, at the time of the death of Pope Pius XII (c. 1959) that symbolized the end of one era and the beginning of another. The next Pope (John XXIII) really started to make enormous reforms—but he didn't live long enough, and the reforms did not essentially disturb the power of the Establishment.[22]

To document this he used newsreel footage of the funeral of Pius XII shown on television while the boys, unconcerned about current events, boisteriously play their games. The director also saw this year as a shift from the semifascist politics of Pius XII to the same spirit of dialogue and openness that Pasolini praised in the peasant-pope John XXIII. Bellocchio paralleled this moment to the Russian destalinization period following the death of the Soviet dictator.

Bellocchio draws a very unflattering picture of the Catholic Church in which he grew up, but which he admits has changed with the Second Vatican Council in the mid-sixties. He saw it in its earlier phase as subservient to the class in power. To remain in power it had to resort to repressive actions, as seen in the film. Authority and discipline are the two guiding lights. The priests who carry out the policies of the Church appear as nothing more than morbid eccentrics, power-hungry tyrants, or utter simpletons.

The Catholic education system perpetuated by the clergy over the centuries directed the students toward positions of power, usually in support of the status quo. Bellocchio observes the underlying policy of the religious teachers:

> . . . They wanted to mold us into solid Christian Democrats, not intransigent reactionaries, saints, or knights of the faith, ready to sacrifice their lives to defend Western Civilization, but level-headed, tolerant, and passive agrarians who were completely apolitical.[23]

In the film, Angelo could not accept this educational goal, nor could he tolerate the stifling, repressive atmosphere of the institution. Every night they were locked in their cells, nothing more than tolerated incarceration paid for handsomely by the wealthy parents. Angelo's refusal to spend the night behind locked doors initiated a wave of rebellion that filtered down through the ranks.

The education of the young boys was meant to be a sexless experience. The physical and psychological growth through puberty is ordinarily traumatic and tumultuous, but more exaggerated in this enclosed and restricted environment. Lectured on the evils of self-abuse, they are made to feel guilty with the Lord's wrath hovering over them like a Damoclean, castrating sword. A la Buñuel, Bellocchio satirizes the frustrations of the young Marsilio in this guilt-ridden milieu by having him masturbate in the back pew while the priest lectures against self-pleasure. The Madonna appears to the boy and gently comforts him in his distress.

Class struggle makes its appearance here, even in a religious institution dedi-

cated to Christian values. As in *China,* Bellocchio is none too kind to the proletariat. He describes the occupants of this nether world as the dregs of society
who passively accept the paternalism of the religious administrators. Even their
strike—led by the symbolically named proletarian messiah, Salvatore—terminates in failure and the dismissal of the instigator. The students who come from
bourgeois backgrounds demonstrate a hostile attitude toward their fellow victims
of oppression. They do not back them in their rebellion. The students are bent
on their own revolution, for less religion, better teaching, and a less oppressive
system. A lack of solidarity weakens the two-pronged attack against the administration.

Bellocchio recognizes himself in the film as psychologically part Angelo, part
Franc. These two sides of his personality, although in apparent conflict, still com-
plement each other. The first is the secular aspect of Bellocchio's personality
represented by Angelo. Jay Cocks succinctly sizes up this disturbing and disturbed character:

> Angelo (Yves Beneyton) is a sort of patrician Nazi with a cultivated superi-
> ority that passes, in the eyes of his fellow students, for power, He also possesses
> a well-developed cynicism which, combined with a taste for psychological vio-
> lence, has a carbolic effect on the school.[24]

Angelo is further characterized by his high technocratic aspirations, a desire for
perfection, as well as a rebellious streak. His super-rationalism borders on fascism.

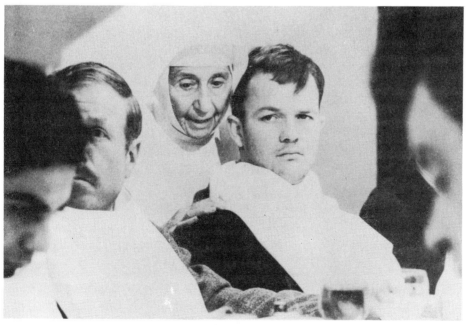

Bellocchio's *In the Name of Father.* Salvatore (Lou Castel), *right,* helps to lead a revolt of the
boarding students against the school officials. *(Courtesy of National Film Archive, British Film
Institute.)*

Franc, on the other hand, suggests the religious side of the director's temperament. He exhibits a certain discretion toward reality and hesitates to act. Yet he
demonstrates a strong will power inculcated by a solid Catholic education, heavily
laden with religious values.

Politics, religion, family, and education—these four institutions served as primary targets in Bellocchio's three autobiographical films. His presence within
them can hardly go unnoticed—in the characters of Alessandro, Camillo, Angelo, and Franc, and in their particular dilemmas. This cynical, yet enlightening,
trilogy serves as a spiritual or psychological confession of his rich but painful
experiences in adolescence.

Let's Discuss, Discuss; Paola; Long Live Red May Day: Collective Militancy

Because of a driving need for political self-expression, several Italian and
French directors in the post-1968 era dabbled in militant or ideological films to
support one cause or another. Bertolucci and Pasolini are noteworthy examples
of this political *engagement* in cinema. Such was also the situation of Marco Bellocchio in late 1968 and early 1969. He first had an opportunity to add his political
reflections, in episode form, to those provided by Lizzani, Bertolucci, Pasolini,
and Godard in *Love and Hate*. His work, *Let's Discuss, Discuss*, replaced Zurlini's
Seated at His Right (*Seduto alla sua destra*, 1968), which became a feature film.
Bellocchio's contribution to this series of shorts on biblical themes radically differed from the others. It did not consciously illustrate a biblical text with a contemporary parallel, although Bellocchio said that the school in the film is a type
of synagogue or religious learning center.

For this short, final episode of the collective film, Bellocchio relied upon the
assistance of his screenwriter-actress Elda Tattoli. Together with a group of University of Rome students whom he described as antiauthoritarian and professing
assorted leftist ideologies, they assembled a script that spoke to the political temper of the times. The tone would be somewhat opposed to that of his earlier films
with respect to the young. This time they assume the role of hero.

*The simple staging for the film consists of posters of Ho Chi Minh and Che Guevara as
well as revolutionary slogans on the walls surrounding the professor's desk and the rows of
students' seats. The camera is as casual in movement and involvement as the students. The
director plays the part of the university professor in confrontation with a group of students.
Their dialectical debate touches upon the issues of authority, culture, and academics, but the
dean, professor, and police appear to be on the losing side of the confrontation. The students
idolize Brecht and Mao, and condemn Croce to a literary hell by burning his book. Like
Angelo and Franc, they criticize the educational system for not teaching students how to live
but only how to imitate through repetition.*

Like many of the 1968–69 militant productions, *Let's Discuss* seems didactic,
dated, and simplistic. The urgency of the political message has faded away. Now
the confrontative words of the students come across as those of leftist reactionaries, as in Godard's *La Chinoise*. The improvisation and nonprofessional acting

fill the film with a clear-cut naturalness and account for the underground or experimental effect of the work. Tullio Kezich in *Bianco e nero* succinctly puts the film into perspective:

> We may consider it an hypothesis on didactic, neo-Brechtian cinema, sustained by an element of Italian improvisational theatre. This is a more interesting line of development for the director than the provincial caricature and mediocre political satire of a film like *China is Near*.[25]

Bellocchio shares his ideas on political film with Fred Tuten for *Cinéaste* in 1969, the same year he made *Paola* and *Long Live Red May Day:*

> 'Revolutionary cinema,' in and of itself doesn't mean anything. But cinema can be put at the service of the revolution. First, though, we have to see what *kind* of revolution, made by *whom*, in the name of *what*. Because, you know, there are many revolutions. Even fascist governments define themselves as revolutionary. Anyway, once you've established the principles, the ideas in the name of which a certain revolution is being made, then cinema—within the limits of those principles—can contribute something to that revolution, and therefore can qualify as revolutionary.[26]

The two revolutionary films made while Bellocchio was a militant member of the Union of Communists illustrate these precepts. As an artist in the press and propaganda division of the Marxist-Leninist party, he put his talents at the service of *their* idea of revolution. It was primarily humanitarian, leftist, and pro-proletariat. Bellocchio's ideas had to be totally subservient to his producer or sponsor, though his earlier producers from Vides and Doria gave him significant artistic leeway in their collaboration with him. In the editing process the party would have the final word. Bellocchio was predisposed to accept their directives, feeling weighed down by a political inferiority complex and a sense of guilt at having his roots in the bourgeois class, he acknowledged.

Paola, a feature-length film made in the southern region of Calabria, highlights the political activities of the Marxist-Leninist group. It is an investigation into the physical conditions of the city Paola, cell meetings of the party, occupation of the *"case popolari,"* and preparations for the 2 March (1969) demonstration. Bellocchio recounts to Goffredo Fofi the background of the production:

> It was filmed from an idea that was theoretically correct: the protagonist was to be the people of Paola. The ideas of the people are right, so it is therefore the people who should express them. The members of the party should not speak for the people, but should restrict themselves to organizing and synthesizing the people's ideas. They ought to help them resolve their contradictions, etc. This was the point of departure, but reality contradicted it somewhat: in the study that we did in the poorest sections of Paola, we especially found evidence of an absence of confidence and optimism, and instead a tragic fatalism about the present as well as the future, and a political consciousness that was hardly existent.[27]

The purpose of the production lay first in raising the class consciousness of the people of Paola and then documenting these experiences for future political action. In the interviews and filming process, the crew—Bellocchio, cameraman

Dimitri Nicolau, and party militants—made their way into ghettoes teeming with poverty-stricken workers, sick children, and poorly-cared-for women in child-birth. Social problems were legion.

Following an a priori schema, the party wished to reveal a people exploited and suffering, explained Bellocchio to Fofi, but also involved, optimistic, and revolutionary. This was certainly not always the case, as they discovered on location. Party politics demanded that certain repugnant aspects of the misery be edited out of the documentary footage. Any of the defeatist material filmed was therefore eliminated. Fofi suggested to Bellocchio that this type of editing falsifies the true picture. The director agreed, noting that this type of militant activity primarily followed the plans—"the Chinese schemas"—of art in the service of the people. Bellocchio and the party members had to accept responsibility for the results of *Paola,* for at any moment the director was free to discontinue his revolutionary cultural role.

The first of May in Italy and other European countries is a time for celebration and demonstration. Banners with revolutionary slogans lead the almost religiously formed processions to show party unity. Bellocchio's second film with militant objectives, *Long Live Red May Day,* documents a revolutionary triumphalism in the organization of the annual May Day demonstrations in several Italian cities.

The controversial period of ideological involvement in 1969 was for Bellocchio *"una grande illusione,"* the director told Sandro Bernardi in July 1977, with eight years of hindsight. The type of political filmmaking witnessed in *Paola* and *Long Live Red May Day* was no longer viable in Italy, he felt. Yet for him this temporary commitment to the revolution provided him with a fresh and close-up look at the political machinery in society. In one sense, he looked almost nostalgically at his participation in the Marxist-Leninist group. Filming *Paola* he learned much about how the other half lived. In another sense, he believed that he and his fellow cinéastes were never fully integrated into the Union of Communists. Their comrades accused them of lacking political enthusiasm. These working class artists, nonetheless, felt themselves still shackled by old bourgeois habits that isolated them from their comrades in the avant-garde of the ephemeral revolution.

Rape on the Front Page/Slap the Monster on Page One, Fit to Be Untied, Victory March: More Institutions under Attack

In the American cinema, attorney-filmmaker Fred Wiseman has very systematically and most effectively studied institutions from mental hospitals for the criminally insane *(Titicut Follies),* through the educational system *(High School),* to the military *(Basic Training).* What Wiseman has been able to achieve in the documentary Bellocchio has been able to do in the political fiction film. In three works of varying quality, Bellocchio analyzes the press, mental hospitals, and the army. As Wiseman found, the reality of the institutions differs from the public's image of it and the administrator's intentions in directing it.

When cinema handles journalism, normally it deifies the heroic journalist who, against all odds and pressure from some powerful force, manages to uncover key sources of injustice. Costa-Gavras's *Z* and Alan Pakula's *All the President's Men* bear this out. Bellocchio's treatment of the press and the institution of journalism in *Rape on the Front Page* (*Sbatti il mostro in prima pagine,* 1972) takes the opposite perspective. The press, primarily personified by the editor Bizanti, manipulates facts and persons for its own purposes. The monster of the Italian title is not the young man accused of rape, but the same unethical editor.

Sergio Donati, filmmaker as well as screenwriter for Sergio Leone's "spaghetti western," *Once upon a Time in the West,* had signed a contract with Ugo Tucci for Jupiter Films to make *Rape on the Front Page.* The script was drawn up and the shooting began with Gian Maria Volonté in the lead role. Donati suddenly fell sick—some say he and Volonté did not work very well together—and Tucci asked Bellocchio to take up the film where Donati left off. This would be a major challenge for the young director. In essence, he considered his work more a lifesaving gesture than a personal film. In conscience he could not complete exactly what Donati had already accumulated as a script. Drastic modifications were in order. He called upon his colleague and critic Goffredo Fofi, who had collaborated with him in the politico-cultural journal *Quaderni piacentini,* edited by Bellocchio's brother. After several days of deliberation, they began their project. Their decision was to politicize the original scenario to the maximum. During the day Fofi would write and both would revise in the evening. The next day Bellocchio shot what they had decided upon. Gian Maria Volonté and Laura Betti, the fascist Lady Macbeth of *1900,* helped construct their own roles in the film. Although Volonté disagreed with Bellocchio's jeopardizing treatment of the Communist party, they were able to come to a working compromise. Their collective participation resulted in a tense work of fiction, enhanced by elements of the Hollywood thriller, police, detective, and adventure film.

In the northern city of Milan, in the course of the Spring 1972 elections, the conservative newspaper Il Giornale *is supposedly attacked by leftist radicals. The editor Bizanti (Gian Maria Volonté) viciously aims to discredit the Left in view of the forthcoming elections. He finds the opportunity when a young girl of an upper class family is raped and killed. Bizanti accuses her boyfriend, an extreme Leftist, of having committed the crime. He splashes the front page with this sensational news. The owner of the paper, Monicelli (John Steiner), agrees with the editor's action. Roveda (Fabio Garriba), the journalist, undertakes his own investigation and discovers the real culprit, a perverted individual who had a passion for the young girl. Bizanti fires Roveda and tells Monicelli that the truth about the real criminal must not be disclosed until after the elections.*

In his cinematic treatise on the manipulative editor and conservative press—patterned on the *Corriere della Sera* of Milan—Bellocchio set out to inculpate the real criminals of society. In a didactic fashion he points out the evils of Bizanti's yellow journalism. The editor deliberately distorts the facts in a serious crime in order to swing the elections. His power, ruthlessly wielded, controls the lives of many people around him. For this reason he readily enters into collusion with police and politicians. He has no scruples. For him any personal end justifies any conceivable means. Not too dissimilar to the officials of the Third Reich, Bizanti and his cohorts instill fear of the Left in the hearts of their readers in order to obtain a fascist order. The enlightened industrialist Monicelli, a mild version of Citizen Kane, even cites the Reich's propaganda minister Joseph Goebbels.

Bellocchio astutely blends historical fact and documentary footage with fictional thriller material. The critic Sandro Bernardi assembles the underlying historical facts which comprise the action of the film:

> There are references to news reports, such as the murder of Milena Sutter and the accusation by the witness Rosanna Zublema, goaded by the commissioner Calabresi, charging the anarchists with the 25 April 1969 bombing at Fiera Campionaria; the examining magistrates' leak to the press, most notably to the *Corriere della Sera;* the attack of the "katanga" against this same newspaper shortly before; the ties of an eminent industrialist and owner of a chain of newspapers with the fascist squads; and the massacre at Piazza Fontana, treated in relation to the investigations which made scapegoats of Valpreda and Pinelli. On the other hand, there is the compilation of documented material, such as the two councils of Almirante, the one of Forlani, Feltrinelli's funeral and the demonstrations of the first of May.[28]

Didactic and partisan, *Rape on the Front Page* does have an aura of militancy about it, confirms Sandro Scandolara of *Cineforum*.[29] Bellocchio took what he and Fofi considered an inadequate script, revitalized it, and struck out against the machinery of fascist finance and political power. Although no longer a member of the Union of Communists, he was still motivated to make a not too subtle, pro-Left political statement.

In 1973, Bellocchio reentered the documentary world by accepting the invitation of Mario Tommasini, Health Director of the commune of Parma, to make a film on the state of mental health facilities in the region. *Fit to Be Untied (Nessuno o tutti/Matti da slegare*, 1974), was to document the care of the psychologically disturbed and to demonstrate the possibilities of integrating these individuals into society. It was almost ten years prior to this production that Bellocchio had shockingly treated in fiction form the mental problems of a provincial family— epilepsy, trauma, and hypertension. The subject still fascinated him. He undertook the project proposed by the commune and selected a crew that could help him film it. Stefano Rulli and Sandro Petraglia came from film criticism. Silvano Agosti had worked as film editor with Bellocchio since *Fists in the Pocket*. The four went to their work with no preconceived notions and only a skeleton of a shooting script. They wanted their narrative to emerge gradually from their footage. Following a first important phase of research, they began shooting in black and white and in 16mm. The crew amassed 25,000 meters of film, replete with lengthy, soul-searing interviews and informative discussions. The first version that they completed lasted three hours and contained two distinct parts: "Tre Storie" (Three Stories) and "Matti da slegare" (Mad as a Hatter). This integral version furnished the responsible medical staff with very graphic images of the current conditions of mental health in their region. A second version under the title *Matti da slegare* was made by blowing up the film into 35mm. and at the same time editing it to a more manageable two hours and fifteen minutes. Both offer keen insights into alternative psychiatry.

Three revealing case studies comprise the first part of the film. The interviews with the young patients, such as Paolo and Marco, and their families uncover layer after layer of personal and social scars over the years. The mother of Marco, a schizophrenic youth, for example, recounts how her mother, out of necessity, put her on the street as a prostitute at the age of ten, and now how her daughter, Marco's sister, has also become a prostitute. The second part of the film exposes the spectator-witness to the testimony of those responsible for caring for the mentally handicapped. It gives the social context from which the mental patients derive, and underlines the fact that insanity must also be regarded as a social disease. It can often be cured only by reintegrating the patient into a human, civic milieu.

This microcosm of the daily life of a mental patient recalls the subhuman world of the mentally handicapped in Milos Forman's *One Flew over the Cuckoo's Nest*, but without a fictional handling of the material. *Fit to Be Untied* demonstrates a documentary style marked by brilliant reportage. Bellocchio notes that the crew's work in the film suggests Chris Marker's approach in *Le joli mai*. It is informative, accusational, and above all, highly personal. We not only look through the window of mental hospitals, but we stare right into the very souls of the patients. Through the revealing interviews with the patients, families, and medical staff, the traditional psychiatric processes are called into question. Bellocchio sees society at fault for the large number and poor conditions of mental patients today. Society, gradually eroded by prostitution, poverty, and juvenile delinquency, has gently pushed—or abruptly shoved—into hospitals individuals who could not cope with these daily pressures. Bellocchio demonstrates how society should now accept the responsibility of rehabilitating these ostracized persons in its midst once again. This clinical study of the conditions of mental health in the general region of Emilia-Romagna ultimately raises the question, as does Philippe de Broca's *King of Hearts:* "Where is the true insanity, inside or outside the walls of a psychiatric ward?"

Although less autobiographical than his trilogy, *Victory March (Marcia trionfale,* 1976) does emanate in part from Bellocchio's personal experiences during his military service. He felt as uncomfortable as his hero Paolo Passeri in his first encounters with the army, for he was an intellectual from a petit bourgeois family totally uprooted and set into an intolerable and dehumanized environment. After a short time, Bellocchio was discharged for reasons of health—more simulated than not, he confesses. His brief stint in the army filled him with a hatred for the utter stupidity of the system, the director later lamented. Unfortunately his hatred, he admits, also had spread to the peasant and the common soldier whom he generally found crass—a sentiment of antipathy that he also had for some of the militants in the Union of Communists.

With unrelenting, brutal realism Bellocchio situates a ménage à quatre *in the context of military life. The characters, heavily burdened psychologically, are consciously or at times unconsciously trapped by the system. Paolo Passeri (Michele Placido), fresh from university studies in literature, finds himself in the alien world of the military. As a fresh recruit in basic training, he is subjected to the usual harassment by his military superiors as well as his already initiated peers. He learns to defend himself, "like a man," through a lesson in violence from the paternal but semifascist Captain Asciutto (Franco Nero). Once fully under the Captain's wing, Passeri is asked by him to keep his young wife Rosanna (Miou-Miou) under surveillance for any extramarital activity. Passeri and she, however, initiate a mutual, consoling relationship, interrupted on occasion by the perverted demands on her by Lieutenant Baio (Patrick Dewaere). Asciutto's relationship with his wife becomes more infernal for his macho attitude toward her. She abandons him. The captain, in an ultimate death-wish gesture, forces a sentry to fire at him under the eyes of the stunned Passeri.*

In making this type of *document-pamphlet,* as Aldo Tassone rightly labels it, Bellocchio ran into serious production problems, exactly as Yves Boisset did in his recent film *Allons, enfants* (1980) on a French military school for young boys. The Italian minister of defense attempted to block the filming. The Italian army refused to cooperate in providing necessary locations and uniforms. Army veterans rallied against the production.

Fred Wiseman's documentary *Basic Training* is a profound revelation of negative as well as positive aspects of military life. Bellocchio stops at the negative in his incrimination of the military. In a very tight script written by Sergio Bazzini, the director stacks his cards against the army. No single redeeming value can be attributed to this way of life. The general atmosphere which pervades the barracks existence suggests incarceration. These young men cannot escape as easily as did Bellocchio with a discharge. As a result they are forced to tolerate the dehumanization process that eats away at their souls while their bodies get into shape. Annihilation of freethinking individuals takes place.

Captain Asciutto and Lieutenant Baio, as officers, represent the military hierarchy. Neither is at all sensitive. The powerhappy Asciutto manipulates and terrorizes his wife just as he does his underlings at the barracks. He beats, threatens, and spies on Rosanna. For him the male is meant to be strong, aggressive, and, if necessary, violent. He advocates a "Might makes Right" philosophy. The female should be subservient to the male. Tension arises when Rosanna refused to abide by this age-old custom. She would not want a child by this sadistic creature and would immediately abort a fetus. Asciutto tells Passeri that he would like a son that he could *form* or *mold* as a true male. He tells the recruit that he loves to see soldiers transformed before his very eyes. When a whimpering raw recruit comes to him, Asciutto can change him in twelve months. Think of what he could do with a son over his whole lifetime, he says. He would have his son bathe in cold water, spend summers outdoors, then send him off to the prostitutes. Gianluigi Bozza refers to Captain Asciutto's philosophy of life as "existential fascism."

Lieutenant Baio appears in no more favorable a light than Asciutto. The perverted young officer makes love to the captain's wife surrounded by an arsenal of pornography shop gadgets, lights, and music. He brutalizes Rosanna and treats her like an object. Making love he must remain dressed while she must be nude, thus accentuating his power over her.

Bellocchio further brings out the anal orientation of barracks existence. The soldiers carry out vendettas on the designated victims by dousing them with buckets teeming with liquidy excrement. At night they play at converting their buttocks into flamethrowers. Asciutto forces Passeri to read him poetry in the lavatory. Much of this is to be expected in a closed institution for males, however, whether it be the boarding school of *In the Name of the Father* or the casern of *Victory March.*

In this situation, which seems unnatural, rage and humiliation well up in the sensitive individual. At the opening of the film, Passeri is forced to go through a dehumanizing ordeal of identifying himself properly. He calls out louder and louder so as to be heard at ten, fifteen, twenty, twenty-five yards: "Soldier Paolo Passeri, second company, second platoon, third squad, at your command!" At the end of the film, nothing has changed. Another humiliated victim of a merciless sergeant takes a few more paces, and cries out his name and company.

There is a sense of liberation, however, at the conclusion of this engrossing analysis of the tragic mechanisms of power. Rosanna finally shakes loose from her destructive, overpowering husband. Her exposure to Asciutto and the military life has scarred her deeply, but she now has at least escaped the physical pain and mental anguish of this deplorable existence. Furthermore, in a gesture that Bertolucci would symbolically appreciate, Passeri sees his paternal figure destroyed before his eyes. He now becomes independent. A growth of consciousness has taken place.

The extreme Left reproached Bellocchio for not having made a militant film

Bellocchio's *Victory March.* Captain Asciutto (Franco Nero) manipulates his military charges as well as his wife. *(Courtesy of National Film Archive, British Film Institute.)*

of this material. The director responded by saying that for him this would be too didactic, too cold an undertaking. He needed a story and characters to flesh out his ideas. At the same time the Right and Center criticized Bellocchio for depicting the military in such a hostile fashion. Although *Victory March* seems most realistic and credible, the spectator must also understand that the material presented by Bellocchio is highly dramatized for effect.

Leap into the Void: **Full Circle**

Bellocchio has remarked on occasion that in his everdeveloping opus, he enjoys handling the same themes, but with each work he attempts to deepen the experience for the viewer. His *Leap into the Void* (*Salto nel vuoto,* 1979) especially bears this out. The brother-sister relationship merging with the theme of insanity has its origins in the searing study of provincial family life of *Fists in the Pocket*. Bellocchio compares both films, especially in terms of sexuality and sensuality:

> *Leap into the Void* is a more chaste film but in which a sensuality emerges, at least I think so, that makes it possible to go beyond the blind rage of *I pugni in tasca;* it is this sexual investment that makes it possible to go beyond blind rage. . . . If one flies into a passion without a plan he can only go on killing; *I pugni in tasca* did not go any further. With *Leap into the Void* I have the feeling I've progressed: there's a plan and it's a plan that has something to do with Eros.[30]

With *Leap into the Void,* his cinematic essay on decadent family life plagued with insanity, he develops his material more intricately and ambiguously. At the film's screening at the 1980 Cannes Film Festival Bellocchio wrote about his fascination with the family:

> I like to tell stories and have always tried to dismantle the machinery of institutions like the family, the school, the armed forces.
> But first and foremost, it is the family that interests me. There is no tragedy, no suffering, that has not been prepared by our childhood.[31]

In the family apartment house in Rome, Marta Ponticelli (Anouk Aimée) lives with her brother Mauro (Michel Piccoli), a judge. On the brink of menopause, she realizes she has poured out her life for her brothers as governess, mother, and servant, and now has nothing to show for it. Her bitterness, depression, and tantrums increase. Mauro fears that madness may overcome his sister as it did one of their brothers. He decides to have her eliminated by a migrant actor, Giovanni Sciabola (Michele Placido), who may have been responsible for urging his mistress to jump to her death from a window. Once Marta and Giovanni meet, a simple loving relationship develops. Her whole bearing radically changes. Marta begins to relate tenderly to the maid Anna (Gisella Burinato) and her small son Giorgio (Piergiorgio Bellocchio). She becomes independent of Mauro at last. Feeling abandoned and depressed, Mauro supposedly casts himself out the window.

Apart from the documentary *Fit to Be Untied, Leap into the Void* could be considered Bellocchio's most intricate sociopsychological work to date. It will prepare the way for a profound study of a has-been actor (played by Lou Castel) in *The Eyes, the Mouth* (1983). In an original fashion in *Leap into the Void*, Bellocchio simultaneously removes the masks from society and reveals the scarred, ancient face of madness. He sets out to bare the human soul and succeeds. His process alternately repulses the spectator and draws him or her further into the psychodrama. It becomes a dance of death on a razor's edge.

The film could be entitled "The Life of a Couple," suggests Bellocchio, for this brother and sister form a couple, the basis of society. More than a married couple, who meet and wed at age twenty, Mauro and Marta share a childhood full of memories and fears. At the outset of the film, their relationship is one of dependence, especially Marta upon Mauro. It is not incestuous, however, for the director feels that incest should not be an everyday commodity in film.

In the course of the film it becomes clearer and clearer that Judge Ponticelli, like Captain Asciutto, is used to controlling everything and everyone around him. He can only relate to her in terms of control. He is terrified that she could lead a life on her own. His ethical sense leaves something to be desired here. When Marta's discreet madness turns into boisterous delirium, it embarrasses him in front of his neighbors. He thus decides that their relationship must be

Bellocchio's *Leap into the Void.* Judge Mario Ponticelli (Michel Piccoli) suggests to Giovanni (Michele Placido) that he murder the judge's sister Marta. *(Courtesy of Clesi Cinematografica, S.p.A.)*

Bellocchio's *Leap into the Void.* Marta (Anouk Aimée) learns the precious beauty of independence. *(Courtesy of Clesi Cinematografica, S.p.A.)*

terminated . . . for good. To do the job he manipulates Giovanni with a threat to reveal the real circumstances surrounding the death of the youth's mistress. When his scheme to have Giovanni dispose of Marta backfires, a reversal of roles occurs. Mauro becomes psychologically dependent upon Marta. The shift in psychology evolves subtly in the hands of Bellocchio.

Through implications, suggestions, and cursory shots or scenes, Bellocchio proposes love to be the true healing and liberating force in society. This ray of hope through love reflects a philosophy similar to Bergman's, Bellocchio observes, but the Swedish director usually has a greater tendency toward pessimism. The viewer is led to believe that a strong, unique relationship between Marta and Giovanni is constructed over a short period of time. Love destroys the bitterness and rage built up within Marta over the countless years of sacrifice. Love is the balm that soothes her wounded soul, then frees it. Bellocchio handles this emancipation of a woman in a complex society in a fascinating manner. Once out from under the thumb of her brother, Marta develops enough inner strength through love and self-assurance to evolve in another direction. She now feels free to go off to Ostia beach with her maid Anna and Anna's son Giorgio, leaving her brother to care for his own needs. He is unable to do so. His own self-confidence disintegrates.

Bellocchio shows Marta's awakening out of the range of the bourgeois judge's value system, as André Cornand writes.[32] Her contacts with the disadvantaged actor Giovanni give her a new lease on life. Anna, her maid, provides her with healthy companionship, despite the class gulf. The final shot of the film reveals Marta sensitively and tenderly climbing into bed with the maid's child, Giorgio.

Despite the almost linear development of the plot, Bellocchio manages to weave a web of ambiguity around the characters. The film opens with the enigmatic suicide of a woman who turns out to be Giovanni's mistress. It terminates with Mauro's leap from a window, which could be his own fantasm or Marta's nightmare at Ostia beach. In a surrealistic manner Bellocchio constructs a burglary of Mauro's home by Giovanni and his friends. Several children in nightshirts inexplicably wander through the place at the time. Is this an obsessive fear of the judge gradually losing his grip on reality, or did the scene actually occur? The final shot of the film also leaves the viewer with a heightened sense of bewilderment. At Ostia, Marta is awakened by a nightmare and suddenly feels liberated. The specter of her overpowering brother has vanished, but is it a symbolic or real disappearance?

Bellocchio implies past madness in the family history of Mauro and Marta. His treatment of this psychological theme is original, and yet its source in society is obvious. He situates personal mental illness in the wider context of contemporary society:

> I've been asked why I go on taking such an interest in madness. But it's obligatory if you want to try and understand the world we live in. In this unjust society, many people don't even have the indispensable to live on, but there are also many people who have more than enough and who act as if even the indispensable were lacking, are terrified of tomorrow, hoard gold and stuff their iceboxes with food, possessed by the terror of dying of hunger, of losing everything, of ending their days in the poorhouse, of sleeping under bridges (the great obsessions of the petty bourgeoisie have surfaced again, the same ones that permitted the rise of Fascism), and even go so far as to carry capsules of cyanide on them because, they say, they couldn't bear torture.[33]

Bellocchio poignantly shows that Marta's madness, an utter inability to cope with everyday pressures, is in reality "normal madness." As Victor Frankl points out from his concentration camp experiences, to act abnormally in an abnormal situation is indeed normal. Marta rightfully lashes out at the perversity of her brother in keeping her subservient in a claustrophobic milieu. Mauro, on the other hand, leads a normal, professional life. It is he, however, who is abnormal in keeping the emotional wraps on his sister. He abuses their relationship to such an extent he would coldly transgress the very law he represents to have her eliminated. In a complex society that reeks with madness, Bellocchio indicates in the film, the apparently mad are sane, and the supposedly normal are indeed abnormal.

The Seagull and *The Cinema Machine:* Invitation into the World of Television

In the oscillating patterns of Bellocchio's professional career, his creative works are not isolated islands. Each is intrinsically connected to something else— a theme, an autobiographical occurrence, an ideology. The two productions of

The Seagull (*Il gabbiano,* 1977), and *The Cinema Machine* (*La macchina cinema,* 1978), both destined for television, are similarly connected with other aesthetic experiences. Before the director undertook Chekhov's *Seagull,* he already had some acting experience at the Centro Sperimentale di Cinematografia almost twenty years earlier. In 1966, he played in Liliana Cavani's *Francis of Assisi* and three years later staged Shakespeare's *Timon of Athens* in the Piccolo Teatro di Milano. Bellocchio found the Eugenio Montale version of the Shakespeare play suffocating in view of the domination of theatrical structures and overwhelming presence of the actor Salvo Randone as Timon. He also discovered that a stage director is almost incidental in the eyes of the public. Nonetheless, in 1977 he undertook an adaptation for television of Anton Chekhov's *Seagull,* for which he assumed the roles of film and drama director.

Marcel Pagnol and Sacha Guitry in France during the first half of the century proved, with international success, that with "filmed theatre" it was still possible to be imaginative and entertaining. Both littérateurs-cinéastes were able to incorporate their own philosophy of life—sometimes optimistic, sometimes bitter—into a stage production that was then filmed. The Marseilles trilogy of Pagnol and the Paris boulevard plays of Guitry, most of which have been preserved on celluloid, testify to this. In his "filmed theatre" Bellocchio goes a step further.

In 1977, Bellocchio took Angelo Maria Ripellino's version of Chekov's nineteenth-century Russian play, staged it for Italian television (RAI), and then assured its international distribution as a film. Although he had read the play in secondary school and at the university, it was not until his 1964–65 stay in England that he had felt the true dramatic and psychological depth of the piece. He witnessed Tony Richardson's stage production of *The Seagull* with Vanessa Redgrave in the role of Nina. In a way, the play nostalgically recalled his own adolescence in the country, a life which he laments has disappeared because of mass consumerism today. In a preproduction statement Bellocchio mentioned: "*The Seagull* is one of my great literary passions, a text that I have always loved. I find certain autobiographical resonances in it."[34]

Bellocchio received financial backing from Italian television and collaborated with artists who had worked with him on numerous occasions—the actress Laura Betti *(In the Name of the Father),* the musician Nicola Piovani *(Victory March),* and the film editor Silvano Agosti *(Fists in the Pocket).* This was Bellocchio's first opportunity to adapt a script or literary text that was not his own in some way. Even the original script of *Rape on the Front Page* underwent drastic changes before the director began filming. Despite the adaptation, the production bore the personal stamp of Marco Bellocchio.

Gradually and amid pregnant silences, the characters emerge from the void: Constantin (Remo Girone), the young idealist poet who believes he can modify reality by his creation; his mother Arkadina (Laura Betti), a celebrated actress with a Mother Courage talent for domination and manipulation; her lover, the successful writer Trigorin (Giulio Brogi), suffocating in his compromises and contradictions; Nina (Pamela Villoresi), an aspiring actress who seeks the love of Trigorin as well as the fame of Arkadina; the young Mascia (Gisella Burinato), who complicates things by loving Constantin, who in turn loves Nina.

The relations oscillate between deepening and splitting. Constantin's beloved Nina escapes the provincial viper's tangle by pursuing an acting career in the city. She returns two years later, still in love with Trigorin. Constantin, utterly disillusioned, finds suicide the only realistic solution to his emotional and professional dilemmas.

In this adaptation of *The Seagull,* Bellocchio remains far removed from the political fiction and militant films of the late sixties. Instead he recreates the universe of his earlier works such as *Fists in the Pocket* and *China Is Near*—a closed, provincial, bourgeois milieu where emotionally wraught characters dramatically play out their morbid lives of madness, jealousy, and hostility. Bellocchio reflected on these powerful emotional motifs of the Chekhov play: "*The Seagull* plunged me back into this madness [of *Fists*], this anger which corresponded with a deep-seated need to modify reality."[35] Bellocchio told Aldo Tassone that the film represented for him a synthesis of themes which he found in his own life and other films, such as impotence, hatred, jealousy, and the temptation to suicide.[36] Their juxtaposition in Chekhov's play immediately attracted him.

Bellocchio recognizes himself in the characters of Constantin and Trigorin:

> I was Constantin (and perhaps still am), the young writer without fame or fortune who refuses to compromise, and for a time I was Trigorin (and still risk becoming him), the successful writer who considers himself beyond all question.[37]

The director had an instinctive sympathy for the young aspiring writer Constantin, although he does not share his final solution of suicide: "Even if the reality in which we live is shameful, we cannot abdicate from our struggle to master it."[38] During the production Bellocchio saw himself returning to his adolescence with the character of Constantin and then evolve into an adult through the personage of Trigorin. The director stated that he does not want to be Trigorin, even if the public considers him this type of individual.

In the society of gradual decomposition depicted in *The Seagull,* the artist is in jeopardy. Trigorin reflects the race of artists who willingly or unwillingly compromise their inner values to succeed. At the other extreme lies the purist Constantin, finally done in by failure and disillusionment when he refuses to compromise his ideals. For the director it was like having a constant dialectic taking place within him and around him while filming.

The television production of *The Seagull* was one of the most challenging undertakings in Bellocchio's career, he admitted. It held up a mirror to his professional life with respect to aesthetics and psychology. It also took its toll:

> Leaving aside the artistic result, which isn't for me to judge, I can say that I've never made a more depressing film, and that I've never wanted so much to flee or disappear. This anguish and despair have left their mark on the film. It's in the atmosphere of sickness and death, and also in the kind of detachment: the images seem to me to congeal, arranged according to a rhythm that doesn't want to get started, as if I wanted to keep them as far away from me as possible. I hope that I'll be more stable in the future, so that I never come to repeat such a crazy experiment.[39]

A second invitation into the television world came a year after *The Seagull* was aired. With the seasoned crew of *Fit to Be Untied*—Silvano Agosti, Sandro Petraglia, and Stefano Rulli—Bellocchio filmed five episodes of a series entitled *The Cinema Machine* (*La macchina cinema*). These episodes of forty-five minutes each were screened on five consecutive Wednesdays in November 1978.[40] A shorter version, like that of the second *Fit to Be Untied*, was planned for distribution on the usual parallel circuit of film clubs, classrooms, and special screenings.

Bellocchio places research among his highest priorities. This becomes most apparent in *The Cinema Machine*. As a result, the series is a fresh view of the cinema world from outside the border of a strip of celluloid. With his crew he tried to grasp the dual function of cinema—a mercantile one which draws in profit, and an entertaining one which provides dreams to dispel the ennui of everyday life. Through these several programs Bellocchio was able to demonstrate the personal as well as the collective aspect of cinema, and the financial as well as the therapeutic role of the medium.[41]

As with his other films on institutions, Bellocchio attempts to get at the inner workings of this octogenarian institution of cinema. Since his entry into the Centro Sperimentale in 1959, he had witnessed the challenges of acting and directing, as well as the problems of producing a' film, whether it be a documentary, militant film, or commercial feature. He now wished to reveal this world to the vast television public not in the traditional, objective manner that reflected a network's "ideology of pluralism," but with a partial perspective that reflected his own thesis about the viscissitudes of life in cinema. The five-part series laced with interviews was unequal in quality, but most revealing in tone and content. From frustrated directors with no future in the cinema world, to has-been actresses whom no one ever greets any more, Bellocchio runs the gamut of disheartening experiences. These individuals are on the periphery of cinema life now, appearing to emerge from a sequel to Robert Florey's *Life and Death of a Hollywood Extra*. In the editing of these numerous interviews, Bellocchio not only gives a documentary view of the double aspect of cinema as an industry and a dream world, but interprets the material. Once again this collective approach to cinema-television expands the director's personal world as well as the spectator's view of the media. He shares his insight into the results of his collaboration with the other members of the crew:

> The real world of cinema . . . is extremely contradictory, full of duplicity, and we ourselves lacked the enthusiasm needed to overcome some of these internal contradictions. Evident in the outcome is an ideological and stylistic compromise, the result of contradictions among the four of us that were not resolved.[42]

Conclusions

Bellocchio's fifteen-year output demonstrates a vast and eclectic series of experiences, none of which he regrets, most of which he can honestly assess and criticize several years after the fact. His personal life, interests, fears, and concerns motivated him to choose and create the works that make up his repertoire. His zigzagging career, to use his expression, brought him into contact with the short episode, the project, the collective film, the documentary, the militant tract, the commercial feature, and television production. In these undertakings, his protagonist, usually an antihero, suffocates from an overexposure to a corrupt and intransigent society and struggles for survival. Institutions, with their traditional power structures, oppose and sometimes destroy him. Madness, suicide, or compromise are the only other viable options.

Bellocchio's itinerary closely resembles the trajectory of several Italian filmmakers such as Bertolucci and Pasolini who evolved from the angry young man characteristic of the sixties to the mature, questioning cinéaste-psychologist of the seventies. These filmmakers' political analyses have been superseded by their almost clinical and psychological treatment of the pressure points in society, whether it be in Bertolucci's *Luna,* Pasolini's *Pigsty,* or Bellocchio's *Leap into the Void.* The films of these three directors thus indicate the correlation of politics and psychology in contemporary Italian culture, reopening the sores of a society beset with many ills.

At the release of Bellocchio's *Fists in the Pocket,* Pasolini fittingly brings to a close their epistolary debate over the film. It sheds some light on Bellocchio's vocation as a cinematic gadfly and his career as a deeply committed filmmaker:

Dear Bellocchio:
  To conclude our debate of loners, I would like you to go on disturbing the conscience of the Army, the Magistracy, the reactionary clergy, and lastly the Italian petty bourgeoisie to which we have the dishonor of belonging.[43]

5

GILLO PONTECORVO:
At the Perilous Crossroads of History

> Cinema can be a way of revitalizing a people's deadened
> responses. We have been conditioned to absorb a false vi-
> sion of reality that is dominated by the tastes, morals, and
> perceptions of the 'establishment.' To forego the possibility
> of opposing the *fictions* diffused by this establishment is at
> least irresponsible. That is why I believe in a cinema which
> addresses itself to the masses and not a cinema for the elite.
>
> —Pontecorvo, 1972

Gillo Pontecorvo differs greatly from the Italian politically oriented filmmakers presented thus far—Rosi, Pasolini, Bertolucci, and Bellocchio. His subjects touch on non-Italian events and are financed through major European or American coproductions. Instead of a feature film on the average of every two years, as has been the case for the others, Pontecorvo completes one every four or five years. To date he has made five films over more than twenty years. Politically, he saw more action than the other cinéastes, clandestinely fighting in the Resistance during World War II and then later working full-time as a Communist militant. Unlike Pasolini and Bellocchio, whose Catholicism had returned to haunt them, Pontecorvo has his religious roots in Judaism. Yet such evidence is rarely seen in his films, save for *Kapò*, dealing with the concentration camps. For his films, he makes use of his political experiences, interests, hobbies, and talents, but differing from Bertolucci or Bellocchio, does not allow his autobiography, however rich it may be, to come to the surface in his cinematic work.

Gillo Pontecorvo, born in Pisa in 1919, belongs more to the generation of Rosi and Pasolini than to Bertolucci's and Bellocchio's. Like Pasolini, he made his first feature as he was approaching forty. Gillo was one of ten children born to a scientifically oriented family; his father was an industrialist and his mother from a family of doctors. The critic Massimo Ghirelli, describing the biographical background of Pontecorvo, notes that it was the custom in the family that the young men take up the sciences, and the young women literature.[1] Such was the case with the eldest son, who became a biologist, and two others, physicists. One

182

of them, Bruno, allegedly offered British nuclear secrets to the Soviets in 1950. Gillo dutifully followed the family tradition by studying chemistry at the University of Pisa. He was dissatisfied with his exposure to the academic world and abandoned his chemistry studies. The time spent in it, however, brought him into contact with many antifascist professors and students. He left Pisa because of anti-Semitic laws and went to Paris where journalism became a major interest. He enrolled in a journalism program that eventually led to a position with Agence Havas (Agence France-Presse today) and later to a job as Paris correspondent for *La Repubblica* and *Paese Sera*. In his travels to the north of France to report on a mining strike, he became more and more interested in the photography and documentary side of journalism. Social and political questions began to draw his attention more and more.

In 1941, Pontecorvo joined the Italian Communist Party. His clandestine party activities centered around the north of Italy, where he assisted in creating a network of partisans. He participated in the guerrilla activity of the Garibaldi Brigade. From 1943 to the Liberation in 1945, under the *nom de guerre* of Barnaba, he was a leader in the Resistance in Milan.

Pontecorvo's work with the party during the war furnished him with invaluable political and military experience. Following the Liberation he stayed with the party as a full-time militant member, despite the fact that from 1948 to 1956, according to Franco Solinas, it was a difficult time to be a Communist. As a party worker he had a double responsibility. He first served in the leadership of the youth movement during and after the war. Giorgio Amendola witnessed Pontecorvo's commitment and leadership in this area of the party's activities: "In a brief time, the *Fronte della gioventù*, under the direction of Gillo, became an essential force in the struggle of the people of Turin."[2] His second duty was to assist in the preparation of newsreel materials for the archives of the Communist party. He manifested an absolute fidelity to the party ideology until 1956. Then came the Hungarian crisis. The Soviet role in the intervention was one of several factors that brought on his exit from the party. Many of his Italian comrades had their faith in the party shaken by these events of 1956, just as others in France and Italy in 1968 and 1979 would have at the time of other Soviet interventions. Although Pontecorvo formally left the party in 1956 because he no longer totally agreed with its policies, he did not completely break his ties with its general direction or underlying Marxist principles. He is still on "friendly" terms with the party.

As with his journalistic work prior to and during the war, his involvement with the Communist party led him to greater reflection on sociopolitical problems in society. His outlet for this interest would soon be cinema. One day in Paris at the Salle Pleyel, he saw for the first time Rossellini's *Paisà* (1946). He compared the experience to being struck by a lightning bolt. The entire film, but especially the sixth episode about the Po, deeply moved him. It was at that moment, he later acknowledged, that he decided to switch from journalism to cinema.

Pontecorvo's apprenticeship in film came through working as assistant for Yves Allégret (*Les miracles n'ont lieu qu'une fois*, 1950), Giancarlo Menotti (*La medium*), as well as Mario Monicelli (*Le infedeli*, 1952, and *Totò e Carolina*, 1955) from whom Pontecorvo learned the most about technique. Pontecorvo had already been somewhat initiated into the film world in 1946. He served as Aldo Vergano's third assistant for *The Sun Still Rises* (*Il sole sorge ancora,* 1946). In view of budgetary restrictions the technicians were asked to play secondary roles in the film. Pontecorvo convincingly became a martyred partisan. His readings of the neorealist critic and theoretician Umberto Barbaro and of the Marxist critic and philosopher Georg Lukács brought him closer to the sociopolitical cinema. Viewing the politically committed masterpieces of Rossellini and the other neorealists and such works as Nicolai Ekk's *The Road to Life* (1931) opened new avenues of interest to him.

From his first short documentary *The Timiriazev Mission* in 1953 to the most recent feature *The Tunnel* in 1979, Pontecorvo allowed the three currents of leftist politics, journalism, and cinema to weave in and out of his life. Relying upon extensive research and documentation, collaborating especially with his screenwriter Franco Solinas, and making use of Marxist procedures, Pontecorvo has given a significant impetus to the political film, both documentary and fiction. Once a producer assures Pontecorvo of adequate financing for his project, the director turns to the co-creator of most of his feature films, the novelist, journalist, and screenwriter Franco Solinas. He is an absolutely essential part of the production, serving as the source of ideas on the one hand, and an echo on the other. Director and screenwriter spend several months in the discussion and research stage, and then Solinas tranquilly writes at the edge of the sea, sometimes for several months before the two artists are content with their product. The Sardinian writer came to Rome during World War II, joined the Resistance at age sixteen, and at the close of the war, the Communist party. His work for Pontecorvo has alternated with scriptwriting for Francesco Rosi (*Salvatore Giuliano*), Damiano Damiani (*Quien sabe?*), Costa-Gavras (*State of Siege*) and Joseph Losey (*Monsieur Klein*). Most importantly, the screenwriter shares Pontecorvo's perspective on political cinema:

> Let's first say that movies have an accessory and not a decisive usefulness in the various events and elements that contribute to the transformation of society. It is naïve to believe that you can start a revolution with a movie and even more naïve to theorize about doing so. Political films are useful on the one hand if they contain a correct analysis of reality and on the other if they are made in such a way to have that analysis reach the largest possible audience.[3]

Until his sudden death in 1982, Solinas's continued membership in the Communist party and his Marxist reading reinforced his sense of discipline and responsibility in his research and helped guide him in the choice of realistic historical and political themes.

At the outset of their project, Pontecorvo and Solinas advance their initial ideas with a vast series of records and documents and then interviews with participants in the particular historical event. The themes that attract these two Marxist individuals—Nazism, imperialism, colonialism, terrorism—come right from crucial moments of recent history. They situate themselves at the crossroads of history and ask the ultimate hows and whys. Then together filmmaker and writer work out the concrete details of the script. The two perfectionists belabor the text. Solinas writes and rewrites the same page up to twenty times, he mentioned in our 1981 interview. They synthesize politics and history with the hope that they can make the latter more comprehensible to a mass public today.

The political stance that they take in their scriptwriting, primarily leftist, revolutionary, and anti-Establishment, leans toward the underdog engaged in a battle against a powerful and destructive force. They back the individual and the collective group who are oppressed and degraded, whether it be by National Socialism or British colonialism. The characters that they forge from the actual reality personify the major historical forces in conflict. In this way their Marxist dialectic becomes an instrument of enlightenment in their hands. Through their depiction of painful moments of degradation and growth in contemporary history, they deliberately set out to be didactic. They insert into the mouths of the protagonists and antagonists political messages that would oblige the public to reflect on a particular issue. In this manner they update Rossellini's desire for an educational, instructional cinema.

From Journalism to the Documentary

Pontecorvo's political background gave him a strong basis for his sociopolitical filmmaking of the fifties. He purchased a 16mm Paillard camera and financed his own production. The results were fifteen or twenty short documentaries, examples of serious filmmaking. One of the first films he completed dealt with the 1951 floods of the Po delta. In 1953, he shot a thirty-minute short *The Timiriazev Mission* (Missione Timiriazev) in 16 mm and then afterwards had it enlarged to 35 mm. The following year he made two documentaries with Rome as the setting—*Dogs behind Bars (Cani dietro le sbarre)* and *The Portese Gate (Porta Portese).* *Dogs behind Bars* shows the city dog pound where the animals were prepared for death, recalling the old man's search for his pet in De Sica's *Umberto D.* His other film dealt with the activity of a flea market in the capital. In 1955, he filmed two other shorts *Festivities at Castelluccio (Festa a Castelluccio)* and *Men of Marble (Uomini del marmo).* Ghirelli speaks of the first as a celebration in the northern plateau region to dispel winter boredom, and the second as a testimony to hard work on the slopes of the Alpi Apuane.[4] Perhaps the most successful of the documentaries was *Bread and Sulphur (Pane e zolfo)* filmed in 1956 with the financial assistance of the Ministry of Labor. Pontecorvo shot the film at Cabernardi in Sicily. The work dealt with a group of striking miners who occupied the mine. It described their daily existence from their strenuous everyday labors to their Sunday celebrations. The director was right on location for the strike and was challenged by the strikers when he began filming.

For Pontecorvo these few documentaries served as a hiatus between his photographic experience as a journalist and his documented political fiction films. In his dual professions his quest for absolute veracity—if that were possible—

obliged him to work under "the dictatorship of truth," to spend months scrutinizing all sides of an issue, and to photograph a reconstructed event. He thus had as his goal the recreation of reality with dramatic intensity.

Giovanna: An Episode of Commitment

The genre of the episode or sketch film, in which Bertolucci, Bellocchio, and Pasolini had invested their talent, became for Pontecorvo a testing ground to prove himself as a filmmaker and a launching pad for his personal political ideology. In 1956, the year of the Soviet intervention in Hungary and Pontecorvo's concomitant departure from the Communist party, the young documentarist offered his contribution to Joris Ivens's *The Windrose (Die Windrose).*[5] The Women's International Democratic Federation sponsored a film in episode form that would treat various problems women experienced in contemporary society. The Dutch political filmmaker Joris Ivens *(The Spanish Earth, Know Your Enemy: Japan, La Seine a recontré Paris)* assumed the responsibility for the coordination of the various episodes to be filmed by an international representation of cinéastes—Alex Viany, Wuo Kuo-Yin, Sergei Gerasimov, and Yannick Bellon. The producer Giuliano De Negri, very committed to political films, invited Pontecorvo to direct the Italian segment of the film. Alberto Cavalcanti would assist Ivens in the supervision of the production and take care of the prologue. Ivens describes the approach taken in the organization of the film:

> The order and content of the five sequences were decided. First Brazil, telling the story of Estella (played by Vanja Orico), an agricultural day laborer. Then in the Soviet Union Nadezhda (played by Zinaida Kiriyenko), a girl from a collective farm who is leaving for the south to help cultivate the new land. Third would be Italy with a strike by textile workers (one of the workers played by Klara Pozzi). In France the struggle of a progressive teacher (played by Simone Signoret) and in China the position of women in the new cooperatives in the villages (the protagonist played by Yen Mei-yi). . . . The task given to me in Berlin was to help in defining the final form of these national productions and to coordinate all the artistic efforts.[6]

Pontecorvo's contribution would be a modest one, but he enjoyed an absolute freedom only comparable to what he experienced in the *Battle of Algiers* production, remarks Massimo Ghirelli.[7] Franco Solinas, then novelist and critic from *L'Unità,* collaborated with him on the script. Giuliano Montaldo who would go on to become a firstrate filmmaker with, for example, *Sacco and Vanzetti,* served as first assistant and production director. The actors would be nonprofessionals, the beginning of a very positive experience for Pontecorvo.

A double growth in consciousness occurs in a proletarian couple. A group of workers occupies a textile plant. One of the factory workers, Giovanna (Clara Pozzi), wishes to become involved in the political action, but her husband (perhaps Communist), a metallurgical laborer, is opposed to it. He believes that a political protest is no place for women. Defiant, she decides to lend her support to the movement. Feeling very much separated from her family, Giovanna leaves the factory to join them. She suddenly realizes that her true place is with the strikers and returns. Finally her husband begins to understand his wife's political vocation.

In this period of intense politicization of the masses during the Cold War, Pontecorvo shows the political involvement of the workers in their solidarity against labor injustices. At the core of the film, however, is a woman's understanding of her role in the political action. Pontecorvo thus refers to *Giovanna* as a feminist film *ante litteram*.[8] It has its analogue in Herbert Biberman's *Salt of the Earth* (1954) in which the wives of striking miners take up the protest when the husbands are prevented by law from striking and eventually win their cause. Pontecorvo's forty-five minute film may be considered propaganda for the Women's International Democratic Federation. It is filmed nonetheless with a very human optic and touches a pressure point in society.

The French critics at the time of the 1956 Venice Film Festival, according to Pontecorvo, spoke of *Giovanna* as reflecting "the purest of neorealist styles."[9] The director often referred to himself as "a late son of neorealism," following especially in the footsteps of Rossellini. In fact, Pontecorvo believes, his ideal director would be comprised of three-quarters Rossellini and one quarter Eisenstein. *Giovanna* exemplifies the neorealistic tradition and the Soviet classic propaganda film, even though both movements had almost faded out. The social realism, nonprofessional actors, and leftist orientation which characterize *Giovanna*, give it a sociopolitical flavor that will later strikingly mark the director's opus.

The Long Blue Road/The Rift: A False Start

Pontecorvo's very positive experience with *Giovanna* in collaboration with artists who shared his sociopolitical vision disappeared like gunsmoke on a windy day. *The Long Blue Road* (*La lunga strada azzurra*, 1957) became possible through a collaborative effort of the Italian and Yugoslav film industry. The work, dealing with an anarchistic fisherman from Sardinia—but filmed off the coast of Dalmatia—was the exact opposite of the earlier, ideal working situation. The factory milieu of *Giovanna* turned into a Cinecittà-type atmosphere. It resulted in "a very bad film," Pontecorvo told Harold Kalishman.[10] The director wanted to shoot in black and white for greater realism as he had seen in Visconti's *The Earth Trembles*. Instead, the producer required color for commercial reasons. For the lead characters, weathered fishermen torn by misery, Pontecorvo hoped for nonprofessionals. Little known actors would not attract the general public, believed the producer. Pontecorvo instead got Yves Montand and Alida Valli, neither of whom would have the physical composure of a lower-class individual struggling for existence. Compromises therefore had to be made, especially when it was a question of a young director's first feature film. The limited budget and the tight shooting schedule further hampered Pontecorvo's creativity. He considered dropping the project, but Franco Solinas, from whose short novel *Squarciò* came the idea of the film, convinced the director otherwise.

In a little port in the Adriatic, the local fishermen eke out an unfortunate existence. A manipulative wholesaler keeps them oppressed. Squarciò (Yves Montand), with an expectant wife, Rosetta (Alida Valli), and two children, survives on his own by illegally fishing with depth charges. His close friend Salvatore (Francisco Rabal) struggles to establish a cooperative. Squarciò is not interested. He continues to fish illegally and has a few encounters with the law. As a result of an explosive blast, Squarciò is mortally wounded. He dies advising his two sons to go to Salvatore and join the cooperative.

Pontecorvo felt he could only salvage three or four sequences from this *"brutto film."* Even though Franco Solinas's novel had all the right sociopolitical ingredients, the exigencies of the production "Hollywoodized" them. The struggle of an oppressed group against a powerful force—the daily heroism of the poor—took on a melodramatic form which dampened the realism of the motifs. Yves Montand, in hindsight, considered the film "rather schematic," possessing "a Manichaean side to the story."[11]

Kapò: An Early Holocaust Study

Four decades have passed since the German labor camps were transformed into extermination centers for European Jews and political dissenters. The survivors pledged never to forget what happened at Dachau, Auschwitz, and Mathausen. Documentary films like Alain Resnais's *Night and Fog* (1956) or C. Lanzmann's *Shoah* (1985), feature films of reconstruction such as Wanda Jakubowska's *The Last Stop* (1948), and television docudramas—*Holocaust* (1978) and *Playing for Time* (1980)—opened the wounds of our civilized society and remind us, as did Resnais at the end of his brutal documentary, that it could happen again.[12]

In 1959, Solinas and Pontecorvo decided to cooperate on another film. This time they would try to evoke the historical tragedy of the concentration camps through images of human degradation and frailty. For this Italo-French-Yugoslav production the writer and director travelled about Europe for eight months to document their work. With tape recorder in hand they interviewed one deportee after another until they could piece together every minor detail of the tragic life in the camps. Once Solinas and Pontecorvo had the raw material on hand, they were able to weave a narrative that could speak honestly to the historical events. The basis of their story in *Kapò* was an actual incident of an escape by a group of Red Army soldiers from Treblinka.

A doctor in a Nazi concentration camp saves the life of a young Jewish girl, Edith (Susan Strasberg), by giving her a new identity—Nicole, political prisoner 10099. The frail Nicole is helped greatly by the tender Teresa (Emanuelle Riva), a translator. Teresa eventually commits suicide by running into the electrified barrier. Nicole proceeds to exchange body and soul for survival, comfort, and power. When a group of captured Russian soldiers arrives in camp, she falls in love with one of them named Sacha (Laurent Terzieff). To redeem herself she assists in the escape of the Russians, but is shot shortly after she sabotages the electrical fence. Sacha, alone amidst the pile of dead prisoners, screams out in anguish.

To create a look of authenticity, the film crew constructed a realistic concentration camp a few miles from Belgrade and shot in black and white. After several experiments in the laboratory, Pontecorvo produced a grainy effect and high contrast by taking a negative from the positive. This process of "dupe negative" added an unrefined, historical tone to the quasi-documentary material.

In this anti-Nazi film Pontecorvo graphically traces the descent of a human being—Nicole—to the lowest possible level before salvation comes. The brutality of the S.S., as well as the animalistic tendencies of the women prisoners, show the grim, subhuman side of life in the camps. Except for Teresa, only Sacha and a few of his Russian comrades come across as warm human beings.

Despite the realism emanating from the raw material and technique of the production, as well as the most credible acting of Susan Strasberg (Anne Frank on Broadway) and Laurent Terzieff, *Kapò* suffers from a double weakness. The final sequences of the love affair of Nicole and Sacha turned the tragic historical scene into an unrealistic melodrama. Pontecorvo finds this fifteen-minute part of the narrative artificial, overly sentimental, and old-fashioned, he admitted to Harold Kalishman. At the time this type of tone in commercial film was in vogue, and even the neorealist films had emotional endings, for example *Bicycle Thieves, Open City,* and *Umberto D.* In our interview of January 1982 he accepted the full responsibility for the inclusion of the love story into the script. The material and tone of the film were too stark, Solinas and Pontecorvo felt. Both debated for over a week about the addition and then decided to go with the relationship to lighten the atmosphere. Pontecorvo realizes that this was a major mistake, for it brought about a significant shift in tone and therefore destroyed the unity of style as a result. Pontecorvo said that if he had to do the film over again, he would eliminate the romance.

The second detrimental factor is the melodramatic music which accompanies this relationship. In the earlier part of the film, the emotional depth of Carlo Rustichelli's and Pontecorvo's score underlines the tension and anguish of the women's lot. When it provides the background aural atmosphere for the love affair, it tears one away from the harsh realism of the actual horrors.[13] If it were not for the melodramatic conclusion of the film, most critics believe that *Kapò* would have been one of the most striking testimonies to the concentration camp experience.[14]

The Battle of Algiers: The Painful Birth of a Nation

On 7 January 1981, a polemic film festival began at the St. Séverin cinema house in Paris's Latin Quarter. It featured films made about the Algerian struggle for independence: Laurent Heynemann's *La question;* René Vautier's *Avoir vingt ans dans les Aurès;* Michel Drach's *Elise ou la vraie vie;* Jean-Luc Godard's *Le petit soldat;* and Pontecorvo's *Battle of Algiers* (*La battaglia di Algeri/La bataille d'Algers*, 1966). The lobby of the theatre was filled with information on the war. Propaganda posters representing all sides of the question lined the walls. One illustrated a parachutist's call to action, while another showed a demonstration by the Socialist party against the war. Still others communicated a call to arms for the OAS (Organisation armée secrète) or the French Algerians. Coming almost twenty years after the declaration of independence, one would have thought the dust of hatred, bitterness, and division had settled. The war was not over for some. The theatre was fire-bombed by a group of Fascists—some say OAS—just a few days after the program began. For the rest of the festival the lobby bore traces of the attack—a reminder of the terrorism of the war so emotionally described in Pontecorvo's film. To grasp the complex nuances of the film one must resort to a historical flashback.

The war for Algerian independence from the French—beginning with a series of "disturbances" throughout Algeria in November 1954 and ending with the Evian Accords in March 1962—has its roots in French colonial policies. French settlers first arrived in Algeria in 1830. A few decades later greater waves of French disembarked in the North African country to settle in the major cities. French and Arab lived side by side in these cities, but with hardly any contact. The European settlers brought their own culture and language with them, and did not mingle or marry with the Algerians in principle. While the French built up a strong economic, educational, and cultural system, the native Algerians sunk lower into the socioeconomic quagmire of their daily existence. The Arab population encountered widespread unemployment (or menial jobs as unskilled laborers), poor educational facilities, and inadequate housing. In the early fifties, ten million or so native Algerians more fully realized that they were in fact menial pawns in the service of the one million *pieds noirs*, the European settlers. The time was ripe for the Algerians to remove the colonialist burden from their shoulders.

The film begins: "Not one foot of newsreel has been used in this reenactment of the Battle of Algiers."

Dawn, 7 October 1957. A tortured Algerian nationalist reveals to Colonel Mathieu (Jean Martin) the hiding place of the sole surviving guerrilla leader, Ali la Pointe (Brahim Haggiag). The army surrounds the cache, prepared to dynamite it if Ali does not surrender. From the faces of the four pensive Algerian freedom fighters within—Ali, the boy guerrilla Omar (Mohammed Ben Kassen), the young woman Hassiba (Fawzia El Kader), and the newly married Mahmoud—there is a flashback to 1 November 1954. A message from the National Liberation Front incites the Arab population of the Casbah to break loose from the bonds of colonial misery. The struggle commences.

Over the next three years terrorist attacks increase on both sides. An innocent Arab worker, Lardjane Boualem, is accused of killing a policeman. In retaliation, a French assistant commissioner has a bomb placed near the Arab's residence in the Casbah. The National Liberation Front seeks vengeance. Three women from the Casbah penetrate the heavily guarded French sector and plant bombs in a milk bar, cafeteria, and Air France

terminal. Colonel Mathieu and his parachutists systematically eliminate cells of the guer-
rilla movement. When they finally arrest the intellectual Ben M'Hidi and the key leader
Saari Kader, known as Djafar (Yacef Saadi), only Ali remains. Following his death, the
Battle of Algiers comes to a close, a victory for the French. But in 1960, the phoenix of the
revolutionary movement rises out of the Casbah and wins its independence in 1962.

Shortly after completing *Kapò,* Franco Solinas and Pontecorvo undertook a
new collaborative project called *Para,* short for *Parachutiste,* the sophisticated,
highly trained French paratrooper. It was to deal with a polished and articulate
paratrooper from the French upper middle class who fought in Indochina and
Algiers. He represented for Pontecorvo the efficient but hollow class in society.
The former paratrooper returns to Algeria as a reporter for the equivalent to
Paris Match, and his eyes are opened wide by what he sees. For documentation
Solinas and Pontecorvo went to Algiers while the *pieds noirs* were making their
last stand on the eve of Algerian independence. They assembled the script and
had even thought of an actor like Paul Newman or Warren Beatty for the major
role. The producer and distributor, however, feared OAS retaliation for the proposed film and so discontinued their support. This film project was necessarily
shelved.

Several years later, in 1965, Yacef Saadi, president of Casbah Films and former
leader of the Algerian resistance movement, came to Italy to create an Italian-
Algerian coproduction dealing with the war of liberation. Three directors were
considered: Francesco Rosi, Luchino Visconti, and Gillo Pontecorvo. Rosi was
unable to accept the invitation in view of his commitment to *More Than a Miracle*
(C'era una volta) in Spain. Visconti was not interested in the project. Pontecorvo
accepted, but with several conditions that would provide him more artistic freedom than he had with his earlier feature films. The Italian producer Antonio
Muso came to terms with Saadi on financial matters, equipment, crew, and locations. The production of *The Battle of Algiers* was now underway.

Six months of intensive research preceded another six months of scriptwriting. For the film, the three-year period covered in the history of the bloody birth
of a nation was documented by interviews with former paratroopers and officers
in Paris as well as Arab revolutionaries in Algeria. Guerrilla dynamiters furnished minute details about their missions. Saadi provided his view from the top.
Newsreel footage, police reports, and newspaper accounts gave a day-to-day account of the struggle. Further materials came from the writings of Franz Fanon
on colonialism in *The Wretched of the Earth,* and from Saadi's own account of the
battle, *Souvenirs de la bataille d'Alger* (1961). The meticulously prepared *Para* script
provided only the basic inspiration, "the conflict between Western civilization and
the filth of the colonial regime," Franco Solinas specified.[15]

For *The Battle of Algiers* Pontecorvo demanded documentary realism in a reconstructed series of historical events. His expectations were met. One would almost
believe that the director integrated into the film newsclips, for example, of the
massive feverish demonstrations against the French shortly prior to independence. At the time of the film's nomination for an Oscar, Pontecorvo's American

friends suggested a preface to the film to dispel the belief that it was a documentary. His achievement of this heightened realism resulted from several factors. The documentation was detailed, precise, and it recorded the actual events with dramatic intensity. Solinas had access to the police archives, for example, and he was thus able to give the precise time, date, and place of each police assassination, as well as the tone and content of the police interrogations that took place. Solinas and Pontecorvo juxtaposed differing perspectives on the conflict, most fairly well delineated and nuanced. Because of the cooperation of the Boumedienne government in Algeria, Pontecorvo was able to shoot on the actual locations in the European sector of the city of Algiers as well as the Casbah.

For his actors, primarily nonprofessional, Pontecorvo used Algerians who either participated in the war or heard inside reports of the military activities from family and friends. Getting Arab women to play various roles such as those on the bombing mission was a major challenge, given the very restrictive national customs. The French in the film came from groups of Europeans who settled in the city after independence. Yacef Saadi, the producer, played himself, the rebel leader responsible for the dynamiting retaliations. His vivid description of actual urban guerrilla warfare fills the screen at the key moments of struggle. For Ali la Pointe, Pontecorvo discovered in the market place Brahim Haggiag, an illiterate peasant who would become the impulsive rebel. The revolutionary boy prodigy Omar was the nephew of Saadi. For Colonel Mathieu Pontecorvo chose the theatre and film actor Jean Martin.[16] The French actor lost his job at the Compagnie Barrault-Renaud in Paris for affixing his signature to the anti-Algerian war statement, *"Manifeste des 121,"* which favored draft resistance to the colonial war.[17] With this blend of committed actors, primarily nonprofessional, Pontecorvo realistically evoked the actual characters in their historical context.

The physical starkness and the documentary tone of the film resulted from the photographic developing process and the usage of lens. With *Kapò*, Pontecorvo and his director of photography, Marcello Gatti, experimented on producing a newsreel effect by making a negative of the positive in the laboratory. In preparation for *The Battle of Algiers,* Pontecorvo and Gatti experimented again with the process, shooting in 16mm and 35mm, this time before the actual filming. They could thus compensate with other technical factors during the shooting and control the tone more closely. In this fashion they were able to get the desired grainy newsreel effect in their black-and-white photography, a type of hyper-realism. For more than a decade the public was fed on television news reporting. At a safe distance from the action, a news reporter and cameraman stood, filming with a 200 or 300mm lens and commenting upon the particular event. Truth at a distance! To reproduce this sensation of a media report Pontecorvo and Gatti used the same type of telephoto lenses. To give the effect of documenting a quasi-Martian invasion, according to Pontecorvo, he filmed Colonel Mathieu and the paratroopers with a 600mm lens. The blanched images of the general strike and the final demonstrations with frenzied gestures, banners, and screams could easily be considered television footage on the Six O'Clock News.

There exists an underlying philosophy behind this reconstructed realism, and it is integrally tied into Pontecorvo's correlation of truth and history. PierNico

Solinas in the introduction to his translation and study of the script and film presents the kernel of the complex problem:

> For Gillo Pontecorvo the remaking of history, or shooting under what he calls "the dictatorship of truth," is not simply a re-creation of past events through *cinéma vérité* technique, nor the repiecing of history for history's sake; it is, rather, a deliberate rearrangement of chosen fact for a didactic purpose. Without adding fiction to the facts he seeks to probe beneath the surface, by stripping history of the superfluous and reducing it to its essentials, to re-examine and re-evaluate the basic concept of the historical event in point. In exploring its most significant implications, he seeks to draw from history a critical conclusion that can exist independently of the Algerian struggle.[17]

Gillo Pontecorvo not only edits for didactic purposes but obviously dramatizes and telescopes the events. He takes a calculated risk in fictionalizing the material. His professional work in journalism shaped his desire for truth in the revelation of an occurrence, but also brought out his sensitivity to historical development. A further influence upon his perception of history derives from his fifteen-year affiliation with the Communist party. As with his other films, a Marxist perception of history characterizes Pontecorvo's *The Battle of Algiers*. Pauline Kael once referred to the director as "a Marxist poet," the most dangerous of Marxists. Franco Solinas, who shares this Marxist vision of history, specifies: "So for me *The Battle of Algiers* is the result of those Marxist procedures: an analysis of two conflicting forces motivated by contingent rather than idealistic terms."[18] In collaborating with Pontecorvo, Solinas manifests the same sensitivity to history, but further notes that there is no such thing as objectivity, absolute truth. Honesty and integrity should be guiding lights, he affirms. The director and screenwriter must, above all, show sound reasons for their actions and choices.

Pontecorvo personifies the two historical forces of the Algerians and the French with the characters of Ali la Pointe and Colonel Mathieu. Others also play a major role in this segment of the revolution, such as Omar, Hassiba, Djabar, and more importantly, the inhabitants of the Casbah, the "choral protagonist," according to Pontecorvo, with whom the public is meant to identify. In hostile confrontation, Ali and Mathieu create a greatly sought-after dialectic in the director's didactic schema. Ali, this "Third World Salvatore Giuliano," represents his people. He is an illiterate man of the lower class who evolves into a revolutionary firebrand. Misery was a major factor that led him to this vocation of anti-European dissident. The guillotining of a political prisoner shouting "Long Live Algeria" rekindles it. Martyrdom is not too high a price to pay for his ideals.

Colonel Mathieu, a composite of three or four French officers, notably Colonel Bigeard and General Jacques Massu, is a more complex force. This "latter day Caesar," to use David Wilson's expression, is, on the one hand, a most rational and articulate individual. He is a product of a higher structure in a supercivilized society, the bourgeoisie. On the other, this Machiavellian soldier cooly accepts the principle of torture, even though he sees it as a dehumanizing means to a desired end—eventual victory. Mathieu represents the colonialists, present for 130 years, who believe that Algeria should still be French. He is their military instrument in

Pontecorvo's ***The Battle of Algiers.*** Guerrilla leader Ali la Pointe prior to his recruitment by the FLN. *(Courtesy of Trastevere Film Theatre.)*

Algeria, their hope to win the war. John Talbott's description of General Jacques Massu in his military context has a fitting parallel to Colonel Mathieu:

> General Jacques Massu, the Tenth Division commander [of paratroopers], in effect took over as police chief of Algiers. But the Special Powers Law made him a special kind of chief, independent not only of the municipal authorities, by virtue of his military status, but also of the military chain of command. A veteran of the prewar Army of Africa, of the Free French Forces, of Indochina and Suez, a man whose rough-hewn looks and reputation as a warrior reminded observers of one of Napoleon's Imperial Guardsmen, Massu had the operational responsibility for conducting what quickly became known as the "Battle of Algiers." His division of eight thousand men was composed in large part of regiments shot to pieces in Indochina, then rebuilt and renamed. The paratroopers faced the task of restoring order in a hilly seaport roughly the size of San Francisco.[19]

Yacef Saadi is another important figure in the revolution. As Djabar in the film, he appears cool, resourceful, and fearless. Like Mathieu, he is ruthless when it comes to military tactics. Sentiment has no place in military battle. He engineers the bombing missions, realizing the innocent French lives that would be lost, but more fully understanding that it is a bloody means needed to obtain the long-hoped-for end—liberation. He was condemned to death in 1958 for his role in the revolution, but was pardoned by de Gaulle. John Talbott offers another reading of Saadi:

> Residents of the Casbah regarded Yacef as a loafer, a soccer enthusiast, a ladies' man. The French police knew his record as a political agitator—he had belonged to the short-lived Organisation Secrète—but they did not suspect he was the chief terrorist of Algiers.[20]

On a more general ideological level, Pontecorvo pits the dialectical forces of colonialism and revolution against each other. Repression, racism, and paternalism characterize the French colonialists. They follow misguided principles in order to retain their power in a colonialist position that is untenable in contemporary society. Pontecorvo's thesis, often mistaken for anti-French, could be more aptly considered anticolonialist. The producer Yacef Saadi reiterated the anticolonialist intentions in filming *The Battle of Algiers:*

> I have substituted the camera for the machine gun. . . . The idea of reliving those days and arousing the emotions I felt moved me greatly. But there is no rancor in my memories. Together with our Italian friends, we desired to make an objective, equilibrated film, that is not a trial of a people or of a nation, but a heartful act of accusation against colonialism, violence, and war.[21]

In a more positive light, Pontecorvo presents the revolutionaries struggling against insurmountable odds, especially with the arrival of Mathieu's crack military force. The director shows the irreversibility of the revolutionary process once the people become conscious of their national identity. He describes the revolution as a surging river that has flowed underground for more than a century and now finally breaks out into the open. With a more violent image he

Pontecorvo's **The Battle of Algiers.** One of the final struggles for independence from French rule. (*Courtesy of Trastevere Film Theatre.*)

considers it a weapon that has been loaded for many years and has finally been fired. Consequently, *The Battle of Algiers* has the immediacy of a guerrilla handbook in the midst of the flames of revolution. In fact, in the trial of thirteen Black Panthers in 1970, the prosecution reportedly stated that the militant group screened the film for recruits to convince them to kill police. Step by step Pontecorvo and Solinas sketch the progress of the revolution. With mandates from the leadership of the FLN, there is a purging of the ranks, eliminating traces of colonialist corruption—prostitution, drugs, and alcohol. The chieftains recruit by testing the sincerity of the initiate with some type of terrorist activity, for example, shooting a policeman. Then they organize the fresh recruits into three-men pyramidal cells. To succeed, the movement must get as much support from the people as possible. To show the people and the enemy the extent of the movement, terrorist activity becomes necessary. The people must then manifest their solidarity by engaging in a general strike, even if it means labelling themselves in the eyes of the colonialists as nationalist sympathizers. Above all, the leaders and the people must persevere despite retaliation by the authorities.

In schematizing the two major forces in opposition in Algeria, Pontecorvo and Solinas run the risk of stereotyping the characters, or of outright Manichaeanism, as the French critics have been wont to put it. Although the Mathieus and the Alis symbolize two philosophical positions, there are others which reveal the complexity of the war.

The Algerian cause, even though it has one primary goal—liberation—has a full range of means. The characters in the film personify each position. Ali, an impulsive and illiterate militant, is convinced that terrorism is the only means. Ben M'Hidi, an older intellectual, sees terrorism useful only in the beginning; then, he feels, must come the backing of the people. Djabar, rational and farseeing, guides the revolution in armed terrorism, but believes in the necessity of progressing slowly, step by step. The Arab people, at first reluctant to share the leaders' revolutionary ideals, eventually swell with incredible militant fervor, willing to risk death for personal and collective freedom. Only the conservative, bourgeois Arabs are not depicted—which would more honestly show a divided Arab front.[22] Some of these were executed on the orders of the FLN for being collaborators.

Nor is the other side unilinear in its ideology and action, as the press conference with Colonel Mathieu proves. Mathieu primarily represents the French bourgeois investment in Algeria. The total populace of France, however, does not fully support him. With clearthinking and realistic procedures, he carries out his counterrevolutionary plans. He does not believe in practicing a false humanitarianism toward his enemy, which would lead to military impotency. Yet he does not hesitate to admit that he admires the moral strength, intelligence, and unwavering idealism that Ben M'Hidi exhibited.

Many of the Europeans in the film possess a racist streak. Young French-speaking men on a street corner trip and taunt Ali at the opening of the film. When a bomb explodes at a racetrack the Europeans in attendance let loose their wrath on an innocent little Arab vendor. Yet a French policeman courageously saves the boy's life. Following the assassination of a policeman, bystanders accuse a meek laborer Larjane Boualem of the murder. He is found guilty by the assistant commissioner but on flimsy evidence consisting of hearsay, speculation, or false assumption.

Besides the professional military stance and the pervasive racist attitude of the Europeans toward the Arabs, there exists an even more perilous position in the confrontation—terrorism. Once the assistant commissioner labels the innocent Boualem guilty, he seeks vengeance against the man's family. He plants explosives near the man's dwelling in the Casbah and destroys the lives of a number of innocent civilians—men, women, and children.

As one can readily perceive, Pontecorvo and Solinas do not offer a simplistic view of either of the two major forces in confrontation. Shades of rationale and emotion pervade each side. He furnishes an emotional reason for terrorism among the nationalist Arabs and the colonialist French. Pontecorvo graphically reveals the atrocities of both sides and is not as partial to the militants as some of his critics say. He does indicate, nonetheless, that the three bombs planted among the European civilian population were a specific means of retaliation against the bombing by the assistant commissioner. It was only then that the nationalists supposedly used violence against civilians. The haunting ethereal music in the wake of the colonialists' bombing of the Casbah residence inculcates in the spectator hatred of the power force and sympathy for the blameless Arabs who were killed.

More complex than the ethical issue of bombing is that of torture.[23] In a calm, precise way, Colonel Mathieu rationalizes the use of torture interrogation, as would Philip Michael Santore in Costa-Gavras's *State of Siege,* also written by Solinas. Mathieu admits that torture is not in his orders, but given the fact that the interrogated guerrillas need be silent for only twenty-four hours so that the rebel organization can modify its structures, the soldiers must be quick to procure the information needed from them. The professional soldier replies to a journalist's question about the application of torture:

> We are soldiers and our only duty is to win. Therefore, to be precise, I would now like to ask you a question. Should France remain in Algeria? If you answer "yes," then you must accept all the necessary consequences.

The "perch," dunking, beating, shocking, and burning—all applied very clinically and systematically to the detainees—eventually draw out the necessary information. This, in the mind of Mathieu, will help remove the last part of the guerrilla tapeworm from the sickly body of Algerian society. Talbott's discussion of torture is perhaps the answer Mathieu was seeking during the press conference:

> Some of the thousands questioned by the paratroopers volunteered information; others were forced to talk. Torture was the army's response to terrorism. In a revolutionary war, it has been argued, the one follows the other as the night the day. The army's choice lay between putting an end to terrorism by the quickest and most efficient means at hand or abandoning Algiers to the terrorists and withdrawing from Algeria. The government had decided to keep Algeria French; the soldiers who resorted to torture believed themselves to be meeting the requirements of the government's policies.[24]

Ironically, many of the experienced soldiers had been in the Resistance and some suffered through brutal torture sessions at the hands of the Gestapo. Now these men were using the same techniques as the Gestapo, but with ten years of refinement.

The incidents of terrorist bombings and torture are tense and repelling. The spectator witnesses the decomposition of human and ethical values. To tone down the graphic, repulsive effect of torture, for instance, Pontecorvo and Ennio Morricone arrange music, making it a political and lyrical experience. The music is designed to play on a hidden psychological level. A Bach chorale accompanies the excruciating images of the torture of an Arab detainee. Pontecorvo discusses the rapport of the music and the torture:

> The torture used by the French as their basic counterguerrilla tactic is the low point of human degradation caused by the war. It seemed to me that the religious music I used in those sequences emphasized with even greater authority the gravity of that degradation. But at the same time torture creates a sort of relationship between those who do it and those who undergo it. With human pity the common bond, the music served to transcend the particular situation making them symbols of an all-encompassing characteristic—that of giving and enduring pain.[25]

Some of the French press *(Combat, Le Figaro)* labelled *The Battle of Algiers* a partisan, pro-Arab film while others considered it a blatant anti-French work. There is some truth to these allegations, but all sides of the political issue should be considered. The film was indeed sponsored by the victors, the Algerians, and produced by the rebel leader Yacef Saadi. These associations make it a potentially propagandistic film. Taking into consideration the entire film, the spectator does become more sympathetic with the Algerian cause. We see Ali, Djabar, and peers waging their nationalist war against oppression. They are the underdogs. Images of child revolutionaries (Omar), women terrorists (Hassiba), gentle and wise intellectuals (Ben M'Hidi), and handsome militants (Djabar) give a human and emotional ring to the liberation movement. Despite the tanks, sophisticated military weaponry, and systematic torture, the little people achieve their victory. It is the classic case of losing the battle but winning the war. In their battle, as Pontecorvo points out, the Arabs are not without guile, which gives the film a more realistic and credible tone. Upon seeing *The Battle of Algiers*, Lieutenant Colonel Roger Trinquier, veteran of the Tenth Division of Paratroopers and author of *Modern Warfare* (1964), believed that the film was an honest representation of the battle, and in a sense, a tribute to the French army.

With *The Battle of Algiers*, Pontecorvo and Solinas primarily wished to provoke the audience to take a position in the controversy after some reflection. Provoke they did. The French delegation at the Venice Film Festival in 1966 boycotted the official screening of the film as well as the award ceremony when the film merited the Golden Lion prize.[26] Despite its pedigree of international awards, *The Battle of Algiers* was banned by the French government and not screened there until 1971. An attempt had been made a year earlier to get rid of the censorship, but bomb threats to the potential distributors and continual harrassment by the veterans of the Union Nationale des Combattants d'Afrique du Nord and right-wing students from Restauration Nationale forced the screening to be put off to a later date. The bombing of the St. Séverin cinema in 1981 proves that controversial films such as *The Battle of Algiers* are not insignificant fiction films, but are like mini-antipersonnel weapons—they could gravely wound but not kill the objective.

Burn!: A Second Panel to an Anticolonialist Diptych

The frescoes of Diego Rivera in Mexican government buildings and museums review in high glossy forms the incredible manipulation, injustice, and destruction brought to the Mexican world by the Spanish *conquistadores*. In one work a fat monk destroys the native religion while the merchant fills his coffers with New World treasures. Pontecorvo's second anticolonial film, *Burn!* (*Queimada*, 1969), makes as strong and colorful a statement as Diego Rivera's. Originally this celluloid weapon was to be aimed at the Spanish, but United Artists, fearing the loss of the sensitive Spanish film market, changed the target to the Portuguese and English.[27]

Pontecorvo's intentions in filming *Burn!* recall his earlier purpose in making *The Battle of Algiers:*

> *Keymada*[*sic*] is an attempted marriage between a classic adventure and even romantic film, and a weaker vein *(filon)*, but still rich with hope, an ideological film, a film of ideas. It is a highly dramatized parable on a third world theme.[28]

In this exotic epic film Pontecorvo and his scriptwriters Giorgio Arlorio and Franco Solinas collaborated to reveal the bloody roots of colonialism in a nonexistent—but at the same time highly universalized—Portuguese island in the Antilles, Queimada (literally, "burnt"). On one level, as Pontecorvo notes, the film is an adventure story, having all the excitement of rebellion, battle, and the hunt. On another level, it is the confrontation of two ways of thinking. It thus has all the earmarks of an exciting political fable.

In the mid-nineteenth century, William Walker (Marlon Brando), a British agent provocateur, arrives on the Portuguese island of Queimada in the West Indies. With patience and skill he schools a fiery Black native, José Dolores (Evaristo Marquez), to lead a rebellion of the cane growers against the Portuguese. Once the revolution succeeds, Walker has the white bourgeois landowners under Teddy Sanchez (Renato Salvatori) assume the powers of government. Sanchez is later shot for high treason.

A decade later in England, two agents for the Royal Sugar Company convince Walker, now an arrogant street fighter, to quell a rebellion against the English led by José Dolores. Walker returns to Queimada and wages a fierce antiguerrilla campaign. The English troops, following Walker's wise military counsel, finally track down Dolores. Walker, fearing eventual martyrdom for Dolores, offers the captured rebel an opportunity to escape, but the revolutionary refuses. Dejected, the agent makes his way to the boat. He is stabbed to death before he reaches it.

Filmed in Columbia in an original Spanish colonial city (and then in Morocco when Brando got bored with Columbia), *Burn!* has a lush beauty to it. Pontecorvo often compares it to a lavish nineteenth century novel in tone, form, color, and music. For him, the film has a formal quality superior to *Kapò* and *The Battle of Algiers,* despite its structural weaknesses. Most impressive is the technical and aesthetic richness of the film, with its flow of images of humans or horses in the rhythms so precious to the director. The finely sculpted faces of the nonprofessionals like Marquez or the delicately nuanced moods of Marlon Brando, product of Lee Strasberg's Actors Studio, reflect the intense cooperation—and at times frustration—that existed between actor and director. The mass scenes of bread distribution have a dynamic orchestration to them. The credits on a split screen with ragged edges, and accompanied by a sensual musical theme, reveal a highly refined technique. Ennio Morricone's exuberant musical score enriches the film experience, although some critics point out that this overtly exotic music detracts from the political import of the work. French film reviewers (Gérard Langlois, Gilles Jacob, Jean de Baroncelli, and Robert Chazal) in one way or other imply that these attractive effects minimize the possibility of transmitting the ideological message of anticolonialism. Pauline Kael in her review casually chides the director for using such vibrant effects which make of the work an "old heart-stirring swashbuckler."[29] One of the most honest appraisals of *Queimada* is Joan Mellen's rereading of the work. Her fine political and critical sense puts all of this in perspective.[30] She sees the weaknesses of this type of film, but respects the work for its political astuteness.

As with *The Battle of Algiers,* an underlying current of Marxist dialectic flows through *Queimada.* The Walker-Dolores confrontation replaces that of Mathieu-Ali. It thereby situates the spectator in the immediate position of grasping a significant and timely lesson in historical forces—colonialism versus rebellion, oppressor versus oppressed. The personification of these conflicting forces provides a human touch to an abstract historical process.

Sir William Walker, representing the powerful intricate system of a politico-economic culture, is "a super-cool C.I.A.-type mastermind crossed with Lawrence of Arabia," according to Pauline Kael.[31] Like Mathieu, Walker is an erstwhile product of a democratic bourgeois society who believes in progress. Dedicated professionalism runs through the fibers of his Machiavellian being. Walker sails to Queimada to do his job—to transform the Portuguese burdens on the shoulders of the native population into British ones. To foment revolution, the British agent leads Dolores in Pygmalion fashion through the steps of bank

Pontecorvo's *Burn!.* The director explains the brawl scene to Marlon Brando. *(Courtesy of Director Gillo Pontecorvo.)*

robbery and confrontation with the law, and Sanchez through assassination and
economic manipulation. Through this process he wears the facade of a friend of
the oppressed, sincerely desirous of a more humane world. When Walker returns to the island ten years later his character has somewhat changed. He still
reeks of a colonialist approach to life, but now, as Pontecorvo suggests to Joan
Mellen, "he does the same things he did before, but like a mercenary, without
belief in anything."[32] Pontecorvo in *Cinéaste* puts Walker's evolution in a broader
political framework:

> In the second part of the film, ten years later, the experience of this brilliant
> man has shown that all he had thought about progress, about the development
> of the English bourgeoisie, was wrong, completely wrong. He becomes com-
> pletely empty, doing the same things as before but without believing in them
> any longer. He does them out of Vitalism. I think he is typical of the early
> period of development of the democratic bourgeoisie during the last century.
> And I think that to show, as it were, the bloody roots of capitalism, the matrix
> of our white civilization and the origin of the present threats, is not a bad
> idea.[33]

In either phase of his colonial tactics Walker just follows orders. Without a basic
set of ethical principles, he manipulates Dolores and tries to destroy this revolutionary he shaped when he is no longer useful to the colonialist cause. In the
hands of Walker and the British Crown, the Black leader is only a simple pawn,
with the real stakes a rich, expanding sugar market.

Just as complex a historical force is José Dolores. This dormant giant, a single
but representative element of the oppressed, is awakened by taunts from the
agent provocateur. From sympathetic porter he is transformed into a bank robber,
then respected rebel leader of his people. Nonetheless he serves as a weapon in
the hands of the British, but is disarmed in the post-revolutionary days for fear
of rebellious enlightenment. When he possesses total consciousness of the plight
of the oppressed, he must be destroyed by the dominating force.

The final encounter of Walker and Dolores brings to light the cumulative personal and collective tensions of the film. Dolores has understood that he was used
and discarded by Walker whom he had so absolutely trusted. For this reason his
deep personal antagonism fills the air during their discussion following Dolores's
capture. Walker realizes that although he and the colonialists have won the battle,
they have given birth to a martyr whose images may encourage further revolution. The fiery militant refuses Walker's hand and the opportunity to escape.
Using very modern concepts, Dolores shows that he prefers shameless martyrdom to shameful subservience. Morally speaking Walker and the British have
lost. Pontecorvo explained the import of this scene:

> You know, a large part of the Left and Third World people believe that there
> is no dialogue possible between the oppressor and the oppressed. This scene is
> an allusion to that position. Dolores does not even want to speak to him and
> this silence is one of the heaviest, most important things in the whole film.[34]

In their deliberately didactic production, Pontecorvo, Solinas, and Arlorio
have fleshed out the schema of the dialectic with their treatment of slavery, revo-

lution, and economics. In the class struggle vividly portrayed in *Burn!*, all of these factors serve as motivational material for the central confrontation. At the outset of the film, slavery under the minions of the Portuguese emits a ghastly stench. Mercilessly whipped and forever overworked, the Black slaves are kept as beasts of burden. When Santiago and his rebels attempt to overthrow the Portuguese, they are garrotted and their heads chopped off. Walker subsequently assists Dolores to escape from his enslavement to the Portuguese. The consequences, however, include an economic slavery. The emancipated slaves, working as underpaid cane cutters, become more subservient to the English bourgeois plantation owners. They exchange physical slavery for economic slavery. Pauline Kael assesses the director's treatment of this theme:

> And *Burn!* is perhaps the least condescending film that has ever dealt with slavery. No doubt the dignity of the slave victims is ideological, but clearly Pontecorvo is not distorting his vision to fit his ideology; when he endows them with nobility, it rings esthetically true.[35]

To date, perhaps with the exception of Herbert Biberman's *Slaves* (1969), only the television epic *Roots,* has been able to show the long, painful evolution from slavery to freedom with an honest view of the inner workings of this phenomenon.

In both *The Battle of Algiers* and *Burn!*, Pontecorvo lays out the intricate mechanisms of revolution. The double revolution in *Burn!* reveals a dual perspective on the subject. When the British liaison walks the potential leader through the steps of rebellion, he presents it in economic not ideological terms. Walker mentions to Dolores that, if he told the Black porter to rebel for an abstract idea, together they could not pull off the revolution. But Dolores and his comrades understood how to rob a bank, defend themselves against the law, and protect their innocent loved ones. Dolores thus learned the steps involved in revolution, and gathering momentum, rebelled against his new masters. He uses the ideology of class struggle, oppression, and unjust working conditions as a basis for the revolution. The irony of the second rebellion is that it was not sanctioned by the British Crown and had to be squelched.

Slavery and revolution thus have at least one thing in common—economics. In a quasi-revisionist manner, Pontecorvo points an accusing finger at the capitalist and colonialist societies of Portugal and Britain. Portugal keeps the slaves subservient in order to control the island, primarily for the sugar market. England, greatly in need of the same product, organizes the revolution and puts its own bourgeois pawns into government to assure its proper direction. In both cases, economics determines the national politics. With this in mind, director and scriptwriters make allusions to present-day imperialistic tendencies in Latin America. The British agent—not too different from an American military advisor in 1969—also tells Dolores that he's off to Indochina.

Despite the disenchanting defects of its slick appearance, major funding through United Artists, a celebrated star in the central role, and insufficient character development (in the mind of Solinas), *Burn!* still transmits an ideology that is anticolonialist and antiimperialist. In considering a faroff, imaginary island in the nineteenth century, Pontecorvo holds up a political mirror to contemporary society and follows in the "didascalic" footsteps of Rossellini. The film had its momentary impact, giving, says Pontecorvo, Third World filmmakers such as Miguel Littin the courage to continue political filmmaking.

The Tunnel: Revolutionary Oratorio

Few countries today have not known the violence, fear, and tension of an urban guerrilla movement, whether it be the FLN in Algeria, the Tupamaros in Uruguay, the IRA in Ireland, the Baadar-Meinhof in Germany, the Red Brigades in Italy, or the ETA in Spain. Costa-Gavras's *State of Siege* and Pontecorvo's *Battle of Algiers* testify to their philosophy and tactics. The field of battle is no longer the jungle or the mountain path but the streets of the city. The code of military behavior is no longer that proposed by the Geneva Conference. Instead the urban guerrilla's tactics include bombings, blackmail, sabotage, and kidnapping. Innocent civilians could become victims of the militants during a terrorist action.

Prior to and shortly after the execution of Italian parliamentary leader Aldo Moro (1978), few producers wished to risk making a film on terrorism. Producers were saying that the current political scene in Italy was too complex to represent adequately, and that the public did not wish to see films that portrayed the same violence that comprised their everyday lives. Then came a breakthrough with *The Tunnel, Three Brothers,* and *Tragedy of a Ridiculous Man.*

For Pontecorvo, the topic of terrorism in film in 1978–79 could be just as controversial as it was during the production of *The Battle of Algiers* ten years earlier. When Ugo Pirro, Giorgio Arlorio, and he were writing the script for *The Tunnel* (*Ogro,* 1979) on the ETA (Euskadi Ta Askatasuna) assassination of the prime minister of the Spanish government, Carrero Blanco, Italy was shocked by the kidnapping and execution of Aldo Moro by the Red Brigades. Film negotiations and preparations had already been underway since 1976. United Artists was afraid that Spain might bar the film from distribution. Franco had died on 19 November 1975, but the major production company still had some franquist sympathies. The Moro affair could also have dealt a final blow to the production, as it did with Massimo Pirri's *Italy, Last Act* (*Italia, ultimo atto*)—the story of an assassination of a prime minister. This film was withdrawn from circulation following the Moro kidnapping. After the project of *The Tunnel* was blocked for a year and a half, the Italian-French-Spanish coproduction was allowed to go through. Surprisingly enough, the film was able to be screened without complications in Spain, the home base of the ETA militants. Pontecorvo did explain in our interview, however, that only two problems occurred, one with the extreme Right's harrassment during the production, and the other from the terrorist branch of the guerrilla movement (ETA-Militar), which felt the director made the film against this group.

1978. A young woman in the Basque area of Spain enigmatically follows a young man to his apartment. Amajur (Angela Molina), the wife of militant Txabi (Eusebio Poncela), shares her love and sense of political tension with her husband. A flashback takes them to

1973. Four Etarras, Txabi, Ezarra (Gian Maria Volonté), Luken (Saverio Marconi), and Iker (José Sacristan) arrive in Madrid with one objective in mind—to kidnap Franco's righthand man, Admiral Luis Carrero Blanco. One day, as Carrero Blanco, now Prime Minister, attends his usual morning Mass at the Jesuit church, the militants discover that with his added security the action is impossible. Instead they decide to execute him, especially after one of their key leaders in the Basque country is eliminated by the police. Carefully tunnelling and laying dynamite under the street through which the official's car will pass after Mass, the four Basques blow his car five stories into the air and successfully escape north. Five years later Txabi is shot after he assassinates a police officer. At his bedside his wife and friends who had already discontinued their terrorist activity grieve over his dying, but do not sympathize with his ideology of armed revolution.

As with all of his films, Pontecorvo, in collaboration with his screenwriters, relies on accurate documentation. During the research and scriptwriting, screenwriter Ugo Pirro said, they had recent international acts of terrorism to serve as illustrations of this growing threat to society. They also had in mind the Red Brigades but at the same time felt that it was not possible to compare the Red Brigades with the ETA of 1973, the time of the action of the film.[36] Pontecorvo's journalistic experience further obliged him to work constantly under his "dictatorship of truth" mentioned earlier. In the course of his preparations he met with two of the four guerrillas responsible for the assassination of Carrero Blanco on 20 December 1973. One of the group was killed in 1978 during a terrorist action. From the two he received all the details necessary to give a precise rendering of the assassination. Eva Forest's *Operación Ogro* was also helpful in supplying concrete facts about the terrorist action, although she later criticized the film for being "Eurocommunist and jesuitical."[37] Other details came from Julen Agirre's book *Operación Ogro*.[38] The essence of the film is contained in Agirre's interviews with the four terrorists Jon, Mikel, Iken, and Txabi. The monograph contains in great detail photos of the buildings involved, street plans, sketches of the results of the explosion, and communiqués from the ETA on their responsibility for the action.

Based on interviews and readings, the director and screenwriters were able to recount an ideological but also very human narrative. From an introduction to the Basque question via a map and news footage of Franco's death in 1975, the director proceeds to give glimpses of the Basque struggle for cultural and political autonomy. Flashbacks to a few decades earlier show young boys beaten by their teacher because they insist on speaking Basque instead of standard Spanish. Another flashback shows a priest leaving his profession to fight in the cause of liberation. These preliminaries provide the background to the ETA movement and the eventual assassination.

The central portion of the film, contained in the major flashback from 1978, develops the four major characters. It offers Pontecorvo an opportunity to present the general ideology of the ETA—anti-Fascist, anti-Franquist, antirepression—the basis for most contemporary revolutionary movements. The original plan of kidnapping Carrero Blanco and holding him hostage in order to procure the release of countless ETA militants in prison appears reasonable to the terrorists. It is only at the moment when this becomes impossible that a deeper, ideological debate begins. In their discussions the four show various approaches to the use of terrorism in the struggle for national autonomy. In the preparation for the dynamiting, the militants deliberate on its effects on their movement. They question how much violence they must use to attain their goal. Perhaps they should resort to more organizational means of transforming society as does the leftist organizer in Madrid in his politicizing of the construction workers?

In the film and in their subsequent interviews, the terrorists—who prefer to be called Basque revolutionaries and not assassins—state outright why they had to execute "this important enemy" of democracy. They saw Carerro Blanco living in the shadow of Franco, patiently awaiting his passing. In the meantime he was preparing meticulously for the moment when he could carry on in the spirit of Franco. Since 1961, Carrero Blanco symbolized "pure Franquism" with his creation of information networks and police systems. To eliminate him would be an assurance that the repression of the Franco regime would not continue.[39] The reasoning of the ETA appeared clear in the film, although the action was violent, extremist, and as unethical as the repressive forces of the regime. On the other hand, argue the militants, if Carrero Blanco continues to abide by the same principles as Franco, there will be more oppression of the Spanish and Basques, more torture and deaths of revolutionaries who speak out against the regime. At the close of the political discussion in the film, it almost appears that the final decision for assassination was an either-or-choice, the death of the Prime Minister or the continuation of oppression.

In *The Tunnel* Pontecorvo attempts to demonstrate how terrorist activity is a viable alternative against the fascism of the Spanish dictator, but *not* after this threat to democracy has been eliminated. The director makes it clear that he is antiterrorist, even though he showed the terrorist act of 1973 in a dynamic, suspenseful, and favorable light. His concluding scene at the bedside of the mortally wounded terrorist Txabi reflects his personal ideological position. He brilliantly uses pathos to underline Txabi's comrades' present rejection of terrorism in a democratic system.

Claire Sterling, in *The Terror Network,* offers a personal account of the ideological detour by the Etarras and parallels it with the experience of the Irish IRA:

> The story I heard from old Basque friends, in the weeks I spent among them at the end of the seventies, bore a striking resemblance to Northern Ireland's. Here, too, was a long-persecuted ethnic minority, valiantly defended at first only to be used and defrauded later, for an occult cause that could bring nothing but misery. "The terrorists are trading on our sentiments today, reminding us of how stupendous they used to be when Franco was on our backs," said a Basque journalist I've known for years. "They *say* they're killing for the sake of Basque nationhood, but their whole purpose has changed. They're really doing it to destabilize the Spanish state—to hit the police, the army, judges, institutions, for the same reasons the Baader-Meinhof Gang does, or the Italian Red Brigades." Or the Provisional IRA, he might have added.[40]

Just as in *The Battle of Algiers*, there is a gamut of diverse political actions possible in this national struggle. Unlike the Arab-French confrontation, however,

The Tunnel does not sufficiently penetrate the ideology of the Right. Carrero Blanco is only a moving target in the film. He and Franco have no human side to them; they simply represent oppression. Nor do the people of Madrid have any character development or even a say about this type of violence destroying their society. In this sense, the ideological development and import of the film is weaker in its integrity than its predecessor's.

The Tunnel has not had as wide a distribution as Pontecorvo's earlier works. Nonetheless, those critics who have come to grips with the terrorist theme in the film are very insightful. Antonello Trombadori sees the film as a type of lamentation, a discourse of Mark Antony over the cadaver of Julius Caesar, and adds a sacral note to his remarks by comparing the work to a sorrowful lament at the foot of the cross in a sacred work of art. *The Tunnel,* he finally adds, reads like an oratorio.[41] Paolo Spriano refers to the film as a classic Pontecorvo film with a taste for dramatic efficacy and a scrupulous concern for detail in faces, places, and dialogue. In Gramscian terms, he observes, *The Tunnel* shows Pontecorvo's "dialogical passion" *(passione dialogica).*[42]

Despite the tension accentuated by Ennio Morricone's music, the attractive but not brilliant cinematography of Marcello Gatti, and the natural, low-keyed acting of Gian Maria Volonté as the older guerrilla, *The Tunnel* does not have the same power as political fiction as did Pontecorvo's preceding works.[43] The ideological weaknesses accruing from the imbalance of the script destroy the power of the film to convey honestly the full rationale of the ETA movement, if that were possible on celluloid. The human side of the guerrillas does emerge but subsides all too quickly, dominated by the technical side of the assassination preparation and the ideological debate. At the conclusion of the film, as the gravely wounded guerrilla speaks for the last time to his former comrades-in-arms, the spectator still remains a bit on the periphery of the characters, although much closer to comprehending the terrorist gesture of 20 December 1973 and the antiterrorist philosophy of Pontecorvo.

Conclusions

If a graph were to be drawn up representing the films of Gillo Pontecorvo, in the light of the critics' and public's assessment of them, the results would closely resemble a sine curve. Starting with the documentaries, the curve ascends toward the director's work with Ivens on *Giovanna* but declines with his first feature *The Long Blue Road,* a failure in one respect but an important experience in another. This was also true with *Kapò,* an intense historical drama but with the tragic flaw of an impossible love affair. Then came the masterpiece, *The Battle of Algiers,* which holds a prestigius position as the most technically astute and most controversial film in Pontecorvo's career. *Burn!* and *The Tunnel* occupy a lower position in a diagram of his opus. They are more colorful, commercial, and compromising, but also more ambitious. Pontecorvo's five political fiction features deliberately purport to be didactic, message films that should ideally help to instruct the viewer on a number of contemporary burning issues. In this respect they are most successful. They further reflect rich but controlled experimentation in photography, music, and editing. With few exceptions, Pontecorvo has educed incredibly persuasive performances from the actors—professionals such as Marlon Brando and Susan Strasberg, or nonprofessionals such as Brahim Haggiag and Evaristo Marquez. Technically and aesthetically, few flaws can be detected in the works of Pontecorvo.

These same films, however, reveal a series of paradoxes, contradictions, and unresolved conflicts that detract from their political impact. Although Pontecorvo frowns upon the criticism, yet his personal leftist orientation, Marxist background, and anti-Establishment topics conflict with the fact that films such as *Burn!* and *The Tunnel* can be made with capitalist money.[44] Pontecorvo discounts these contradictions by underlining the fact that, if the message is to reach the public, some type of commercial means must be used. He does not fear or hesitate to use these institutional means toward his personal end, yet at the same time encourages an alternative cinema.

Pontecorvo's treatment of history emerges from his deep-seated belief in the Marxist dialectic. Most of his films pit one striking oppressive force against a weaker, unrecognized entity. He says he creates the tension between these conflicting forces, as seen in his films, because that is how reality is. Other political, social, and economic elements are certainly at work in the concentration camps, sugar cane plantations, and Casbah streets. He may deliberately restrict himself to this structured duality even though he is aware that a *tertium quid* may lie right at hand.

In his transposition of reality he and Franco Solinas attempt an honest, extensive series of research studies of an actual recent historical event. However, no documentary can reflect absolute truth, nor can a political fiction film. The mere selection of the facts and their ordering indicate some type of interpretation of the event. This already follows from a thesis-type paradigm in the minds of Pontecorvo and Solinas.

The protagonists in his films—Nicole, Ali, Mathieu, Dolores, Walker, Txabi— all embody forces in history, be they imperialistic, Nazi, or revolutionary. Within the space of two hours Pontecorvo can hardly be able to delineate fully his complex characters or reflect a highly nuanced individual or collective force in society. For example, the spectator learns little about the life of Mathieu and the rationale of his professional military career aside from a few moments before the journalists. Other characters, like Mathieu's enemy Djabar, run the risk of being walking ideologies.

In the blend of politics and fiction in Pontecorvo's quasi-documentary genre of filmmaking there is unresolved tension. On occasion, in certain films such as *Kapò* or *Burn!*, the politics succumb to the fiction. The ideology becomes too superficial. Even though Pontecorvo attempts to show several ideologies at work, a two-hour film is insufficient to develop adequately those that are presented. For the most part, various, differing ideologies in confrontation are suggested and underlined, but also diluted in order to make the film narrative comprehensible at one screening. The other pole—fiction—is not omitted, as can be judged by *The Long Blue Road* or *Kapò*. Pontecorvo inserts emotional material to reveal the human aspect of the ideological conflict. The melodramatic use of children hurts his political thesis, as witnessed in the child revolutionary Omar in *The Battle of Algiers,* the little Basque girl in *The Tunnel* greeting the terrorists in Madrid, and the captured child in *Burn!* holding up his hands in imitation of the Warsaw ghetto raid. Brechtian "distantiation" has no place in these particular situations in Pontecorvo's films.

Most of the director's films ingeniously cast contemporary universal problems in prior historical moments, like the imperialist theme in *Burn!* For this Pontecorvo has inherited the label revisionist. On the one hand, in the course of the film there is a sense of urgency about the particular political problem for the spectator. On the other, the immediacy of the issue at times fades with the final credits. Nonetheless each film has the potential of planting a seed of desire to learn more about the unjust situation at hand.

In assessing their own work, both Pontecorvo and Solinas honestly perceive the weaknesses of a particular film. Neither attempts to be defensive about his work, but offers the rationale operative at the time of the production. Solinas, in our discussion of 1981, listed a series of precise moments that he found detrimental to the success of individual films. With respect to the ideological significance of his films, Pontecorvo is especially realistic. He sees films only as a modest means toward a very idealistic goal of consciousness-raising. It seems to him a way of clarifying complex sociopolitical ideas. When asked by Harold Kalishman of *Cinéaste* what he can hope for in terms of the political impact of his films upon an audience, Pontecorvo concluded:

> Honestly, I don't think that a movie can do very much. But if what we do, the little that we do, is on a large front, I think that it helps. If you reach a large front of people, you make a little step forward. It is something very valuable and useful. But having said what I just said, I must also say that we must not rely on movies. Movies are movies. The cinema is the most important of the arts, as Lenin said, but in any case it is still an art. It is not, directly, action.[45]

6

ELIO PETRI: A Kafkaesque Moralist (Often) above Suspicion

> I don't believe in the effectiveness of the militant film. I
> think it's necessary to make films which oblige the public to
> reflect on political issues. There is no type of film that is
> more political than the one referred to as the "escape" film.
>
> —Elio Petri

Elio Petri's roots are in the Roman working class, unlike those of Bertolucci or Bellocchio, directors who came from the provinces and from a bourgeois environment. His origins in part account for his sociopolitical perspective as well as his interest in film. "I come from a family of poor laborers. Instinctively, I have chosen to side with the workers. These circumstances have led me to a career in film."[1] Elio Petri was born in the capital city on 29 January 1929. His father was an artisan, a coppersmith by trade. His family—father, mother, and grandmother—was steeped in the politics of antifascism.

Attending the parochial schools of San Giuseppe and Pio IX, Petri saw how the other half lived. In this Catholic milieu he learned to be a Fascist and to believe in the national Italian spirit. Although dismissed from Pio IX for disciplinary reasons, he profited from his experience in these schools. Following this encounter with the bourgeoisie, he felt that he was no longer inferior to members of the upper classes.

In secondary school around the close of World War II, from age thirteen to fifteen, Petri experienced several changes within him and around him. At this time he says he lost his Catholic faith—which gives rise to a cynical anticlericalism in his films. He also witnessed the process of dismantling the fascist structures of an Italy over which the spirit of Il Duce still hovered. He listened attentively to family political discussions. He began to see the world with different eyes. His readings gave him more extensive, vicarious experiences to rely on. Over the next few years he would fall under the spell of the Italian writers Moravia and Pirandello. An international host of writers further influenced him, made up of Stendhal, Kafka, Tolstoy, Proust, Dostoevsky, and Gide. From 1944, Marx became one of his faithful guides along the socialist trail. Academics all of a sudden meant little. He dropped his studies at the Instituto Tecnico Superiore without completing a degree.

Still in his teens, Petri became obsessed with cinema. He would see three or four films a day. Visconti's *Obsession* and Rossellini's *Rome, Open City* traumatized him. These neorealist films, as well as the American films of the 1930s, left an imprint upon him especially obvious in his early feature films. For the local film clubs he wrote the program notes. His friend Gianni Puccini, director of the film journal *Cinema* and screenwriter for Visconti's *Obsession,* was the one responsible for finally drawing him into the front ranks of cinema. Puccini introduced Petri to director Giuseppe De Santis, marking the start of a dynamic collaboration between the two. Together De Santis and Petri worked on six films from 1952 to 1960, the most famous of which may be *Rome, the Eleventh Hour (Roma, ore undici,* 1952).[2] In the meantime he also worked on scripts for Enzo Provenzale, Gianni Puccini, Carlo Lizzani, and other filmmakers. In all, he signed sixteen scripts over a ten-year period, but most often with other scriptwriters.

Like Gillo Pontecorvo, Petri combined his interests in politics, journalism, and cinema. He wrote for the Communist daily *L'Unità* under the guidance of the critic Tommaso Chiaretti. At *L'Unità* he experienced a surprising form of censorship. He was not allowed to be critical of Soviet films. Petri also wrote for the Communist youth paper *Gioventù nuova* and reviewed for *Mondo operario* such films as Rosi's *The Challenge* in September 1958.

His experience with the Communist party over several years, at first refreshing and enlightening, soon turned sour. The crisis of the Soviet intervention in Hungary in 1956 elicited a strong negative reaction from Petri. In October 1956, with artists, scientists, professors, littérateurs, and philosophers, Petri signed the famous *"Manifesto dei 101"* concerning the events in Hungary—for which the members of the Communist party considered him a political adversary.[3] Petri and the other signers were critical of the Soviet Union's interference in Hungary and felt the USSR lost its socialist innocence by this gesture. The rebels also confronted the party for its general policies and lack of a democratic process.

At the same time Petri formed part of a group of Communists from Tommaso Chiaretti of *L'Unità* to the painter Lorenzo Vespignani, that established the radical journal *Città aperta* (Open City). Only a few issues were published. Several of the group felt constrained to leave the party in view of the political tension during this period. Shortly after the Twentieth Party Congress and right in the midst of the destalinization process, Petri abandoned the ranks of the Communists. His class roots, however, would not allow him to be anticommunist. He still remained a militant, a part of the traditional Left, but a critical one. He perceptively analyzed some of the issues surrounding socialism:

> The problem with socialism is that it does not want to abandon its paternalist spirit. The entire structure of the Communist party is based on the importance of the father figure. If one wants the citizen only to be an obedient son, however, this will prevent him from growing up into an adult. We have to begin telling the truth to the children.[4]

In 1979, he conveyed his reactions about communism to Alfredo Rossi:

Do I consider myself a Communist? In all sincerity, the answer is no. This is not solely because I am not regarded as one by the various communist circles, old or new. Rather, it is because, in the light of my long experience as a militant, being communist means accepting the discipline of the party, sacrificing one's subjectivity to the reasoning of the party, and living each moment for the party. This I cannot accept.[5]

In the long run, Petri wished to remain independent and non-Communist, while his leftist films reflect a conscious anti-Establishment perspective.

Although his cinematic style evolved from the more political, there are certain common elements that pervade most of his opus, which was terminated by an early death in November 1982. He presented various themes for collective discussion in order for the filmgoer to understand a sociopolitical situation from within. Like Francesco Rosi, Petri had a keen desire to treat the subject of power and the self-destructive obsession with power. In Petri's films the phenomenon of power readily leaps to the eye, as it appears in fascist authority roles in the clerical realm, the economic world, and the political and police forces. The display of power extends to sexuality when the immature, perverted individual uses power sexually to manipulate another person—not too different from Bertolucci's development of the leitmotif in *Last Tango in Paris* and Pasolini's in *Salò*. The philosophies of Freud and Reich weave their way in and out of Petri's repertoire. Sex is commonly linked with power and violence.

Petri makes negative, disturbing statements about society. With Bellocchian grimness he captures the darker side of life. He shows the alienation of the individual in a society that is crumbling. Noncommunication prevails. Death lurks everywhere, and not a natural death, of course. Neurosis and schizophrenia rear their ugly heads as well. In setting these themes before the public, the director eventually hopes to help society grow, but with a caustic tone he goads certain sectors of society to change. His sharp eye for the foibles of society always provided him with sufficient targets.

The cinematic style of Petri, a hybrid of harsh realism and grotesque expressionism, brings out the worst in his characters. In a Kafkaesque and at times Brechtian fashion he captures the carnival of buffoonish clowns and intellectual dwarves cavorting on the political stage. Petri felt that the Italian people accepted too readily the folly of the political scene and took it for granted. To highlight the ridiculousness of this sphere, Petri caricatures his political figures and paints them in exotic colors. From *Investigation of a Citizen above Suspicion* to *Good News* the director shows a flair for the grotesque as he makes the asinine features of these individuals stand out. With this satirical style he makes the viewer laugh in order to set in motion a serious thought process.

In his cinematic opus Petri simultaneously displays a fine sensitivity to art. He appreciated painting and has expounded his own theories on it during many of his interviews. For example, he sees the images of Pop Art used in *The Tenth Victim* as an aesthetic reinforcement of the revolutionary spirit surrounding the student movement of the late sixties. He mounts the credits of *The Days Are Numbered* and *Property Is No Longer a Theft* on the art work of Lorenzo Vespignani. The apartment of the inspector's mistress in *Investigation* is exotically designed in the art deco style of the turn of the century. Petri discusses his perception of the depth of art in terms of a contrapuntal dialectic between the dynamic of the unconscious and the artist's need to express himself or herself explicitly and publicly.[6]

A pleiad of artists and technicians helps provide Petri with inspiration and unique results. In the crew of actors, Salvo Randone, Marcello Mastroianni, and Gian Maria Volonté each has his own specific dynamism to bring to the production. Mastroianni's brother Ruggero usually edits Petri's films. Ugo Pirro, a close friend and former member of the Communist party, often provides the scenario, and Luigi Kuveiller, the photography. Ennio Morricone adds a musical score to the finished product. The novels of Leonardo Sciascia on occasion serve as the source of the adaptations. The all-round collaboration thus teems with intensity and creativity and thrives in the political environment resulting from such artists.

Two Shorts: Testing Ground

Petri had a very brief exposure to actual filmmaking while he was writing scripts for well-known directors. In 1954, he made a documentary on the evolution of a professional athlete, *A Champion Is Born (Nasce un campione)*. Three years later he filmed *The Seven Peasants (I sette contadini)*. The seven Cervi brothers were shot down by the Nazis in northern Italy during World War II.[7] The film, not a very good one, admits Petri, was produced by the National Association of Italian Partisans (ANPI). "I made this film at a very dark political moment, immediately following the Hungarian events, as if to demonstrate that my dissidence in the confrontations with the Italian Communist party did not minimize my political zeal."[8]

The Lady Killer of Rome and *The Days Are Numbered:* Colorful Black-and-White Studies

For his first feature Petri chose to make a film that skillfully blends psychology, politics and suspense in a thriller-type work. His fascination for detective stories thus found an outlet in *The Lady Killer of Rome* or *The Assassin (L'assassino,* 1961).

One morning Alfredo Martelli (Marcello Mastroianni), an antique dealer, is unexpectedly accused by the police of having murdered his former mistress Adalgisa De Matteis (Micheline Presle). All the evidence seems to point to him. The police commissioner Palumbo (Salvo Randone) has him arrested and jailed. Here he has the opportunity to reconsider his shallow existence. Eventually the police track down the real murderer and release the innocent Alfredo. This incident has changed his life.

A Kafkaesque cloud dangles over the heads of the characters. Alfredo is arrested without knowing the details. Inspector Palumbo eavesdrops on the alleged criminal through a one-way mirror in his office. The heaping up of accusa-

Petri's *The Lady Killer of Rome.* Alfredo Martelli (Marcello Mastroianni) is suspected by police commissioner Palumbo (Salvo Randone) of murdering his mistress. *(Courtesy of Titanus Films.)*

tions against Alfredo reaches an absurd level. Innocence and guilt merge in this study of the rapport between the individual and society. Petri explained the subject of the film to Aldo Tassone:

> *The Assassin* is a sign of the changing times. There appeared a new generation of social climbers who were abandoning all moral scruples. The film narrates the search into the conscience of an individual from the lower class who uses agreements and complicity to further himself, forsaking a certain way of life. The self-examination is accomplished in the film much like an involuntary *rictus:* the inquest to which the protagonist is subjected by the police is a mechanical device used to mimic those sentiments and morality which he no longer possesses. They are now dead in him and in society. The film was a small omen of things to come.[9]

The director uncovers the moral apathy and egotism of the cynical Alfredo. He takes a general stab at society, which suffers from similar maladies, and then a particular one at the police force. Petri originally had the police speak in a rough Sicilian accent to show in a condescending way their origins in the lower class of society, as the Romans perceive it. He changed it. Palumbo uses surveillance to trap Alfredo in his office, and then sets up two "detainees" to share the cell with Alfredo and procure a confession from him. Palumbo's use of any means appears warranted to him. As a result of the anti-Establishment tone of the script, the censors made ninety modifications of the original submitted, according to Petri.

With his first film, Petri shows himself to be a most capable cinéaste. His flowing narrative style holds the film together and keeps the rhythm moving at a dynamic pace. The flashbacks will become an integral part of his style, revealing a nonlinear structure that breaks away from the traditional. This will also mark Petri's first use of Marcello Mastroianni in one of his films, and the cinema debut of the theatre star Salvo Randone.

The following year Petri continued with another film that was heavily psychological, *The Days Are Numbered (I giorni contati, 1962)*. The series of alternate titles in English—*Borrowed Time, No Time Left,* and *Counted Days*—sheds some light on an oft-treated subject, the imminence of death. As noted earlier, Kurosawa's *Ikiru,* Bergman's *Wild Strawberries,* and De Sica's *Umberto D* reveal the plight of elderly men on the threshold of death. The Bergman film, made several years earlier, helped Petri get the necessary existential tone, acknowledged the director. Part of the inspiration for the film also comes from the situation of his father. At the age of fifty-three, the coppersmith refused to continue to work. He had begun his first job forty-two years earlier and was simply tired of sweating out his days.

Riding in a tram in Rome one day, Cesare Conversi (Salvo Randone) is traumatized by the sudden death of one of the passengers. The abrupt cessation of life forces Conversi to rethink how he will spend the rest of his own days. He quits his plumbing job and takes advantage of things for which he never found time earlier—art studios, casual conversations, card playing. He tries to renew his relationship with Giulia (Regina Bianchi). Eventually he finds he cannot survive without money and attempts an insurance ploy with some fellow conspirators. At the last minute he backs out. Enlightened somewhat about the meaning of life, and in particular his life, he resumes his work. He reads in the newspapers that the Russian astronaut Titov has returned to earth. One evening aboard the tram, he surrealistically accompanies the vehicle deep into the eerie night.

The Days Are Numbered has a poignancy all its own. It tells of an individual's refusal of society, a radical decision to discontinue working when he no longer psychologically wishes to do so. Petri situates the film in its sociopolitical context: "It was the first antilabor film, and in its own way, a political film. Against productivity in 1962, the film dealt with the division that separates economical from existential time."[11] The philosophical, political, and psychological currents in the flow are strong. The most graphic, aesthetic elements—the surrealistic atmosphere, unusual geometric shapes, bizarre paintings—further help make *The Days Are Numbered* an original work, despite its cinematic competition.

The Teacher of Vigevano and *Sin in the Afternoon:* **Modest Endeavors**

For a brief time following *The Days Are Numbered* Petri found himself unemployed. Dino De Laurentiis proposed financing the next Petri film if the director would use the comedian Alberto Sordi. Petri agreed, and with other scriptwriters such as Ettore Scola and Ruggero Maccari, began to piece together a script. The result was *The Monsters (I mostri)*, a sixteen-episode work that had a strong political bent. In the film Ugo Tognazzi and Vittorio Gassman incarnate various monsters of the bourgeois class. The work, however, was eventually filmed not by Petri but by the prolific Risi, more recently known for *The Bishop's Room (La stanza del vescovo)*, *The New Monsters (I nuovi mostri)*, and *Lost Soul (Anima persa)*.

A short time later the director used Sordi for the lead role of his next film, *The Teacher of Vigevano (Il maestro di Vigevano*, 1963). Petri adapted the autobiographical novel of Lucio Mastronardi entitled *The Shoemaker of Vigevano (Il calzolaio di Vigevano*, 1962). The director transformed Mastronardi's protagonist, a shoemaker, into a teacher.

Professor Mombelli (Alberto Sordi), a pompous petit bourgeois, cannot quite adapt either to his home life or his academic milieu. His rebellious wife Ada (Claire Bloom) takes a job in the factory, beneath the dignity of a professor's wife. At school he is awkward and has but one friend, Nannini (Guido Spadea), who unfortunately commits suicide. Mombelli resigns his post. His situation goes from bad to worse as his wife becomes the mistress of the factory owner and then abandons her husband completely. In time he returns to his teaching, but a humiliated man.

This tragicomedy showed once again the talent Petri has for detecting the moral weaknesses of society. In a way it echoes the humiliation experienced by the professor in Josef von Sternberg's *The Blue Angel*. With a ferocious cutting edge he sculpts the character of Mombelli into a curiously unique individual.

Following the sixties popularity of the episode film, Petri offered his own contribution to a four-part work entitled *High Infidelity (Alta infedeltà*, 1964). Franco Rossi filmed *Scandalous (Scandalosa)*, Luciano Salce *Sighing (La sospirosa)*, and Mario Monicelli *Modern People (Gente moderna)*. Petri's intention in *Sin in the Afternoon (Peccato nel pommeriggio)* was to satirize his compatriot Michelangelo Antonioni. To play the feminine role he invited Monica Vitti, a veteran of the existential films of Antonioni—*Eclipse (L'eclisse)*, *The Adventure (L'avventura)*, and *Night (La notte)*. Understanding his satirical intentions, she declined, and Claire Bloom assumed the role of Laura and Charles Aznavour that of Giulio. Petri only wanted to make of the film "pure and simple entertainment."[12] The *divertissement*, however, would include moral problems, as can be seen from the plot.

Giulio (Charles Aznavour), a bourgeois businessman, meets and marries Laura (Claire Bloom). Marriage problems arise, which they try to resolve by simulated infidelity. In the end, tranquillity is restored.

This short film neither enhanced nor detracted from the reputation of Elio Petri. It simply filled in the gap between features.

The Tenth Victim and *We Still Kill the Old Way:* Mean Streets

It is easy to observe, but more difficult to explain, how violence has made such an impact upon our society today. Petri witnessed this growing phenomenon, already cancerous almost two decades ago. He made a double statement about it.

In 1979 Robert Altman's *Quintet* portrayed a ruthless game of execution in a futuristic Siberia-like wasteland. More than a decade earlier Petri filmed *The Tenth Victim* (*La decima vittima*, 1965) derived from Robert Sheckley's novel, first published in *Galaxy* magazine in 1953. The similarities with the Altman film appear obvious, but may only be coincidental.

In a science fiction world of the Twenty-First Century, where war no longer exists, an international game called The Big Hunt *channels human aggression from warrior instincts to competitive encounters. The goal of the legalized venture is to amass ten kills, thus earning for oneself unlimited privileges in society.*

The publicity-hungry Caroline Meredith (Ursula Andress) stalks her tenth victim Marcello Polletti (Marcello Mastroianni) in Rome. She plans to execute him on a live television broadcast. Mutual fascination, however, prevents each from slaying the other. Subsequently Caroline drugs Marcello and leads him to the Colosseum, where the final kill will take place before the television cameras.

With an inclination toward satire, Petri examines the underpinnings of society. In a type of modern allegory, using Sheckley's novel as a springboard, he satirizes a mechanized Orwellian society dominated by electronic computers programmed by Freudian psychologists. He takes a critical look at religion, Italian divorce, militarism, art, automation, and mass media. With a caustic verve he discloses the cruelty of human relationships in a society that legitimizes individual violence in order to prevent collective aggression. In the mid-sixties, the director pinpointed his concern about this type of society:

> Everything you will see in "The Tenth Victim" exists today. We have humorously exaggerated current ideas and institutions to show entertainingly and in a nonliteral way what man may someday make of himself. These absurdities could become frightening realities in a world devoted to technological progress at the expense of spiritual growth. . . . They are metaphors designed to make the point that everyday civilized life has almost reached the intensity of physical violence.[13]

Petri's development of the dehumanizing process at work in society recalls Hannah Arendt's phrase, "the banality of evil," from *Eichmann in Jerusalem*, in Saul Kahan's view.[14]

Petri refers to *The Tenth Victim* as "un film d'industrie," a commercial product which demands certain compromises but reaps some positive fruits.[15] Carlo Ponti produced the film, which already implied a certain type of popular film— big name stars, large budgets, exotic locations, and the usual romantic sentiments. At the same time Petri would be assured of a more extensive distribution. His efforts resulted in a film that is part James Bond, part Alfred Hitchcock, and part George Orwell, according to the production notes. It capitalizes on the interest of the sixties in science fiction entertainment captured in Truffaut's *Fahrenheit 451*, Kubrick's *Dr. Strangelove* and *2001: A Space Odyssey*, and Godard's *Alphaville*. Despite the popular, commercial tone of *The Tenth Victim*, Petri is able to include an apocalyptic vision that serves as a hypothesis for the future.

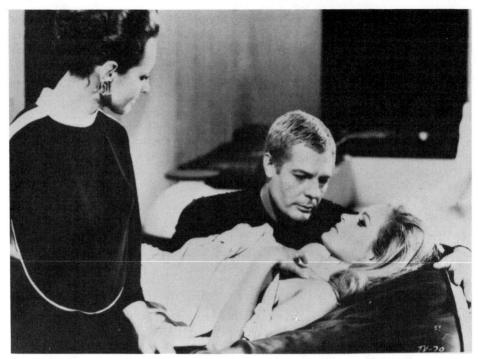

Petri's *The Tenth Victim.* Caroline Meredith (Ursula Andress) and Marcello Polletti (Marcello Mastroianni) are involved in the killing game of "The Big Hunt" in a science-fiction thriller. *(Courtesy of Movie Star News.)*

We Still Kill the Old Way (*A ciascuno il suo,* 1967) pursues further the theme of violence. The source for the film on the Sicilian Mafia is a 1966 novel by Leonardo Sciascia, adapted by Petri and Ugo Pirro within a week. For the protagonist Petri chose Gian Maria Volonté whom he had seen in Nanni Loy's *Four Days of Naples* (*Le quattro giornate di Napoli,* 1962).

In the miniscule Sicilian town of Cefalù, pharmacist Arturo Manno (Luigi Pistelli) and doctor Antonio Roscio (Franco Tranchina) are murdered while hunting, after the pharmacist received a series of threatening letters. An investigation takes place, but the Sicilian pledge of silence—omertà— prevents the authorities from making any headway. Professor Paolo Laurana (Gian Maria Volonté) undertakes his own investigation, only to learn that the intended victim was the doctor not the pharmacist. The lawyer Rosello (Gabriele Ferzetti) had Doctor Roscio murdered since he knew (and documented) much of the attorney's illegal activity. Laurana is seized by force and blown to pieces in a mining shack. Rosello marries the doctor's widow, his accomplice and cousin Luisa (Irene Papas). The couple had intended to marry but their blood relationship prevented it. The archpriest now arranges for the necessary dispensation.

In *We Still Kill the Old Way* we breathe in the Sicilian air polluted by crimes and power plays, corruption and cover-up. Complex intrigues and the code of *omertà* heighten the suspense. The two positive forces of good—the doctor and professor—both seeking after the truth, are removed. They pose a threat to the existence of the larger, clandestine force of power, a "sickness," in Petri's words. The power is centralized in the person of the Big Boss, Attorney Rosello. Maria-Teresa Ravage underlines the sociopolitical implications of the film, perhaps underestimating the Mafia aspect of the film:

> *A Ciascuno il suo* is less interested in dealing with the Mafia itself than with denouncing a tragic human and historical condition: lives dominated by fear, injustice and exploitation; political games where everyone is equally corrupt, where salvation is no longer expected or even hoped for; a situation where the "law" of silence is stronger than the knowledge of crime, the desire for justice or even moral indignation.[16]

The various themes indicated by Savage provide a literary, sociological, and political framework for the film. Like Rosi's *Lucky Luciano, Salvatore Giuliano* and perhaps *Mattei, We Still Kill the Old Way* is an attempt to bring the dark sinister world of the Mafia to light. It is a hermetic world that is reluctant to allow its secrets to come to the surface. Mystery thus pervades the film because of the subject matter, but also because of the gripping style of editing.

The character of Laurana has a special interest for Petri. The professor is an intellectual of the Left who struggles against corruption. Yet he is not a realist. Petri in a way makes of him a symbolic type of castrated intellectual, for he believes that intellectuals in an industrialized society are all castrated.[17] Laurana's school becomes his refuge. Fascinated by the Communists, Laurana—like Petri— still feels that they are constrained individuals, obliged to work within a system.

Petri's *We Still Kill the Old Way.* Professor Laurana (Gian Maria Volonté) discovers a murder and cover-up in Sicily. *(Courtesy of Movie Star News.)*

Although Antonio Gramsci is one of his heroes, Marilyn Monroe and Marcel Proust—in poster form—still vie for his allegiance. As Laurana painstakingly evolves from ignorance to discovery, he must be able to accept the penalty for uncovering the truth. Petri terminates the film with Laurana's suffering the same fate Doctor Roscio did at the hands of the Big Boss.

A Quiet Place in the Country: Hallucinatory Turning Point

From a subject written earlier, dropped, and then picked up in 1968, Petri makes *A Quiet Place in the Country* (*Un tranquillo posto di campagna*, 1968) in which madness and aesthetic creation oscillate in an artist's life. For this twilight zone of an artist's mind, Petri received inspiration from Huysmans's *A rebours*. The French novelist cast his hero, Jean des Esseintes, into the rich and noble life of decadence for which he gradually feels great disgust. Hallucinations and sensuality accompany him on his search for solitude.

The young artist Leonardo Ferri (Franco Nero) and his mistress Flavia (Vanessa Redgrave) set off from Milan to their dream home in the country, an eighteenth-century villa. Mysterious occurrences—poltergeists—disturb their existence. They learn that the house is haunted by the phantom of Wanda (Gabriella Grimaldi), the daughter of a count. She made love to a German and was stabbed by Attilio, the butcher (Georges Géret). Leonardo barricades himself in the house and has violent hallucinations about Flavia's death. Flavia and the police finally break in. Leonardo is hospitalized and draws bizarre paintings which Flavia will soon exhibit.

Petri expounds on the importance of this film for him:

> The film was a real turning point for me. . . . I had to confront the problems of an artist who had lost his inspiration, in the romantic sense of the word, and who sought to rediscover his own sense of reality. He deceives himself, however, by mistaking illusion for reality, and consequently, he once again gives reality a romantic meaning. It was then that I decided to make only political films. I understood that the artist was right, but that it was important not to slip back into illusion. The character in the film was correct in feeling himself useless, believing painting to be an institution and a futile consciousness that was asocial and without a sound basis in life except as a metaphysical reference.[18]

Petri defends the film as a type of portrait of the artist as a young intellectual. Leonardo tried various formulae, broke old forms, but finally became trapped in commercial mass production. The director thus criticizes the bourgeois intellectual, but he does so while understanding the plight of the artist in confrontation with modern society. He recognizes the tension and almost speaks in the first person. Petri laments: "Ours is a world that has no need of art; it has no desire for art because it has no will to live."[19] Petri also spoke from firsthand experience of the art world; he completed a 16 mm documentary on the young American painter James Dine, part of the Pop Art movement of Johns, Oldenberg, and

Rauschenberg, and a representative of action painting, an artistic trend in the sixties. For *A Quiet Place in the Country* Dine painted twelve canvases in a Pop Art style. Franco Nero, as the artist Leonardo, simply touched them up in the course of the film.

The film has the tone and style of a modern horror film, with beatings enacted with violent realism, a body slashed to pieces, shocking hallucinations, strange séances, and upsetting nightmares. The scenes of madness rival Bellocchio's treatment of this subject. These diverse elements offer a juxtaposition of illusion and reality which the director situates at the core of his aesthetic theories.

This allegory, bordering on the surrealistic, marks the end of one phase of Petri's cinematic career, he reflected. His earlier films were simply "individual caprices" *(capricci individuali).* [20] With the turbulent events of 1968 and the serious politicizing of many aspects of society, he would launch out into a more political stream of filmmaking. He briefly remarked about this desire to change radically his approach to film direction: "I felt the necessity to make films that had a practical purpose." [21]

Investigation of a Citizen above Suspicion, The Working Class Goes to Heaven and *Property Is No Longer a Theft:* An Ideological Trilogy

In hindsight, Petri considers these three films a trilogy of political works on the schizoid elements of our society. *Investigation* deals with the relationship of power

Petri's *A Quiet Place in the Country.* Disturbed artist Ferri (Franco Nero) is offered comfort and support by his mistress Flavia (Vanessa Redgrave). *(Courtesy of Movie Star News.)*

to the average citizen; *Working Class* with the rapport of worker to productivity; and *Property* with the attitude of the individual to possessions. The director considers each of these films a type of *huis clos*, a "no exit," as well as an inferno in the Dantesque sense, where power, money, and work damn the individual's soul.[22] He also considers the triptych as autobiographical: "I have lent certain of my characteristics to the characters of these films. To make a film is to undergo self-analysis, with certain limits, obviously."[23]

> *The police inspector from homicide (Gian Maria Volonté), promoted to head of the political section of the department, cuts the throat of his mistress Augusta Terzi (Florinda Bolkan). Obsessed with the fact that his position puts him above suspicion, he deliberately leaves clues at the scene of the crime that could lead to him. When the police official eventually confesses to the murder, his colleagues implore him to deny the charges. His guilt would jeopardize the credibility of the department. He confesses his innocence and the cover-up begins. The film concludes with a quote from Kafka's* The Trial: *"Whatever impression he may give us, he is a servant of the Law. He therefore belongs to the Law and is beyond human judgment."*

With the same spirit as Francesco Rosi in his attack on the illegal use of authority, Petri strikes out at the arbitrary use of power in society. He discloses the mechanisms of power and authority that supposedly maintain an equilibrium in a society based on law and order. The Italian police department in Rome is a microcosm of all oppressive forces. Consequently he subjects the police to one of the most critical treatments that the Italian cinema had seen, although this would be popular in France with Yves Boisset's *Un condé (A Cop)* and later Michel Drach's *Le pullover rouge (The Red Sweater)*, and in the U.S. with Sidney Lumet's *Serpico*. In *Investigation*, Petri caustically presents the police as a plague on society. "The police are extremely important in my mind; they are the club of the *padrone*, the strap of the father."[24] Petri describes in his notes how he decided upon this subject with his scriptwriter Ugo Pirro and actor Gian Maria Volonté:

> On 10 April 1969 I wrote: Luciano, a friend from Milan, tells me that the police killed two people at Battipaglia; I decide to make *Investigation*. The film did not come about by chance, for Pirro, Volonté, or me. Above all, the film emerged from the group, as a clear and explicit decision on our part to make a film *against the police*.[25]

In fact, while Pirro and Petri were collaborating on the script, a police commissioner did commit a murder but was sent to prison, unlike their protagonist. The director also felt that the police commissioner Palumbo (Salvo Randone) in *The Lady Killer of Rome* (1961)—manipulative, repressive—may already have been an unconscious first draft for *Investigation*.

The police of *Investigation* are immune to sanctions because they serve power. Their work justifies any means of action, be it unethical, inhuman, or fascist. Depicted as instruments of repression, they represent or carry out the wishes of the political and economic powers of the bourgeois state. With all the ultra-modern technological means available, the head commissioner (Gianni Santuccio) steps up his witch hunt for leftists. The Inspector-Assassin meanwhile says to his police colleague: "The revolution is like syphillis. They have it in their blood." During the course of his promotion speech to his subordinates on the police force he gives statistics; he already has dossiers on 10,000 subversives and 600 homosexuals.[26] Freedom is getting out of hand, he claims. There are too many liberal journals, protests, and so on. His crowning remark is:

> The people are minors, the city, sick. Others have the task of caring for and educating. Our job is to repress. Repression is our vaccine. Repression *is* civilization!

Petri shows the average citizen is subservient to the whims of authority figures or helpless to attack and destroy them when they are corrupt or unjust. The young leftists in the film who will not conform but continually lash out against authority immediately find their revolutionary energy snuffed out by harrassment, surveillance, and torture.

The abuse of power and authority is personified in the Sicilian police assassin, dramatically played by Gian Maria Volonté. Petri sketches his character not only in political but psychological and sexual terms as well. His primary lust is for power. It blinds him to the aberrancies from his ethical code. The relationship here between fascism and sexual degeneracy is closely related to Wilhelm Reich's studies of this subject, as discussed in the treatment of Pasolini's *Salò*. Sexually immature and perverted, the assassin turns to sadomasochistic games with his mistress Augusta to stimulate their encounters. Guy Braucourt thus refers to him as "a high-placed civil servant of crime [who] is evidently only a little bureaucrat of love."[27] When Augusta attacks the Inspector's sexual inadequacy, he takes his revenge on her. She is only a sexual object to him anyway.

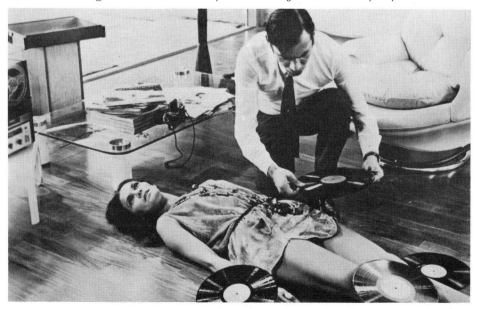

Petri's *Investigation of a Citizen above Suspicion.* The police inspector (Gian Maria Volonté) elaborately contrives the murder of his mistress (Florinda Bolkan). *(Courtesy of Movie Star News.)*

Investigation of a Citizen above Suspicion placed Elio Petri into the midst of major international circles, as did *Z* for Costa-Gavras about the same time. It established him as a true political filmmaker and a perceptive moralist as well. With an audacity not often realized in commercial films, Petri diagnoses the weaknesses of society in the unethical convictions and actions of the police force as it places itself above the law. Instead of his usual satire, Petri resorts to a more direct confrontation with the problems on the one hand and casts them into a grotesque form on the other. The issues of the rapport of the police to society are concretely delineated. At the same time, the film transcends the realistic and natural to attain a grotesque picture of Mediterranean bureaucracy, not unlike Eisenstein's method in *October* with Kerensky or Brecht in *Threepenny Opera*. The tone is reinforced by the brilliant editing and photography that make the film a technical masterpiece as well as an insightful political declaration.

In *Modern Times* (1936) Charlie Chaplin made a farcical yet perceptive observation about life in a factory progressing into the technological age. Petri's insights in *The Working Class Goes to Heaven/Lulù the Tool* (*La classe operaria va in paradiso*, 1971) are equally profound, but certainly not as humorous. He relates his intentions in making this second panel of the filmed triptych: "I wanted to do a film concerning an average worker, about his mentality, his weaknesses, and his heartrending problems. I did it in a popular language."[28] To offer a slice of proletarian life in a realistic fashion, Petri and Ugo Pirro, his scriptwriter, visited the Lebole factory in Arezzo. It was here that the workers first cut back on the cadence of the machines, resulting in a healthier working climate but lower profits for their *padroni*. Pirro and Petri thus got on-the-spot documentation for their script. Once Gian Maria Volonté was contracted to play Lulù, the metal worker, the actor met with many factory employees to discuss problems about their working conditions and their health. He learned the Milanese accent and spoke in short sentences. In this way the character of Lulù was fashioned concretely in the milieu itself.

> *For a fistful of lire, thirty-one-year-old lathe operator Lulù Massa (Gian Maria Volonté) becomes a model worker at the BAN factory of Milan, imitating the famous Russian worker Stakhanov. As industrial robot, he gradually begins to lose his identity and meaning in life. His domestic life is topsy-turvy—he shares his home life with his mistress Lidia (Mariangela Melato) and has an explosive encounter with his wife when he visits with her.*
>
> *The workers around Lulù are caught between unions and Maoist students. After an industrial accident and recuperation, he visits a former worker, Militina (Salvo Randone), whom he fears he may follow to the mental hospital. Returning to the factory with a fiery, revolutionary zeal, Lulù now sides with the militant students. He is fired for his political tactics, but the union pressures the management to rehire him. He continues his work, without heart, without hope. The final scene shows him recounting to his comrades on the assembly line the dream he had: The workers finally batter down the walls to paradise. Beyond the walls, however, lies only fog.*

This cynical study of the lot of the contemporary proletariat has its ambiguities. Petri at one time called the film "propaganda for the working class," but to

Gérard Langlois he stated that he detested propaganda and deliberately tried to avoid it in his work.[29] Petri further shows the dehumanized process at work in the factory environment, which represents physical and psychological incarceration. His realistic and yet allegorical tale should be put in a broader perspective, as noted in *Cinéaste:*

> Except for a few films by Ugo Gregoretti (even these more apologetic than thoughtful), Italian cinema has never passed through the factory gates. This was true in the years of "neo-realism," right through to the late '60's when workers resumed radical struggles. Therefore this new film by Elio Petri represents an important contribution. Where Italian cinema has gotten us accustomed to certain commercial and superficial speculations on the most controversial social questions, *The Working Class Goes to Heaven* actually comes to grips with them. The life of the worker is not mystified. We see specific problems of speed-up, union indifference, unsafe working conditions and inferior pay not as specifics of a single private life, but as a social milieu.[30]

The everyday problems of dangerous working conditions and accelerated assembly lines result in the madness of Militina and the neurosis of Lulù. The proletarians become the victims of the capitalist management, Petri poignantly shows. The society of mass consumers brings this on, and Lulù unconsciously has been taken by it; at home he is surrounded by worthless bric-à-brac such as Donald Duck and stuffed dolls. Using the dialectic of the unions versus the extremist students, Petri highlights the political and economic tension of a society gone as haywire as Charlie Chaplin's assembly line.

Petri strikes another ambiguous note, besides that of his propagandistic intent in making the film, when he makes his protagonist an antihero. Lulù has many negative traits. His life is at first cluttered up with consumer goods, awkward relationships, and a slave philosophy. His conversation with Militina radicalizes him, for the demented ex-worker serves as a reminder that it could happen to him. Once he changes political sides he is alienated. He fits on neither side.

Lulù realizes he is simply another gear in an industrial machine; keep it oiled and it can go on forever, or so management thought. Besides referring to his body as a machine to be broken in or repaired, he sees it as a "crap factory," into which raw materials are stoked and then processed. Like the Inspector of *Investigation,* Lulù is beset by his own sexual problems. In bed he is mechanically minded, and at work he is sexually oriented. He releases his sexual frustrations in a macho manner with a young, virginal worker in the front seat of his miniscule car. James Roy MacBean addresses the mechanical-sexual relationship in the context of human development:

> Petri in this film explores the way in which even the supposedly deep-seated character-structures of sexuality are not necessarily "fixed," once and for all, in earliest childhood, as most Freudians would maintain, but may on the contrary be constantly in process of formation even well into maturity and perhaps all through one's life. And significantly, what Petri concentrates on in *The Working Class Goes to Heaven* are the relations between sexuality and the machine-patterns imposed on the life of the mature adult factory worker in industrial capitalism . . .[31]

The factory psychiatrist tells Lulù a castration complex linked with his lost finger is at the root of his neurosis, showing Freudian psychology going a bit astray. Penelope Gilliatt imaginatively describes the encounter:

> (Massa) is catechized by the factory psychiatrist, a pallid, invertebrate-looking man who bends like a filleted sole. The wetly sympathetic inquisitor makes a laborious Freudian point about the lost finger. He pretends to be concerned for Massa's sexual prowess, but all he is really concerned for, of course, is his prowess at work. The psychiatrist is a mercenary of truisms of management, including the truisms of debased Freudian theory, which the Marxist Petri obviously wants us to note as having taken root most functionally in the industrialized West.[32]

Yet Freud and Marx are complementary forces and have their source in the economy Petri mentioned to Gérard Langlois.[33] The director also believes that one can be a Marxist, Freudian, and existentialist at the same time. This was the case with Wilhelm Reich, whose work inspired Petri in the film.

The Working Class provoked lively discussion and much reflection, living up to the intentions of the director. Petri wanted the film to speak to the general lot of the worker and not to the issues of any specific party. The Italian Communist party criticized the film, despite its attack on capitalist society. It felt it misrepresented the relationship of the worker to the party. *Ombre rosse*, the radical political film journal, in the person of one of its editors, Goffredo Fofi, strongly attacked the film: "It's Kafka and Freud viewed from Rome. The ideology of Petri is a very confused ideology, very mixed."[34]

Over the past ten or fifteen years since the conception of *The Working Class*, countless other films have shown the tensions of the proletariat—Paul Schrader's *Blue Collar*, Andrzej Wajda's *Man of Marble* and the sequel *Man of Iron*, Lina Wertmüller's *Seduction of Mimi*, Michel Carmin's *Blow for Blow*, and Martin Ritt's *Norma Rae*. Few have the sting of *The Working Class*; few raise the *cri d'alarme* so stridently.

Petri's last film of the trilogy—*Property Is No Longer a Theft (La proprietà non è più un furto*, 1973)—retains some of the same ambiguity as the earlier films but also moves in a more imaginative direction. Petri comments on the essence of the work: "This is a film on the uselessness of possessions, and therefore, on the uselessness of theft."[35] After his acute—some say distorted—vision of the police and the proletariat, Petri now takes on the ogre of capitalism in the form of possessions. Property is the root of all evil, conclude Petri and Ugo Pirro, his scriptwriter for the film.[36]

The credits appear over the art work of Lorenzo Vespignani. Total (Flavio Bucci), a bank employee, is allergic to money and handles it with gloves. He has become a victim of the capitalist system. One day Total watches the butcher (Ugo Tognazzi) receive an exorbitant loan from the bank. His attempt to get a more than modest one fails. Total decides to take revenge on the butcher, representative of the capitalist world, by stealing first the butcher's knife, hat, jewels, car, and then his wife. The butcher dares not put the police on the thief's trail lest his own illegal monetary dealings come to light. To eliminate this thorn in his side, the butcher finally strangles Total.

Petri was very fond of Erwin Gofman, an American sociologist who did detailed studies of closed institutions like hospitals, mental asylums, convents, and prisons. Petri felt that private proerty was itself a closed institution in a consumer society, not unlike a prison. *Property* delves into the relationship of the individual to the economic functioning of society. Petri, coming from poorer origins, asserts that property ownership is not theft, but a malady that has struck our contemporary society and grown to epidemic proportions. Alienation results. Property has become a sign of our personality, an extension of our interior being. It offers us a sense of social identity, as well as proof of our existence: "I possess, therefore I am." In the early stages of our human development property supposedly fulfills the function of a god. The bank becomes the new temple, and takes on an ecclesiastical image, not unlike Ferdinand Céline's view of it in *Voyage au bout de la nuit*.[37] The Church, in return, takes on economic characteristics, which Petri will develop in his next film, *Todo modo*.

The butcher exercises his territorial imperative, attempting to protect his goods surrounding him. In *On Aggression*, Konrad Lorenz shows how various species of the animal kingdom exercise this type of protection of one's boundaries. The butcher pushes this concept to its limits by eliminating Total.

Petri presents his ideological criticism of the economic structures of society through a satirical fable that gets at the roots of a detrimental system of haves and have-nots. His protagonist, Total, defines himself as a "mandrakian Marxist," perhaps a type of Marxism of the comic book generation. As a thief, he and the capitalist have one thing in common—the amassing of goods. One does the acquiring illegally, the other legally.

Petri's style in *Property* is both Brechtian and expressionist. The viewer immediately experiences the "distantiation" of Brecht with the concomitant reflective awareness. The monologues of Total, the butcher, and others directly facing the camera, make the film self-conscious. At the same time the director presents this critique of the economic facet of society in a popular manner on the one hand, and in a grotesque, macabre fashion on the other. A confused, nervous laugh is usually emitted by the viewer, who is challenged by this imaginative work.

As with *The Working Class*, the Communist party took a dim view of *Property*, especially following one projection of the film. Petri was unconcerned, for he felt that the party was primarily made up of little tradespeople just like the butcher. He reacted to their criticism by saying that the Communists do not like to speak of this malady presented in the film, but only of Stalinism. His remarks against Stalinism in *Jeune cinéma* for November 1973 were warranted, he said. Petri was brought up on Stalinism and saw the intellectual mess caused by the diehard Stalinists. *Property* simply illustrates the political scene on celluloid.

Hypotheses in *Documents on Giuseppe Pinelli:* The Militant Film

On 12 December 1969, a bomb went off in the Agricultural Bank of Milan. the police suspected it to be the work of anarchists. They picked up Giuseppe Pinelli, a pacifist and anarchist, whom they had earlier tried to blame for the August 1969 bombing of the train station in Milan. Shortly after midnight of 15-16 December, the police reported that Pinelli "jumped" to his death during the interrogation. In early 1970, there took place a court trial with Calabresi, the head investigator, suing the radical organization, *Lotta continua*, for slander. *Lotta continua* accused the police of having *pushed* Pinelli out the window during the questioning. In the course of the trial all the evidence was stacked against Pinelli, "proving" that it was a suicide. Yet the Left could hardly believe that Pinelli, held in a room that was the size of a bathroom, rushed through the ranks of several policemen, jumped up onto the high window ledge, and threw himself out the window. The window was supposedly open, despite the chilly December night. The trial was discontinued when Calabresi was mysteriously assassinated on 17 May 1972.[38]

Five groups of filmmakers representing the Associazione Nazionale Autori Cinematografici and the Associazione Autori Cinematografici Italiani, in a stand against repression, were scheduled to contribute material for the documentary film on the Pinelli case. Cinéastes like Visconti and Bellocchio were unable to synthesize their material in the given time. Only Petri and Nelo Risi, director of *We Will Go to the City (Andremo in città)* and *A Season in Hell (Una stagione all'inferno)*, were able to complete their projects. Risi's material, more extensive than Petri's, concentrated on Pinelli's background.[39] *Hypotheses (Ipotesi)*, Petri's fifteen-to-twenty-minute segment with Gian Maria Volonté and Luigi Diberti, documents the several explanations or hypotheses concerning Pinelli's "suicide." Petri's understanding of the situation is that the police report lied. It was impossible for Pinelli to have jumped from the window given the physical circumstances.

The film, resembling a type of cinétract or Godardian film pamphlet, was collectively signed in solidarity by seventy directors, among them Pontecorvo, Rosi, Bellocchio, and Bertolucci. Eventually the film was destined for the "popular" circuit of communist and socialist film clubs, unions, and cultural centers.[40] This would be Petri's only exposure to the pure militant film.

Todo modo: The Ruling Class Does Not Go to Heaven

Petri's bitterness against the Establishment grew with each film. His earlier films attack the law, psychiatry, police, and capitalism. With *Todo modo* (1976), Petri's aim is more accurate, his targets more personal. He now descends into the nether regions of contemporary Italian politics for his material. To see the film several years after its release would leave one with an uneasy feeling. One of the primary bull's-eyes of the work was Aldo Moro, head of the Italian Christian Democratic party. In March 1978, Moro was kidnapped by the Red Brigades, and after a long painful imprisonment was executed. His body was dumped by the urban terrorists in the area near the headquarters of the Communist party and the Christian Democratic party in Rome.

The Spiritual Exercises of Ignatius Loyola, founder of the Jesuit Order, begins, "Todo modo para buscar y hallar la voluntad divina." (One must use every means to seek and find the divine will.) Using the title from the Ignatian dictum, Sicilian novelist Leonardo Sciascia published *Todo modo* in 1974. It was designed as a satire of the Church and Italian government, especially the Christian Democratic party. His novel highlights the observations of a painter at the retreat house Zafer, where a group of the Establishment is making a retreat based on the Spiritual Exercises of Saint Ignatius.

Petri adapted Sciascia's novel almost two years later and made the author's satire even more pointed and cutting. The filmmaker traced for Tassone the source of the film project to several factors. One of Petri's most negative experiences as an adolescent was a retreat he made with a quasi-mad Jesuit who terrorized the retreatants with images of hell, fire, and damnation. Rereading the Spiritual Exercises later, Petri was intrigued with them on the one hand, and repelled by the perverse cartesian separation of the body and soul on the other. He also read Roland Barthes's study *Sade, Fourier, Loyola* which fascinated him in its analysis of the Spiritual Exercises. For the political bent of the film, Petri reflected on the "decomposing of institutions," a type of putrification that the director saw coinciding with Aldo Moro's fifteen years of governing. All of these ingredients made their way into the film in one form or other.

The political leader M. (Gian Maria Volonté) appears at the retreat house of Zafer to make the Spiritual Exercises with other government figures. The retreat director Don Gaetano (Marcello Mastroianni) facilitates the sessions in an atmosphere which appears to be more political than spiritual. Very enigmatically, three of the retreatants are murdered. An investigation ensues. Shortly before the close of the retreat Don Gaetano is also eliminated. In his room are discovered compromising dossiers on the retreatants, various false uniforms, and a parcel of dollars. Upon leaving the retreat house, M. also mysteriously meets his death.

In discussing the conclusion of the film, Petri admits he does not know who is responsible for the murders. Perhaps Gaetano ordered them and then became a victim himself. As in the political realm, no one knows all the real answers. The deaths in the film, he says, are meant to be symbolic of this type of clandestine political activity.

Luigi Barzini in 1964 acutely juxtaposes the myth and the reality of the ideologies of the more popular political parties in the Italian government. He places the Christian Democrats in this political theatre, in which Italians see the members playing out their collective farce:

> They are, reading from left to right, the Communists, the Socialists, the Christian Democrats, and the Fascists, or, as they prefer to call themselves, the *Movimento Sociale Italiano*. Together, these now represent about 85 percent of the electorate. None are especially interested in freedom. Fascists, Communists, and left-wing revolutionary Socialists notoriously deride liberty as a silly and sentimental weakness of their enemies, a *petit bourgeois* prejudice, which can be utilized to provoke disorders, to disrupt the functioning of the State and carry on preparations for their particular revolutions with greater ease. Christian Democrats and right-wing Socialists, on the other hand, praise liberty, mention it a number of times in every speech, exalt it in their anthems and marching songs; the Christian Democrats even have its Latin name inscribed on their escutcheon, *'Libertas'*. But when these parties' ideals are ana-

lyzed, they appear so confined by limitations, provisos, theological preoccupa-
tions, controls, class prejudices and arbitrary shackles, that one must conclude
they are really wary of liberty, want only a little of it, at best, safely diluted, and
at times, none at all.[41]

Petri said that his disgust and even hatred for the Christian Democratic party
had been welling up within him since his adolescence. Since 1967, he had
thought of making a film against the Christian Democrats. He wrote a political
script entitled *Nostra Signora Metedrina* about a member of this conservative party
who took drugs, and suddenly became evangelical and revolutionary. The film
was unable to be produced.[42] Almost a decade later the political situation in Italy
had not significantly evolved, despite the events of 1968. The filmmaker now,
however, could take greater risks with his subject matter. As he adapted the
novel with the assistance of Berto Pelosso, he took into consideration the political
changes of June 1975. He called the elections a signal for the beginning of the
end of the Christian Democratic party. Petri deliberately set out to do the maximum harm to the Christian Democrats. He saw the party as responsible for the
degradation of society, for the continuation of fascism today, and for the creation
of capitalist models over thirty years. He refers to this "cancer" as a type of
"Americanization of the country." For his vendetta he chose the weapon of political satire. He describes the results as "a pamphlet in which I have violently expressed my own rage, as well as that of the collective, anti-Christian Democratic
sentiment over thirty years."[43] Even more vehemently, he says that there is no
possible compromise with this type of people. They *must* be destroyed, he asserts.

This allegory, which is an amalgam of satire, surrealism, and thriller, conjures
up the unpardonable sins of the Church and state. Supposedly two distinct entities, the two institutions work in collusion with each other. Petri thus directs his
caustic wit against not only the Christian Democratic party, but the more general
modus operandi of Italian politics, and then at the Church's link with the inner
workings of the right-wing political organization.

The Church and its priests do not fare very well in *Todo modo*. Petri shows the
Church siding with the forces of authority—the powerful, rich and influential. It
uses the weapons of guilt, sin, and death to manipulate the people, and thus
preserve existing social structures. Don Gaetano represents the militant and economic Church. Petri characterizes him as an enterprising businessman and
wealthy bandit, an important figure in the spiritual multinational. He is an expelled atheist ("un athée refoulé"), says Petri, a leader interested only in temporal
power and not in the spiritual well-being of his flock. Religion only serves as a
means toward this secular end. Jean Rochereau refers to him as a Savonarola
who has mistaken the century.[44] The fiery sermon of Don Gaetano (Mastroianni)
carries the same judgmental theology as the Jesuit preacher (John Gielgud) in
the screen adaptation of Joyce's *A Portrait of the Artist as a Young Man*, or the
preacher in Bellocchio's *In the Name of the Father*.

Petri's diatribe against the Christian Democratic party is equally venomous.
The director shows no mercy as he presents the influential political leaders as
mediocre and buffoonish. Their hypocrisy matches that of the members of the

Church, both defending each other's rights. This ruling class is destined for political suicide, feels Petri. It must pay for its crimes, gone too long unpunished.

The politician M. is primarily based on Aldo Moro, as indicated earlier. Petri and Volonté studied Moro very closely in order to caricature him in the film. Consequently, M. has many many of Moro's tics. Petri recounted to Jean Gili the reasons for choosing Moro as his target:

> Among all the Christian Democrats, it seemed to me that Aldo Moro was the most symbolic and also the most dangerous. Moro was the protagonist in the Center-Left experience. He succeeded in drawing the Socialists into the coalition of the sixties when already the serious crisis of the model of development was being sketched out, a crisis that has reached its limits today. Moro readily succeeded, therefore, in making the Socialists co-responsible for all the errors that the Christian Democrats had been able to commit over the course of the preceding fifteen years. He is now trying to play the same card with the Communists. He is a sweet-talker.[45]

To the tics of Moro, Petri adds those of other politicians as well. In fact, Petri wanted to make his protagonist a type of universal politician conditioned by Judaeo-Christian principles. The director surrounds him with mystery—did he murder his cohorts? Was the criminal acting under the orders of the CIA, the Fascists, or political competitors? Petri felt that the characters who inspired the film were more horrifying in real life. The grotesque and at times expressionistic style of *Todo modo*, however, makes the film less realistic but does not reduce the impact of the satire. At the film's release during the elections of 1976, Petri knew that the film was effective. The hostile reaction to its image of the Church and the Christian Democratic party was overwhelming. Petri's cinematic torpedo did the job. Leonardo Sciascia, author of the novel, underlined the confrontative work of Petri: "The trial that Pasolini wanted to put the Christian Democrats through, Petri accomplished today."[46]

Dirty Hands and *Good News:* Encounter with Television

In the fifties Petri had thought of making a film on Stalinism:

> Following the Twentieth Congress of the Bolshevik Communist Party—I was not yet making films—I proposed to Cristaldi a film entitled *Is Stalin Dead?*. In those days, the communist intellectuals had been swept up in a dramatic moral and political crisis, provoked by Khrushchev's indictment of Stalin's crimes. It was a crisis which also changed many personal destinies. But at the same time, making political films was considered taboo. For a good many years matters were not openly known by their real names. . . . *Is Stalin Dead?* was obviously never made.[47]

Filming Jean Paul Sartre's *Dirty Hands* (*Les mains sales,* 1948) for television was a substitute for his original intention. In the back of his mind, Petri understood full well that the spectre of Stalin still hovered over the European political scene—which was also Artur London's and Costa-Gavras's conclusion in their collaboration on *The Confession* (*L'aveu*, 1979). Petri's decision to make *Dirty Hands* (*Mani sporche*, 1979) for Channel One (RAI) came from his desire to recreate the existential drama of Sartre but also to give it some local, contemporary color.

> *The action takes place in the fictitious central European country of Illiria, occupied by Nazis, as the end of World War II is approaching.*
>
> *The young Hugo (Giovanni Visentin) returns from a two-year prison term for homicide and speaks with his fellow comrade Olga (Anna Maria Gherardi). Representation from the Communist party will arrive shortly to determine if Hugo is ideologically "salvageable." If not, they will eliminate him. In a type of flashback to March 1943, Hugo explains how he and his wife Jessica (Giuliana Di Sio) went to the partisan headquarters of Hoederer (Marcello Mastroianni) with the intention of executing him. Rumor had it that Hoederer was going to sell out his Communist allies for a tripartite government at the close of the war. The cowardly petit bourgeois Hugo hesitates to carry out his mission for the party, and is only forced to execute Hoederer when he discovers his wife in his arms. As the party representatives are about to enter, at the close of the flashback, Hugo tries to make some sense of his act, but he ultimately faces them with a suicidal "not salvageable" (non récupérable).*

Petri adds a type of revolutionary postscript to the original work. Hugo gets up at the applause of the audience. There follows an exchange of revolutionary slogans: "Provocateurs!", "The Truth is revolutionary!", "No compromise with the bourgeois!", "Long live national unity!" Stalin's image overhead is the last to fade.

The director relies on Sartre's historical appreciation of the postwar dilemma in the restructuring of society and government. At the same time he captures the timeliness of the Hoederer-Hugo tension. Hoederer is a classical realist, but not an opportunist. He sees the final days of the six-year struggle against the tyranny of fascism coming to its end. He seriously considers a tripartite government as the most feasible and meets with the necessary political leaders to assure this. In the back of his mind he has a plan to retain some power and prevent possible insurrection during the forthcoming political chaos. In this way he hopes to help the country and not simply follow an abstract ideal. Expedience, and not party unity, is his priority, and the compromising means will justify his political end.

Hugo, on the other hand, a bourgeois intellectual anarchist, blindly believes in absolute party purity and following orders for the cause. He wants nothing to do with a coalition, especially where his comrades would retain a very weak voice. Ideological integrity is of greater importance to him than political expediency. He is characterized by Petri as an adolescent, false, abstract, and cold, contrasted to Hoederer who is paternal, virile, and warm.

Petri handles the confrontation in dialectical fashion. He can detect traces of this debate in Italy from the historical compromise of the sixties to the present. More personally, like Bellocchio during the production of Chekhov's *The Seagull*, Petri senses the inner tension of his two major characters:

> Hoederer and Hugo are in a position, analogous to the elections of 1948, of having to choose. Like this pair, I feel myself divided. Some of Hugo's words

are timely. These thirty years of "dirty hands"—accepting the principle of a bourgeois reality—have caused confusion, disorientation. . . . But I also wonder how one cannot agree with Hoederer when he speaks of "dirty hands" and the love of humanity.[48]

It is thus that a thirty-year old French play takes on a new face under Petri's direction.

Petri's experience with the television medium in directing *Dirty Hands* provided him with a springboard for his next film, *Good News* (*La personalità della vittima ovvero le buone notizie*, 1979). His central character comes from the television industry and is played by the actor and coproducer, Giancarlo Giannini.

The nameless protagonist (Giannini) works for Italian television (RAI), supervising television monitors. Around this Keatonesque character unfolds a curious political and sexual psychodrama which recalls somewhat Albee's Who's Afraid of Virginia Wolff?. *Living out their own personal ideologies, two couples are involved in complicated relationships—the television functionary and his wife Feodora (Angela Molina), and his Jewish friend Professor Gualtiero Milano (Paolo Bonacelli) with his wife Ad (Aurore Clement). The macho protagonist is constantly in search of his true sexual identity. Meanwhile his friend Gualtiero dies a violent death in a mental hospital. Returning from the funeral service, Feodora admits to her husband that she is pregnant by his friend. The child's name shall be Gualtiero. Once back in his office, the television supervisor finds a parcel left by Gualtiero marked "DO NOT OPEN." Fearing a bomb, he opens it in the garden. The parcel ironically contains materials to delete typing errors.*

The fascinating and provocative themes of Petri's earlier films reappear in *Good News,* again presented in a grotesque tone. In the film, primordial fear of death, male domination, sexual inadequacy predominate. Marital infidelity, the terrorism of violence, and the obsession with the growing impact of the mass media and technology all feed into the psychodrama which Petri calls "a sophisticated comedy of the Left."[49] To personalize his thesis the director casts the television operator as a pathetic creature who lives only on the level of reflex action, symptomatic of our technological society. His reality is filtered through television, a surrogate for the actual life around him. He finds himself in an existential abyss, and the news reports on the various monitors simply reinforce this state. The television, a transmitter of authority, power, and religion, is also a major symbol of production in an increasingly industrialized society. In Petri's vision, it serves as the purveyor of a society on the apocalyptic edge of doom.

Conclusions

Elio Petri's film career until his untimely death in 1982 was extensive. From journalism to the documentary, to feature political fiction and militant ideological film, and concluding in television production, Petri traversed the vast scope of the media world. His own scriptwriting and co-production work supplemented this extensive experience. Like Pontecorvo in this, Petri graduated from militancy in the Italian Communist party to become a fellow traveller as well as a critic of the party on occasion. With his Commedia dell'Arte style, he studied the various institutions that comprise contemporary society. He made the filmgoer laugh in order to reflect its weaker points—and they are many, he admits—and to ameliorate the general human condition. His purpose was thus moralistic. Consequently, the spectator does laugh, but nervously. The material sometimes hits too close to home in one or more of the sectors of society that he criticizes. Here he cannot camouflage his leftist, partisan views toward the police, clergy, or Christian Democrats. His films thus become a cudgel, knocking the viewer to attention or, as some critics complain, beating him or her over the head until the message is grasped. The political, psychological, sexual, and aesthetic—all provide the director with a unique tone and a rich context in which to communicate ominously his sociopolitical message about alienation in a modern technological society.

7

LINA WERTMÜLLER:
The Politics of Sexuality

> My films are deliberately provocative, intended to agitate
> problems and bring them out in the open. This is my aim—
> to provoke and discuss.
>
> —Lina Wertmüller, 1976

For a variety of sociological reasons, very few women filmmakers have attained international success in the fiction film realm. Agnès Varda and Marguerite Duras in France, Claudia Weill and Susan Sontag in the United States, Gillian Armstrong in Australia, and Liliana Cavani and Lina Wertmüller in Italy, have made a name for themselves, but not without great frustrations, in the male-dominated film industry.[1] In the seventies, Lina Wertmüller surpassed most of her international comrades-in-arms in reputation and productivity. Eclectic, unorthodox, and at times bitterly sarcastic in her works, she has often found herself at the center of a storm of controversy. Her thirteen films primarily dealing with politics and sexuality nonetheless reveal a brilliant originality and incredible vitality. Consequently she has become the object of an American cult whose quasi-religious power has only mildly spread to England and France, and she has hardly been accepted in her native Italy. Not even a cinematic prophet is accepted in his or her own land.

She was born Arcangela Felice Assunta Wertmüller Von Elgg Spagnol Von Braucich on 14 August 1928, with her origins in a Roman family. Her remote roots were in Zurich. Her great-great-grandfather of noble rank left Switzerland for Naples, following a duel over a woman. Her father was a wealthy lawyer practicing in Rome. As a child, she was sent to the best of private religious schools. Each of these fifteen institutions dismissed her for disciplinary reasons. "It's interesting," she recalled to Jerry Tallmer of the *New York Post* (27 January 1978), "I grew up in an era that still had the sense of authority of parents, church, school; the sense of sin, of guilt; therefore also the sense of revolution." Inevitably she did revolt. Like Bellocchio in similar circumstances, she broke with organized religion at the age of thirteen, discounting a good and omniscient God who creates a hell in which to send those who fall, as she told Ernest Ferlita.[2] The existence of hell and possible eternal damnation would color her perception of the Church in her films, even though she would not insist upon this theme as does Bellocchio, who came out of the religious experience less resilient than she.

Following the war Lina Wertmüller attended the Academy of Pietro Sharoff where the Stanislavsky method of acting was taught. Her interest was primarily in drama—her first love—and then choreography. Another love was music, as reflected, for example, in her thinking in musical phrases as she plots out a film. At the academy she took a course in theatre direction. "In 1951, with friends, I formed a theater group called Harlequin. It was supposed to be avant-garde, but it might be better to call it 'rear guard.' The group dissolved as its members, one by one, left to work as cinema extras."[3] Cinecittà was blossoming. Celluloid dreams seduced her company. She persevered, however, and became a disciple of the celebrated actor-director Edoardo de Flippo and worked as assistant director to Guido Salvini and Giorgio DeLullo.

For about ten years Wertmüller worked in theatre and television, writing plays and filming television musicals. Two of her more important works for the stage were *Love and Magic in Mamma's Kitchen (Amore e magia nella cucina di mamma)* on the tragic story of murderer Leonardo Cianciulli, drawn from Arnold Wesker's *The Kitchen* (1970), and *Two and Two No Longer Make Four,* written by her in 1969 and staged by Franco Zeffirelli. For television, in 1965 she adapted *The Diary of Gian Burrasca (Il giornalino di Gian Burrasca)* of Vamba (Luigi Bertelli) with actress Rita Pavone, whom she would also use in the television musicals *Rita the Mosquito (Rita la zanzara,* 1966) and *Don't Sting the Mosquito (Non stuzzicate la zanzara,* 1967). She signed *Rita the Mosquito* with the name George H. Brown. In our interviews of 25–26 April 1981 in Rome, the director admitted that these two television productions were the work more of an artisan than an artist. The projects, however, kept her employed. In 1981, she was still interested in television. She completed a reportage on the earthquake which struck Naples in late 1980, in which she was asking the ultimate question, "What do you say to the irrationality of Nature?" The filmed document is her response, made so we do not forget this tragic blow by Destiny. In it she used the basic principles of the neorealists, the recognition of and the witness to the problems of the south.[4]

Wertmüller engaged in other unusual aesthetic activities before she turned to cinema. She worked with hand puppets. With the Maria Signorelli puppet troupe she toured all over Europe. The performances were oriented more toward Kafka than Punch and Judy. Her experience with puppets added another dimension that would enhance her vision of the general art world and pave the way for a blend of the serious and absurd in her film work.

Like many of the other Italian cinéastes, Lina Wertmüller thrived on cinema from her teenage years. She grew up in the Regina Cinema in Rome, filled with the illusions of a mythical Hollywood. Her formal entry into the film world came in 1962. Flora Carabella, her close friend from convent school days and later wife of Marcello Mastroianni, introduced her to Federico Fellini. He would be the catalyst in her career, accepting her as an assistant for *8½* (1963). For the three months that she worked with the film maestro, she was able to learn directly the ins and outs of the film world. From him she gained not so much a knowledge of technique, but a cinematic *Weltanschauung.* Fellini was a light, a god, a liberator for her, she acknowledges today. He showed her the freedom of an artist, enlightening her about the myriad of possibilities in film direction. The grotesque and the tragic, curious bedfellows in Fellini, become part of Wertmüller's narrative. Making a film, the director of *8½* suggested, is like telling a joke to friends; one must have the ability to tell a good story. Other cinematic influences in her career came from Pietro Germi, Luigi Comencini, and Carmelo Bene.

Her personal political philosophy was coming into better focus about the time she met Fellini and during the filming of her first work *The Lizards (I Basilischi,* 1963). Yet her sociopolitical formation began as a child. Her father had become a Fascist in 1923, several years before Lina was born. The following year he severed his ties with the Fascists when he wrote against the government. During World War II, the family hid a group of Jews in their home. The house was filled with more and more anti-Fascists as time went on. As children, Lina and her playmates imitated Mussolini although they also had great respect for *Il Duce.* She compares images of Mussolini in the context of the Cold War:

> We were taught that he was a god, the savior of Italy, that everything would be ruined after his death. . . . In Italy after the war, many people took the left position. Those two polar worlds—America and Russia—they burst, both of them. The real drama of my generation was to discover the wreckage of both ideologies: Stalin on one side, Hiroshima on the other. And one has to fight very hard to build up a world less divided than it is now.[5]

Following World War II, Wertmüller entered the Communist-oriented Circolo Giovani. She was a member of the Communist party until 1956. Like Pontecorvo and many other Italian intellectuals, she left the party at the Soviet invasion of Hungary. She then joined the Socialist party. There she experienced greater freedom of thought. Less leftist than the Communists, the Socialists worked very conscientiously for reform. Her idol in the early days in the party was Giacomo Mancini, then leader of the Socialist party. She was most enthusiastic about socialism, especially his brand, and saw it as the way of the future. She later became a member of the Central Committee of the party and only abandoned this position around 1978 when she could no longer continue with all of her political responsibilities. Her politics would sometimes take her to the public square, where she would demonstrate for divorce and abortion. Today she appreciates the many and diverse parties in the Italian political system. Despite the infighting and complexity of this type of governing—in 1982 occurred the forty-second government since the war—there is a better sense of representation for everyone, she believes.

Her politics are not abstract or purely ideological. She has her finger on the pulse of a struggling society, as the topics of our interviews indicated: paralyzing terrorism, youth and drug problems, proletarian conflicts, economics as a basis for politics, the feminist movement, parliamentary representation, the power of the mass media, and so on. She addressed these issues in a simple, colloquial manner that shows that they have entered into her everyday life and are not simply pious political platitudes.

From her films one can construct a sociopolitical perspective that emerges gradually in the sixties and blossoms in the seventies. She directs these works at the masses, she says, forcing them to reflect on certain major societal issues: "My films are deliberately provocative, intended to agitate problems and bring them out in the open. This is my aim—to provoke and discuss."[6] As a result she creates a more popular type of political film than a Godard with his recherché opus.

Wertmüller exhibits great sympathy for the poor, the downtrodden, and the proletariat. This sentiment can take the shape of depicting the south of Italy, a Third World, she believes; her first feature *The Lizards* proved it, and her recent documentary on the Naples earthquake reinforced it. Rosi's interest in the Mezzogiorno or southern question is also hers. She has a personal interest in this question since part of her family comes from Puglia in the south. She elaborates on the significance of this region: "The South is a symbol. . . . We are all black people. It's all the same in life, the relationship between men and women, the south and the north, the exploiters and exploited, the civilized and the un-civilized."[7] Born into the bourgeoisie, she says she continually wages a constant war against it. Sympathetic toward the poor, she encourages them not to become materialistic like the members of the upper class.

The director's protagonist usually comes from the poorer regions of the south. She has a warm feeling for him, yet she does not whitewash him. He is a loving but naive creature, sharing attractive and repelling characteristics simul-taneously. Wertmüller depicts this Chaplinesque underdog as confronted by powerful forces—the government, Church, Mafia, bosses, Nazis, police, and bourgeoisie. In her mind these power structures dominate and at times destroy the underpinnings of a civilization. They also attempt to crush the individual like a worm underfoot. Weak and immature, the little man cannot cope with them. He capitulates. This is especially evident in her sensitivity to the lot of the Italian bluecollar worker, as Thomas Bohn and Richard Stromgrem point out:

> In *Love and Anarchy* he is a peasant whose mission to assassinate Mussolini is subverted by a sexual foray. In *Swept Away* he is a Marxist *Admirable Crichton* whose sexual/political confrontation takes place on a deserted island. And in *Seven Beauties* he is the murderer of a pimp, having his own sexual encounter with a female guard of a Nazi concentration camp. In all of these he is in the person of Giancarlo Giannini, Wertmüller's star underdog who becomes a pawn of the political system as well as a victim of his own and others' sexual drives.[8]

In a sociopolitical manner, Wertmüller further expresses a genuine moral con-cern about this individual trapped by these forces. She usually situates him in a political and ethical dilemma. Unfortunately he can only survive unemployment, imprisonment, or shipwreck by compromising his moral principles. Her realism in this treatment of the leading character sometimes borders on nihilism.

Although Wertmüller has been a member of the leftist but slightly conservative

Italian Socialist Party, on occasion an unusual anarchistic streak runs through her films and her ideology. It comes to the surface, for example, when she speaks of the family, although perhaps somewhat naively. As it is structured now, she senses, the family is an outmoded and paralyzing phenomenon. It curtails the psychological growth of women and puts a burden on the economy. She and her artist-husband Enrico Job have no children, "but all my films are my children. Anarchy is utopia."[9]

Through all her films from *The Lizards* in 1963 to her 1981 reportage on the earthquake Wertmüller weaves political themes that speak to society's current anguish and moral decadence. She is not idealistic in her approach to the political impact of her films: "You cannot make the revolution on film."[10] Avoiding any heavy propaganda for or against a cause, she tries to balance her politics with her aesthetics. To John Simon she remarked, "Ideology must not devour but illuminate art."[11] This has been the basic principle operative in most of her filmmaking.

Wertmüller's uniqueness lies in her flamboyant style, only rivaled by Bellocchio in *In the Name of the Father.* This style serves as a well-oiled vehicle for her profound social criticism directed to a large, popular audience. As the "Italian Aristophanes," she hopes to uncover the foibles of society in order that the public may take a long, hard look at the fragility of this society.[12] In order to do this she leans heavily on the biblical form of the parable, harking back to her interest in the biblical parable of the talents. She comments on this biblical form:

> I have always been struck by the parable of the talents in the Gospel, of the wonderful opportunity given exclusively to man to invest, as best he can, the coin of life. As a consequence, I am also struck by every neglect and every waste.[13]

Ferlita and May develop an analysis of her work using this biblical form or genre as a framework. The parable, a type of allegorical story in the New Testament, narrates an everyday reality in simple, universal terms—encounters of kings, shepherds, laborers, fishermen, and tax-collectors. The narrative offers on several levels an insight into our human and moral lives.

In the contemporary parables of Wertmüller there are harlots, anarchists, proletarians, aristocrats, Mafiosi, and Nazis. They become types which can be interpreted in several ways. She positions the cast of characters in metaphorical situations, as Ferlita states: quarry, island, concentration camp, kitchen, brothel.[14] This may be a stumbling block for her critics who take these situations at face value, instead of accepting her sweeping universal application.

Although her political perspective is serious, her presentation of it is deliberately humorous, but not without its tragic overtones. She discusses her evolution from the seriousness of her early work to the genuinely tragicomic in her more recent films:

> I proceeded with a great faith in the power of laughter, and tears, without fearing to be too obvious or to appear banal, always trying to communicate and entertain and hoping, in the end, that people would leave my films with

problems to think over and analyze. I feel that I have succeeded in reaching a popular audience in many parts of the world in this way.[15]

This simultaneously comic and tragic tone expressed in her films derives from her interests in theatre, especially the Commedia dell'Arte. Giancarlo Giannini, the protagonist of most of her films, plays the buffoonish Harlequin, a Chaplinesque Everyman in confrontation with a hostile society. In his clownish manner, he becomes the antihero, the butt of Wertmüller's jokes. She feels laughter is the best defense the poor can have, an excellent antidote against the drug of power. To achieve this laughter, which she feels liberates the individual, Wertmüller runs a full gamut of comedy—slapstick, satire, wit, black humor. The colorful namecalling which escalates between the couple in *Swept Away*, the symbolic leap of the anarchist Pedro of *Seven Beauties* into the pit of excrement, the imitation of the Holy Family flight into Egypt seen in *Seduction of Mimi*, Mimi's encounter with the bovine Amalia, and Pasqualino's seduction of the Nazi guard in *Seven Beauties* stir the audience to laugh heartily. But just as with Chaplin in *Modern Times* or *The Great Dictator*, the laughter reinforces the political message. When asked by McIsaac and Blumenfeld if this comic approach does not ultimately mock politics, thus rendering the message ineffectual, Wertmüller replied:

> Why should serious political points necessarily be made in a serious manner? This is not the only way to present political problems. On the contrary, experience shows us that the opposite can be true; the serious approach may make its point less effectively than the comic. In fact, in Italy, the severe, macabre approach to politics drives people away. It intimidates them, making them feel politics is only for the experts. But politics is not divorced from our lives; each of our acts has political consequences. Every familiar experience partakes of all of life—which is tragic and horrendous, yes, but also wonderful. Why should we choose only to look at the tragic and heavy face of politics?[16]

Given this comic thrust to her works, the spectator must be prepared to change gears quickly when Wertmüller introduces a simultaneous serious element. Pasqualino's seduction of the enormous Nazi officer draws gales of laughter, but underlining this comedy of situation is the sad tale of what must be done in order that Pasqualino survive. He must then choose six camp prisoners to execute or else she will have the whole group destroyed. The acting of Giannini, which carefully depicts this shift, and the ironic use of music help achieve and accentuate the tragicomic juxtaposition. Even in a tragedy such as Tunin's attempted suicide with an empty pistol in *Love and Anarchy*, the facial expression of the actor can bring humor to the situation. The sound track especially can bring this out. In *Seven Beauties* Nazi powerhouse Hilde sings a piece from a Wagner opera while Pasqualino eats to prepare himself for lovemaking with her. The caustic "Oh Yeah!" refrain to the song that opens the film adds a comic note to a serious song of love, compromise, belief and struggle. As Mimi arrives in the northern city of Turin from his native Sicily, a tenor off-screen sings from the opera *Il trovatore:* "We have arrived. This is the land where the political prisoners weep . . . Ah! This is where the poor man was brought to." As in a Shakespearean play, there is something for everyone—bawdy language for the groundlings, and sophisticated symbolism and plays on words for the intellectuals. These comic and tragic elements of the film cannot be separated. Together they show the oscillating emotional elements of our everyday lives, as Terrence Des Pres succinctly notes: "Her films are just that: part cartoon, part tragedy, life's sorrow smeared in farce. This is an art faithful to life as we live it, half in joke and half in deadly earnest."[17] In essence, the director's work, where art and life amusingly intersect, is paradoxically traditional and original.

Much of Wertmüller's style of the grotesquely comic springs from her own fertile imagination, though one can readily see parallels with Fellini in his use of comic and tragic elements such as three-hundred-pound frolicking maidens or sexual ambivalence. Other sources of inspiration in her films come from her husband Enrico Job and Giancarlo Giannini. Job, once a sculptor and artist, has invested his creative energy in designing all the sets of Wertmüller's films. The apartment of the ex-Maoist virgin Raffaella in *The Seduction of Mimi* reflects the innovative architectural and aesthetic touch he contributes to the film collaboration. His masterpiece may be an old paper factory near Tivoli converted into the eerie, expressionistic concentration camp of *Seven Beauties*. The very earthy Giancarlo Giannini was born in Genoa but was brought up in Naples. Like Lina Wertmüller he also came from the theatre. His earliest film appearances with Wertmüller were *Rita the Mosquito* and *Don't Sting the Mosquito*. His facial expressions—drooping eyes, bedroom eyes, bulging eyes—lend a fresh dramatic tone to acting. With great exuberance he plays the role of "the worm," "the Mediterranean larva," or the "Neapolitan macaroni."

Giannini, Job, and Wertmüller work closely on the project right from the very beginning. Once Wertmüller has her insight into the content of the film—usually arising from a real-life situation, almost never from a written source—she sits down to write her script. (She had already had some experience writing scripts for other directors.)[18] This most often takes two to four months, as she gets further ideas from her two collaborators. With a lengthy script before her, generally approved in advance by the production company, she undertakes her venture. She also feels a certain freedom within her to become inspired during the shooting and to alter completely a minutely prepared scenario. Giannini plays before a mirror with a series of grimaces and they shoot the scene several times. Wertmüller tries the scene from various angles, adds new materials. At times she edits during the shooting, at other times in the month(s) following. In the end she has at her disposal more than ten times the amount of footage necessary, giving her a wide choice of shots. The rich unique results bear her mark but credit must also be given to her two artistic partners.

The Lizards and Let's Talk about Men: Before the Cultic Revolution

For Lina Wertmüller, *Lizards* and *Let's Talk* serve as stepping stones to the success which eventually came in 1971 with *Seduction of Mimi*. While driving through the southeastern region of Puglia and Basilicata in the heel of Italy, the director had the idea to make a film on this land of some of her ancestors. Since she was involved with Fellini in the filming of *8½*, she looked to him for counsel. He offered her more than that. Fellini helped Wertmüller obtain funding for the project and shared some of his *8½* crew with her in order to assist in the filming. She was given three months to prepare the script. She examined many documents about life in this region before beginning. Within three days she completed the script. In order to make it appear as if writing were not a hasty task, she waited a week and then submitted it. It was accepted and shooting was done in Minervino Murge. *The Lizards (I Basilischi*, 1963) was shot directly from the script with almost no modifications.[19]

In a small provincial town of southeastern Italy, life drags on without incident. Social paralysis has set in. Antonio (Toni Petruzzi) escapes this fossilized existence by going to Rome. Disillusioned, he eventually returns to his home town. And life goes on.

Several titles were proposed for this study of provincial life: *Oblomov di provincia (A Provincial Oblomov)*, *Un colpo di vita (A Blow from Life)*, and *Ragazzi seduti (Seated Kids)*. The title chosen, *I Basilischi* recalls Fellini's *I vitelloni (The loafers/The Young and the Passionate)*, about the ennui and restlessness of young men in a similar provincial setting. The characters of the Wertmüller film could leap right out of the Fellini work. The English title, *The Lizards*, captures perfectly the feel of the young people in this milieu. They are psychologically and socially immobile, like lazy lizards basking in the noonday sun. Wertmüller reveals the key to the thematic structure of the film: "The central theme develops two motifs: on the one hand, the process of giving way to laziness, to disintegration; on the other hand, my personal views on the bourgeoisie, particularly the bourgeoisie in the south of Italy."[20]

In a slow, meditative, and almost painful manner, the director recreates the impotent provincial life that she saw in the southern sections of Italy. In the film the young have no drive, ambition, or sense of destiny. The young males stalk their female prey, play cards, and spend the remainder of their energy on endless banter, as did the characters of Pasolini's *Accattone*. For Wertmüller's characters this is a *huis clos*. Only those few who have dreams are able to escape the rigor mortis. This slice of life was most accurate, most realistic. The public and the critics viewing it understood that. The film won approximately fifteen prizes. Twenty years later, Wertmüller believes that little has changed in the region since she made the film.

She calls her next film, *Let's Talk about Men (Questa volta parliamo di uomini*, 1965) "my theatrical film" and that it is. To the wave of episodic films in Italy in the sixties Lina Wertmüller made her own contribution. The producers wanted to lessen risks and attract stars and celebrated directors. This was seen as a solution to the growing financial crisis in the Italian cinema which has been ever-present in the industry over the past two decades. The four episodes of the film feature Nino Manfredi, whose reputation in the United States was made with Franco Brusati's *Bread and Chocolate (Pane e cioccolata)*.

Wertmüller's **The Lizards.** The director sets up a scene for the film. *(Courtesy of Director Lina Wertmüller.)*

A research fellow at Rome's Institute for Tropical Diseases (Nino Manfredi), alone in the apartment of his friend, accidentally locks himself out in the course of his shower. Embarrassingly naked, he attempts to get back in. Certain remarks by or encounters with the neighbors evoke four fantasies which enlighten the scholar:

—*"A Man of Honor" ("Un Uomo d'onore"): The financially comfortable Federico is distraught that his wife Manuela (Luciana Paoluzzi) has been stealing jewelry and concealing the booty in her bureau. In the meantime, the world economic situation is such that Federico may be reduced to poverty. He resorts to a sophisticated form of dishonesty by arranging for a chic evening party for jewel-bedecked guests. . . .*

—*"The Knife Thrower" ("Il Lanciatore di coltelli"): Pedro, "The Infallible Morgas," veteran circus knifethrower, shows himself less than infallible in his art: his wife Saturnia (Milena Vukotic) sports a wooden leg and a patch over her eye as a result. In his reverie, the youthful Pedro miscalculates, and Saturnia slips off into the nether world without his realizing it.*

—*"A Superior Man" ("Un Uomo superiore"): Ironically this "superior" man is well shy of the mark both physically and psychologically. The scientist Rafael limps and has a perverted view of sexuality. The attempts of his wife Marquessa (Margaret Lee) to murder him are in vain. They are reconciled following his ruse of feigning death.*

—*"A Good Man" ("Un Brav' uomo"): The stereotype of the macho Italian male is sketched out here. Salvatore, a Sicilian, rises late, spends his day at the bar, plays cards, and ends up inebriated. He only comes home when he has to fulfill his other needs. His sexual desires once sated, his exhausted wife (Patrizia De Clara) can now return to her endless chores.*

At the close of the film the uncomfortable situation of the scholar has worsened. The neighbors take him for an exhibitionist.

Let's Talk about Men is a clever exercise in style and technique, using as a framework the predicament of the naked man. It passes from comical to surrealistic and then to neorealistic, all the time shedding light on crumbling human nature. The women in Wertmüller's film are shaped by tradition and culture, and reinforced in their passivity by their insensitive husbands. Fragile, weak, inferior, and dishonorable, the men are hardly "superior." These various types of men will be further developed in the director's evolving opus. The fourth model, the macho who oppresses his slave-wife, will predominate. In Salvatore are the seeds for the characters of Mimi and Pasqualino.

Seduction of Mimi, Swept Away, Seven Beauties: Allegories of Survival

In the Darwinian jungle of contemporary society it is not only the strongest that survive. It is those who possess the ability to *adapt* to life in such fundamental environments as a deserted island, competitive industry, or a concentration camp. It may mean leaving behind some ethical baggage, but at least one saves one's skin. Integrity is only skin-deep, and human dignity is necessarily in abeyance. Such are the conclusions of a majority of Wertmüller's characters in this series of allegories or parables.

Following her two little-known musicals for television—*Rita the Mosquito* (*Rita la zanzara*, 1966) and *Don't Sting the Mosquito* (*Non stuzzicate la zanzara*, 1967), with Rita Pavone and Giancarlo Giannini, Wertmüller launched out in international waters with *The Seduction of Mimi* (*Mimi metallurgico ferito nell' onore*, 1971). Distribution of the film in the United States in 1974 brought her success and initiated her Manhattan cult that was especially fervid during the late seventies.

A news item, a personal experience, or a true story told by a friend often serve as a starting point for Wertmüller's films. For *Mimi* it was a political situation in Sicily. When the director read that the Communist city of Catania in the southeast sector of the island had gone Fascist, she was puzzled by the ideological shift. In our April interview she recounted that, when she was in Catania and inquired about this political change, one man replied, "My wife's handbag was snatched, so I voted for law and order." In a region of the country at times marked by crime, vendetta, Mafia law and little or no order, this response could be well comprehended. Wertmüller's film traces the evolution of a young man in a political swing of the pendulum from Left to Right. Giancarlo Giannini was contracted for the role of the protagonist. To prepare for this part the Neapolitan-bred actor spent several weeks in Sicily with camera and tape recorder, documenting the speech and mannerisms of the local Sicilians. He recounts how he creates a character such as Mimi from the exterior (milieu) to the interior (soul):

> Once I've formed an idea of a character . . . I confront him from the outside. I start with the spinal cord, which is basic to his carriage, his entire nervous system. I must decide how he stands and carries himself in the world. Next his arms—how does he reveal himself through his arms? Then his body rhythms—slower or faster than mine? Once all this is clarified, I'm prepared to hide myself inside.[21]

Carmelo Mardocheo, better known as Mimi (Giancarlo Giannini), is a leftist quarry-worker in Sicily. He alienates the Mafia when he refuses to vote for their proposed candidate in the elections. To find employment, Mimi is obliged to leave Sicily and his wife Rosalia (Agostina Belli). He arrives in the northern industrial city of Turin where he lands a job as a metallurgist. He joins the Communist party and falls in love with the ex-Maoist precious flower of a virgin Fiore (Mariangela Melato). He is soon transferred to his native Sicily with Fiore and their son. He leads a double life of love until he discovers that his wife is pregnant by the customs officer Almicare Finochiarro. To preserve his honor, he seduces the officer's wife, the bovine Amalia (Elena Fiore). In his confrontation with Almicare, Mimi witnesses a Mafia gunman shoot the officer and drop the weapon near him. Framed, Mimi serves out his sentence in jail, only to emerge as the father of a herd of eight children. He becomes easy prey for the Mafia and finds himself alone, reduced to a lackey, campaigning among the quarrymen for the Mafia candidate.

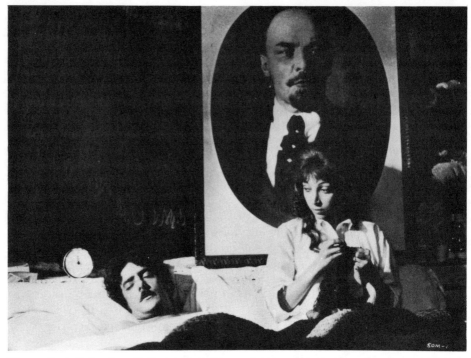

Wertmüller's *Seduction of Mimi.* Mimi (Giancarlo Giannini) dozes under the watchful eye of his radical wife Fiore (Mariangela Melato). *(Courtesy of Donald Velde, Inc.)*

Wertmüller constructs a humorous carnival shooting gallery in which the seducer and the seduced are moving targets. The leftists, primarily Communists, are weak and ineffectual in the film. Despite their ideologies, the quarry-workers succumb to voting for the Mafia candidate. Later in the film, Fiore describes her former political experiences. When Mimi tells Fiore that the only true left-wing is made up of eight million workers belonging to the Communist party, she bursts out in laughter and responds: "On the one hand there are those [leftists] planting bombs, on the other they're all on strike. We're all left-wingers, but instead of being united we're fighting among ourselves. . . ."

The director is also critical of the Mafia in *Mimi*. They are omnipresent, as Wertmüller humorously shows with continuous zoom shots to the faces of the triple-moled representatives (played by Turri Ferro). Peter Biskind considers the haunting face of the Mafioso, ever-present to Mimi, as "an external fate which he is powerless to elude."[22] The Mafia keep the populace under their thumbs through fear and pressure. They jockey susceptible individuals like Mimi into such a position that these victims cannot help but accept the Mafia's "assistance." Her image of the Sicilian brotherhood has some basis in reality. When she began researching in Calabria she was threatened. Then while shooting, one of the cameras was mysteriously destroyed and the tires of the cars slashed. Shortly afterwards, she was called in by the local authorities and handed a plane ticket back to Rome. "I'm sure the Mafia was behind it. To me, they're the most clever parasitic infrastructure of Italian society."[23]

Other power structures are evident in the film as well. The police, for example, are not interested in justice. Fiore tells Mimi that when the Fascists were beating up the left-wingers, the police simply looked away. Nor are the *padroni* in the least concerned about ethical principles in their relationships with the workers. When Fiore arrived at her job in a department store with Mao's Little Red Book in her bag, the boss made sexual advances on her, threatening to fire her for being an anarchist.

The Sicilian male in *Mimi* has a tragicomic air about him. He is guided in general by three principles: honor *(onore)*, silence *(omertà)*, and revenge *(vendetta)*. Wertmüller, for example, parodies Mimi's sense of honor in the famous seduction scene with the custom officer's wife.[24] Mimi's honor obliges him to take revenge on the officer by committing an act that is most repulsive to him, seducing the man's enormous wife. Ironically Mimi is devastated by the fact that his own wife made love to Almicare, but sees nothing wrong in his setting up a second household with Fiore. The double standard is in full operation. The macho side of the Italian male is also obvious throughout the film. Closely linked with all of the other factors mentioned above, *machismo* distinctly sets a man above a woman, gives him all the rights and privileges but no concomitant duties and responsibilities.

Wertmüller above all satirizes the common man trapped by destiny. Mimi begins as an outspoken Communist who defies the Mafia. Unemployment and love alter his ideology. With a second wife and a new son to worry about, Mimi moves closer to the center. Then he wants to make of his son a consumer, a budding capitalist. He wants no more strikes. Order must prevail, he tells his colleagues. Finally he is seduced into working for the Mafia Commie-haters. His politics have swung to the other side from when we met him at the outset of the film. Mimi, the survivor, experienced jail, rejection, adultery, cuckoldery, unemployment with his honor supposedly intact. His Faustian soul, unfortunately, was eventually sold to the Mafia.

With the film's release in Italy, it was Lina Wertmüller who became the moving target. The Communist party, upper class, and feminists, each individually, waged a verbal attack on her. She felt immune to the harsh criticism after one very positive, revealing experience. *Mimi* was screened in Turin for a gathering of 3000 metal workers, as the director recounts:

> Then I was really terrified; here I was confronted with my real audience, not the critics or the intellectuals or the bourgeoisie. And the response was incredible, wonderful. They got my meaning. And you must understand, this was a very political audience.
> I was terribly nervous because the unions in Turin are very strong and the theme of the film was very threatening to them, since the central character was a worker who was apparently becoming a leftist, but ended up working for the fascists because of his incomplete political understanding. You can see that the film was potentially very explosive.[25]

Wertmüller's **Seduction of Mimi.** Mimi (Giancarlo Giannini) seduces the custom officer's wife Amalia (Elena Fiore) in retaliation for the loss of his own personal honor. *(Courtesy of Donald Velde, Inc.)*

In our interview she mentioned that Mimi's seduction of the hefty Amalia was the cathartic moment of the film for the leftist metal workers. At this point, they dropped all their ideological pretentions and entered into the spirit of the director.

The Seduction of Mimi also seduced the American public and critics. Wertmüller and Giannini (and to a much lesser extent Melato) would soon become household gods in the religiously attended cinema houses of the U.S.[26]

In Peter Brook's film adaptation of William Golding's *Lord of the Flies,* the reversion to primal needs, instincts, and gestures is most graphic and disturbing. Wertmüller in *Swept Away (Travolti da un insolito destino nell'azzurro mare d'agosto,* 1974) captures the same primitive violence and tension in a couple stranded on an uninhabited island, although she lifts it to a more allegorical level. Through this confrontation the director narrates a metaphysical tale of struggle between two classes (proletariat and bourgeois), sexes ("macho" male and "bitchy" female), and geographies (regressive south and industrial north). It could very well be a modern-day Aesopian fable entitled, "The Bourgeois and the Proletarian."

The high-strung, capitalist, northern, anti-Communist bitch Raffaella (Mariangela Melato) lords it over the odorous, bungling, red Sicilian crew member Gennarino (Giancarlo Giannini) on the yacht Esmeralda II. Sailing in a small raft, trying to catch up with the other members of the boating party, Gennarino and Raffaella get swept up on a deserted island. Their roles are soon reversed; he becomes the dominant individual who verbally and physically attacks his boss while she is obliged to take orders from him. Raffaella gradually evolves from feisty harpy to masochistic slave, to adoring concubine, and then beloved mistress. Their Adam-and-Eve existence comes to an end when they are rescued. Raffaella then flies off in a helicopter with her husband while the demoralized Gennarrino is left to work things out with his tempestuous Sicilian wife, Tutuzza.

At the heart of the film is a poignant socioeconomic statement about the master-slave relationship in a caste system historically analyzed by Marx and Engels. This thesis is only rivalled on the metaphorical level by Pozzo and Lucky in Beckett's *Waiting for Godot*. At the outset of *Swept Away*, the Sicilian crew member is submissive to his wealthy, spoiled employer. He dares not rebel since his livelihood depends on healthy relations with the *padrone*. In his Stalinist-Communist heart, however, he harbors undying hostile sentiments toward the ruling class. His crewmate Pippo differs from him and plays up to the vacationers, kissing their capitalist derrières in order not to displease them. Throughout the hostile jeremiads of Raffaella, it is obvious that she represents the industrial world oppressing the masses of the Third World. She criticizes not only the lackey's preparation of the coffee and spaghetti, but his ideology, his native background, and his biological odors. The worker becomes victim to the oppressing class wielding power through money.

On the island, the tables are turned. The oppressed becomes the oppressor in order to teach a lesson in class-consciousness. Gennarino forces lily-white-

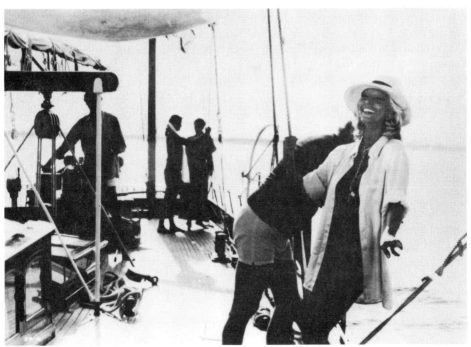

Wertmüller's *Swept Away*. Raffaella (Mariangela Melato) aboard the luxury yatch Esmeralda II. *(Courtesy of Donald Velde, Inc.)*

handed Raffaella to wash his underwear so that she might experience the menial lot of the disadvantaged. He throws food into the fire to teach her that the capitalists do the same to raise prices. Gennarino accentuates the fact that the poor are always in this deprived condition created by the capitalists, a fact alien to Raffaella's bourgeois worldview.

A storm of criticism descended upon this film when it was released in the U.S. in September 1975. The unusual metaphor and the ambiguity of the film stirred the critics and public to judge her severely. The negative critiques of the film pointed to the male chauvinism of the protagonist and supposed misogynist views of the director. Ellen Willis remarks, "To begin with, an allegory of class struggle that casts the woman as the bourgeoisie and the man as the proletariat is inherently corrupt."[27] Another criticism often voiced was that the film does not satirize and challenge traditional sexual attitudes but upholds and reinforces them.

At the core of this negative film criticism is a flaw. These critics interpret the fable literally. They do not realize Wertmüller raises the conflict of Raffaella and Gennarino from the obvious sexual level to the political level. When he slaps her it is a blow against the bourgeoisie—he calls her "an industrial slut"—and not against women. Their relationship is more along power lines than sexual ones. At the close of the film the class and sex distinctions finally dissolve, and the island couple show their true fragility. Two fallible creatures are then safely back on the shores of civilization. She goes off to a world of few needs and he to his uncomfortable proletarian hovel where he may once again find solace in his half-baked ideological platitudes about the oppressors. A temporary truce has taken place in the politicized war of sex and oppression.

Following World War II, almost impenetrable silence shrouded the awesome experience of the death camps. The pain, the horror, the shock had to settle, had to be reflected upon in order to get some perspective on man's most incredible and systematic destruction of fellow human beings. Thirty years later, books, films, memoirs, lectures, and television productions have enlightened the disbelieving public, but at the same time made of the hallowed experience a commercialized product. The concentration camps administered by the ruthless Nazis have entered into our popular mythology. The docudrama *Holocaust* proved this by spreading televised images of the horror to all corners of the world. Lina Wertmüller takes a different approach; she stylizes this phenomenon, putting it into a metaphorical or parable form. The lesson to be communicated is the cost of survival.

While shooting *Mimi*, Wertmüller had to construct a scene in a jail. She went looking for a connoisseur of prisons. Someone on the set told her to make inquiries of one of the extras who had spent a good deal of his life moving in and out of Italian jails. Wertmüller thus discovered what she needed for the organization of the jail scene in *Mimi*. Shortly afterwards, she had the idea of using this man's background for the basic outline of her next film, *Seven Beauties (Pasqualino settebellezze,* 1975). In our interview she called him "a dark type of Candide." He had been in both mental hospital and concentration camps. Today he is still very much alive and has fourteen children. Wertmüller's film is less violent than the real life story of this individual, she insists, and the original character much more ridiculous than her protagonist.

A montage of images of Hitler, Mussolini, and the horrors of war is accompanied by a tongue-in-cheek song with the sarcastic refrain, "Oh Yeah!" Two Italian deserters, Pasqualino Frafuso (Giancarlo Giannini) and Francesco (Piero di Orio), are completely lost behind German lines. Not wanting to get involved they passively watch as some Nazis execute a group of Jews. A flashback returns us to Pasqualino's cavorting in Mussolini's prewar Italy. Pasqualino plays the king rooster in the family nest where his mother and seven sisters make a living by stuffing mattresses. To save his honor, besmirched by "Eighteen Carats" Totonno (Mario Conti) who turned his beefy sister Concettina (Elena Fiore) to prostitution, he murders the villain and sends the butchered carcass in luggage destined for several cities. Pasqualino's subsequent destiny leads him from prison to an insane asylum, then into the army and finally a concentration camp. To stay alive he makes love to the enormous Nazi officer of the camp, Hilde (Shirley Stohler), and executes his best friend on her whim. He manages to survive. Returning to his native Naples, he discovers his young beloved Carolina (Francesca Marciano) involved in prostitution. They will marry and populate the earth with twenty-five or thirty kids, he hopes.

Seven Beauties follows the form and style of a picaresque work, not unlike *Tom Jones, Tin Drum, Lazarillo* or *Candide*. The picaresque rogue Pasqualino stumbles from one predicament to another. Naive and humorous, he hardly appears to be in control of his destiny.

Wertmüller's *Swept Away.* Raffaella (Mariangela Melato) and Gennarino (Giancarlo Giannini) become separated from the boating party. *(Courtesy of Donald Velde, Inc.)*

Wertmüller's *Seven Beauties.* Pasqualino (Giancarlo Giannini) disrupts life in a Neapolitan brothel. *(Courtesy of Donald Velde, Inc.)*

One could read the film simply on a historical level, but this would do an injustice to the work. Those who have done so have erred seriously. The film must be considered in all of its metaphorical possibilities. This is certainly in agreement with Wertmüller's intentions of having her films viewed from multiple perspectives. Pasqualino could be the traditional Everyman, caught in the absurd forces of human history. Tom Allen of *America* sees him as representing Italy, muddling its way through World War II.[28] On a similar level Pasqualino symbolizes Italy's desire to survive, be it with honor and dignity or as a subhuman Mediterranean larva, in confrontation with the Nordic inhumanity of the Nazi guard.

Though a great deal of humor, often grotesque, prevails in *Seven Beauties,* Wertmüller still expresses several quasi-theses. As Pasqualino begins to choose six prisoners for execution in compliance with the wishes of "The Great Beast,"[29] the sympathetic anarchist Pedro (Fernando Rey) jumps into the latrine full of liquid excrement, crying out, "Man in disorder!" Life is not better than this vat of excrement, believes Pedro. He had earlier explained to Pasqualino and Francesco his theory of the need for a "new man." "A new type of man must hurry up and appear . . . not the type of beast which has unbalanced the harmony of nature up to now, but a civilized man, a man who would be able to find peace and harmony within himself." Pedro sees the barbarous Nazis as men of order. The only hope of a civilized culture is a man in disorder.[30] The anarchist Pedro prefers to die in the latrine rather than survive and watch Pasqualino's capitulation to the abhorrent values of the Nazis.

Wertmüller distributes the responsibility for the degradation of human life during World War II beyond the parameters of the Nazis. When Pasqualino returns to Naples, he discovers his Carolina a victim of prostitution. Innocent girls like her were drawn into the profession because of the massive influx of American soldiers in the European landing. Carolina probably enlisted in the ranks of the women of mercy in order to survive the poverty resulting from circumstances of war, a situation recounted in gross detail in Liliana Cavani's *The Flesh/ The Skin (La pelle,* 1981).

Luigi Barzini, in his analysis of the male in the Italian family, balances his all-important honor and duty against the mere law of survival, which offers some insight into the character of Pasqualino:

> There have been men in Italy who, in wars not of their liking, often did only what was necessary merely to return alive to their homes and no more, men who could be technically accused of cowardice; the same men often face, when it becomes necessary, in peacetime, almost unbearable sacrifices and mortal dangers for the sake of their parents or children. Fathers, brothers, sons, grandsons (mostly from the south and the islands, but frequently also from the more advanced north) daily risk death to protect their women from outrage and themselves from dishonour. Many of these champions of the family respectability end up in prison for life, but with a clear conscience. They carry themselves proudly, head high. They know they have done their duty and have obeyed one of the few valid laws they recognize. . . .[31]

Pasqualino is politically naive. His conversation with the socialist professor in the train station offers a dialectic of opinions on the significance of *Il Duce:*

Wertmüller's *Seven Beauties.* Pasqualino's seven Neapolitan sisters, whose honor he defends. *(Courtesy of Donald Velde, Inc.)*

. . . As a matter of fact I rather like him . . . after all, he did make some changes . . . he gave us great roads, created an empire . . . foreigners all envy us because we have such a great leader . . . when he appears on his balcony . . . those eyes, that voice . . . well, everyone has great respect for him . . . Look, before he came people used to spit right in our faces. He really straightened things out, before he arrived everyone was always on strike, things were really a mess.[32]

The professor listens patiently to Pasqualino and then sets him straight:

Sure, he cleaned up the peripheral things, wiped out the labor unions and the class struggle. As a result, the cost of living is twice what it used to be in 1919 and wages have gone down. You say everyone envies us our Mr. Mussolini, but I say to you that it is the bosses who envy him and they alone. The Italian people are still hungry, and what do they get? Nice words from him when he shouts down from his balcony.[33]

In De Sica's *Garden of the Finzi-Continis* and Bertolucci's *The Conformist*, certain serious moral problems concerning Mussolini's brand of fascism arise. At the outset of *Seven Beauties*, Francesco and Pasqualino stumble upon a Nazi massacre of Jewish men, women, and children. As they watch, Francesco acknowldges their complicity simply by not doing anything. He realizes, "we're the allies of the dregs of humanity."[34] Pasqualino prefers to save his skin and not get involved. To try to do anything, he argues, would be suicide. Francesco appears to have more of an ethical awareness of the situation than Pasqualino. Francesco feels that something should have been done. "No! It wouldn't have been futile. A decent man should rebel when faced by certain abuses. One should say no; instead I said yes . . . yes to Mussolini, to orders!"[35] This question of passivity before evil has been foremost among ethical issues from the Second World War to the Vietnam War. Two critics of *Seven Beauties* elaborate on the ethical aspects of the film. In view of Pasqualino's silence before the genocide, Jerzy Kosinski, author of the horrifying and brutal *Painted Bird,* is correct in pushing the question of Pasqualino's passivity further. Instead of asking "How did this world get like this?", Kosinski suggests asking "How did I get like this?"[36] He thus recommends Wertmüller shift the question from collective to personal responsibility, which would be more constructive and realistic. As it is, argues Kosinski, this treatment of the ethical issues in the film is self-delusional, with a less-than-meaningful image of the camp in Grand Guignol style. In the end, the author maintains, it is a caricature of the reality, despite the inherent tragic elements.

Bruno Bettelheim's analysis of the moral problems presented by Wertmüller is more detailed—twenty pages—and more penetrating. It emerges from his own experiences as a survivor of Buchenwald. Although he accepts the film as a work of art with concomitant liberties taken for dramatic reasons, he nonetheless considers the film dangerous and questionable entertainment. It neutralized the horror, Bettelheim thinks. Wertmüller presents her protagonist in terms of self-justification. Pasqualino degrades the notion of surviving, he feels, for it is at any price—from rape to murder. Human dignity, therefore, is only a sham.

Though Bettelheim clarifies many of the issues which are ambiguous or superficial in the film, he may fail to appreciate the deliberate irony of Wertmüller. Pasqualino does survive, but without honor or dignity. For Wertmüller, he is more an antihero than a pure hero who cleverly saves his skin. On the criticism of the stand of silence that Pasqualino takes, Bettelheim does well to speak in terms of Hannah Arendt's "banality of evil." He praises the heroism of those inmates of the camps who were able to be altruistic in such excruciating circumstances as described in Victor Frankl's study *Man's Search for Meaning* or Alain Resnais's film *Night and Fog*. He may mistake Wertmüller's ambiguous treatment of Pasqualino's realistic approach in keeping silent during the Jewish execution for support of Pasqualino's reasoning. Wertmüller in fact does not say that this approach is good, but presents it as part of a healthy dialectic with Francesco. One can readily understand Bettelheim's sensitivity to the topic and his uneasiness with Wertmüller's tongue-in-cheek treatment of a delicate subject. His insights into *Seven Beauties* and the general phenomenon of survival in all of its ethical aspects are a moving contribution to the discussion of the situation, and then, secondarily, to the aesthetic worth of the film. He furthers the dialogue on the relationship of art to reality, thus fulfilling one of the primary intentions of Wertmüller in her filmmaking.

Love and Anarchy: The Sexual-Political Dilemma

The assassination attempts on the life of Hitler and Mussolini are legion. Never before, however, have they been treated in film with such dark humor and personal tragedy as in Wertmüller's *Love and Anarchy (Film d'amore e d'anarchia,* 1973). For the protagonist-assassin of this film, Wertmüller created a synthesis of three different persons, one of whom was Gaetano Bresci, a Tuscan anarchist who assassinated Umberto I on 29 July 1900.

The film begins with a montage of green-filtered stills of Mussolini and states that his enemies were Anarchists and Socialists. A peasant farmer and Anarchist, Antonio Soffiantini called Tunin (Giancarlo Giannini), decides to assume the responsibility for the assassination of the fascist dictator after his friend was killed by the police. While awaiting the precise moment to eliminate Il Duce, *he cavorts in a Roman brothel under the guise of being a cousin of the* puttana *Salomé (Mariangela Melato). In the meantime, he falls in love with Tripolina (Lina Polito). On the morning of the scheduled assassination, Tripolina prevents Salomé from awakening Tunin. Once awake, he goes beserk, shooting several police. In prison he is interrogated and beaten by the Fascist Spatoletti (Eros Pagni), head of Mussolini's bodyguard. The police report his death as a "suicide." The film ends with a quote from the turn-of-the-century Anarchist, Enrico Malatesta:*

I would like to stress my horror of the attempted assassinations. These gestures are not only evil, but they hinder the cause they are meant to serve. . . . One must admit, though, that these murderers are heroes as well. . . . When their extreme gesture will be forgotten, we shall celebrate the ideal which spurred them.

Wertmüller proceeds with a multifaceted technique, blending, juxtaposing, or accentuating the various elements of her material throughout the film. On a metaphorical level, the *bordello* is Italy, as the director mentioned in the course of our interview. It is the face of Italy, full of love but also replete with many of the foibles, antagonisms, and problems seen in the work. She also called the brothel "the maternal womb" of Italy where the clients found solace in difficult times.

The director enters into the stereotypical realm in her characterization of the Fascist Spatoletti, although this type of image appears to be a common phenomenon in some of the Italian political films such as Bertolucci's *The Conformist*. Mussolini's chief bodyguard possesses all the characteristics of a typical Fascist— loud, aggressive, insensitive, vulgar, as well as womanizing and manipulating. He is an avid admirer of emperor Marcus Aurelius, but this ruler is now being replaced by HIM *(Il Duce)* in his personal pantheon.

With the pitting of Tripolina against Salomé, Wertmüller situates the viewer in the heart of the dialectic. On the one hand, Salomé, despite her profession, is a hardened antifascist. When her lover, Anteo Zamboni, was falsely accused of an assassination attempt on Mussolini's life in Bologna and was torn apart for it, Salomé swore to make the Fascists pay for his death. As far as her relationship with Tunin goes, politics comes before love. On the other hand, the prostitute Tripolina provides the other pole of tension. She is young, fresh, full of life. Above all, she puts love before politics. Basically apolitical, she realizes that Tunin will assuredly go to his death if he attempts to assassinate the dictator. She has the power to convince Salomé of this eventually, and they mutually agree not to awaken Tunin on that fateful morning. It is ironic that their loving colleagues on the staff of the *bordello* are strong women who rebel against militarism and the patriarchal order. When all is said and done, however, love supersedes politics.

Through the dilemmas posed by the confrontation of sex and politics, Tunin exhibits a peculiar philosophy of life, filled with lukewarm ideologies and tormented by emotional tensions. He describes to Spatoletti how a dog, if beaten too many times, will eventually turn on his master and kill him. Tunin feels he is the dog-victim who has been pushed too far. His ideological reasons for assassinating Mussolini do not appear too profound. All the ramifications of his action have not been worked out in advance. In a way Salomé's political commitment is both deeper and more rational.

The film concludes with a phrase from Enrico Malatesta, a supposedly harmless anarchist who was tolerated by Mussolini "to prove" *Il Duce's* openmindedness. He was allowed to live unmolested in fascist Italy. Wertmüller sings his praises:

> Malatesta was a wonderful human being. He was the philosopher of an impossible utopia. But within his utopian dream is the core of a very important principle—that of the freedom of the individual. This idea should enlighten all of us and inspire us to create the "Man in Disorder."[38]

Wertmüller uses Malatesta's comments on an assassination attempt against Mussolini in Milan to enlighten the public on terrorism. While filming *Seven Beauties* she felt that some of the political insights of that period were still applicable to the political turmoil of the present.

All Screwed Up, A Nightful of Rain, and *Blood Feud:* **Triple Play**

Wertmüller's reputation as a filmmaker or political commentator was not greatly enhanced by these three films. Some critics feel she had really struck out. On the one hand, her public expected one thing and she gave them another. They recalled only too well the impact of *Mimi* and *The Lizards.* On the other, her production companies only offered her certain parameters in which to work. With their veto power they held a Damoclean sword over her head.

All Screwed Up (*Tutto a posto e niente in ordine,* 1973) was the first installment of this series and was filmed after *Love and Anarchy.*

In the city of Milan, another planet from Wertmüller's usual southern realm, a dilapidated apartment building houses a group of peculiar individuals. From rustic backgrounds, they arrive in this industrialized city to improve their lot. Life in the big city radically alters their primitive worldview. Adelina (Sara Rapisarda) struggles to make a success of herself on the urban scene. In her attempts she loses her virginity to her proletarian boy friend Carletto (Nino Bignamini). While fending off his advances, she preferred to catch her falling color television set to preserving her virtue. Gigi (Luigi Diberti) chooses petty crime to succeed. Isotta (Isa Danieli) opts for whoredom in order to provide for the family she left behind. Carletto meanders from one position to another, finally getting a job at a restaurant where a social whirlwind ensues. He is swept along with it until a fascist bombing of the restaurant disrupts the centrifugal force of the group. Things settle down momentarily, until suddenly everyone jumps back on his or her vertiginous carnival ride.

This parable about Western civilization on the brink of chaos does not separate the comic wheat from the tragic chaff, but juxtaposes both in order to drive home diverse sociological lessons about life in an urban society. Tom Allen points out some of the tension spots in society:

> Basically, Wertmüller, who poses as the most sympathetically male-oriented of female directors and who again inserts an outrageously embraced rape by a professional virgin hoisted between her honor and her pocketbook, is chillingly depicting the emasculation of migrating male workers from a host of nerve-prostrating urban pressures, including housing shortages, up-tight police, capitalist wages and child-rearing pressures. At the same time, the unattached females wax into voracious caricatures of the consumer society.[39]

Gary Arnold is less impressed with the blend of "social satire and soapbox editorializing," calling it a "mishmash" and "an indiscriminate jumble of buffoonery and hysteria."[40] Nonetheless, like Brusati's *Bread and Chocolate,* Wertmüller's *All Screwed Up* can readily poke fun at society while stating that there are certain

Wertmüller's *All Screwed Up.* The filmmaker offers stage directions to one of the actors.
(Courtesy of Director Lina Wertmüller.)

sectors of it that must be altered, or else the world will be reduced to even greater
chaos than it experiences now.

The first English-language picture of a European director is always a risk. The
public often has conservative expectations, pigeonholing the foreign filmmaker.
The director usually finds it a challenge to grasp the nuances of an English-
speaking production. He or she confronts head-on the innumerable conditions
imposed by the American company, conditions not experienced by the director
on native terrain. Much depends on the director's ability to adapt to all of the
new circumstances while still maintaining some aesthetic and personal integrity.
Resnais *(Providence),* Forman *(One Flew over the Cuckoo's Nest),* and Zeffirelli *(Romeo
and Juliet)* adapted well and achieved some success. Bergman *(The Serpent's Egg),*
Truffaut *(Fahrenheit 451),* and Polanski *(Cul de sac* and *Repulsion)* enjoyed a less
favorable reception. The mystical and exotic flavor of some of the directors disappeared, the critics felt. A transplanted director has a minimal chance of flour-
ishing on foreign soil.

After pre-release screenings of *Seven Beauties,* Warner Brothers offered Lina
Wertmüller a contract for four English-language films. She accepted, although
she was wary of such a contract with a major company. *A Nightful of Rain (La fine
del mondo nel nostro solito letto in una notte piena di pioggia,* 1978) was the first production in the series. It was originally to have been called *Perhaps, Perhaps, Because It's Brando's Fault.* Wertmüller clarifies her purpose in making this film
about an American woman photographer and an Italian Communist:

I wanted to create a bridge between Italy and America. The space of the bed indicates the nucleus of the family in this night full of rain that may indicate the great universal flood. Often water is also a symbol of renewal . . . a new cycle. My new film is born out of this whole problematical basis and it cannot offer solutions; it only records them and proposes . . . because there never was such equality between sexes.[41]

A lively folksong from a Neapolitan play Cinderella the Cat (La gatta Cenerentola) *opens the film.*[42] *Lizzie (Candice Bergen), a feminist bourgeois American photographer, has been married for ten years to a macho, romantic Italian leftist, Paolo (Giancarlo Giannini). Their marriage, begun when they were both quite young, has had its share of tempests. They incarnate the age-old marital dilemma—they cannot live with one another, nor can they live apart. Lizzie wishes to leave Paolo in order to find herself. Nevertheless she still loves him. Throughout their marital discussion an on-screen Greek chorus provides some resonance to the crisis.*

Lina Wertmüller on one level helps this couple ask the ultimate question, "Can we live together?" On a more allegorical level, however, she subtly raises the question, "Can civilization continue?" The director articulates her idea of Lizzie's and Paolo's relationship in the greater context of the film's meaning:

Nightful of Rain is not about a couple, it is about the end of the world. Love stories don't interest me. It's all a means to an end, a way of telling a story. I think the movie is a social service, a very big way to speak about the problems of life indirectly and symbolically.[43]

Once again she speaks metaphorically in using the rain (water) as a symbol of the deluge, the wiping out of civilization and the beginning anew. For Wertmüller this is a symbol of change, perhaps even like Hemingway's use of it as a metaphor for death.

The dual interconnecting themes of the film—profeminist and antifamily—are not readily accepted by the more traditional public and critics. The ambiguities leave them unsettled. Wertmüller proposed that the family is a prison for the woman. Through childbearing it becomes an oppressive force that stifles her. The contemporary form of the family must go, she insists. It is a nonviable institution that has lost its meaning and true function. However, the director sees that no alternative has yet been developed, although the commune and the kibbutz have offered the most promising options. Her radical thesis here is quite opposed to the more traditional view of Luigi Barzini:

The first source of power is the family. The Italian family is a stronghold in a hostile land: within its walls and among its members, the individual finds consolation, help, advice, provisions, loans, weapons, allies and accomplices to aid him in his pursuits. No Italian who has a family is ever alone. He finds in it refuge in which to lick his wounds after a defeat, or an arsenal and a staff for his victorious drives. Scholars have always recognized the Italian family as the only fundamental institution in the country, a spontaneous creation of the national genius, adapted through the centuries to changing conditions, the real foundation of whichever social order prevails.[44]

Wertmüller's *Nightful of Rain.* The religious procession draws a crowd of curious onlookers. *(Courtesy of Director Lina Wertmüller.)*

Wertmüller already poked fun at Pasqualino at the end of *Seven Beauties* for wanting to have twenty-five to thirty children. In *A Nightful of Rain* she warns that overpopulation will be a natural disaster and bring on the end of the world. Without realizing that China has taken such legislative steps in curbing child-bearing, she argues further:

> For woman, the [bearing of] children is a trap. I think that the first child should be absolutely paid by the state, the second not so much, the third you pay, the fourth you lose your job, the fifth you go to jail. . . . How can you have courage to give birth to little children in this world?[45]

A Nightful of Rain was far from the success that Warner Brothers expected when they made the contract with Wertmüller. Warner Brothers' approach to the film displeased the director no end. After the film was cut, it was poorly distributed because the company did not appreciate it, she felt. The relationship between Wertmüller and the producers was thus strained.

In October 1978, Warner Brothers and Lina Wertmüller went their separate ways, legally and mutually terminating the contract for the other English-speaking films. Dealing with a major production company was alien to the director and impinged upon her creative process in making a film. Submission of first script, all successive script changes, constant decision-making, slowed down the rhythm that the director needed.

When Wertmüller was flying from New York to London for the opening of *Swept Away* in March 1978, she sketched out the basic plan for her next film, *Tragic Incident between a Widow and Two Men (Fatto di sangue fra due uomini per causa di una vedova. Si sospettano moventi politici)* released in U.S. as *Blood Feud*. Once in London she requested a typewriter and wrote the first twenty pages of the script. Later she and the executive producer from Liberty Films, Arrigo Colombo, flew to Paris to offer the lead female role to Sophia Loren. Shortly afterward in Rome, Wertmüller completed the lengthy 600-page script. She shot most of the film on location in Sicily from 24 July to 8 October 1978. Set in the 1920s, the film was meant to capture the sociopolitical atmosphere of the period between the start of the decade and Mussolini's March on Rome in 1922.

The voluptuous Titina Paterno (Sophia Loren) is abruptly cast into widowhood when her husband is gunned down in a local feud in a Sicilian village. Her widow's weeds are still fresh when she finds the seedy-looking Spallone (Marcello Mastroianni), a socialist intellectual and attorney, very much interested in her. The lusty gangster Nico Sammichele (Giancarlo Giannini), recently returned from the Prohibition-ridden streets of New York, also has an eye on her. The not-too-uncommon eternal triangle is now operative as Titina seeks justice on the Mafia-infested island. Pitted against the strong-arm members of "the Family" and the Mussolinian Black Shirts, the hapless and helpless trio has no chance to win or even survive. After a final battle with the enemy, Titina cradles the two heroes in her arms as they lie dying.

Despite her humorous tongue-in-cheek approach, Wertmüller slashes away at the powerful threats of the Black Shirt Fascists and the ruthless *barone* or Mafiosi. The melodrama of romance and the occasional "spaghetti Western" tone give way to an acerbic treatment of those unhealthy sociopolitical forces on the island. She reveals the complicity of the two representatives of power in Acicatena, a Mafia henchman who assumes the fascist leadership in the Sicilian village when Mussolini bursts onto the political scene. Acicatena's attempted rape of Titina only underlines the use of uncontrollable power not only politically but sexually.

Wertmüller's male heroes are not without blemish, either, however. Socialists like Spallone are weak and ineffectual. Too theoretical and disorganized, they cannot make an impact upon the peasant population. The American-schooled gangster Nico boasts of having eliminated a few dozen men in New York in order to preserve his honor. His unethical tactics are no purer than those of the home-town baronial figures who casually dispose of any competition. Spallone and Nico are impotent in attaining Titina's much-sought-after retribution. Justice does not win out in the end.

Lina Wertmüller's feud over the film began when she saw it at the Oxford Film Festival. She was irate at the liberties that the producers/distributors took. The film had been drastically cut. The director said she could not recognize her work in the final distributed product and asked that her name be stricken from the credits. She bemoaned this attack on artistic integrity in the course of our interview in Rome. Wertmüller stressed vehemently that she can only survive artistically if she is given the full freedom she needs to exercise her sexually and politically fertile imagination.

Sophia Loren is the nexus with Lina Wertmüller's next project, *Tieta*. In June

1982, the actress's return to Italy to spend some time in the quasi-country-club atmosphere of a Roman prison for tax evasion could leap right out of a Wertmüller script. She had extended privileges and socialized extensively, spending her brief time in prison in a spirit of jest and scorn, in order to pay for her financial sins. The other purpose of the return of the exiled wife of Carlo Ponti was the film *Tieta*, which Lina Wertmüller was scheduled to begin shooting in Florence the following month, July 1982.

> Tieta is the name of the heroine of the story, based on a novel by Jorge Amado, a Brazilian writer, that follows a girl's life in an idyllic Brazilian town. She goes to the big city, works in a brothel, meets a man who transforms her into a high-class courtesan, buys the brothel and caters to rich businessmen and influential politicians. She sends money to her family, which is embroiled in a dispute at home. The town is divided over a chemical plant's locating there, and Tieta saves the town.[46]

The project unfortunately came to naught. Wertmüller's most recent films, however, are *A Joke of Destiny Lying in Wait around the Corner like a Bandit* (1983), *Sotto, sotto* (1984), and *Un complicato intrigo di donne vicoli e delitti.*

Conclusions

With love/sex alternating with politics/ideology in the foreground and sometimes in the background of her films, Lina Wertmüller entertains, cajoles, and disturbs her audiences. Her work is replete with paradoxes and contradictions. She woos the public with a romantic scene one moment only to shock them with a grotesque or violent action the next. The language her characters use is highly political, but is equally vulgar and graphic. She directs her films at the masses, yet she attacks the masses as possessing the law of the anthill, not understanding their individual responsibility in society. Wertmüller claims to be a feminist filmmaker in her own right and strongly upholds feminist causes, but her sympathetic macho protagonists (Mimi, Carletto, Pasqualino, Paolo, and Gennarino) seduce and/or rape their way to a woman's heart in her films. In the meantime the women—bitch, bourgeois, or bovine—do not come across as the most positive creatures in God's creation. This provokes Molly Haskell in the *Village Voice* to describe Lina Wertmüller colorfully as "a radical chick with an eye for the rooster."[47] She meticulously researches the historical, political, and social dimensions of a particular topic, only to render the image of it caricatured, grotesque, or surrealistic. Her photography is rich, colorful, exotic; the subject matter, however—a blubbery Nazi officer in a stylized concentration camp, a vat of excrement, violent macho attitudes in her protgaonists—verges on questionable taste for some critics and public. As a result, her work teems with ambiguities and has become ultracontroversial.

Wertmüller unfortunately has been coolly received in her native Italy, as Lino Miccichè explains. For the most part, she has not been taken seriously. Although she is a very clever woman, most cultured, with clear political ideas and convictions, the style and language of her films make them seem reactionary. He considers this vulgarity of form very dangerous.[48]

The majority of criticism, both positive and negative, has come from this side of the Atlantic. In the U.S. she has been enthroned as a cinematic goddess by many for her unique, radical and controversial treatment of serious subjects. Others have decried her perspective as promacho and antifeminist. Both sets of critics always touch upon the unusual blend of politics and sexuality, for better or for worse. "In the end," she often says, "I always make the same story—the problems of men and women in relation to society, especially the problems of sex and politics."

The Achilles heel of the political characterization of her protagonists appears to be the eclectic, comic, and grotesque approach to anarchy, fascism, or communism. It tones down the seriousness of the political message. The leftist individuals in her films are walking examples of half-baked ideologies; their political philosophy will never be fully digested in a hostile or alien world. One would only have to read the article of Wertmüller's assistant for *Swept Away,* Lucy Quacinella—"How Left is Lina?"—to perceive that the political or revolutionary moral of a film such as *Love and Anarchy* is shaky. As it did with Petri's *Working Class Goes to Heaven,* the Communist party reacted negatively to her supposedly inaccurate depiction of the impotent Left in *The Seduction of Mimi.* None of this, however, disproves her profound political consciousness or her intense commitment to assist humanity in renewing itself.

To appreciate fully the politicial and aesthetic value of Wertmüller's films, the air must be finally cleared over her treatment of sexuality. The ambivalence in her characterization of the leading males and females in her works cannot be dismissed, yet her handling of the subject is carefully thought out. This has made her the target of radical feminists. Barbara Garson in *Ms.* magazine, Lillian Gerard in *American Film,* and Ruth McCormick in *Cinéaste* offer balanced views of Wertmüller's opus. They support her risky cinematic ventures. These critics see the weaker elements in the director's repertoire, but they grasp her intentions and uniqueness. This is certainly not the case with Molly Haskell, Pauline Kael, and Ellen Willis, who have been known to string together a list of pejorative labels for the director—reactionary, misogynous, double-dealing, hypocritical, and perverse. Wertmüller considers that the radical feminists, especially the American ones, are blind to the real issues. They see sexuality as the only problem, she maintains. The director implies that these critics do not fully comprehend the larger societal issues of class differences, radical politics, historical and contemporary fascism, and so on. In a popular assessment, they miss the political forest for the sexual trees.

Wertmüller is often referred to as a "woman filmmaker."

I reject that entirely. . . . I am a filmmaker who happens to be a woman. A human being at work. Of course I always try to show the woman's situation in my films. I become very passionate when I think of the plight of many women. But I am also passionate and worried about the situation of many men.[49]

The label is limiting and Wertmüller considers it sexist. It is only when the public and critics cease to categorize her in terms of her sex that her films can be assessed as works which break categories, genres, traditions, and taboos. In essence, she thus proves herself to be a politically and socially enlightened cinéaste who transcends genders in making films that reflect her concern for society.

Conclusions

Within the past four decades the Italian cinema has evolved from the fascist or neutral "white telephone" films of the thirties to the antifascist neorealist films of the forties, through a type of existential period of Antonioni and Fellini in the fifties, finally to the anti-Establishment works of "neo-neorealists" in the sixties and seventies. The seven filmmakers at the nucleus of this critical work—Rosi, Pasolini, Bertolucci, Bellocchio, Pontecorvo, Petri, and Wertmüller—were formed by their neorealist masters and their communist idols and ideals. Their first films retain this double mark. During their early careers in documentary or fiction film, some of them, notably Pontecorvo and Petri, considered their work primarily political and at times militant. Pasolini had already been separated from the Communist party when he began filming, but he continued to serve the cause of Marxism through his films. Bellocchio and Bertolucci joined the Communist ranks later, in connection with the May '68 student and union dissent. Their films of the early seventies reflect this commitment. Rosi maintained the Marxist dialectic in film without being a militant in the Communist party. Lina Wertmüller switched allegiances from the Communist party to the Socialist party. Her works manifest humanitarian and socialist concerns. Some of these filmmakers, disillusioned as a consequence of the Hungarian crisis, broke their ties with the Communist party. Their militant committed cinema turned into an acerbic civilian cinema which possessed unusual psychological strains. They became moralizing filmmakers. Their new targets primarily emerged from everyday life in Italy. For some directors like Petri and Bellocchio the cinematic work would be the settling of accounts with certain oppressive institutions. The overall purpose of these cinéastes was to preach not only to the already convinced, but also to the uninformed general public.

The seven filmmakers succeeded in reaching the masses because they were able to adapt to the new political and economic scene. In this respect they wished to follow Costa-Gavras's philosophy of aiming at a large public through popular political film as opposed to an anarchistic, esoteric, and art-for-art's-sake cinema. Some critics call this pragmatic and shrewd, while others see it as a necessary economic compromise. The purists, however, consider it opportunistic and "selling out to the Establishment." The most critical political reviewers feel that the commercially backed films of a Petri, Pontecorvo, or Wertmüller diametrically militate against the politically oriented content, especially if it is a leftist message.

In such cases, the politics appear to be diluted in order to make of the work a slick, marketable, comprehensible, and commercial product.

Where the neorealists accentuated the social and political difficulties of society, more and more the following generation of filmmakers developed the personal and psychological crises of the individuals in society, face to face with the powerful and destructive systems at work. With the political the new wave of directors mix the psychological and sexual. Sigmund Freud and Wilhelm Reich exert their influence on the filmmakers of the seventies, more than Karl Marx and Antonio Gramsci. As a result, the films reflect explicit sexual themes that have been controversial to some, alien to others, and shocking to the general public. Bertolucci's *Last Tango in Paris*, Petri's *Investigation of a Citizen above Suspicion*, Wertmüller's *Seven Beauties*, and Pasolini's *Salò* created stirs in the seventies.

Instead of the serious and melodramatic treatment of social themes characteristic of the earlier generation—Rossellini, De Sica, and Visconti—these heirs of neorealism evolved in the use of the grotesque and hyperrealistic. Petri's *Todo modo* makes its point against the Christian Democratic party and the Catholic Church through the use of parody. Bellocchio's *Victory March* and Pasolini's *Salò* favor sadistic violence in order to drive home the message.

The diverse sociopolitical messages of these filmmakers are, as well, not confined to the cinematic ghettos of the elite in university filmclub circles or little art houses. Italian television (RAI) has taken considerable steps to finance artistic productions by Bellocchio, Rosi, and Bertolucci and thus assure the directors a wider public. The cross-fertilization of the two media has created not an ugly hybrid but an attractive and provocative *objet d'art*.

The seven Italian political filmmakers of our study have not remained at a standstill. They continue to inveigh against rampant social and political injustices. Nor are they alone. A legion of others struggle with them in their ranks. Tinto Brass, Damiano Damiani, Gianfranco De Bosio, Vittorio De Seta, Nanni Loy, Carlo Lizzani, Francesco Maselli, Mario Monicelli, Giuliano Montaldo, Valentino Orsini, and Paolo and Vittorio Taviani have developed political themes in their works.

In 1966, Fellini observed: "Out of Italy's chaos a few good directors always emerge. Rebellion is a healthy sign, but I don't think Italy's young have raised their voices high enough yet."[1] Almost two decades later we have seen that at least seven politically committed directors have emerged from the chaos of a shaky industry. They are no longer young in age or lacking in experience, but are politically and technically mature. In many cases they have raised their rebellious voices very high against the Establishment. On occasions these forces attempted to stifle them. The artists have survived. Their echoing voices are still heard around the world.

Filmography

Francesco Rosi

The Challenge (*La sfida*, 1958)
The Weavers/Con Men/Swindlers (*I magliari*, 1959)
Salvatore Giuliano (1961)
Hands over the City (*Le mani sulla città*, 1963)
Moment of Truth (*Il momento della verità*, 1965)
More than a Miracle (*C'era una volta*, 1967)
Just Another War (*Uomini contro*, 1970)
The Mattei Affair (*Il caso Mattei*, 1972)
Lucky Luciano (*A proposito Lucky Luciano*, 1973)
Illustrious Corpses (*Cadaveri eccellenti*, 1976)
Eboli (*Cristo si è fermato a Eboli*, 1978)
Three Brothers (*Tre fratelli*, 1981)
Bizet's Carmen (1984)

Pier Paolo Pasolini

Accattone (1961)
Mamma Roma (1962)
La Ricotta in *RoGoPaG* (1962)
Rage/Hatred (*La rabbia*, 1963) with Giovanni Guareschi
Forum of Love (*Comizi d'amore*, 1964)
Gospel According to St. Matthew (*Il Vangelo secondo Matteo*, 1964)
Hawks and Sparrows (*Uccellacci e uccellini*, 1966)
The Earth Seen from the Moon (*La terra vista dalla luna*) in *Le streghe* (*The Witches*, 1966)
What Are the Clouds? (*Che cosa sono le nuvole?*) in *Capriccio all'Italiana*, (1967)
Oedipus (*Edipo re*, 1967)
Teorema (1968)
Medea (1969)
Sequence of the Paper Flower (*La sequenza del fiore di carta*) in *Love and Anger* (*Amor e rabbia*, 1969) (feature title changed to *Vangelo '70*)
Pigsty (*Porcile*, 1969)
The Walls of San'A (*Le mura di Sana*, 1969)
Notes for a Film on India (*Appunti per un film sull'India*, 1969)
Notes on an African Oresteia (*Orestiade Africano*, 1969)

12 December (Dodici dicembre, 1971)
The Decameron (Il decamerone, 1971)
Canterbury Tales (I racconti di Canterbury, 1972)
Arabian Nights (Il fiore delle mille e una notte, 1974)
Salò (Salò o le 120 giornate di Sodoma, 1975)

Bernardo Bertolucci

The Grim Reaper (La commare secca, 1962)
Before the Revolution (Prima della rivoluzione, 1964)
The Petroleum Route (La via del petrolio, 1965)
Agony (Agonia) in *Love and Anger (Amor e Rabbia/Vangelo '70, 1969)*
Partner (1968)
The Spider's Stratagem (La strategia del ragno, 1970)
The Conformist (Il conformista, 1970)
The Poor Die First (I poveri muoiono prima, 1971)
Last Tango in Paris (Ultimo tango a Parigi, 1972)
1900 (Novecento, 1976)
Luna (La luna, 1979)
Tragedy of a Ridiculous Man (La tragedia di un uomo ridicolo, 1981)

Marco Bellocchio

Fists in the Pocket (I pugni in tasca, 1965)
China Is Near (La Cina è vicina, 1967)
Let's Discuss, Discuss (Discutiamo, discutiamo, 1969)
Paola (1969)
Long Live Red May Day (Viva il Primo Maggio rosso, 1969)
In the Name of the Father (Nel nome del padre, 1972)
Slap the Monster on Page One/Rape on the Front Page (Sbatti il mostro in prima pagina, 1973)
Fit to be Untied (Matti da slegare, 1974)
Victory March/Triumphal March (Marcia trionfale, 1976)
The Seagull (Il Gabbiano, 1977)
The Cinema Machine (La macchina cinema, 1978)
Leap into the Void (Salto nel vuoto, 1979)
The Eyes, the Mouth (Gli occhi, la bocca, 1983)
Henry IV (Enrico IV, 1984)

Gillo Pontecorvo:

The Timiriazev Mission (Missione Timiriazev, 1953)
The Portese Gate (Porta Portese, 1954)
Dogs behind Bars (Cani dietro le sbarre, 1954)
Festivities at Castelluccio (Festa a Castelluccio, 1955)
Men of Marble (Uomini del marmo, 1955)
Bread and Sulphur (Pane e zolfo, 1956)

Giovanna in *The Compass/The Windrose (Die Windrose*, 1956)
The Long Blue Road/The Rift (La lunga strada azzurra, 1957)
Kapò (1959)
Battle of Algiers (La battaglia di Algeri, 1966)
Burn! (*Queimada*, 1969)
The Tunnel (Operazione Ogro/Il tunnel, 1979)

Elio Petri

A Champion is Born (Nasce un campione, 1954)
The Seven Peasants (I sette contadini, 1957)
Lady Killer of Rome/The Assassin (L'assassino, 1961)
The Days Are Numbered/No Time Left/Borrowed Time/Counted Days (I giorni contati, 1962)
The Teacher of Vigevano (Il maestro di Vigevano, 1963)
High Infidelity (Alta infedeltà) in *Sin in the Afternoon (Peccato nel pomeriggio*, 1964)
The Tenth Victim (La decima vittima, 1965)
We Still Kill the Old Way (A ciascuno il suo, 1967)
A Quiet Place in the Country (Un tranquillo posto di campagna, 1968)
Investigation of a Citizen above Suspicion (Indagine su un cittadino al di sopra di ogni sospetto, 1970)
The Working Class Goes to Heaven/Lulu the Tool (La classe operaria va in paradiso, 1971)
Ipotesi (Hypotheses) in *Documents on Giuseppe Pinelli*
Property Is No Longer a Theft (La proprietà non è piu un furto, 1973)
Todo modo (1976)
Dirty Hands (Mani sporche, 1979)
Good News (La personalità della vittima ovvero le buone notizie, 1979)

Lina Wertmüller

The Lizards (I Basilischi, 1963)
Let's Talk about Men (Questa volta parliamo di uomini, 1965)
Rita the Mosquito (Rita la zanzara, 1966)
Don't Sting the Mosquito (Non stuzzicate la zanzara, 1967)
Seduction of Mimi (Mimi metallurgico ferito nell'onore, 1971)
Love and Anarchy (Film d'amore e d'anarchia, 1973)
All Screwed Up (Tutto a posto e niente in ordine, 1973)
Swept Away (Travolti da un insolito destino nell'azzurro mare d'agosto, 1974)
Seven Beauties (Pasqualino settebellezze, 1975)
Nightful of Rain (La fine del mondo nel nostro solito letto in una notte piena di pioggia, 1978)
Blood Feud (Fatto di sangue fra due uomini per causa di una vedova. Si sospettano moventi politici, 1978)
Earthquake (Terremoto, 1982; for RAI)
A Joke of Destiny Lying in Wait around the Corner like a Bandit (Scherzo, 1983)
Sotto, sotto (1984; English title not available)
Un complicato intrigo di donne vicoli e delitti (English title not available)

Notes

Introduction

1. To trace the origins of neorealism from the "white telephone" epoch, read Massimo Mida and Lorenzo Quaglietti, *Dai telefoni bianchi al neorealismo* (Rome-Bari: Laterza, 1980). Often in these films depicting upper-class life, an exotic actress could be seen talking on a white telephone.

2. Ibid., pp. 115–79.

3. The two scholarly journals *Cinema* (with antifascist writers Gianni Puccini and Domenico Purificato) and *Bianco e nero* (founded by Umberto Barbaro and Luigi Chiarini in 1936) promoted a serious study of these movements.

4. For further insights into the origins and evolution of neorealism consult Roy Armes, *Patterns of Realism* (South Brunswick, N.J.: A. S. Barnes, 1971); Pierre Leprohon, *The Italian Cinema* (New York: Praeger, 1972); Raymond Borde and André Bouissy, "Nouveau cinéma Italien," *Premier plan*, Special Issue 30 (1963); and Carlo Lizzani, *Il cinema italiano: 1895–1979* (Rome: Editori Riuniti, 1979). For a development of the heritage of neorealism see Peter Bondanella, *Italian Cinema: From Neorealism to the Present* (New York: Frederick Ungar, 1982).

5. Lino Miccichè interview with author, Rome, 15 January 1982.

6. Visconti's *Obsession* was based on James Cain's *The Postman Always Rings Twice*. Bob Rafelson in his 1981 remake with Jack Nicholson and Jessica Lange chose a more erotic and psychological perspective over a neorealist approach.

7. In the documentary film *Neorealism: The Italian Cinema* (1972), one older person, almost twenty years after the movement faded out, objected to the earthy nature of these films. According to him, they showed "the rotten teeth" of Italian society.

8. For further reading examine Quintin Hoare and Geoffrey Nowell-Smith, *Selections from the Prison Notebooks of Antonio Gramsci* (New York: International, 1971), or Lynne Lawner, *Antonio Gramsci: Letters from Prison* (New York: Harper and Row, 1973).

9. For the Communist party's call to youth, see Nello Ajello, "Togliatti, Croce, e i giovani," *Intellettuali e PCI,1944–1958* (Rome-Bari: Laterza, 1979), pp. 27–34.

10. Pierre Billard, "Un cinéma au-dessus de tout soupçon," *Le Point*, 1 May 1978, 97.

11. For a treatment of this division see Ajello, "I fatti di Ungheria" and "Il dopo-Ungheria e la diaspora," in *Intellettuali e PCI*, pp. 397–428 and 429–52, respectively.

12. Lino Miccichè reviews some of the political situation as it affects cinema in "Quindici anni di cinema italiano, 1958–1973," *Novità in cineteca* (Bologna), March 1979: 2–6.

13. To observe the increase in the Communist vote compare the two elections of 1972 and 1976. In the 1972 election, the Communist party took 9,068,961 votes (27.1 percent) while the Christian Democratic party obtained 12,912,466 votes (38.7 percent). Four years later the Communists had 12,614,650 votes (34.4 percent) and the Christian Democrats 14,209,519 votes (38.7 percent). This data is adapted from Howard R. Penniman (ed.), *Italy at the Polls* (Washington, D.C.: American Enterprise Institute for Public Policy Research, 1977), p. 33. For earlier election comparisons (1946–1960), consult Norma Kogan, *The Government of Italy* (New York: Thomas Y. Cromwell, 1962), p. 42.

14. See Goffredo Fofi, "Dopo il '68" and "Ritorno alla politica" in *Il cinema italiano: servi e padroni* (Milan: Feltrinelli, 1977).

15. Lino Miccichè, interview with author, 15 January 1982.

16. Joan Mellen, "Film and Style: The Fictional Documentary," *Antioch Review* 32 (1972): 24–25.

17. Alberto Moravia, interview with author, Rome, 13 January 1982, with the assistance of Susan A. (Ross) Michalzcyk.

Chapter 1. Francesco Rosi

1. For the best full-length biographical and political studies of Rosi see Michel Ciment, *Le dossier Rosi: cinéma et politique* (Paris: Stock, 1976); Jean Gili, *Francesco Rosi: cinéma et pouvoir* (Paris: Editions du Cerf, 1976); and Sandro Zambetti, *Francesco Rosi* (Florence: La Nuova Italia, 1976).

2. Francesco Rosi, "Introduzione," *Luchino Visconti: "La terra trema"* (Bologna: Cappelli, 1977), p. 9.

3. See Pierre Leprohon, *The Italian Cinema* (New York: Praeger, 1972), pp. 109–14.

4. "A colloquio con Rosi," June 1964, quoted in Nino Ferrero, *Francesco Rosi* (Turin: Edizioni A.I.A.C.E., 1972), pp. 10–11.

5. Gramsci addressed the questions of the south "Il Mezzogiorno e il fascismo," in *Scritti politici* (Rome: Editori Riuniti, 1967), pp. 549–52. For a more popular grasp of the situation, read Luigi Barzini, "The 'Problema del Mezzogiorno,'" *The Italians* (New York: Atheneum, 1964), pp. 234–51.

6. David L. Overbey, "Rosi in Context," *Sight and Sound*, Summer 1976, 174.

7. Michel Cournot, "Beauté interdite," *Nouvel observateur*, 21 June 1971, 48.

8. From a compilation of interviews with Michel Ciment, Bernard Cohn, and Jean-François Held, in "Francesco Rosi," *Filmoteca nacional* (Madrid), February 1976, section 4.

9. John Francis Lane, "Moments of Truth," *Films and Filming*, September 1970, 10.

10. Ciment, *Le dossier Rosi*, p. 85.

11. For a more recent German view of the lot of an Italian worker in the diaspora see Werner Schroeter's *Palermo oder Wolfsburg* (1980), a study of a Sicilian worker Nicola Zarbo in a Volkswagen plant in Wolfsburg.

12. Aldo Tassone, *Parla il cinema italiano*, Vol. 1 (Milan: Il Formichiere, 1979), p. 288.

13. Jean Gili, "Francesco Rosi," *Le cinéma italien* (Paris: Union Générale d'Editions, 1978), p. 254.

14. Ciment, *Le dossier Rosi*, p. 85.

15. Leprohon, *The Italian Cinema*, p. 190.

16. See also Arnaldo Cortesi, "Bandit Giuliano Is Slain in Sicily: Killer of 100 Falls with Guns Ablaze," *New York Times*, 6 July 1950, pp. 1, 15.

17. Edoardo Bruno accentuated this quest for realism in *"Salvatore Giuliano: ritorno alla verità,"* *Filmcritica*, January 1952, 677–79.

18. This article is reproduced in the most important documentation on the film by Tullio Kezich, *Salvatore Giuliano* (Rome: Edizioni F. M., 1961), pp. 18–25.

19. Rosi attended a May Day celebration in the same location to verify the events and the people's perspective on the massacre. It was then that he had the idea of having the shots come from the mountain, thus depersonalizing the murderers, according to Ciment in *Le dossier Rosi*, p. 92.

20. Ibid., p. 93.

21. Maria-Teresa Savage, "The Mafia on Film: *Salvatore Giuliano*," *Film Society Review*, October 1971, 33.

22. Ciment, *Le dossier Rosi*, p. 94.

23. Geoffrey Nowell-Smith, *"Salvatore Giuliano,"* *Sight and Sound*, Summer 1963, 143.

24. Paolo Gobetti, "Entretien avec Rosi," *Positif*, May 1965, 9.

25. P. H. Frankel, *Mattei: Oil and Power Politics* (London: Faber and Faber, 1966), p. 15. For further documentation on Mattei's life see Francesco Rosi and Eugenio Scalfari, *Il caso Mattei: Un 'corsaro' al servizio della repubblica* (Bologna: Cappelli, 1972). The photos between pp. 48 and 49 reveal significant events in the life of Mattei, with parallels in the film between pp. 112 and 113.

26. For further connections of Mauro de Mauro with the Mattei case, consult Riccardo De Sanctis, *Delitto al potere: continchiesta* (Rome: Edizioni Samona and Savelli, 1972), pp. 61–86.

27. Colin McArthur's *Underworld USA* (New York: Viking Press, 1972), treats the Mafia film on pp. 34, 35, and 68. For a further treatment of this genre see Jack Shadoian, *Dreams and Dead Ends: The*

American Gangster/Crime Film (Cambridge: MIT Press, 1979).

28. Two colorful colloquial biographies are worth noting: Martin A. Gosch and Richard Hammer, *The Last Testament of Lucky Luciano* (Boston: Little, Brown, 1974), and Sid Feder and Joachim Joesten, *The Luciano Story* (New York: David McKay, 1954).

29. Gary Crowdus and Dan Georgakas, "The Audience Should Not Be Just Passive Spectators," *Cinéaste*, Fall 1975, 5.

30. In 1961, a very favorable film, *The Lucky Luciano Story*, was scheduled to be made with the collaboration of Luciano. The Mafia leader suggested Frank Sinatra to play the lead role, but it was later agreed that Dean Martin would take it. "The Little Man" (Meyer Lansky) in New York, according to Gosch and Hammer, pressured Luciano not to go through with the film in light of the then current publicity surrounding the television production *The Untouchables*.

31. Crowdus and Georgakas, "The Audience Should Not be Just Passive Spectators," p. 5.

32. Kezich, *Salvatore Giuliano*, p. 189.

33. Ciment, *Le dossier Rosi*, p. 148.

34. Gili, *Le cinéma italien*, pp. 256–57.

35. In Gosch and Hammer's account, Luciano states that there is no truth to his helping the Americans in Sicily with his contacts. He left there when he was nine, he said. Jack Higgins has fictionalized this aspect of the Mafia leader's life in his novel *Luciano's Luck* (1982).

36. John Horne Burns, *The Gallery* (New York: Harper, 1947). This is an excellent mirror of Americans and Neapolitans interacting on many levels.

37. Michel Ciment and Michel Delain, "La Mafia selon Rosi," *L'Express,* 22 October 1973, p. 108.

38. McArthur, *Underworld USA,* pp. 35, 38. Rosi, in our May 1981 interview in Rome, stated that Giannini's death actually occurred in this manner, and that the mythology of the gangster's death had its basis in reality.

39. Crowdus and Georgakas, "The Audience Should Not Be Just Passive Spectators," p. 5.

40. From the Museum of Modern Art program notes for a Rosi retrospective, 27 February to 11 March 1975. The distributors, said Rosi, did not want to use this quote for the publicity.

41. Ciment, *Le dossier Rosi*, p. 162.

42. *"Main basse sur la ville"* (script), *L'avant-scène cinéma,* 1976, 6.

43. Callisto Cosulich, ed., *"Uomini contro" di Francesco Rosi* (Bologna: Cappelli, 1970), p. 58.

44. Ibid., p. 60.

45. See a similar description in photo #9, following p. 96 in the Italian script of *Uomini contro*.

46. Leonardo Sciascia, *Il conteso* (Turin: Einaudi, 1971).

47. Gili, *Francesco Rosi*, p. 118.

48. For critical reviews and debate about the film, see Lorenzo Codelli, *"Cadavres exquis* sous trois angles," *Positif,* May 1976, 24–33, and John Francis Lane, "Films and Politics in Italy: Francesco Rosi," *Films and Filming,* May 1976, 16–17.

49. Gili, *Francesco Rosi*, p. 62.

50. For an esthetic parallel, listen to Jacques Brel's "Les Taureaux" which symbolically portrays a bullfight, but the arena is war and the bulls (soldiers) are sent out to the slaughter.

51. Alberto Moravia, *"C'era una volta . . . ," Alberto Moravia al cinema* (Milan: Bompiani, 1975), p. 87.

52. Lane, "Moments of Truth," p. 6.

53. In translation, *Christ Stopped at Eboli* (New York: Farrar, Straus, 1947).

54. Giovanni Falaschi, *Levi* (Florence: La Nuova Italia, 1971), p. 3.

55. For a detailed study of Levi's life and work, and especially *Eboli*, consult Gigliola De Donato, *Saggio su Carlo Levi* (Bari: De Donato, 1974), notably, pp. 75–119.

56. Reproduced in the program notes for New World Pictures' distribution of *Three Brothers* in the U.S.

57. Judith Slatin, "Brothers in Grief," *Screen International,* 13 May 1981, 17.

58. Michel Ciment, "Francesco Rosi's *Three Brothers,*" *Sight and Sound,* Winter 1981/82, 46.

59. Rosi, in an interview in *Corriere delle Sera,* 27 March 1981, printed in the program notes for New World Pictures' distribution.

60. Carrie Rickey, "Trinity Holy and Unholy," *Village Voice,* 23 February 1982, 52.

61. Ciment, "Francesco Rosi's *Three Brothers,*" p. 47.

62. Stanley Kauffman, "Good Intentions," *New Republic,* 21 April 1982, 24.

63. David Ansen, "Politics on Celluloid," *Newsweek,* 22 February 1982, 68.

Chapter 2. Pier Paolo Pasolini

1. Enzo Siciliano in *Pasolini* (New York: Random House, 1982; trans. John Shepley) dedicates the first and last chapter of his work to the director's death. Siciliano describes in detail Pasolini's encounter with the assailant Giuseppe Pelosi, the youth's clubbing of Pasolini and running him over with the director's Alfa Romeo, then the court case, and finally the impact of his death upon the film world.

2. "Pier-Paolo Pasolini," *Cahiers du cinéma,* July–August 1976, 100.

3. William Weaver, "Report from Italy—Pasolini: Writer, Director, Murder Victim," *Attenzione,* August 1979, 6. Oriana Fallaci talked with someone who claimed to have seen three men beat up Pasolini. The source was also severely beaten up as a warning not to disclose further information.

4. Mavrikos's film included remarkable newsreels of the director's funeral. There have been other films made on Pasolini, mostly during his lifetime, for example, by Maurizio Ponzo (*Il cinema di Pasolini,* 1966); Giovanni Bruno Solaro (*Pasolini in carne ed osse,* 1966); Carli Di Carlo (*Mondo e personaggi di Pasolini,* 1967); Primo Piano (*Pier Paolo Pasolini: cultura e societa,* 1967); Carlo Hayman-Chagey (*Pasolini,* 1970); and Jean-André Fieschi on French television, 15 November 1966 (*Pasolini l'enragé,* in the series "Cinéastes de notre temps").

5. See also the *Corriere delle Sera, L'Unità,* and *Il Messaggero* for 3 and 4 November 1975 for reactions to the director's death.

6. Christin Lord, "Pasolini, Italian Movie Director, Is Bludgeoned to Death near Rome," *New York Times,* 3 November 1975, 38.

7. Excerpt from "A Desperate Vitality" ("Una disperata vitalita") in *Poems in the Form of a Rose* (*Poesia in forma di rosa,* 1964), translated by Norman MacAfee and Luciano Martinengo, in *Christopher Street,* June 1977, 24.

8. Lord, "Pasolini, Italian Movie Director," p. 100.

9. Pasolini's close friend, actress Laura Betti, has edited materials dealing with the director's various trials, in *Pasolini: cronaca giudizaria, persecuzione, morte* (Milan: Garzanti, 1978).

10. Marc Gervais, "Pasolini: Contestatore," *Sight and Sound,* Winter 1968/69, 3.

11. Sandro Petraglia in *Pasolini* (Florence: La Nuova Italia, 1974) and Luigi Bini in *Pier Paolo Pasolini* (Milan: Letture, 1978) assess Pasolini's cinematic work from the point of view of poetic inspiration, often showing the conjunction of his poetry with a specific film. Marc Gervais in *Pier Paolo Pasolini* (Paris: Seghers, 1973) and Adelio Ferrero in *Il cinema di P. P. Pasolini* (Venice: Marsilio, 1977) develop the sacral side of his cinematic production. Enzo de Paoli in "Da Marx a Freud attraverso l'umorismo tragico" (*Cinema nuovo,* 1975) and Guido Aristarco in his essays reveal the psychological elements of the director's work with respect to his personal life and temperament. Ferrero and Petraglia include detailed bibliographies.

12. Quoted in a Brandon film brochure on Pasolini, originally from an interview with *Cahiers du cinéma.*

13. Bini, *Pier Paolo Pasolini,* p. 7.

14. Bernardo Bertolucci's father, the poet and critic Attilio, believes that a volume of Provençal lyrics with an Italian translation may have served as a model for Pasolini's work in dialect.

15. Siciliano, *Pasolini,* pp. 158–59.

16. Giuseppe Zigaina, "Pier Paolo Pasolini e il dialetto," *Italian Quarterly* 82–83 (Fall 1980–Winter 1981): 81. This special issue of the *Italian Quarterly* includes twenty-one papers given at the Yale conference on Pasolini, 23–26 October 1980.

17. Pasolini dedicated *Mamma Roma* to Longhi, to whom he was indebted for his aesthetic training.

18. Oswald Stack, *Pasolini on Pasolini* (Bloomington: Indiana University Press, 1969), pp. 19–20.

19. In 1962, Paolo Heusch and Brunello Rondi adapted *Una vita violenta* for the screen.

20. Enzo Siciliano, "Pier-Paolo Pasolini: Témoignages," *Cahiers du cinéma,* July–August 1976, 100.

21. Pier Paolo Pasolini, *Mamma Roma* (Milan: Rizzoli, 1962), p. 145. These remarks are also quoted in Siciliano's *Pasolini,* p. 232.

22. Herbert Mitgang, "Publishing: New Interests in the Work of Pasolini," *New York Times,* 21 November 1980, p. C26.

23. Siciliano, *Pasolini,* p. 29.

24. Ibid., pp. 86–90. In a letter to his friend Luciano Serra dated 21 August (1945), Pasolini describes Guido's resistance activities and gives the date of death as 7 February (1945), in *Lettere agli amici: 1941–1945* (Lodi: Guanda, 1977), pp. 46–47.

25. Stack, *Pasolini on Pasolini,* p. 19.

26. He explains his dismissal to Stack in different terms: "I did join the party for about a year in the period of 1947–48, but when my membership card lapsed I didn't bother to renew it." (p. 22).

27. Aggeo Savioli, interview with author, Rome, 16 April 1981. Enzo Siciliano in *Pasolini* has a similar reading: "In the fierce climate of the cold war, political and moral schematism was obligatory." (p. 136)

28. Alberto Moravia, interview with author, Rome, 12 January 1982.

29. Alberto Moravia, "Pasolini poeta civile," *Italian Quarterly* (Fall 1980–Winter 1981): 10–11.

30. From the publicity materials for the French distribution of *Arabian Nights.*

31. Gideon Bachmann, "The 220 Days of 'Salò,'" *Film Comment,* March–April 1976, 42.

32. Fluvio Stinchelli, "Il discorso di Pasolini: continuate a lottare," *Il Messaggero,* 5 November 1975, 2.

33. Bachmann, "The 220 Days of 'Salò,'" p. 43.

34. William Weaver, "Report from Italy," p. 8.

35. Stack, *Pasolini on Pasolini,* p. 30.

36. Publicity materials for the distribution of *The Gospel According to St. Matthew,* p. 72.

37. Pier Paolo Pasolini, *La religione del mio tempo* (Milan: Garzanti, 1961), p. 172.

38. Alberto Moravia, "Immagini al posto d'onore," *L'Espresso,* 1 October 1961, quoted in Siciliano, *Pasolini,* p. 238.

39. To follow the successive stages of Accattone's consciousness, see Randal Conrad, *"Accattone," Film Quarterly,* Winter 1966/67, 28–33.

40. "Pasolini—Press Conference, New York Film Festival, 1966," *Film Culture,* Fall 1966, 102. See also the transcript of the television production *Pasolini l'enragé,* in the special issue of *Cahiers du cinéma* (1981), pp. 48–49.

41. From the Italian edition of the screenplay *Accattone* (Rome: F.M., 1961), quoted in the Pasolini retrospective at the Museum of Modern Art (New York), following the director's death.

42. "Pasolini l'enragé," *Cahiers du cinéma* (1981), 47.

43. Stack, *Pasolini on Pasolini,* pp. 38–39.

44. "Pasolini Press Conference, New York Film Festival, 1966," p. 103.

45. "Pier Paolo Pasolini: An Epical Religious View of the World," *Film Quarterly,* Summer 1965, 32.

46. Petraglia, *Pasolini,* p. 6.

47. A few years later, in June 1965, Pasolini delivered a paper at the Pesaro Festival entitled "Il cinema di poesia."

48. The bedridden man is played by Lamberto Maggiorani who calls out "Stop, thief", as he does in De Sica's *Bicycle Thief* when his bicycle is stolen.

49. Giulio Cesare Castello, "Cinema Italiano 1962," *Sight and Sound,* Winter 1962/63, 33.

50. Jeanne Cordelier's experience as a prostitute in the French film *La dérobade* with Miou-Miou shows that the problem is not uncommon.

51. Stack, *Pasolini on Pasolini,* p. 49.

52. Claude Trémois, "*Mamma Roma:* Dans la lumière blanche du désespoir," *Télérama,* 7 November 1976, 70.

53. Stack, *Pasolini on Pasolini,* p. 14.

54. The film was also distributed under the title *Laviamoci il cervello.* The other contributors were Rossellini ("Illibatezza"), Jean-Luc Godard ("Il nuovo mondo"), and Ugo Gregoretti ("Il pollo ruspante").

55. A brief glimpse of political power is seen in the film as the reporter threatens the director with writing a bad review of the film. The director (Orson Welles) is not concerned, for the producer also owns the newspaper, and therefore controls both media.

56. Pasolini's poem, "To a Pope," in *The Religion of My Time* created a minor stir in the Vatican. The poem was an accusatory jab at the vicar's inactivity, a perspective later shared by Rolf Hochhuth in *The Deputy.*

57. The filming here resulted in *Sopraluoghi in Palestina* (1963–64) a type of travelogue of fifty minutes filmed by the cameraman Aldo Pennelli. In the film Pasolini discusses the radical transformation of the biblical sites.

58. Mark Stevens and Sari Gilbert, "Death Imitates Art," *Newsweek,* 17 November 1975, 75.

59. To John Bragin in "Pasolini: A Conversation in Rome," *Film Culture,* June 1966, 104, he said he reproduced the actual Christ of Matthew, "a figure who was man and God at the same time."

60. René Jordan, "The Gospel According to St. Matthew," *Films in Review,* January 1966, 54.

61. Stack, *Pasolini on Pasolini,* p. 155. Pasolini published the literary text of *Teorema* in 1968 with Garzanti. The frontpiece reads, "Instead God led the people by the roundabout way of the wilderness." (Exodus 13:18).

62. Alberto Moravia, *"Teorema," Alberto Moravia al cinema* (Milan: Bompiano, 1975), p. 107.

63. Dominique Noguez, "Teorema," *Take One,* November–December 1962, 23.

64. Carmen Tessier, "L'Abbé Marc Oraison," *Journal du dimanche,* 16 March 1969, 12.

65. John Bragin, "Pier Paolo Pasolini: Poetry as Compensation (Part Three)," *Film Society Review,* March 1969, 35.

66. Quoted in Petraglia, *Pasolini,* p. 94.

67. *"Teorema* Director Disowns His Awards," *Film and Television Daily,* 1 April 1969, 4. Pasolini always distinguishes between the religious institution and the sacred sentiment. In this article he contradicts himself in praising modernism and the industrial age which he normally condemns, especially in his "Trilogy of Life."

68. Philip Hartung, "Pasolini's Parable," *Commonweal,* 16 May 1969, 266.

69. *"Edipe roi* et *Téoreme," L'avant-scène cinéma,* November 1969, 47.

70. Originally in *Rinascita* of 21 May 1966, quoted in Gervais, pp. 153–54.

71. Stack, *Pasolini on Pasolini,* pp. 103, 106.

72. Siciliano, *Pasolini,* p. 296.

73. Totò is a "popular" Italian comic who comes from a Neapolitan subculture. A typical Totò comedy would be *Totò al giro d'Italia* (1949), a Mephistophelean comedy in which he sells his soul to win the Italian bicycle race. For further details consult Franco Faldini and Goffredi Fofi, *Totò: L'uomo e la maschera* (Milan: Feltrinelli, 1977).

74. Bini, *Pier Paolo Pasolini,* p. 39.

75. From the Brandon Films publicity materials for *The Hawks and the Sparrows,* p. 30.

76. In our 12 January 1982 interview, Moravia credited Pasolini with the whole idea of the film. He also said that most people approached by the director were reluctant to talk about sex and love. Musatti, according to Stack (p. 66), later denounced Pasolini for his methodology and called the film "reactionary."

77. Gervais, *Pier Paolo Pasolini,* p. 33.

78. Jean Narboni, "Rencontre avec P. P. Pasolini," *Cahiers du cinéma,* July–August 1967, 31.

79. Pasolini's treatment of incest would be closer to Louis Malle's development in *Murmur of the Heart* or Bertolucci's *Luna,* than Visconti's graphic or violent handling of the subject in *The Damned.*

80. Guido Aristarco, "Feto adulto alla ricerca dei fratelli," *Cinema nuovo,* January–February 1968, 16–19. See also his "Jung et De Seta, Freud et Pasolini," in *Cinéma '69,* April 1969, 93–104.

81. Pier Paolo Pasolini, *Oedipus Rex,* trans. John Mathews (London: Lorimer, 1971), p. 9.

82. Ibid.

83. Enzo Siciliano, in *Pasolini* (pp. 332–33), points out that the operatic singer Maria Callas was chosen because she was intricately connected with this role since she first performed it in 1953 at Milan's La Scala under the direction of Leonard Bernstein. He also notes that a legend grew around the Callas-Pasolini relationship at this time. See also Arianna Stassinopoulis, *Maria Callas: The Woman behind the Legend* (New York: Ballantine, 1981). Pasolini referred to her as a modern woman with ancient conflicts (p. 282).

84. Petraglia, *Pasolini,* p. 101.

85. Derek Elley, *"Medea," Films and Filming,* July 1975, 45.

86. Bini, *Pier Paolo Pasolini,* p. 67.

87. Ron Cohen, "Film," *Open Stage*, October 1980.

88. Filmoteca Nacional, *Pier Paolo Pasolini*, February 1976.

89. Siciliano, *Pasolini*, p. 342.

90. Richard Roud, "Roman Summer," *Sight and Sound*, Autumn 1971, 199.

91. David Bevan, "Pasolini and Boccaccio," *Literature/Film Quarterly*, Winter 1977, 29.

92. Told to Guy Flatley, "Bertolucci Is All-Tangoed Out," *New York Times*, 11 February 1973, 15.

93. Vincent Canby, "'Arabian Nights,' Last in Pasolini Trilogy," *New York Times*, 25 May 1974.

94. Quoted in an interview of Pasolini by Georges Moraux in publicity materials for *Arabian Nights*.

95. Wilhelm Reich, *The Mass Psychology of Fascism* (New York: Farrar, Straus & Giroux, 1970), pp. 29–30. The italics are Reich's.

96. One of the survivors in Piers Paul Read's *Alive: The Story of the Andes Survivors* described the eating of human flesh as holy communion.

97. One can readily perceive here the allusions to the complicity between the political and industrial worlds during the Third Reich, for example, in Bayer, I. G. Farben, Krupp, and other industries.

98. Alberto Moravia, *"Porcile," Alberto Moravia al cinema* (Milan: Bompiani, 1975), p. 92.

99. Joan Mellen, "Fascism in the Contemporary Film," *Film Quarterly*, Summer 1971, 2–3.

100. To this list one could later add the special issue of *Obliques* 12–13 (1979), edited by Michel Camus. Of the writers included, Barthes and Klossowski will be quoted in the film.

101. Bini, *Pier Paolo Pasolini*, p. 93. For a further discussion of sex and power see also Ugo Finetti, "Nella struttura di *Salò:* la dialettica erotismo-potere," *Cinema nuovo*, November–December 1976, 428–33.

102. James Cameron-Wilson, "What's on in London," 10 March 1978, from the British Film Institute Archives on Pasolini.

103. Bachmann, "The 220 Days of 'Salò,'" p. 43.

104. Siciliano, *Pasolini*, p. 388. See also, Richard Roud, "Pier Paolo Pasolini," *Cinema: A Critical Dictionary* (New York: Viking, 1980), p. 771.

105. Louise Barnetti, "Pasolini's Reputation in the United States," *Italian Quarterly* 82–83 (1980/81): 56.

106. André Cornard and Dominique Maillet, "Entretien avec Pier Paolo Pasolini," *Revue du cinéma*, January 1973, 91–92.

107. Gideon Bachmann, "Pasolini in Persia: The Shooting of *1001 Nights*," *Film Quarterly*, Winter 1973/74, 25.

108. The director develops this in "Pasolini: 'Je suis un enragé,'" *Télérama*, 13 November 1966, 29.

109. Published in *Christopher Street*, June 1977, 28.

Chapter 3. Bernardo Bertolucci

1. The theme of the voyage, along with that of ambiguity, death, and the quest for the father, forms the nucleus of Francesco Casetti's monograph, *Bernardo Bertolucci* (Florence: La Nuova Italia, 1975).

2. "Bernardo Bertolucci: A Film. Biography with Comments," a composite of interviews (unpaginated) from United Artists production notes for *1900*.

3. "Bernardo's Passion: *The Tragedy of a Ridiculous Man*," *Screen International*, 24 May 1981, 62.

4. Fabio DiVico and Roberto Degni, "The Poetry of Class Struggle," *Cinéaste*, Winter 1976/77, 7.

5. Daniela Morera, "1900: On the Set with Bertolucci," *Interview*, July 1975, 34.

6. Casetti, *Bernardo Bertolucci*, p. 30. In the small volume of poetry *In Search of Mystery (In cerca del mistero)* Bertolucci dedicated the poem, "A mio padre," to his father.

7. Bernardo's brother Giuseppe would also start out writing poetry and then move to cinema.

8. Richard Roud, "Fathers and Sons," *Sight and Sound*, Spring 1971, 61.

9. Gloria Stewart, "Are you Evil and Obsessed?," *The Daily Mail* (London), 19 March 1973.

10. Gideon Bachmann, "Utopia Revisited," *Sight and Sound*, Winter 1974/75, 33.

11. Mel Gussow, "Bertolucci Talks about Sex, Revolution, and 'Last Tango,'" *New York Times*, 2 February 1973, 20.

12. Bertolucci collaborated on the scripts for Gianni Puccini's *Ballata di un millardo*, Sergio Leone's *C'era una volta il West*, and Gianni Amico's *L'inchiesta*.

13. For a popular discussion of Vittorio Storaro's work as cinematographer, read Charles Mann, "Media: Writing with Light," *Attenzione*, November 1980, 66–71.

14. Jean Gili, "Bernardo Bertolucci," *Le cinéma italien* (Paris: Union Générale d'Editions, 1978), p. 63.

15. Deborah Young, "History Lessons," *Film Comment*, November–December 1977, 17.

16. Marilyn Goldin, "Bertolucci on *The Conformist*," *Sight and Sound*, Spring 1971, 66.

17. Amos Vogel, "Bernardo Bertolucci: An Interview," *Film Comment*, Fall 1971, 29.

18. Gussow, "Bertolucci Talks about Sex, Revolution, and 'Last Tango,'" p. 20.

19. Giovanni Di Bernardo, "Red Flags and American Dollars," *Cinéaste*, Winter 1976/77, 4.

20. Joseph Gelmis, "Bernardo Bertolucci," *The Film Director as Superstar* (New York: Doubleday, 1970), p. 113.

21. Attilio Bertolucci, "La teleferica," *Viaggio d'inverno* (Milan: Garzanti, 1971), pp. 33–35. Paul Crinel in *Etudes cinématographiques* 122–26 (1979): 95–96, argues for its being an 8 mm. camera. In our interview, Bertolucci said that his father was not aware of the technical differences, and concluded, "When you're eight you use an 8 mm., when you're sixteen, you use a 16 mm."

22. Casetti, *Bernardo Bertolucci*, p. 32.

23. Gelmis, "Bernardo Bertolucci," p. 113.

24. Bernardo Bertolucci, interview with author, 12 January 1982.

25. Bertolucci said the title came from the Roman poet Giuseppe Gioacchino Belli (1791–1863) who wrote in dialect.

26. Gordon Gow, "Cinema and Life," *Films and Filming*, June 1978, 12.

27. See Linda Williams, "Stendahl and Bertolucci: The Sweetness of Life before the Revolution," *Literature/Film Quarterly*, Summer 1976, 215–21. In French, consult Roger Tailleur, "Les Vacances rouges," *Positif*, May 1968, 31–39.

28. Gow, "Cinema and Life," p. 12.

29. Riccardo Rossetti, "Bernardo Bertolucci," *Con-verzazioni* (Rome: Bulzoni, 1977), p. 173.

30. While in the Suez region for the second episode, he also shot a short twelve-minute film, *Il canale*, which he did not make commercial.

31. Gelmis, "Bernardo Bertolucci," p. 116. The colorful posters tacked on the walls call for "Vietnam Libero."

32. From the publicity materials of Unitalia Films for *The Spider's Stratagem*.

33. Jorge Luis Borges, "The Theme of the Traitor and the Hero," *Labyrinths* (New York: New Directions, 1972). For a further discussion of the adaptation, see Ulrich Wicks, "Borges, Bertolucci and Metafiction," *Narrative Strategies* (Macomb, Ill.: Western Illinois University, 1980), pp. 19–36.

34. Consult T. Jefferson Kline in "Father as Mirror: Bertolucci's Oedipal Quest and the Collapse of Paternity," *Psychocultural Review* (Spring 1979): 91–109. Kline links Tara's name with the seat of the mythical Irish kings, the exotic plantation of *Gone with the Wind*, and the first two syllables of the dreaded tarantula spider. Bertolucci refers to the little town as "a place in one's consciousness," in Aldo Tassone, "Bernardo Bertolucci," *Parla il cinema italiano* (Milan: Edizioni il Formichiere, 1980), p. 73.

35. Joan Mellen, "A Conversation with Bernardo Bertolucci," *Cinéaste*, Summer 1972, 23.

36. Filming in Gonzague and Sabbioneta, between Parma and Mantua, Bertolucci is able to return to his own childhood. His dedication of the film to the new administrative district of Emilia-Romagna, established in 1969, is a signpost along this psychological itinerary.

37. Kline, "Father as Mirror: Bertolucci's Oedipal Quest and the Collapse of Paternity," p. 100.

38. This awareness of Athos, Jr., takes place while the duke's jester, Rigoletto, cries out, *"Ah, la maledizione,"* at the close of act 1 in the opera.

39. In the poem the son Giovanni learns his father was killed on 10 August 1867. His horse returned home all alone. Years later when Giovanni wants to find out more about his father's assassins, he finds all the roads blocked.

40. Michel Ciment and Gérard Legrand, "Entretien avec Bernardo Bertolucci," *Positif*, March

1973, 34.

41. Charles Mann's article on Storaro in *Attenzione* noted earlier shows how closely the cinematographer collaborates with a director to reveal a collective vision, but also how the cinematographer maintains a healthy independence.

42. Alberto Moravia, interview with author, 12 January 1982. For a comprehensive comparison of novel and film, see Daniel Lopez, "Novel into Film: Bertolucci's *The Conformist,*" *Literature/Film Quarterly,* Fall 1976, 303–12.

43. The marquee on the theatre at the opening of the film flashes the title of Jean Renoir's *La vie est à nous* (1936), a propaganda film made by the director for the Communist party even though he was not a member.

44. Mellen, "Conversation with Bernardo Bertolucci," p. 24.

45. Jonathan Cott, "A Conversation with Bernardo Bertolucci," *Rolling Stone,* 21 June 1973, 46.

46. The novel has been published by Robert Alley, *Last Tango in Paris* (New York: Dell, 1972).

47. Alberto Moravia, *"Ultimo tango a Parigi," Alberto Moravia al cinema* (Milan: Bompiani, 1975), pp. 264–66.

48. Cott, "A Conversation with Bernardo Bertolucci," p. 46.

49. Mellen, "A Conversation with Bernardo Bertolucci," p. 24.

50. Joan Mellen, "Sexual Politics and *Last Tango in Paris,*" *Film Quarterly,* Spring 1973, 19.

51. Jean-Louis Tallenay, "Bernardo Bertolucci parle de *1900,*" *Télérama,* 29 November 1976, 63.

52. Ibid., p. 62.

53. As Bertolucci was filming *1900,* not too far away was his friend Pasolini making his last film *Salò.*

54. During the production of *1900* Giuseppe Bertolucci filmed a one-hour documentary in 16 mm., *The Cinema According to Bertolucci (Bertolucci secondo il cinema,* 1975).

55. Guy Flatley, "Bertolucci Brings Liv Ullman to Brooklyn," *New York Times,* 25 November 1977, 66.

56. DiVico and Degni, "The Poetry of Class Struggle," p. 8.

57. Bachmann, "Utopia Visited," p. 29.

58. Jacques Siclier, "Les secrets de *La luna,*" *Le Monde,* 14 October 1979, 18.

59. Ibid.

60. Bertolucci said he felt very much like Joe when he arrived in Rome from Parma at the same age as the protagonist.

61. Claire Clouzot, "Le fils à maman," *Le Matin de Paris,* 3 October 1979.

62. Eric de Saint Angel, "Bertolucci: l'atroce confusion de la vie actuelle," *Le Matin* (Special Cannes), 24 May 1981, iii.

63. Pierre Montaigne, "Tognazzi: rapt à l'italienne," *Le Figaro,* 25 May 1981, p. 20E.

64. Joan Dupont, "Bertolucci's 'Ridiculous Man' is Typically Italain," *Film français,* 24 May 1981, 2.

65. de Saint Angel, "Bertolucci: l'atroce confusion," p. iii.

66. Dupont, "Bertolucci's 'Ridiculous Man,'" p. 2.

67. Yet in our 12 January 1982 interview Bertolucci referred to Primo Spagiarri as having a symbolic maternal function in the film, "someone who gives milk."

68. In 1980, about the time that *Tragedy of a Ridiculous Man* was in production, Carlo Donat-Cattin, vice-president of the Christian Democratic party, resigned because of his son's terrorist affiliations. He warned his colleagues that he had a list of forty-one names of leading Italian personalities who had sons in similar situations. The Donat-Cattin case points out that many terrorists come from solid Roman Catholic, Christian Democratic families, says Henry Tanner in "For Italians, Ideological Splits Stretch from Home to Rome," *New York Times,* 8 June 1980, p. E3.

69. de Saint Angel, "Bertolucci: l'atroce confusion," p. 3.

70. Bertolucci says that the style in *Tragedy* differs from that of his other works, for the film was done not in operatic language but prose. This resulted when director of photography Carlo di Palma (Antonioni's *Red Desert* and *Blow Up*) replaced Vittorio Storaro who was on the Coppola set for *One from the Heart.*

71. Vincent Canby, "Screen: A Kidnapping As Seen by Bertolucci," *New York Times,* 12 February 1982, p. C21.

72. Gelmis, "Bernardo Bertolucci," p. 120.

Chapter 4: Marco Bellocchio

1. Jean Gili, "Marco Bellocchio," *Le cinéma italien* (Paris: Union Générale d'Editions, 1978), p. 17.
2. Sandro Bernardi, *Marco Bellocchio* (Florence: La Nuova Italia, 1978), p. 17.
3. "Marco Bellocchio: An Interview," *Film Society Review*, January 1972, 34.
4. Nuccio Lodato further develops these themes and symbols in *Marco Bellocchio* (Milan: Moizzi, 1977), pp. 53–87.
5. This is quoted in publicity materials for *Leap into the Void* (p. 15), distributed by Clesi productions, first published in an interview with Callisto Cosulich in *Paese Sera*, 26 January 1980.
6. Goffredo Fofi, "La place de la politique," *Positif*, April 1972, 11.
7. Fred Tutten, "China Is Near," *Cinéaste*, Summer 1970, 25.
8. In publicity materials for *Leap into the Void* (p. 10), from an article published by Bellocchio in *Il lavoro*, 23 February 1980.
9. Susan Sontag in *Sickness as Metaphor* (New York: Farrar, Straus & Giroux, 1978), opposes the use of physical sickness as a metaphor for moral decadence.
10. Christian Braad Thomsen, "Bellocchio," *Sight and Sound*, Winter 1967/68, 15.
11. In publicity materials for *Leap into the Void* (p. 22), from an interview in *Amica*, 19 February 1980.
12. Luigi Barzini, *The Italians* (New York: Atheneum, 1964), p. 192.
13. Goffredo Fofi, "La place de la politique," p. 10.
14. Braad Thomsen, "Bellocchio," p. 15.
15. Tommaso Chiaretti, "Allegretto con pessimismo," in Bellocchio, *China Is Near* (New York: Orion Press, 1969), p. 10.
16. "Authors on Tape," in Bellocchio, *China Is Near*, p. 21.
17. Ibid., p. 20.
18. John Francis Lane, "Italy's Angry Young Directors," *Films and Filming*, October 1968, 76.
19. Marisa Rusconi, Su *La Cina è vicina*," in *La macchina cinema di Marco Bellocchio*, ed. Giuliana Callegari and Nuccio Lodato (Pavia: Centro Stampa dell'Amministrazione provinciale, 1979), p. 76.
20. Tuten, *"China Is Near,"* p. 25.
21. Fofi, "La place de la politique," p. 16.
22. "Marco Bellocchio: An Interview," *Film Society Review*, January 1972, 36.
23. Fofi, "La place de la politique, p. 16.
24. Jay Cocks, "Burnt Offering," *Time*, 22 April 1974, 68.
25. Tullio Kezich, "Amore e rabbia," *Bianco e nero*, July–August 1969, 130–32.
26. Tuten, *"China Is Near,"* p. 25.
27. Fofi, "La place de la politique," p. 12. The text was originally published in *Il nome del padre* (Bologna: Cappelli, 1971).
28. Bernardi, *Marco Bellocchio*, pp. 85–86.
29. Sandro Scandolara, *"Sbatti il mostro in prima pagina,"* *Cineforum*, March 1973, 257.
30. In publicity materials for *Leap into the Void* (p. 17) from an interview with Anna Maria Mori, *La Repubblica*, 1980.
31. Ibid., p. 3.
32. André Cornand, *"Le saut dans le vide,"* *Image et son*, June 1980, 32.
33. In publicity material for *Leap into the Void* (p. 10), from Bellocchio's article, "Me, Madness, and Desire."
34. Marco Bellocchio, *"The Seagull,"* Program Notes (21st London Film Festival, 1977).
35. Ibid.
36. Aldo Tassone, "Marco Bellocchio," *Parla il cinema italiano* (Milan: Edizioni il Formichiere, 1980), p. 43.
37. Ibid.
38. Preproduction statement, 21st London Film Festival.
39. Ibid.
40. These episodes were entitled: I. "Era San Benedetto"; II. "Periferie, III"; III. "Il mago Zu Zu"; IV. "Il travagliato sogno di una vita"; and V. "Una vita per il cinema."
41. Tassone, "Marco Bellocchio," p. 19.

42. Ibid., p. 20. For a fuller treatment of *Cinema Machine,* see R. T. Witcombe (New York: Oxford University Press, 1982), pp. 55–56.

43. *Un film di Marco Bellocchio:* I pugni in tasca (Milan: Garzanti, 1967), p. 24.

Chapter 5. Gillo Pontecorvo

1. Massimo Ghirelli, *Gillo Pontecorvo* (Florence: La Nuova Italia, 1978), pp. 24–30.

2. Giorgio Amendola, *Lettere a Milano: Ricordi e documenti* (Rome: Editori Riuniti, 1973), p. 507. When Amendola saw *The Battle of Algiers* many years after World War II, he could detect parallels in the sentiments and motivation of the combatants of both World War II and the Algerian War, as well as the sacrifice and death that led to final liberation.

3. PierNico Solinas, ed., *Gillo Pontecorvo's "The Battle of Algiers"* (New York: Charles Scribner's Sons, 1973), p. 199.

4. Ghirelli, *Gillo Pontecorvo,* pp. 32–33.

5. Joris Ivens, *The Camera and I* (New York: International Publications, 1974), pp. 249–50. For a critical work on Ivens in Italian, see Silvano Cavatorta and Daniele Maggioni, *Joris Ivens* (Florence: La Nuova Italia, 1979), especially p. 100 on *The Windrose.*

6. Ivens, *The Camera and I,* p. 250. Other titles of the film are *The Compass Chart* and *The Compass Rose.*

7. Ghirelli, *Gillo Pontecorvo,* p. 34.

8. Ibid., p. 12.

9. The film was also screened in the seventies at Prato, north of Florence, says Franco Solinas, with the participation of several of the nonprofessional actors who played in the film. Two decades later it still had the fresh aura of the neorealistic about it.

10. Harold Kalishman, "Using the Contradictions of the System," *Cinéaste,* Spring 1974, 4.

11. Alain Rémond, *Montand* (Paris: Henri Veyrier, 1977), p. 71.

12. There is a resurgence of interest in the Holocaust as seen by such films as *The Boat Is Full, Night Porter, David,* and others.

13. Pontecorvo studied music with René Leibowitz in Paris during the forties and assists in the musical compositions in almost all of his films. Like Eisenstein in *Alexander Nevsky* (1938), he strongly believes in the music-image relationship in film.

14. It was rumored that *Kapò,* nominated for an Oscar in the foreign language category of 1960, did not win because of the negative reaction to Gillo's brother Bruno's Soviet ties. Pontecorvo discounts this and praises Ingmar Bergman's *Virgin Spring,* which won the Academy Award.

15. PierNico Solinas, *Gillo Pontecorvo's "The Battle of Algiers",* p. 193.

16. Henri Rode, "Jean Martin: Pour tourner *La Bataille d'Alger,* j'ai quitté la soutane pour l'uniforme du colonel," *Cinémonde,* 23 June 1970, 10–11.

17. PierNico Solinas, *Gillo Pontecorvo's "The Battle of Algiers",* p. ix.

18. Ibid., p. 198.

19. John Talbott, *The War without a Name: France in Algiers, 1959–1962* (New York: Alfred A. Knopf, 1980), p. 83.

20. Ibid., p. 81.

21. From the Igor Film (Rome) publicity material, also reproduced in "Dossier: Tout savoir sur *La Bataille d'Alger,*" *Cinémonde,* 16 June 1970, 20.

22. For a discussion of the revolutionary splinter groups see Alf Andrew Hessoy, *Insurgency and Counterinsurgency in Algeria* (Bloomington: Indiana University Press, 1972), especially pp. 99 and 266. John Talbott's notes and bibliography of English and French works are extensive. They include partisan as well as objective, historical analyses of the eight-year war.

23. Laurent Heynemann's controversial film *La question* vividly shows the torture tactics of the French military.

24. Talbott, *The War without a Name,* pp. 85–86.

25. PierNico Solinas, *Gillo Pontecorvo's "The Battle of Algiers," p. 178.*

26. More liberal French critics pointed out in *Le Monde* of 5 June 1970 that the U.S. sent the biting antimilitary satire *M.A.S.H.* to Cannes at the height of the Vietnam War.

27. The Spanish government had the power to do this, as it proved earlier when it cost Columbia

Pictures millions of dollars by boycotting Fred Zinnemann's *Behold a Pale Horse* (1964).

28. Guylaine Guidez, "Gillo Pontecorvo," *Cinémonde*, 23 June 1970, 25.

29. Pauline Kael, "Mythmaking," *New Yorker*, 7 November 1970, 159.

30. Joan Mellen, "A Reassessment of Gillo Pontecorvo's *Burn!*" *Cinema* (Los Angeles), Winter 1972/73, 39–47.

31. Kael, "Mythmaking," p. 160.

32. Joan Mellen, "An Interview with Gillo Pontecorvo," *Film Quarterly*, Fall 1972, 9.

33. Harold Kalishman, "Using the Contradictions of the System," p. 3.

34. Ibid.

35. Kael, "Mythmaking," p. 159.

36. Mario Scialoja, "'Curcio the Kid,' vietato ai minori di anni cento," *L'Espresso*, 28 October 1979, 81.

37. Corinne Lucas, "'Ogro' et le terrorisme," *Image et Son*, June 1980, 66.

38. Julen Agirre, *Operación Ogro: Como y por qué ejecutamos a Carrero Blanco* (Hendaye: Ediciones Mugalde, 1974).

39. Ibid., pp. 9, 20.

40. Claire Sterling, *The Terror Network* (New York: Berkeley, 1982), p. 168.

41. Antonello Trombadori, "E *Ogro*? Era meglio parlare di Gallinari," *L'Espresso*, 28 October 1979, 79.

42. Paolo Spriano, "Bravo Gillo, continua così," *L'Espresso*, 28 October 1979, 81.

43. For an actor to play the diehard militant Txabi, Pontecorvo had been thinking of an American, for example, Robert De Niro or Al Pacino.

44. There have been three other projects that would call for American backing. Over the past ten years Pontecorvo has considered making a biblical film on the rebellious Jesus, *End Times (I tempi della fine)*, perhaps in Jerusalem. He also completed a script based on Peter Masse's *Made in America*, which he would like to film in the U.S. Also, Marlon Brando, who had not spoken to Pontecorvo after his stormy relationship with this "dictatorial director" (Brando's words), asked him to direct a film on the American Indian for Columbia. Brando was to have played the role of a semihonest lawyer. Nothing came of their discussion. Most recently Pontecorvo has been interested in making a film on the political situation in Nicaragua.

45. Harold Kalishman, "Using the Contradictions of the System," p. 6.

Chapter 6. Elio Petri

1. Alfredo Rossi, *Elio Petri* (Florence: La Nuova Italia, 1979), p. 6.

2. The script was published in Petri's *Roma, ore undici* (Rome: Avanti!, 1956). His other scripts were *A Husband for Anna Zaccheo* (*Un marito per Anna Zaccheo*, 1953); *Days of Love* (*Giorni d'amore*, 1954); *Men and Wolves* (*Uomini e lupi*, 1956); *A Year's Long Road* (*La strada lunga un anno*, 1956); and *The Bachelor's Establishment* (*La garconière*, 1960).

3. Nello Ajello, *Intellettuali e PCI, 1944–1958* (Rome-Bari: Laterza, 1979), p. 404.

4. Jean Gili, *Elio Petri* (Nice: Faculté des Lettres et Sciences Humaines, 1974), p. 20.

5. Rossi, *Elio Petri*, p. 4.

6. Ibid., p. 58.

7. A feature film about the Cervi brothers, *I sette fratelli Cervi* was made in 1967 by Gianni Puccini.

8. Rossi, *Elio Petri*, p. 30.

9. Aldo Tassone, "Elio Petri," *Parla il cinema italiano* (Milan: Edizioni il Formichiere, 1980), p. 239.

10. Jean Gili, "Elio Petri," *Le cinéma italien* (Paris: Union Générale d'Editions, 1978), 39.

11. Tassone, "Elio Petri," p. 240.

12. Ibid., p. 227.

13. Saul Kahan, "*The Tenth Victim*," *Cinema* (Los Angeles), December 1965, 37.

14. Ibid.

15. Goffredo Fofi, "Conversation avec Elio Petri," *Positif*, April 1971, 49.

16. Maria-Teresa Savage, "The Mafia on Film: *A ciascuno il suo*," *Film Society Review*, December 1971, 38.

17. Tassone, "Elio Petri," p. 246.

18. Rossi, *Elio Petri*, p. 61.

19. Tassone, "Elio Petri," p. 228.

20. Ibid., p. 249.

21. Ibid.

22. Gili, *"La proprietà non è più un furto,"* in *Elio Petri*, p. 83.

23. Tassone, "Elio Petri," p. 250.

24. Ibid., p. 230.

25. Fofi, "Conversation avec Elio Petri," p. 40.

26. Two cinematic parallels—Costa-Gavras's *Z* and *Special Section*—show that maintaining surveillance and keeping dossiers on possible dissidents are characteristic of fascist regimes.

27. Guy Braucourt, "L'organe crée la fonction, ou le fascisme en gants blancs," in *"Enquête sur un citoyen au-dessus de tout soupçon,"* *L'avant-scène cinéma*, February 1971, 9.

28. Christian Viviani, "Elio Petri dans son milieu naturel," in Jean Gili, ed., *Elio Petri*, p. 175.

29. Gérard Langlois, "Elio Petri le polémiste," *Lettres françaises*, 31 May 1972, 14.

30. Alberto Cattini, "The Working Class Goes to Heaven," *Cinéaste*, Spring 1972, 24.

31. James Roy MacBean, "The Working Class Goes Directly to Heaven . . . ," *Film Quarterly*, Spring 1973, 54.

32. Penelope Gilliatt, "The Workers Gate-Crash Elysium," *New Yorker*, 19 May 1975, 79.

33. Langlois, "Elio Petri le polémiste," p. 14.

34. Joan Mellen, *"Ombre rosse:* Developing a Radical Critique of the Cinema in Italy," *Cinéaste*, Spring 1972, 52.

35. Rossi, *Elio Petri*, p. 80.

36. Petri and Pirro's text is published in *La proprietà non è più un furto* (Milan: Bompiano, 1973).

37. Ferdinand Céline, *Voyage au bout de la nuit*, Pléiade collection (Paris: Gallimard, 1962), p. 192.

38. See *La piste rouge*, 10/18 collection (Paris: Union Générale d'Editions, 1973), on Giuseppe Pinelli as well as Pietro Valpreda, arrested on 15 December 1969. The Italian playwright Dario Fo has rendered a tragicomic view of the Pinelli case in *The Accidental Death of an Anarchist*.

39. For a discussion of Risi's contribution, read Adelio Ferrero, "Nelo Risi: *Giuseppe Pinelli*," in *Dal cinema al cinema* (Milan: Longanesi, 1980), pp. 369–71.

40. In France, *Documents on Giuseppe Pinelli* was screened with *Angela Davis* by Yolande de Luart. The effect of the Pinelli film was limited since there was no explanation of the political atmosphere that engendered the work.

41. Luigi Barzini, *The Italians* (New York: Atheneum, 1964), p. 114.

42. This would be one of the several projects that Petri would not complete. He had wanted to make a film on Hitler and Mussolini, *Zoo* with Jack Nicholson, *Settore privato* of Paul Léautaud, *Autobus, Quartetto*, Moravia's *Vita interiore*, a theatrical work *Giacobbe*, and a project with Enzo Siciliano on two priests in crises.

43. Sandro Zambetti, *"Todo modo:* Ogni mezzo va bene per cercare di battere il regime DC," *Cineforum*, May 1976, 245.

44. Jean Rochereau, *"Todo modo,"* *La Croix*, 29 January 1977, 8.

45. Jean Gili, "Entretien avec Elio Petri," *Ecran*, 15 January 1977, 55.

46. Gili, "Entretien avec Elio Petri," p. 56.

47. Jean de Baroncelli, *"Todo modo* de Petri: Un film de combat," *Le Monde*, 23–24 January 1977, 31.

48. Tassone, "Elio Petri," p. 235.

49. Giovanni Grazzini, *"Buone notizie,"* in *Cinema '79* (Rome: Universale Laterza, 1980), p. 156.

Chapter 7. Lina Wertmüller

1. See Molly Haskell's *From Reverence to Rape: The Treatment of Women in the Movies* (New York: Holt, Rinehart, Winston, 1973) for a lament over the lack of women in strategic positions in cinema.

2. Ernest Ferlita and John R. May, *The Parables of Lina Wertmüller* (New York: Paulist Press, 1977), pp. 83–84. This monograph has a fine analysis of the director's works as well as a more than adequate bibliography in English. Wertmüller praises this work highly.

3. Melton S. Davis, "Lina Wertmüller Turns to the Stage," *New York Times*, 30 March 1980, 8.

4. "La Wertmuller ha 'girato' fra le macerie del terremoto," *Corriere della Sera*, 23 April 1981, 27.

5. Nora Sayre, "Lina Wertmuller Defines Free-Wheeling Politics," *New York Times*, 5 February 1975, 30.

6. Paul McIsaac and Gina Blumenfeld, "You Cannot Make the Revolution on Film: An Interview with Lina Wertmüller," *Cinéaste*, Spring 1974, 7.

7. Glenys Robert, "Lina Wertmüller: A Thirst for Life," *Times* (London), 25 February 1977.

8. Thomas W. Bohn and Richard L. Stromgren, *Light and Shadows* (Sherman Oaks, Calif.: Alfred, 1978), pp. 412–13.

9. Tom Zito, "Her Offspring: Films Born of Love, Anarchy and Economics," *Washington Post*, 2 February 1976, p. D1.

10. McIsaac and Blumenfeld, "You Cannot Make the Revolution on Film," p. 9.

11. John Simon, "Portrait of the Artist as Workhorse," *New York*, 2 February 1976, 29.

12. Diane Jacobs, "Lina Wertmuller: The Italian Aristophanes?", *Film Comment*, March–April 1976, 48, 50.

13. From an interview for Italian television (RAI), quoted in the Ferlita-May monograph. p. 9.

14. Ferlita and May, *The Parables of Lina Wertmüller*, pp. 19–25.

15. McIsaac and Blumenfeld, "You Cannot Make the Revolution on Film," p. 7.

16. Ibid.

17. Terrence Des Pres, "Bleak Comedies," *Harper's*, June 1976, 26.

18. Ernest Ferlita mentions her scriptwriting for such films as *Les chemins de Kathmandu/Katmandu* (1969); *Città violenta* (1970); *Quando le donne avevano la coda* (1970); *Fratello sole sorella luna/Brother Sun Sister Moon* (also story, 1972); *Cari genitori* (1973).

19. In the course of the filming she visited Francesco Rosi on the day when he was shooting the famous sequence of the "Portella della Gineste" for *Salvatore Giuliano*.

20. From the production notes for *The Seduction of Mimi*.

21. "The Irresistible Force and the Immutable Object," *Time*, 16 February 1976, 60.

22. Peter Biskind, "Lina Wertmüller: The Politics of Private Life," *Film Quarterly*, Winter 1974/75, 13.

23. Judy Klemesrud, "Wertmuller: The Foremost Woman Movie Director," *New York Times*, 9 February 1975, p. D15.

24. In our interview she said, "The actress came from Naples and the derrière from Rome." She added metaphorically, "I am this *culo.*"

25. McIsaac and Blumenfeld, "You Cannot Make the Revolution on Film," p. 7.

26. *The Seduction of Mimi*, however, was released in the U.S. with approximately twenty minutes of the film cut, lamented the director.

27. Ellen Willis, "Is Lina Wertmuller Just One of the Boys?," *Rolling Stone*, 25 March 1976, 31.

28. Tom Allen, "Announcing—Lina Wertmüller Daredevil Aerialist," *America*, 7 February 1976, 100.

29. "The Great Beast" is patterned on "The Bitch of Buchenwald," Ilsa Koch, wife of the commandant of the camp, Karl Koch. She was tried after the war for having instigated 35 murders and attempting 135 others. See "Very Special Present," *Time*, 25 December 1950, 23. Bruno Bettelheim, a former camp survivor, writes, in "Surviving," *New Yorker*, 2 August 1976, 46, that, given the Nazi's idea of prescribed roles of women and men in society, there was no such woman commandant.

30. Lina Wertmüller told Jerry Tallmer of *The New York Post* (27 January 1978) that the U.N. wanted to give her an award for "Woman of the Year," and asked her what phrase she wanted inscribed on it. She told them, "Man in disorder, that's the only hope." The U.N. never sent the medal.

31. Luigi Barzini, *The Italians* (New York: Atheneum, 1964), p. 194.

32. From *"Seven Beauties," The Screenplays of Lina Wertmüller* (New York: Quadrangle/New York Times, 1977), p. 313.

33. Ibid.

34. Ibid., p. 273.

35. Ibid.

36. Jerzy Kosinski, "'Seven Beauties!'—A Cartoon Trying to Be a Tragedy," *New York Times*, Arts and Leisure sec., 7 March 1976, 1.

37. Betthelheim, "Surviving," pp. 31–52.

38. McIsaac and Blumenfeld, "You Cannot Make the Revolution on Film," p. 7.

39. Allen, "Announcing—Lena Wertmüller, Daredevil Aerialist," p. 100.

40. Gary Arnold, "A Need for Chaos Fulfilled on Film," *Washington Post*, 19 February 1976, p. G11.

41. Günter Ott, "Lina Sweeps In," *Cinema Canada*, March 1978, 15.

42. In the play it was sung by washerwomen who have erotic feelings while scrubbing their laundry. Someone from the Warner Bros. production took it for a modern rock song, which indicates the great cultural abyss between America and Italy, says the director.

43. Glenys Roberts, "Lina Wertmuller: A Thirst for Life," *Times* (London), 25 February 1977. Wertmüller explained to Jerry Tallmer of *The New York Post* (27 January 1978) the parallel between the couple in the film and Giancarlo Giannini and his wife, married for ten years and breaking up.

44. Barzini, *The Italians*, p. 190.

45. Tania Brassey, "A Hissing behind the Camera," *Evening Standard* (London), 6 March 1978.

46. "Sophia Loren to Start Wertmüller 'Tieta'," *New York Times*, 22 June 1982, p. C7. At the same time as Wertmüller began *Tieta*, William Morrow published her first novel, *The Head of Alvise*. The work deals with the relationship of two Jewish boys, Sammy and Alvise, from their early days in Venice, through the concentration camps, to America where they meet four decades later.

47. Molly Haskell, "Lina Wertmüller Is a Radical Chick with an Eye for the Rooster," *Village Voice*, 26 January 1976, 12–13.

48. From the author's interview with Lino Miccichè, Rome, 15 January 1982.

49. Rita Dallas, "For Lina, It's Problems, Not Prophecy," *Daily Telegraph* (London), 12 May 1979.

Conclusions

1. "The Double-Neos," *Newsweek*, 21 February 1966, 101.

Bibliography

General

Ajello, Nello. *Intellettuali e PCI 1944–1958*. Rome-Bari: Laterza, 1979.

Armes, Roy. *Patterns of Realism*. South Brunswick, N.J.: A. S. Barnes, 1971.

Baragli, Enrico. "Marxisti e cinema in Italia." *La Civiltà cattolica* 2682 (1962).

Barbaro, Umberto. *Il film e il risarcimento marxista dell'arte*. Rome: Riuniti Editori, 1961.

Barzini, Luigi. *The Italians*. New York: Pantheon, 1964.

Bertetto, Paolo. *Il cinema dell' utopia*. Salerno: Rumma Editore, 1970.

Bondanella, Peter. *Italian Cinema: From Neorealism to the Present*. New York: Frederick Ungar, 1983.

Borde, Raymond, and André Bouissy. "Nouveau cinéma italien." *Premier plan* (Special Issue), 30 (1963).

Bruno, Edoardo. *I film di Filmcritica: I migliori dal 1950–1979*. Rome: Savelli Editori, 1980.

Carpi, Fabio. *Cinema italiano del dopoguerra*. Milan: Schwartz, 1958.

Castello, Giulio Cesare. "Cinema italiano, 1962." *Sight and Sound*, Winter 1962–63, 28–33.

"Cinema nuovo" Staff. "Douze ans de cinéma italien." *Ecran '73*, April 1973, 34–42.

Di Giammatteo, Fernaldo. "'Marienbadism' and the New Italian Directors." *Film Quarterly*, Winter 1962–63, 20–25.

Ferrero, Adelio. *Dal cinema al cinema*. Milan: Longanesi, 1980.

Fofi, Goffredo. *Il cinema italiano: servi e padroni*. Milan: Feltrinelli, 1971.

Gili, Jean, ed. *Fascisme et résistance*. Etudes cinématographiques 82–83 (1970).

Gough-Yates, Kevin. "The Destruction of Neo-Realism." *Films and Filming*, September 1970, 14–22.

Grazzini, Giovanni. *Cinema '79*. Bari: Editori Laterza, 1980.

Jarratt, Vernon. *The Italian Cinema*. New York: Arno, 1972.

Kane, Pascal. "Les fils ne valent pas les pères." *Cahiers du cinéma*, November 1977, 21–23.

Kogan, Norma. *The Government of Italy*. New York: Thomas Y. Crowell, 1962.

Lane, John Francis. "Five Directors Who Are the New Realists." *Films and Filming*, January 1961, 20–21, 46.

————. "The 'Woodstock' of Italy's Leftists." *Films and Filming,* November 1973, 62–65.

Leprohon, Pierre. *The Italian Cinema.* New York: Praeger, 1972.

Liehm, Mira. *Passion and Defiance: Film in Italy from 1942 to Present.* Berkeley: University of California Press, 1984.

Lizzani, Carlo. *Il cinema italiano 1895–1979.* Rome: Editori Riuniti, 1980.

Mellen, Joan. "Fascism in the Contemporary Film." *Film Quarterly,* Summer 1971, 2–19.

————. "Film and Style: The Fictional Documentary." *Antioch Review* (1972): 403–25.

————. "*Ombre rosse:* Developing a Radical Critique of the Cinema in Italy." *Cinéaste,* Spring 1972, 49–52.

Miccichè, Lino. "Quindici anni di cinema italiano, 1958–1973." *Novità in cineteca,* March 1979, 2–6.

Mida, Massimo, and Lorenzo Quaglietti. *Dai telefoni bianchi al neorealism.* Rome-Bari: Laterza, 1980.

Moravia, Alberto. *Alberto Moravia al cinema.* Milan: Bompiani, 1975.

Overbey, David. *Springtime in Italy: A Reader on Neo-Realism.* London: Talisman, 1978.

Penniman, Howard, ed. *Italy at the Polls.* Washington, D.C.: American Enterprise Institute for Public Policy Research, 1977.

Protti, Daniele, and Alberto Cattini. "Political Engagement in the Italian Cinema." *Cinéaste,* Spring 1970, 28–29.

Rondi, Gian Luigi. *Italian Cinema Today, 1952–1965.* New York: Hill and Wang, 1966.

Rondolino, Gianni, ed. *Catalogo Bolaffi del cinema italiano 1979/1980.* Turin: Giulio Bolaffi Editore, 1980.

Roud, Richard. "Roman Summer." *Sight and Sound,* Autumn 1971, 197–202.

Sbarberi, Franco. *I communisti italiani e lo stato 1929–1956.* Milan: Feltrinelli, 1980.

Witcombe, R. T. *The New Italian Cinema: Studies in Dance and Despair.* New York: Oxford University Press, 1982.

Francesco Rosi

Ansen, David. "Politics on Celluloid." *Newsweek,* 22 February 1982, 69.

Amengual, Barthelemy. "D'un réalisme 'épique.'" *Positif,* May 1976, 39–44.

————. "Rosi in Context." *1000 Eyes,* November 1976, 17.

Baby, Yvonne. "*L'Affaire Mattei,* un film de Francesco Rosi." *Le Monde,* 7–8 June 1972, 19.

————. "*Salvatore Giuliano.*" *Le Monde,* 6 March 1963, 13.

Bachmann, Gideon. "Francesco Rosi: An Interview." *Film Quarterly,* Spring 1965, 50–56.

Banacki, Raymond. "*More Than a Miracle.*" *Film Quarterly,* Spring 1968, 59–60.

Benayoun, Robert. "Le cinéaste du centre-gauche." *France observateur,* 14 November 1963, 17–18.

Biraghi, Gugliemo. "*Tre Fratelli* di Francesco Rosi." *Il Messaggero,* 21 March 1981, 13.

Bory, Jean-Louis. "Francesco Rosi." In *Dossiers du cinéma: Cinéastes II,* pp. 169–72. Paris: Casterman, 1971.

Braucourt, Guy. "Gian-Maria Volonté Talks about Cinema and Politics." *Cinéaste,* Fall 1975, 10–13.

Bruno, Edoardo. "*Salvatore Giuliano,* ritorno alla verità." *Filmcritica,* January 1962, 677–79.

Buache, Freddy. "Rosi." In *Le cinéma italien d'Antonioni à Rosi,* pp. 159–66. Yverdon, Switzerland: Edition de la Thiele, 1969.

Chevassu, François. "*L'Affaire Mattei: La classe ouvriere va au paradis.*" *Revue du cinéma,* June–July 1972.

Ciment, Michel. *Le dossier Rosi: Cinéma et politique.* Paris: Editions Stock, 1976.

———. "Entretien avec Francesco Rosi." *Positif,* November 1970, 22–33.

———. "Entretien avec Francesco Rosi: à propos de *Lucky Luciano.*" *Positif,* January 1974, 15–24.

———. "Entretien avec Francesco Rosi." *Positif,* February 1979, 24–32.

———. "Francesco Rosi, artiste-citoyen." *L'Express,* 8–14 September 1975, 16–17.

———. "Francesco Rosi's 'Three Brothers.'" *Sight and Sound,* Winter 1981–82, 46–49.

———. "Neuf propositions pour un étage de Francesco Rosi." *Positif,* May 1980, 2–7.

———. "Rosi: à scénario ouvert." *L'Express,* 17–23 July 1972, 48–49.

———. "Sciascia, Leonardo: Du *Contexte* à *Cadavres exquis.*" *Positif,* May 1976, 34–38.

———. "Vivir Desviviendose." *Positif,* May 1965, 1–2.

Ciment, Michel, Lorenzo Codelli, and Paul-Louis Thirard. "*L'Affaire Mattei* sous trois angles." *Positif,* July–August 1972, 12–30.

Ciment, Michel, and Michel Delain. "La Mafia selon Rosi." *L'Express,* 22 October 1973, 106–8.

Ciment, Michel, Goffredo Fofi, and Paolo Gobetti. "Entretien avec Rosi." *Positif,* May 1965, 4–17.

Codelli, Lorenzo. "*Cadavres exquis* sous trois angles." *Positif,* May 1976, 24–33.

Coleman, John. "Dead Ends: *Illustrious Corpses, The Lost Honour of Katharina Blum, Riddles of the Sphinx.*" *New Statesman,* 13 May 1977, 650.

Cosulich, Callisto, ed. "*Uomini Contro*" *di Francesco Rosi.* Bologna: Cappelli Editore, 1970.

———. "Un vecchio e i suoi figli." *Paese Sera,* 21 March 1981, 3.

Cournot, Michel, "Beauté interdite." *Nouvel observateur,* 21 June 1971, 48–49.

Crowdus, Gary, and Dan Georgakas. "The Audience Should Not Be Just Passive Spectators: An Interview with Francesco Rosi." *Cinéaste,* Fall 1975, 1–6.

de Baroncelli, Jean. "A la recherche d'un monde oublié." *Le Monde,* 13 May 1979, 1, 17.

———. "'Trois Frères' de Francesco Rosi." *Le Monde,* 14 May 1981, 19.

De Donato, Gigliola. *Saggio su Carlo Levi.* Bari: De Donato, 1974.

De Sanctis, Riccardo. *Delitto al potere: Controinchiesta.* Rome: La Nuova Sinistra, 1972.

Durgnat, Raymond. "*Hands over the City.*" *Films and Filming,* October 1966, 18ff.

Durieux, Gilles. "Les choix précis de Francesco Rosi." *Film français,* 13 May 1981, 5–8.

d'Yvoire, Jean. *"Salvatore Giuliano." Télérama,* 17 March 1963, 58.

Falaschi, Giovanni. *Levi.* . . . Florence: La Nuova Italia, 1971.

Ferrero, Nino. *Francesco Rosi.* Turin: Edizioni A.E.A.C.E., 1972.

Fofi, Goffredo. *"I magliari." Positif,* May 1965, 18–20.

Frankel, Paul. *Mattei: Oil and Power Politics.* London: Faber and Faber, 1966.

Gili, Jean. "Un homme contre: Francesco Rosi." *Ecran,* December 1973, 6ff.

———. "Francesco Rosi." In *Le cinéma italien,* pp. 239–73. Union Générale d'Editions, 1978.

———. *Francesco Rosi: Cinéma et pouvoir.* Paris: Editions du Cerf, 1976.

———. "Levi, Rosi, Eboli: Comme s'il y avait deux Italies." *Ecran,* 15 September 1979, 49–52.

Gillett, John. "Cinderella—Italian Style." *Sight and Sound,* Autumn 1969, 214–15.

Gosch, Martin. *The Last Testament of Lucky Luciano.* Boston: Little, Brown, 1975.

Gow, Gordon. *"Illustrious Corpses." Films and Filming,* July 1977, 34–35.

———. *"The Mattei Affair." Films and Filming,* August 1975, 41.

Grazzini, Giovanni. *"Cristo si è fermato a Eboli."* In *Cinema '79,* pp. 33–36. Rome: Universale Laterza, 1980.

Greenspun, Roger. "From Italy, 'Mattei Affair.'" *New York Times,* 21 February 1973, 40.

Held, Jean-François. "Francesco Rosi: 'La Mafia n'a pas de principes.'" *Nouvel observateur,* 29 October 1973, 44–46.

Kael, Pauline. "Francesco Rosi." *New Yorker,* 22 March 1982, 160–64.

Kauffmann, Stanley. "Good Intentions" *(Three Brothers). New Republic,* 21 April 1982, 24–25.

———. *"The Mattei Affair, A Doll's House, The Day of the Jackal." New Republic,* 2 June 1973, 24, 33.

Kezich, Tullio. *Salvatore Giuliano.* Rome: Ed. F.M., 1961.

Lane, John Francis. "Film and Politics in Italy: Francesco Rosi's Example." *Films and Filming,* May 1976, 16–19.

———. "Moments de verité." *Positif,* May 1965, 21–32.

———. "The Moment of Truth." *Films and Filming,* December 1964, 5–10.

———. "Moments of Truth." *Films and Filming,* September 1970, 6–10.

Langlois, Gérard. "Francesco Rosi: *L'Affaire Mattei." Lettres françaises,* 17 May 1972, 11ff.

———. "Francesco Rosi—*Les hommes contre:* Chercher le véritable ennemi." *Lettres françaises,* 9 June 1971, 19–20.

Levi, Carlo. *Christ Stopped at Eboli.* New York: Farrar, Straus, 1947.

"L'Italie fortissimo avec Rosi." *Le programme du festival* (Cannes), 13 May 1981, 1, 3.

"Main base sur la ville" (script). *L'avant-scène cinéma,* May 1976.

Moravia, Alberto. "Machiavelli a cavalla di una bomba: *Il caso Mattei* di Francesco Rosi." *Espresso,* 6 February 1972, 23.

"More Than a Miracle." Filmfacts, 1967, 307–8.

Nowell-Smith, Geoffrey. *"Salvatore Giuliano." Sight and Sound,* Summer 1963, 142–43.

Overbey, David L. "Rosi in Context." *Sight and Sound,* Summer 1976, 170–74.

Padovani, Marcelle. "Les damnés de Mezzogiorno." *Nouvel observateur,* 5 June 1978, 62–63.

Pérez, Michel. "'Trois Frères' de Francesco Rosi." *Le Matin,* 14 May 1981, 24.

Ravage, Maria-Teresa. "The Mafia on Film: *Salvatore Giuliano.*" *Film Society Review,* October 1971, 33–38.

Reggiani, Stefano. "Tre fratelli e un padre in un'Italia confusa." *La Stampa,* 5 April 1981, 19.

Rémond, Alain. *"Cadavres exquis." Télérama,* 27 May 1976, 80–82.

———. "Entretien avec Francesco Rosi." *Télérama,* 26 May 1976, 82–83.

Renaud, Tristan. *"Les hommes contre* de Francesco Rosi." *Lettres françaises,* 9 June 1971, 18–19.

Rickey, Carrie. "Trinity Holy and Unholy." *Village Voice,* 23 February 1982, 56.

Robinson, George. "An Interview with Francesco Rosi." *1000 Eyes,* November 1976, 6–17.

Rosi, Francesco. *"Il caso Mattei": Un consaro al servizio della repubblica.* Bologna: Cappelli, 1972.

Rosi, Francesco and Eugenio Scalfari. *Il caso Mattei.* Bologna: Cappelli Editore, 1972.

St. Jacques, André. *"Il caso Mattei." Cinéma/Québec,* May–June 1973, 45–46.

Sarris, Andrew. "Maverick at the Fall Round-Up" (*Mattei Affaire*). *Village Voice,* 4 October 1973, 61, 72.

Schickel, Richard. "Italian Crude: *The Mattei Affair." Time,* 11 June 1973, p. 70.

———. "Way Station: *Eboli." Time,* 28 April 1980, 76.

Selden, Ina Lee. "Town on Wrong Side of Christ's Path." *New York Times,* 6 June 1978, C5.

Siclier, Jacques. *"Main basse sur la ville." Télérama,* 14 May 1975, 55.

Slatin, Judith. "Brothers in Grief." *Screen International,* 13 May 1981, 17.

Tallenay, Jean-Louis. *"L'Affaire Mattei." Télérama,* 18 June 1972, 55–56.

Tassone, Aldo. "Les *Cadavres exquis* de Francesco Rosi." *Télérama,* 18 March 1976, 86–87.

———. "Le Cinéma de Francesco Rosi." *Revue du cinéma,* June–July 1976, 69–75.

Tassone, Aldo. "Francesco Rosi. "In *Parla il cinema italiano,* pp. 263–307. Milan: Il Formichiere, 1979.

———. "Francesco Rosi: 'Au cinéma la dénunciation devient vite un prêche. . . .'" *Cinéma '74,* January 1974, 88–99.

Tornabuoni, Lietta. "Rosi: più che denunciare oggi e necessario capire." *La Stampa,* 5 April 1981, 19.

Trémois, Claude-Marie. *"Le Christ s'est arrêté à Eboli . . . au-dèla, les damnés de la terre." Télérama,* 30 April 1980, 102–3.

"Les Trois Frères." Informations Gaumont, 31 May 1981, 1, 6.

Visconti, Luchino. *La terra trema.* Bologna: Cappelli Editore, 1977.

Vitoux, Frédéric. "Le pouvoir et ses masques." *Positif,* January 1974, 25–29.

Zambetti, Sandro. *Francesco Rosi.* Florence: La Nuova Italia, 1976.

Pier Paolo Pasolini

"Accattone." Filmfacts, 1968, 164–66.

"Accattone." L'avant-scène cinéma, 15 April 1962, 52.

Aristarco, Guido. "Jung et DeSeta, Freud et Pasolini." *Cinéma '69* April 1969, 101ff.

Armes, Roy. "Pasolini." *Films and Filming,* June 1971, 55ff.

Bachmann, Gideon. "Pasolini in Persia: The Shooting of *1001 Nights." Film Quarterly,* Winter 1973–74, 25–28.

———. "Pasolini on de Sade." *Film Quarterly,* Winter 1975–76, 39–45.

———. "Pasolini Today." *Take One,* May–June 1973, 18–21.

———. "The 200 Days of 'Salo.'" *Film Comment,* March–April 1976, 38–47.

Berry, Leonard. "Pier Paolo Pasolini." *Mexico Quarterly Review* 4 (1969): 15–17.

Bevan, David. "Pasolini and Boccaccio." *Literature-Film Quarterly,* Winter 1977, 23–29.

Bonitzer, Pascal. *"Mamma Roma." Cahiers du cinéma,* March–April 1976, 66.

Bragin, John. "Pasolini—A Conversation in Rome, June 1966." *Film Culture,* Fall 1966, 102–06.

———. "Pier Paolo Pasolini: Poetry as a Compensation." *Film Society Review,* January, February, March 1969—(3 parts).

Braucourt, Guy. "Dernier tango à Salò." *Ecran,* 15 December 1975, 28–29.

Castello, Giulio Cesare. "Cinema italiano 1962: *Mamma Roma." Sight and Sound,* Winter 1962–63, 28–33.

Chapier, Henry. *"Théorème* de Pasolini ou la malédiction des bourgeois." *Combat,* 29 January 1969, 15.

Chappetta, Robert. *"Teorema." Film Quarterly,* 1969, 22–29.

Colport, Gilles. *"Mamma Roma." Revue du cinéma,* October 1976, 228.

"Comizi d'amore (Enquête sur la sexualité). *Revue du cinéma,* October 1977, 101–2.

"A Communist Christ." *Time,* 18 February 1966, 101.

"Con el Nuevo Testamento por guión." *Analisis,* 14 November 1966, 36–37.

Conrad, Randall. *"Accattone." Film Quarterly,* Winter 1966–67, 28–33.

Corbin, Louise. *"The Decameron." Films in Review,* December 1971, 641–62.

Cornand, André and Dominique Maillet. "Entretien avec Pier Paolo Pasolini." *Revue du cinéma,* January 1973, 83–92.

Cros, Jean-Louis. *"Salò, ou les 120 journées de Sodome." Revue du cinéma,* October 1976, 316.

Crowther, Bosley. "'Hawks and Sparrow.'" *New York Times,* 28 July 1967, 15.

———. "The Life of Christ." *New York Times,* 18 February 1966, 23.

Daney, S. "Note sur *Salò." Cahiers du cinéma, July–August 1976, 102–3.*

*"The Decameron." Filmfacts,*1971, 680–83.

de Gramont, Sacha. "Christ in Calabria." *New York Herald Tribune,* 22 November 1974, 32.

Di Giammatteo, Fernaldo, ed. "Lo Scandalo Pasolini. *Bianco e nero,* January–April 1976.

"Edipe roi." L'avant-scène cinema, November 1969, 47.

Elley, Derek. "Pasolini's *Salò: 120 Days of Sodom.*" *Films and Filming,* October 1977, p. 31.

———. *"Medea."* *Films and Filming,* July 1975, p. 45.

Escobar, Roberto. "Pier Paolo Pasolini: *Salò o le 120 Giornati di Sodoma.*" *Cineforum,* April 1976, 183–203.

"Especial: Pasolini." *Cinema 2002* (Madrid), April 1979, 44–90.

Faldini, Franca, and Goffredo Fofi. *Totò: L'uomo e la maschera.* Milan: Feltrinelli, 1977.

Ferrero, Adelio. *Il cinema di P. P. Pasolini.* Venice: Marsilio, 1977.

Finetti, Ugo. "Nella struttura di *Salò* la dialettica erotismo-poetere." *Cinema nuovo,* November–December 1976, 428–33.

Fitzgerald, John E. "The Paradoxical Pasolini." *U.S. Catholic,* March 1967, 27–32.

Foucault, Michel. "Les matins gris de la tolérance." *Le Monde,* 23 March 1977.

Gambetti, Giacomi, ed. *"Ostia": Un film di Sergio Citti.* Milan: Garzanti, 1970.

———. "Pasolini da Boccaccio a Chaucer: Per una 'Trilogia popolare, libera, erotica.'" *Cineforum,* March 1974, 221–29.

Gambetti, Giacomi, ed. *"Uccellacci e uccellini": Un film di Pier Paolo Pasolini.* Milan: Garzanti, 1966.

Gervais, Marc. *"Accatone"* [*sic*]. *Wide Angle,* 1977, 50–51.

———. "Pier-Paolo Pasolini: Contestatore." *Sight and Sound,* Winter 1968–69, 2–6.

Gili, Jean. "D'*Accattone* aux fascistes de Salò et autres lieux." *Ecran,* 15 December 1974, 24–25.

———. "Mort d'un cinéaste." *Ecran,* 15 December 1975, 20–21.

Gow, Gordon. "Pigsty." *Films and Filming,* March 1970, 38.

Green, Calvin. "L'homme politique." *Cinéaste,* Fall 1969, 2ff.

Green, Martin. "The Dialectic of Adaptation: *The Canterbury Tales* of Pier Paolo Pasolini." *Literature-Film Quarterly,* Winter 1976, 46–53.

Grisolia, Michel. "Le sang d'un poète." *Nouvel observateur,* 10 November 1975.

Hart, Henry. *"Teorema."* *Films in Review,* June–July 1969, 376–77.

Hartnung, Philip. "Pasolini's Parable." *Commonweal,* 16 May 1969, 265–66.

"The Hawks and the Sparrows." *Filmfacts,* 1968, 230–32.

Jordan, René. *"Gospel According to St. Matthew."* *Films in Review,* January 1966, 54–55.

Kane, Pascal. "Cinéma et histoire: L'effet d'étrangeté." *Cahiers du cinéma,* December 1974–January 1975, 77–83.

Lane, John Francis. "The Triumph of Italy's Realism." *Films and Filming,* December 1961, 38–39.

Langlois, Gérard. "Un drôle d'ucello pour Pasolini." *Lettres françaises,* 1 March 1972, 15–16.

Lawton, Ben. "The Storyteller's Art: Pasolini's *Decameron* (1971)." In *Modern European Filmmakers and Art of Adaptation,* edited by Andrew Horton and Joan Magretta. New York: Frederick Ungar, 1981.

Lord, Christina. "Pasolini, Italian Movie Director, Is Bludgeoned to Death near Rome." *New York Times,* 3 November 1975, 38.

MacFadden, Patrick. *"Uccellacci e uccellini."* *Take One,* September–October 1966.

Martin, Marcel. *"Salò ou les 120 journées de Sodome."* *Ecran,* July 1976, 47–49.

Maslin, Janet. "Danish Boys and Pasolini Bits; *Notes for an African Orestes,"* *New York Times,* 2 January 1981, p. C11.

"Medea." *Filmfacts,* 1972, 698–700.

Mitgang, Herbert. "Publishing: New Interest in the Works of Pasolini." *New York Times,* 21 November 1980, C26.

Noguez, Dominique. *"Teorema."* *Take One.* November–December 1968, 23.

Nowell-Smith, Geoffrey. *"Accattone."* *Sight and Sound,* Autumn 1962, 193–94.

"Pasolini Cinéaste." *Cahiers du cinéma.* Special Issue, 1978.

"Pasolini: 'Encore deux films et j'arrête." *Photo,* September 1974, 76ff.

Pasolini, Pier Paolo. "Je haïs l'état où je vis." *Ecran,* 15 December 1974, 22–23.

———. *Oedipus Rex.* Translated by John Mathews. London: Lorrimer Publishing, 1971.

———. "Sur 'Salò.'" *Ecran,* 15 December 1974, 25–27.

Passek, Jean-Loup. "La fausse innocence et la sodomystique." *Cinéma '73,* January 1973, 120–22.

Petraglia, Sandro. *Pasolini.* Florence: La Nuova Italia, 1974.

"Pier Paolo Pasolini." *Filmoteca Nacional* (Madrid), February 1976.

"Pier Paolo Pasolini: An Epical Religious View of the World." *Film Quarterly,* Summar 1965, 31–45.

"Pier Paolo Pasolini: A Meeting Five Years Later" (Yale University Symposium, 23–26 October 1980). Proceedings published in *Italian Quarterly,* Fall 1980–Winter 1981, nos. 82–83.

"Pier Paolo Pasolini and the Art of Directing." *Film Comment,* Fall 1965, 20–32.

"Pier-Paolo Pasolini: Témoignages." *Cahiers du cinéma,* July–August 1976, 100–01.

Ponzi, Marizio. *Pier Paolo Pasolini.* Torino: Edizioni A.I.A.C.E., 1972.

Purdon, Noel. *"1001 Nights* and *120 Days."* *Cinema Papers,* July–August 1975, 113ff.

Rayns, Tony. *"Fiore delle mille e una notte."* *Monthly Film Bulletin,* April 1975, 79.

Renaud, Tristan. *"Les Contes de Canterbury:* pour le plaisir." *Cinéma '73,* January 1973, 119–20.

Sarris, Andrew. "Pasolini Leaves a Literary Legacy." *Village Voice,* 17 November 1975, 127.

———. "Pier Paolo Pasolini." In *Interviews with Film Directors,* pp. 366–70. New York: Avon, 1967.

Scobie. W. I. "Pier Paolo Pasolini." *Advocate,* 5 May 1976, 45ff.

Siciliano, Enzo. *Pasolini: A Biography.* Translated by John Shepley. New York: Random House, 1982.

Siclier, Jacques. "Comment ils sont devenus réalisateurs: Pier Paolo Pasolini." *Télérama,* 11 September 1966, 10–11.

Stack, Oswald. *Pasolini.* Bloomington: University of Indiana Press, 1969.

Strick, Philip. *"Pigsty."* *Sight and Sound,* Spring 1970, 99–100.

Stuart, Alexander. *"The Canterbury Tales."* *Films and Filming,* June 1973, 46–47.

Taylor, John Russell. "Pier Paolo Pasolini." In *Directors and Directions,* pp. 44–68. New York: Hill and Wang, 1975.

"*Teorema.*" *Filmfacts,* 1969, 204–7.

Termine, Liborio. "*Il fiore delle mille e una notte.*" *Cinema nuovo,* September–October 1974, 374–75.

Tessier, Carmen. "L'Abbé Marc Oraison." *Journal du dimanche,* 16 March 1969, 12.

Toros, Hilmi. "A Gay Pass Blamed in Rome Killing." *New York Post,* 3 November 1975, 8.

Trémois, Claude-Marie. "*Mamma Roma.*" *Télérama,* 7 January 1976, 70–72.

Vecchiali, Paul. "*Les contes de Canterbury.*" *Revue du cinéma,* October 1973, 86.

Voglino, Bruno, Rolando Iotti, and Nino Ferraro. "Incontro con Pier Paolo Pasolini." *Filmcritica,* January 1962, 686–96.

Weaver, William, "Report from Italy: Pasolini—Writer, Director, Murder Victim." *Attenzione,* August 1979, 6–8.

White, Edmund. "Movies and Poems: *Pasolini, Poems.*" *New York Times Book Review,* 27 June 1982, 8ff.

White, Robert J. "Myth and Mise-en-Scène: Pasolini's *Edipo re.*" *Literature/Film Quarterly,* Winter, 1977, 30–37.

Whitehead, Peter. "*Theorem*" (and) "*Oedipus Rex.*" *Films and Filming,* June 1969, 38–39.

Winsten, Archer. "'Gospel' Film at Fine Arts Theater." *New York Post,* 18 February 1966, 63.

/

Bernardo Bertolucci

Alley, Robert. *Last Tango in Paris.* New York: Dell 1972.

Amiel, Mireille. "Bernardo Bertolucci." *Cinéma '73,* January 1973, 60–63.

Baber, Rob. "After the Revolution." *Soho Weekly News,* 24 November 1977, 23–24.

Bachmann, Gideon. "Films Are Animal Events: Bernardo Bertolucci Talks about His New Film, *1900.*" *Film Quarterly,* Fall 1975, 11–19.

———. "Every Sexual Relationship Is Condemned." *Film Quarterly,* Spring 1973, 2–9.

———. "Utopia Visited." *Sight and Sound,* Winter 1974–75, 28–33.

Badou, Jacques, Alain Calame, and Paul Gayot. *Borges et le cinéma.* Rheims: Maison de la Culture André Malraux, n.d.

"Bernardo Bertolucci." *Etudes cinématographiques,* 112–26 (1979).

"Bernardo Bertolucci Seminar." *Dialogue,* April 1974, 14–28.

Bertolucci, Bernardo. "L'ambiguïté et l'incertitude au miroir." *L'avant scène-cinéma,* June 1968, 7.

———, et al. *Novecento: Atto Primo, Atto Secondo.* Turin: Einaudi, 1976.

Bickley, Daniel. "Bernardo Bertolucci's *1900.*" *Cinéaste,* Winter 1976–77, 1

Blake, Richard. "Plop, Plop, Fizz, Fizzle." *America,* 3 December 1977, 403.

Bory, Jean-Louis. "Bernardo Bertolucci." In *Dossiers du cinéma (Cinéastes I),* pp. 25–28. Paris: Casterman, 1971.

———. "Fabrice et la baleine blanche." *Nouvel observateur,* 17 January 1968, 42–43.

Bragin, John. "A Conversation with Bernardo Bertolucci." *Film Quarterly,* Fall 1966, 39–44.

Braucourt, Guy. "Bertolucci: 'J'ai éventré Moravia.'" *Nouvelles littéraires,* 25 February 1971.

―――. *"Le conformiste:* Comment peut-on être fasciste." *Cinéma '71,* April 1971, 114–20.

―――. *"Dernier tango à Paris* ou le monde entier dans une chambre." *Ecran '73,* February 1973, 7–11.

Cadeau, Emile. *"La stratégie de l'araignée." Télérama,* 29 June 1974, 23–24.

Canby, Vincent. "A Kidnapping as Seen by Bertolucci." *New York Times,* 12 February 1982, p. C21.

Capdenac, Michel. "La fin de la douceur." *Lettres françaises,* 24 January 1968, 19.

―――. "Le principe du camélion." *Lettres françaises,* 24 February 1971, 16–17.

Casetti, Francesco. *Bernardo Bertolucci.* Florence: La Nuova Italia, 1975.

Chappetta, Robert. "The Meaning Is Not the Message." *Film Quarterly,* Summer 1972, 10–18.

Ciment, Michel, and Gérard Legrand. "Entretien avec Bernardo Bertolucci." *Positif,* March 1973, 29–38.

"The Conformist." Filmfacts, 1971, 81–85.

Cornand, André. *"1900." Revue du cinéma,* November 1976, 103–107.

Cott, Jonathan. "A Conversation with Bernardo Bertolucci." *Rolling Stone,* 21 June 1973, 44–46.

Cremonini, Giorgio. *"Ultimo tango a Parigi." Cinema nuovo,* January–February 1973, 53–55.

Dawson, Jan. *"Partner." Sight and Sound,* Winter 1968–69, 34, 51.

de Montvalon, Christine. *"La stratégie de l'araignée." Télérama,* 29 June 1974, 57.

de Saint Angel, Eric. "Bertolucci: 'l'atroce confusion de la vie actuelle.'" *Le Matin de Paris* (Special Festival), 24 May 1981, iii.

Di Bernardo, Giovanna. "Red Flags and American Dollars." *Cinéaste,* Winter 1976–77, 2–9, 50.

"Dialogue: Bertolucci and Aldrich." *Action,* March–April 1974, 23–25.

Douin, Jean-Luc. *"La luna:* Ma mère, mon amour." *Télérama,* 3 October 1979, 109–10.

Dupont, Joan. "Bertolucci's 'Ridiculous Man' Is Typically Italian." *Film français,* 24 May 1981, 2.

Engstrom, John. "Bertolucci's Latest Marks a Comeback." *Boston Globe,* 12 March 1982, 26.

Evin, Martine. *"La stratégie de l'araignée." Revue du cinéma,* 1973, 141–44.

Farber, Stephen. *"Last Tango." Hudson Review* (Autumn 1973): 534–44.

Fields, Sidney. "The Man behind *Tango." Daily News,* 5 February 1973, 38.

Fieschi, Jean-André. *"Prima della rivoluzione." Lettres françaises,* 10 January 1968, 18–19.

Flatley, Guy. "Bertolucci Brings Liv Ullmann to Brooklyn." *New York Times,* 25 November 1977, 66.

―――. "Bertolucci Is All Tangoed Out." *New York Times,* 11 February 1973, 1, 15.

Gardner, Paul. *"1900:* It Won't Be Bertolucci's Last Tango." *New York,* 6 June 1977, 1, 15.

Gelmis, Joseph. "Bernardo Bertolucci." In *The Film Director as Superstar,* pp. 111–20. New York: Doubleday, 1970.

Gili, Jean. *Le cinéma italien.* Paris: Union Générale d'Editions, 1978.

Goldin, Marilyn. "Bertolucci on *The Conformist." Sight and Sound,* Spring 1971, 64–66.

Goldstein, Richard. "Bertolucci Beats the Press." *Village Voice,* 28 November 1977, 42.

Gosetti, Giorgio. "Entretien avec Bernardo Bertolucci." *Ecran '79,* October 1979, 46–49.

Gow, Gordon. "Cinema and Life: Bernardo Bertolucci in an Interview." *Films and Filming,* June 1978, 10–15.

———. *"1900." Films and Filming,* April 1978, 31–32.

———. *"Partner." Films and Filming,* January 1971, 53.

———. *"The Spider's Stratagem." Films and Filming,* February 1977, 42–43.

Grazzini, Giovanni. "*La luna* di Bernardo Bertolucci." In *Cinema '79,* pp. 105–8. Rome: Universale Laeterza, 1980.

Greenspun, Roger. "Before the Revolution." *Film Comment,* May–June 1974, 22–23.

Gussow, Mel. "Bertolucci Talks about Sex, Revolution and 'Last Tango.'" *New York Times,* 2 February 1973, 20.

Heifetz, Henry. *"La commare secca." Film Quarterly,* Winter 1966–67, 44–46.

Hoberman, J. "Das Family: *Tragedy of a Ridiculous Man, Without Anesthesia, Dialogue with a Woman Departed." Village Voice,* 23 February 1982, 48.

Jebb, Julian. "The Visitable Past: Bertolucci's American Dream." *Sight and Sound,* Spring 1973, 80–81.

Kael, Pauline. "Carry Your Own Matches." *New Yorker,* 8 March 1982, 114ff.

———. "Hail Folly!" *New Yorker,* 31 October 1977, 148–61.

———. "Tango." *New Yorker,* 28 October 1972, 130–38.

Kakutani, Michiko. "Bertolucci: He's Not Afraid to Be Shocking." *New York Times,* 4 October 1979, p. C17.

Kauffmann, Stanley. *"Last Tango in Paris." New Republic,* 3 March 1973, 20, 33.

Kline, T. Jefferson. "Father as Mirror: Bertolucci's Oedipal Quest and the Collapse of Paternity." *Psychocultural Review* (Spring 1979): 91–109.

———. "The Unconformist: Bertolucci's *The Conformist."* In *Modern European Filmmakers and the Art of Adaptation,* edited by Andrew Horton and Joan Magretta. New York: Frederick Ungar, 1981.

Kroll, Jack. "Epic of the Century." *Newsweek,* 17 October 1977, 101–2.

Langlois, Gérard. "Bernardo Bertolucci: Qu'est-ce qu'un conformiste?" *Lettres françaises,* 14 January 1970.

"Last Tango in Paris." *Filmfacts,* 1973, 1–7.

Leclerce, Marie-Françoise. "Une femme têtue." *Le Point,* 1 October 1979, 134–35.

Legrand, Gérard. "The Last Time I Saw Hollywood (Sur *Le Dernier Tango à Paris)." Positif,* March 1973, 22–26.

———. "Les panneaux coulissants de Bertolucci." *Positif,* July–August 1971, 35–40.

Leogrande, Ernest. "The Longest Movie." *Daily News,* 30 October 1977, 5.

Lichenstein, Grace. "Bertolucci, the Man and His Epic." *New York Times,* 7 October 1977, p. C8.

Lopez, Daniel. "Novel into Film: Bertolucci's *The Conformist." Literature-Film Quarterly,* Fall 1976, 303–12.

Mann, Charles. "Media: Writing with Light." *Attenzione,* November 1980, 66–71.

Martin, Marcel. "Entretien avec Bernardo Bertolucci." *Ecran '73,* February 1973, 2–6.

Mellen, Joan. "A Conversation with Bernardo Bertolucci." *Cinéaste,* Summer 1972, 21–24.

———. "Sexual Politics and *Last Tango in Paris." Film Quarterly,* Spring 1973, 9–19.

Milne, Tom. *"La strategia del ragno"* (The Spider's Stratagem)." *Monthly Film Bulletin,* January 1977, 10–11.

Montaigne, Pierre. "Tognazzi: rapt à l'italienne." *France-Soir,* 25 May 1981, p. 20E.

Morera, Daniela. *"1900." Interview,* July 1975, 34–35.

Musatti, Cesare. "Il quarto stato nel *novecento* di Bertolucci." *Cinema nuovo,* September–October 1976, 340–44.

Nichols, Bill. *"Il conformista." Cinéaste,* Spring 1971, 19–23.

Orth, Maureen. "A Battle for '1900'." *Newsweek,* 27 September 1976, 107.

Passek, Jean Loup. *"Dernier Tango à Paris:* Le radeau perché." *Cinéma '73,* January 1973, 113–16.

"Prima della rivoluzione" (script). *L'avant-scène cinéma,* June 1968, 8–48.

Quart, Leonard. *"1900:* Bertolucci's Marxist Opera." *Cinéaste,* Winter 1977–78, 24–27.

Rossetti, Riccardo. "Con Bernardo Bertolucci." *Con-versazioni,* pp. 165–82. Rome: Bulzoni, 1977.

Roud, Richard. *"The Conformist." Sight and Sound,* Spring 1971, 62–63.

———. "Fathers and Sons." *Sight and Sound,* Spring 1971, 60–64.

———. *"Last Tango in Paris." Sight and Sound,* Summer 1972, 46–48.

Sadkin, David. "Theme and Structure: *Last Tango* Untangled." *Literature-Film Quarterly,* Spring 1974, 162–73.

Sarris, Andrew. "Films in Focus." *Village Voice,* 25 January 1973, 73–74.

"Self-Portrait of an Angel and Monster." *Time,* 22 January 1973, 51–55.

Siclier, Jacques. "Entretien avec Bernardo Bertolucci: Les secrets de *La luna." Le Monde,* 4 October 1979, 18.

Simsolo, Noel. "Bernardo Bertolucci." *Zoom,* November–December 1974, 98–101.

Speziale-Bagliacca, Roberto. *"Tango* tra un' incognita e un passato irrecuperabile." *Cinema nouvo,* May–June 1973, 188–91.

"The Spider's Stratagem." Filmfacts, 1973, 89–92.

Tailleur, Roger. "Les vacances rouges *(Prima della rivoluzione)." Positif,* May 1968, 31–39.

Tassone, Aldo. "Bernardo Bertolucci." In *Parla il cinema italiano,* pp. 45–82. Milan: Edizioni il Formichiere, 1980.

———. "Entretien avec Bernardo Bertolucci *(Dernier tango à Paris)." Revue du cinéma,* February 1973, 99–110.

———. "*La luna* de Bernardo Bertolucci." *Télérama,* 18 April 1979, 85–86.

Tessier, Max. "*1900:* 1er et 2e actes." *Ecran,* January 1977, 61–63.

Thirard, Paul-Louis. "A propos de 'le dernier tango à Paris.'" *Positif,* March 1973, 27–28.

Thomas, John. "*Before the Revolution.*" *Film Quarterly,* Winter 1966–67, 55–57.

Vogel, Amos. "Bernardo Bertolucci: An Interview." *Film Comment,* Fall 1971, 25–29.

Westerbeck, Colin. "L'amara vita." *Commonweal,* 6 January 1978, 16–18.

———. "*The Last Tango:* Le camera stilo." *Commonweal,* 2 March 1973, 501–2.

———. "Patriotic Gore." *Commonweal,* 23 December 1977, 820–21.

———. "Sex, Death and *Tango,* Part 2." *Commonweal,* 9 March 1973, 15–16.

Wicks, Ulrich. "Borges, Bertolucci, and Metafiction," 19–36. In *Narrative Strategies.* Macomb, Ill.: Western Illinois University Press, 1980.

Williams, Linda. "Stendhal and Bertolucci: The Sweetness of Life before the Revolution." *Literature-Film Quarterly,* Summer 1976, 215–21.

Young, Deborah. "History Lessons." *Film Comment,* November–December 1977, 16–19.

Zaller, Robert. "Bernardo Bertolucci, or Nostalgia for the Present." *Massachusetts Review* 4 (1975): 807–28.

Marco Bellocchio

Ansen, David. "Welcome Back, Bellocchio." *Newsweek,* 24 January 1983, 65–66.

Bernardi, Sandro. *Marco Bellocchio.* Florence: La Nuova Italia, 1978.

Bory, Jean-Louis. "*Les poings dans les poches.*" In *Dossiers du film,* 137–40. Paris: Casterman, 1972.

Bozza, Gianluigi. "Marco Bellocchio: *Marcia Trionfale.*" *Cineforum,* May 1976, 283–93.

Braucourt, Guy. "Brève rencontre . . . avec Marco Bellocchio." *Ecran,* April 1976, 12–13.

Bragin, John. "*La Cina è vicina* and *La Chinoise.*" *Film Society Review,* September 1968, 26–36.

Callegari, Giuliana, and Nuccio Lodato. "Marco Bellocchio: *I pugni in tasca* e *La macchina cinema.*" *Quaderno di documentazione* 14 (1979).

Carcassonne, Philippe, and Bruno Villien. "Entretien avec Marco Bellocchio." *Cinématrographe,* April 1979, 55–57.

Chapier, Henry. "*Les poings dans les poches,* de Marco Bellocchio." *Combat,* 21 April 1966, 6.

Chiaretti, Tommaso. "Allegretto con pessimismo." In Bellocchio, *China Is Near.* pp. 1–12. New York: Orion Press, 1969.

Clouzot, Claire. *China Is Near. Film Quarterly,* Fall 1968, 70–72.

———. "Fous à delier: *Matti da slegare.*" *Ecran,* April 1976, 55–56.

Cocks, Jay. "Burnt Offering." *Time,* 22 April 1974, 68.

Cornand, André. *"Le saut dans le vide."* *Revue du cinéma,* June 1980, 30–33.

Cournot, Michel. "La folie Bellocchio." *Nouvel observateur,* 2 June 1980, 102.

Cros, Jean-Louis. *"La Marche Triomphale."* *Revue du cinéma,* October 1977, 169.

Crowdus, Gary. *"Nel nome del padre."* *Film Society Review,* January 1972, 46.

Delain, Michel. "Bellocchio: La folie Tchekhov." *L'Express,* 24 April 1979.

———. "La dernière bombe de Bellocchio." *L'Express,* 5 February 1973.

Delmas, Jean. "La révolte lucide de Marco Bellocchio." *Jeune cinéma,* February 1977, 10–15.

Dupuich, Jean-Jacques. *"Au nom du père."* *Revue du cinéma,* March 1973, 102–4.

Escobar, Roberto. *"Nel nome del padre."* *Cineforum,* March 1973, 231–50.

Fofi, Goffredo, ed. *" 'Nel nome del padre' di Marco Bellocchio."* Bologna: Cappelli, 1971.

———. "La place de la politique." *Positif,* April 1972, 10–19.

Gain, Danielle. *"Viol en première page."* *Revue du cinéma,* March 1973, 136.

Gili, Jean. "Entretien avec Marco Bellocchio." *Ecran,* February 1973, 13–17.

Gili, Jean. "Marco Bellocchio." In *Le cinéma italien,* pp. 15–39. Paris: Union Générale d'Editions, 1978.

Glaessner, Verina. *"Nel nome del padre* (In the Name of the Father)." *Monthly Film Bulletin,* May 1977, 104.

Kael, Pauline. "Movies as Opera" *(China Is Near). New Yorker,* 13 January 1968, 90ff.

Kauffmann, Stanley. *"In the Name of the Father."* *New Republic,* 23 March 1974, 24, 33.

Kaupp, Katia. "Entretien: Un militant solitaire." *Nouvel observateur,* 21 April 1973, 57.

Kral, Petr. "Marco Bellocchio: Danse sur le fil du rasoir." *Positif,* June 1980, 2–5.

Lane, John Francis. "Italy's Angry Young Directors." *Films and Filming,* October 1968, 74–80.

Lawton, Harry. *"In the Name of the Father."* *Film Quarterly,* Winter 1974–75, 63–66.

Lefèvre, Raymond. "Marco Bellocchio: *La marche triomphale."* *Cinéma '77,* March 1977, 72–73.

Linden, Mathieu. "Italie, année zéro." *Nouvel observateur,* 24 March 1980, 93.

Lodato, Nuccio. *Marco Bellocchio.* Milan: Moizzi Editore, 1977.

Macklin, F. Anthony. "The Art of Marco Bellocchio: *In Nome del padre"* [*sic*]. *Film Heritage,* Fall 1971, 33–36.

"Marco Bellocchio: An Interview." *Film Society Review,* January 1972, 33–40.

Murat, Pierre. *"Le saut dans le vide."* *Télérama,* 14 May 1980, 108.

"New Movies: Two by Bellocchio." *Time,* 12 January 1968, 59.

Niogret, Hubert. "Viol en première page." *Positif,* June 1973, 86–88.

Perissinotto, Maria Regina. "Entretien avec Marco Bellocchio." *Positif,* June 1980, 6–12.

Rabourdin, Dominique. "Marco Bellocchio." *Cinéma '77,* March 1977, 54–57.

Rinaldi, Giorgio. "*Nessuno o tutti* di Bellocchio, Agosti, Petraglia, Rulli." *Cineforum,* October 1975, 737–42.

Rossetti, Riccardo. "Con Marco Bellocchio." In *Con-versazioni.* Rome: Bulzoni, 1977.

Scandolara, Sandro. "*Sbatti il mostro in prima pagina.*" *Cineforum,* March 1973, 251–66.

Seguin, Louis. "Une métamorphose surprenante." *Positif,* December 1967, 25–30.

Tassone, Aldo. "*Le saut dans le vide.*" *Télérama,* 26 March 1980, 96–97.

———. "Marco Bellocchio." In *Parla il cinema italiano,* pp. 7–44. Milan: Edizioni il Formichiere, 1980.

Tessier, Max. "*La marche triomphale.*" *Ecran,* 15 January 1977, 51–53.

———. "Marco Bellocchio: *Au nom du père* et de la politique." *Ecran,* February 1973, 18–21.

Thomsen, Christian Braad. "Bellocchio." *Sight and Sound,* Winter 1967–68, 14–16.

Tuten, Frederic. "*China Is Near:* An Interview with Marco Bellocchio." *Cinéaste,* Summer 1970, 24–25.

Un film di Marco Bellocchio: "I pugni in tasca." Milan: Garzanti, 1967.

Villien, Bruno. "*La mouette.*" *Cinématographe,* April 1979, 58.

Zalaffi, Nicoletta. "Interview with Marco Bellocchio." *Sight and Sound,* Autumn 1973, 197–99, 231.

Gillo Pontecorvo

Agirre, Julen. *Operación Ogro: Còmo y por qué ejecutamos a Carrero Blanco.* Paris: Ruedo Iberico, 1974.

Amendola, Giorgio. *Lettere a Milan: Ricordi e documenti, 1939–1945.* Rome: Editori Riuniti, 1973.

"Behind Barbed Wire." *Time,* 12 June 1964, 116.

Buache, Freddy. "Pontecorvo." In *Le cinéma italien d'Antonioni à Rosi,* pp. 136–40. Yverdon, Switzerland: Editions de la Thièle, 1969.

Capdenac, Michel. "La question du pouvoir." *Lettres françaises,* 27 January 1971, 19–20.

Carzou, Jean-Marie. "Le cinéma politique." *Cinémonde,* 16 June 1970, 11.

Cavatorta, Silvano, and Daniele Maggioni. *Joris Ivens.* Florence: La Nuova Italia, 1979.

Dowd, Nancy Ellen. "Popular Conventions." *Film Quarterly,* Spring 1969, 26–31.

Fink, Guido. "La grande strada azzurra." *Cinema nuova,* March–April 1959, 160.

Ghirelli, Massimo. *Gillo Pontecorvo.* Florence: La Nuova Italia, 1978.

Goodman, Mark. "Overburdened Island." *Time,* 2 November 1970, p. 94.

Green, Calvin. *"Burn!" Cinéaste,* Fall 1970, 35–36.

Guidez, Guylaine. "Tout savoir sur *La Bataille d'Alger." Cinémonde,* 23 June 1970, 20–25.

Hessoy, Aif Andrew. *Insurgency and Counterinsurgency in Algeria.* Bloomington: Indiana University Press, 1972.

Ivens, Joris. *The Camera and I.* New York: International Publishers, 1969.

Kael, Pauline. "Mythmaking." *New Yorker,* 7 November 1970, 159–65.

Kalishman, Harold. "Using the Contradictions of the System: An Interview with Gillo Pontecorvo." *Cinéaste,* 1974, 2–6.

Klein, Michael. *"Burn!" Film Quarterly,* Winter 1971–72, 55–56.

Kozloff, Max. "Shooting at Wars: Three Views." *Film Quarterly,* Winter 1967–68, 27–31.

Lucas, Corinne. " 'Ogro' et le térrorisme." *Revue du cinéma* June 1980, 66.

Mauriac, Claude. "Le temps des aveux." *Figaro littéraire,* 1–7 June 1970, 34–35.

Mellen, Joan. *Filmguide to "The Battle of Algiers".* Bloomington: Indiana University Press, 1973.

———. "An Interview with Gillo Pontecorvo." *Film Quarterly,* Fall 1972, 2–10.

Michalczyk, John J. "Gillo Pontecorvo." In *World Film Directors* (forthcoming).

Rémond, Alain. *"Un dénommé squarcio: La lunga strada."* In *Montand,* pp. 69–71. Paris: Henri Veyrier, 1977.

Rode, Henri. "Jean Martin: 'Pour tourner *La Bataille d'Alger* j'ai quitté la soutane pour l'uniforme de colonel.' " *Cinémonde,* 23 June 1970, 10–11.

Scialja, Mario. " 'Curcio the kid,' vietate ai minori di anni cento." *L'Espresso,* 28 October 1979, 81.

Solinas, PierNico, ed. *Gillo Pontecorvo's "The Battle of Algiers".* New York: Charles Scribner's Sons, 1973.

Spriano. "Bravo Gillo, continua così." *L'Espresso,* 28 October 1979, 81.

Talbott, John. *The War without a Name: France in Algeria, 1954–1962.* New York: Alfred A. Knopf, 1980.

Tassone, Aldo. "Gillo Pontecorvo." In *Parla il cinema italiano* (I), pp. 207–30. Milan: Il Formichiere, 1979.

Trombadori, Antonello. "E *Ogro?* Era meglio parlare di Gallinari." *L'Espresso,* 28 October 1979, 79–80.

Veillot, Claude. "Visa pour l'Algérie." *L'Express,* 1 June 1970, 94–95.

Wilson, David. "Politics and Pontecorvo." *Sight and Sound,* Summer 1971, 160–61.

Yamaguchi, John. *"Burn!" Village Voice,* 3 December 1970, 68, 70, 74.

Elio Petri

Alemanno, Roberto. "Da Rosi a Petri: todo modo dentro il contesto." *Cinema nuovo,* July–August 1976, 266–75.

Andrews, Nigel. *"Investigation of a Citizen above Suspicion." Sight and Sound,* Summer 1971, 166.

Arbois, Janick. *"La propriété c'est plus le vol." Télérama,* 16 October 1974, 72, 77.

Benayoun, Robert. "Cinéma: Requiem pour l'Italie." *Le Point,* 1 May 1978, 96–97.

Billard, Pierre. "Un cinéma au-dessus de tout soupçon." *Le Point,* 1 May 1978, 97.

———, et al. "Les cadavres énigmatiques de Monsieur Sciascia." *Le Point,* 31 January 1971, 79–81.

Braucourt, Guy. "Gian Maria Volonté." *Ecran '72,* June 1972, 20–25.

———. "L'organe crée la fonction, ou le fascisme en gants blancs." *L'avant-scène cinéma,* February 1971, 9–10.

"A chacun son du: Violence, amour et mort. . . ." *Cinémonde,* 5 December 1967, 40.

Chevallier, Jacques. *"Todo modo." Revue du cinéma,* October 1977, 265–66.

Cowie, Peter, ed. *"Indagine su un cittadino al di sopra di ogni sospetto."* In *International Film Guide,* pp. 183–84. London: Tantivy Press, 1971.

———. *"L'assassino." Films and Filming,* December 1963, 31, 38.

de Baroncelli, Jean. *"La Dixième Victime." Le Monde,* 12–13 February 1967, 18.

———. *"Enquête sur un citoyen au-dessous de tout soupçon." Le Monde,* 18–19 October 1970, 19.

———. *"Todo modo,* de Petri: Un film de combat." *Le Monde* 23–24 January 1977, 1, 31.

"Enquête sur un citoyen au-dessus de tout soupçon." (script) *L'avant-scène cinéma,* February 1971.

Ferrero, Adelio. "Nelo Risi: *Giuseppe Pinelli."* In *Dal Cinema al cinema,* pp. 369–71. Milan: Longanesi, 1980.

Fléouter, Claude. "La Classe. . . ." *Le Monde,* 1 June 1972, p. 19.

Fofi, Goffredo. "Conversation avec Elio Petri." *Positif,* April 1971, 39–50.

Gershuny, Ted. "Most Explosive Film in Town: *Lulu the Tool." Soho Weekly News,* 8 May 1974, 24, 28.

Gili, Jean. "Elio Petri." *Le cinéma italien,* pp. 15–39. Paris: Union Générale d'Editions, 1978.

———. "Entretien avec Elio Petri." *Ecran '74,* December 1974, 63–64.

———. "Entretien avec Elio Petri." *Ecran '77,* 15 January 1977, 55–56.

———. *"La propriété c'est plus le vol.' Ecran '74,* December 1974, 62–63.

———. *"Todo modo." Ecran '77,* 15 January 1977, 54–55.

———. "Un cinéma à l'écoute de l'Italie réele." *Ecran '72,* June 1972, 6–15.

———. *Elio Petri.* Nice: Faculté des Lettres et Sciences Humaines, 1974.

Gili, Jean, and Christian Viviani. "Elio Petri." *Ecran '72,* June 1972, 15–19.

Gilliatt, Penelope. "The Workers Gate-Crash Elysium." *New Yorker,* 19 May 1975, 78–81.

Goodman, Mark. "Injustice Is Blind." *Time,* 18 January 1971, 75.

Gow, Gordon. *"Investigation of a Citizen above Suspicion." Films and Filming,* June 1971, 57.

———. *"A Quiet Place in the Country." Films and Filming,* July 1971, 64.

Grazzini, Giovanni. *"Buone notizie* di Elio Petri." In *Cinema '79,* pp. 155–57.Rome: Universale Laeterza, 1980.

Hart, Henry. *"Investigation of a Citizen above Suspicion." Films in Review,* February 1971, 103–5.

Herridge, Frances. "When Workers Fought the Bosses." *New York Post,* 8 May 1975.

Kahan, Saul. *"The Tenth Victim." Cinema,* December 1965, 37–39.

———. *"The Tenth Victim." Films and Filming,* April 1966, 57–60.

Langlois, Gérard. "Elio Petri le polémiste." *Lettres françaises,* 31 May 1972, 14–15.

Lefèvre, Raymond. *"Todo modo:* La classe bourgeoise va en enfer." *Cinéma '77,* March 1977, 91–92.

MacBean, James Roy. "The Working Class Goes Directly to Heaven, without Passing Go." *Film Quarterly,* January 1973, 52–58.

Mellen, Joan. "Cinema Is Not for an Elite but for the Masses." *Cinéaste,* Spring, 1973, 8–13.

———. "Fascism in the Contemporary Film." *Film Quarterly,* Summer 1971, 2–19.

Miccichè, Lino. "Cinéma Italien, 1971." *Ecran '72,* June 1972, 2–6.

Miller, Letizia Ciotti. *"L'assassino." Film Quarterly,* Summer 1963, 52.

Nourissier, François. "Une police au-dessus de tout soupçon." *L'Express,* 12 October 1970, 96–97.

Padovani, Marcelle. "Des bandits et des prêtres." *Nouvel observateur,* 17 January 1977, 38–39.

Ravage, Maria-Teresa. "The Mafia on Film: *A ciascuno il suo." Film Society Review,* December 1971, 37–40.

Rémond, Alain. "Entretien avec Elio Petri." *Télérama,* 19 January 1977, 81.

Rochereau, Jean. *"La proporiété c'est plus le vol." La Croix,* 27–28 October 1974, 10.

———. *"Todo modo:* Insignifiant." *La Croix,* 29 January 1977, 8.

Rossi, Alfredo. *Elio Petri.* Florence: La Nuova Italia, 1979.

Tallenay, Jean-Louis. *"Todo modo:* Un pamphlet politique où tous les moyens sont bons." *Télérama,* 19 January 1977, 80–82.

Tassone, Aldo. "Elio Petri." In *Parla il cinema italiano,* pp. 221–84. Milan: Edizioni il Formichiere, 1980.

"The Tenth Victim." Time, 24 December 1965, 46.

Tournès, Andrée. "Actualité politique d'Elio Petri." *Jeune cinéma,* October 1976, 18–20.

———. "Entretien avec Elio Petri." *Jeune cinéma,* October 1976, 20–25.

———. "L'enfer selon Petri: *Bonnes nouvelles." Jeune cinéma,* September–October 1980, 1–3.

Weiler, A. H. "'Lulu the Tool,' Italian Drama." *New York Times,* 12 May 1974, 39.

"The Working Class Goes to Heaven." *Cinéaste,* Spring 1972, 24.

Zambetti, Sandro. *"Todo modo:* Ogni mezzo va bene per cercar di battere il regime DC." *Cineforum,* May 1976, 245–52.

Lina Wertmüller

Angell, Roger. "Three Beauties." *New Yorker,* 3 March 1980, 112ff.

Allen, Tom. "Announcing—Lina Wertmüller, Daredevil Aerialist." *America,* 7 February 1976, 99–100.

Arnold, Gary. "A Need for Chaos Fulfilled on Film." *The Washington Post,* 19 February 1976, G11.

Astle, Richard. *"Seven Beauties:* Survival, Lina-Style." *Jump Cut,* July 1977, 22–23.

Bachmann, Gideon. "Look, Gideon—." *Film Quarterly,* Spring 1977, 2–11.

Bartholomew, D. "Let's Talk about Men." *Cinéaste,* 1977, 47–48.

Biskind, Peter. "Lina Wertmüller: The Politics of Private Life." *Film Quarterly,* Winter 1974–75, 10–16.

Blumenfeld, Gina. "The (Next to) Last Word on Lina Wertmüller." *Cinéaste,* Fall 1976, 2–5.

Buckley, Michael. *"The Seduction of Mimi." Films in Review,* December 1974, 629.

———. *"Seven Beauties." Films in Review,* February 1976, 123.

Callenbach, Ernest. "Everything Ready, Nothing Works." *Film Quarterly,* Winter 1974–75, 59–60.

Cocks, Jay. "Bordello Politics: *Love and Anarchy." Time,* 20 May 1974, 67–68.

———. "Sexual Politics." *Time,* 22 July 1974, 6.

Coleman, John. "The Couple Solution." *New Statesman,* 10 March 1978, 331.

———. "Crowd Pleaser: *Tribute, Times Square, Blood Feud." New Statesman,* 16 January 1981, 22–23.

———. "Devil Take It *(Seven Beauties)." New Statesman,* 29 April 1977, 578.

Crist, Judith. "Home-grown Horror." *New York,* 24 June 1974, 58–59.

Dalla, Rita. "For Lina, It's Problems Not Prophecy." *Daily Telegraph* (London), 12 May 1979.

Davis, Melton. "I Get Along Well with Wild Personalities." *New York Times,* 6 March 1977, 13, 31.

———. "Lina Wertmüller Turns to the Stage." *New York Times,* Arts and Leisure section, 30 March 1980, 6, 8.

Demeure, Jacques. *"Pasqualino* (Pasqualino Settebelezze)." *Positif,* June 1974, 74.

Des Pres, Terrence. "Bleak Comedies." *Harper's,* June 1976, 26–28.

Everhart, Jane. "Today's Most Provocative Filmmaker, Women in Change: Lina Wertmüller." *Womens Week,* 13 March 1978, 11–12, 18.

Gallo, William. *"Swept Away." Film Heritage,* Spring 1976, 29–30.

Garson, Barbara. "A Reviewer under the Influence." *Ms.,* December 1975, 37–38.

———. "The Wertmüller Ethic: Wanting to Be Popular, Working to Be Popular is the Only Way to Be Taken Serious Politically." *Ms.,* May 1976, 71–75.

Gerard, Lillian. "The Ascendance of Lina Wertmüller." *American Film,* May 1976, 20–27.

Gilliatt, Penelope. "Church-Step Farce." *New Yorker,* 24 June 1974, 80–83.

Gow, Gordon. *"Seven Beauties." Films and Filming,* May 1977, 30–31.

———. *"Swept Away." Films and Filming,* June 1977, 36.

Hammond, Margo. "Wertmüller Raps WB Handling of 'Rain'; Cut It and Brushed It." *Variety,* 3 May 1978, 38, 42.

Haskell, Molly. "Swept Away on a Wave of Sexism." *Village Voice,* 29 September 1975, 128ff.

Hatch, Robert. "Films" *(Blood Feud). Nation,* 15 March 1980, 316–17.

———. "Films" *(Love and Anarchy). Nation,* 4 May 1974, 573–74.

———. "Films" *(Swept Away). Nation,* 4 October 1974, 318.

Hoy, Anne. "The Grotesque World of Lina Wertmüller." *Boston Globe,* 24 September 1978, p. B19.

"The Irresistible Force and the Immutable Object." *Time,* 16 February 1976, 58–60.

Jacobs, Diane. "Lina Wertmüller: The Italian Aristophanes?" *Film Comment,* March–April 1976, 48, 50.

Kael, Pauline. "Seven Fatties." *New Yorker,* 17 February 1976, 104ff.

Kauffmann, Stanley. "The Seduction of Mimi." *New Republic,* 17 July 1974, 20.

———. "Wertmüller." *New Republic,* 14 February 1976, 22–23.

Kay, Karyn, and Gerald Peary. *Women and the Cinema.* New York: E. P. Dutton, 1977.

Klemesrud, Judy. "Wertmüller: The Foremost Woman Director." *New York Times* Arts and Leisure sec., 9 February 1975, 15.

Kosinski, Jerzy. "Seven Beauties—A Cartoon Trying to Be a Tragedy." *New York Times,* Arts and Leisure sec., 7 March 1976, 1, 15.

Kroll, Jack. "Wertmüller's Inferno." *Newsweek,* 26 January 1976, 78–79.

Lawson, Carol. "Lena [*sic*] Wertmüller Directs at La Mama." *New York Times,* 30 January 1980, p. C24.

McCormick, Ruth. *"Swept Away." Cinéaste,* Spring 1976, 41–42.

Modleski, Tania. "Wertmüller's Women: Swept Away by the Usual Destiny." *Jump Cut,* June 1976, 1, 16.

O'Connor, John J. "TV Watches Lina Wertmüller at Work." *The New York Times,* 24 March 1977.

Orth, Maureen. " 'Look This Way. Breathe. Brava!' " *Newsweek,* 26 January 1976, 79.

Ott, Gunter. "Lina Sweeps In." *Cinema Canada,* March 1978, 14–15.

Plumb, Catherine. *"The Seduction of Mimi." Take One,* May–June 1973, 41–43.

Quacinella, Lucy. "How Left Is Lina?" *Cinéaste,* Fall 1976, 15–17.

Rich, Frank. "Water Torture: *The End of the World in Our Usual Bed in a Night Full of Rain." Time,* 6 February 1978, 66.

Riley, Brooks. "Lina Wertmüller: The Sophists' Norman Lear?" *Film Comment,* March–April 1976, 49, 51.

Roberts, Glenys. "Lina Wertmüller: A Thirst for Life." *Times* (London), 25 February 1977.

Rosenstein, Nathan. *"Swept Away." Take One,* July–August 1974, 35–36.

Rubenstein, Lenny. "Love and Anarchy." *Cinéaste,* 1974, 36–37.

Sayre, Nora. "Lina Wertmüller Defines 'Free-Wheeling' Politics." *New York Times,* 5 February 1975, 30.

———. " 'The Seduction of Mimi.' " *New York Times,* 19 June 1974, 40.

Simon, John. "Caste Away." *New York,* 22 September 1975, 70–71.

———. "Wertmüller's 'Seven Beauties'—Call It a Masterpiece." *New York,* 2 February 1976, 24–31.

Sterritt, David. "Lina Wertmüller—Queen of Directors." *Christian Science Monitor,* 6 February 1976.

Stoop, Norma McLain. "Lina Wertmüller Plays a Beautiful Game." *After Dark,* April 1976, 34–43.

Tallmer, Jerry. "Lina Wertmüller: Sex, Politics and Movies." *New York Post,* Entertainment sec., 24 January 1976, 1, 6.

Van Wert, William. "Love, Anarchy, and the Whole Damned Thing." *Jump Cut,* November–December 1974, 8–9.

"La Wertmüller ha 'girato' fra le macerie del terremoto." *Corriere della Sera,* 23 April 1981, 27.

Wertmüller, Lina. *The Screenplays of Lina Wertmüller.* New York: New York Times Books, 1977.

Westerbeck, Colin. "The Screen" *(Swept Away). Commonweal,* 10 October 1975, 470–71.

———. "Sexual Politics: *Love and Anarchy." Commonweal,* 9 August 1974, 430.

Willis, Ellen. "Is Lina Wertmüller Just One of the Boys?" *Rolling Stone,* 25 March 1976, 31, 70, 72.

———. "Wertmüller. . . ." *Rolling Stone,* 25 March 1976, 28, 38.

Wood, Michael. "All Mixed Up." *New York Review,* 18 March 1976, 5, 8.

Zimmerman, Paul. "Love—Sicilian Style." *Newsweek,* 8 July 1974, 69–70.

———. "The Passionate Assassin." *Newsweek,* 29 April 1974, 98–103.

Zito, Tom. "Her Offspring: Films Born of Love, Anarchy and Economics." *Washington Post,* 2 February 1976, pp. D1–2.

———. "The 'in' Film Director Is an Italian Woman 'Feminists Don't Like.'" *Philadelphia Inquirer,* 7 March 1976, pp. 1–2H.

Zocaro, Ettore. "Lina Wertmüller e Franco Brusati." *Filmcritica,* February 1963, 103–7.

Index